Table of Contents

The New Testament

GOSPELS
MATTHEW 1
Mark 34
Luke 55
John 91

ACTS OF THE APOSTLES
ACTS 117

EPISTLES
ROMANS 151
1ST CORINTHIANS 164
2ND CORINTHIANS 178

GALATIANS 186
EPHESIANS 190
Philippians 195
COLOSSIANS 198
1ST THESSALONIANS 201
2ND THESSALONIANS ... 204
1ST TIMOTHY 205
2ND TIMOTHY 209
Titus 211
PHILEMON 213
Hebrews 213

JAMES 223
1ST PETER 227
2ND PETER 230
1ST JOHN 233
2ND JOHN 236
3RD JOHN 237
Jude 237

Prophecy
Revelation 239

Legend

PROPHECY/PROPHECY FULFILLED (REFERENCED IN THE BIBLE)
Note: Many prophecies fulfilled, but not recorded in The Bible are not "ALL CAPPED."
Spiritual Terms Capitalized
the law: laws no longer in effect and secular laws
the Law: mixed; laws no longer in effect and Commandments/Spiritual Law
The Law: Commandments and Spiritual Law

Color Coded:
Dreams/Visions and Miracles
Words of Christ
Words of God
Words of The Holy Spirit

Godspeed LLC
382 NE 191st #9164
Miami, FL 33179
KingJamesVersion2@hotmail.com

The New Testament
King James Version 2 ©
Color Coded

Matthew

Chapter 1

1 The scroll of the generation of Jesus Christ, the son of David, the son of Abraham.
2 Abraham begat Isaac. And Isaac begat Jacob. And Jacob begat Judas (and his brothers.)
3 And Judas begat Pharez (and Zara, of Tamar.) And Pharez begat Hezron. And Hezron begat Aram.
4 And Aram begat Amminadab. And Amminadab begat Naasson. And Naasson begat Salmon.
5 And Salmon begat Boaz (of Rachab.) And Boaz begat Obed (of Ruth.) And Obed begat Jesse.
6 And Jesse begat David, the king. And David, the king begat Solomon (of her that had been the wife of Uriah.)
7 And Solomon begat Roboam. And Roboam begat Abijah. And Abijah begat Asa.
8 And Asa begat Josaphat. And Josaphat begat Joram. And Joram begat Uzziah.
9 And Uzziah begat Jotham. And Jotham begat Ahaz. And Ahaz begat Hezekiah.
10 And Hezekiah begat Manasseh. And Manasseh begat Amon. And Amon begat Josiah.
11 And Josiah begat Jeconiah (and his brothers about the time they were carried away to Babylon.
12 And after they were brought to Babylon) Jeconiah begat Shealtiel. And Shealtiel begat Zerubbabel.
13 And Zerubbabel begat Abihud. And Abihud begat Eliakim. And Eliakim begat Azzur.
14 And Azzur begat Zadok. And Zadok begat Jokim. And Jokim begat Eliud.
15 And Eliud begat Eleazar. And Eleazar begat Matthan. And Matthan begat Jacob.
16 And Jacob begat Joseph (the husband of Mary) of whom, was born Jesus, Who is called Christ.
17 So, all the generations from Abraham to David are fourteen generations. And from David, until the carrying away into Babylon are fourteen generations. And from the carrying away into Babylon to Christ are fourteen generations.

18 Now, the birth of Jesus Christ was on this wise, when, as His mother, Mary was espoused to Joseph, before they came together, she was found with child of The Holy Ghost.
19 Then Joseph, her husband being a Just man and not willing to make her a public example, was minded to put her away privily.
20 But while he thought on these things, behold, the angel of The Lord appeared to him in a Dream saying, "Joseph, you son of David, fear not to take to yourself, Mary, your wife. For that, which is conceived in her, is of The Holy Ghost.
21 AND SHE SHALL BRING FORTH A SON AND YOU SHALL CALL HIS NAME, JESUS. FOR HE SHALL SAVE HIS PEOPLE FROM THEIR SINS.
22 Now, all this was done that it might be Fulfilled, which was spoken of The Lord, by the prophet saying,
23 "BEHOLD, A VIRGIN SHALL BE WITH CHILD AND SHALL BRING FORTH A SON AND THEY SHALL CALL HIS NAME, "'EMMANUEL,'" which being interpreted is, "'GOD WITH US.'"

24 Then, Joseph being raised from sleep, did as the angel of The Lord had bidden him and took to himself, his wife
25 And knew her not, until she had brought forth, her firstborn Son and he called His Name, "Jesus."

Chapter 2

1 Now, when Jesus was born in Bethlehem, of Judaea in the days of Herod, the king, behold, there came wise men from the East to Jerusalem
2 Saying, "where is He that is born, king of the Jews? For we have seen His star in the East and are come to Worship Him."

3 When Herod, the king had heard these things, he was troubled and all Jerusalem with him.
4 And when he had gathered all the chief priests and scribes of the people together, he demanded of them, where Christ should be born.
5 And they said to him, "in Bethlehem, of Judaea. For thus, it is written by the prophet,
6 "'AND YOU, BETHLEHEM, IN THE LAND OF JUDAH, ARE NOT THE LEAST AMONG THE PRINCES OF JUDAH. FOR OUT OF YOU, SHALL COME A

GOVERNOR THAT SHALL RULE MY PEOPLE, ISRAEL.'"

7 Then Herod, when he had privily called the wise men, enquired of them diligently, what time the star appeared.

8 And he sent them to Bethlehem and said, "go and search diligently, for the young Child. And when you have found Him, bring me word again that I may come and worship Him, also."

9 When they had heard the king, they departed and lo, the star, which they saw in the East, went before them, until it came and stood over where the young Child was.

10 When they saw the star, they Rejoiced with exceedingly great Joy.

11 And when they had come into the house, they saw the young Child with Mary, His mother and fell down and Worshipped Him. And when they had opened their treasures, they presented to Him, gifts: gold and frankincense and myrrh.

12 And being Warned of God in a Dream that they should not return to Herod, they departed into their own country, another way.

13 And when they were departed, behold, the angel of The Lord appeared to Joseph in a Dream saying, "arise and take the young Child and His mother and flee into Egypt and remain yourselves, there until I bring you word, for Herod will seek the young Child to destroy Him."

14 When he arose, he took the young Child and His mother, by night and DEPARTED INTO EGYPT

15 And was there, until the death of Herod that it might be Fulfilled, which was spoken of The Lord, by the prophet saying, "OUT OF EGYPT, HAVE I CALLED MY SON."

16 Then Herod, when he saw that he was mocked of the wise men, was exceedingly wroth and sent forth and slew all the children that were in Bethlehem and in all the coasts, thereof; from two years old and under, according to the time, which he had diligently inquired of the wise men.

17 Then, was fulfilled that, which was spoken by Jeremiah, the prophet saying,

18 "IN RAMAH, WAS THERE A VOICE HEARD; LAMENTATION AND WEEPING AND GREAT MOURNING, RACHEL WEEPING FOR HER CHILDREN AND WOULD NOT BE COMFORTED, BECAUSE THEY ARE NOT."

19 But, when Herod was dead, behold, an angel of The Lord appeared in a Dream to Joseph in Egypt,

20 Saying, "arise and take the young Child and His mother and go into the land of Israel, for they are dead, which sought the young Child's life."

21 And he arose and took the young Child and His mother and came into the land of Israel.

22 But, when he heard that Archelaus did reign in Judaea in the room of his father, Herod, he was afraid to go there. Notwithstanding, being Warned of God in a Dream, he turned aside into the parts of Galilee.

23 And he came and dwelled in a city called, Nazareth that it might be Fulfilled, which was spoken by the prophets, "HE SHALL BE CALLED A NAZARENE."

Chapter 3

1 In those days, came John, the Baptist Preaching in the wilderness of Judaea

2 And saying, "Repent you, for the Kingdom of Heaven is at hand.

3 For this is He that was spoken of, by the Prophet Isaiah saying, "'THE VOICE OF ONE CRYING IN THE WILDERNESS, PREPARE YOU, THE WAY OF THE LORD. MAKE HIS PATHS STRAITGHT.'"

4 And the same, John, had his raiment of camel's hair and a leather girdle about his loins. And his meat was locusts and wild honey.

5 Then went out to him, Jerusalem and all Judaea and all the region, round about Jordan

6 And were Baptized of him in Jordan, Confessing their sins.

7 But, when he saw many of the Pharisees and Sadducees come to his Baptism, he said to them, "O generation of vipers, who has Warned you to flee from the wrath to come?

8 Bring forth, therefore, fruits meet for Repentance.

9 And think not, to say within yourselves, "'we have Abraham, to our father.'" For I say to you that, "'God is able of these stones, to raise up children to Abraham.'"

10 And now also, the axe is laid to the root of the trees. Therefore, every tree which brings not, forth Good Fruit is hewn down and cast into the fire.

11 I indeed Baptize you with water, to

Repentance. But, He that comes after me, is Mightier than I, Whose shoes, I am not worthy to bear. He shall Baptize you with The Holy Ghost and with Fire,
12 Whose fan is in His hand and He will throughly, Purge His floor and gather His wheat into the garner. But, <u>He will burn up the chaff with unquenchable fire.</u>

13 Then came Jesus, from Galilee to Jordan, to John to be Baptized of him.
14 But, John forbade Him saying, "I have need to be Baptized of You and come You, to me?"
15 And Jesus answering said to him, "suffer it to be so now, for thus, it becomes us, to Fulfill all Righteousness." Then, he suffered Him.
16 And Jesus, when He was Baptized, went up straightway out of the water and lo, the heavens were opened to Him and He saw The Spirit of God descending like a dove and Lighting on Himself
17 And lo, A Voice from Heaven saying, "This is My Beloved Son, in Whom I am Well Pleased."

Chapter 4

1 Then, was Jesus led up of The Spirit into the wilderness, to be tempted of the Devil.
2 And when He had Fasted forty days and forty nights, He was afterward, a hungered.
3 And when the tempter came to Him, he said, "if You are The Son of God, Command that these stones be made bread."
4 But, He answered and said, "it is written, "'man shall not Live by bread alone, but by every Word that proceeds out of the mouth of God.'"
5 Then, the Devil took Him up into the Holy city and set Him on a pinnacle of the temple
6 And said to Him, "if You are The Son of God, cast Yourself down, for it is written, "'He shall give His angels charge concerning you and in their hands, they shall bear you up, lest at any time you dash your foot against a stone.'"
7 Jesus said to him, "it is written again, "'you shall not tempt The Lord, your God.'"
8 Again, the Devil took Him up, into an exceedingly high mountain and showed Him all the kingdoms of the World and the glory of them
9 And said to Him, "all these things, will I give You, if You will fall down and worship me."
10 Then, said Jesus to him, "get you hence, Satan. For it is written, "'you shall Worship The Lord your God and Him only, shall you Serve.'"
11 Then, the Devil left Him and behold, angels came and ministered to Him.

12 Now, when Jesus had heard that John was cast into prison, He departed into Galilee
13 And leaving Nazareth, He came and dwelled in Capernaum, which is on the Sea coast, in the borders of Zebulun and Naphtali
14 That it might be Fulfilled, which was spoken by Isaiah, the prophet saying,
15 "THE LAND OF ZEBULUN AND THE LAND OF NAPHTALI, BY THE WAY OF THE SEA, BEYOND JORDAN, GALILEE OF THE GENTILES,
16 THE PEOPLE WHICH SAT IN DARKNESS, SAW GREAT LIGHT AND TO THEM, WHICH SAT IN THE REGION AND SHADOW OF DEATH, LIGHT IS SPRUNG UP."
17 From that time, Jesus began to Preach and to say, "Repent, for the Kingdom of Heaven is at hand."

18 And Jesus, walking by the Sea of Galilee, saw two brothers, Simeon, called Peter and Andrew, his brother, casting a net into the Sea, for they were fishers.
19 And He said to them, "Follow Me and I will make you fishers of men."
20 And they straightway, left their nets and Followed Him.
21 And going on from there, He saw other two brothers, James, the son of Zabdi and John, his brother, in a ship with Zabdi, their father mending their nets and He called them.
22 And they immediately, left the ship and their father and Followed Him.

23 And Jesus went about all Galilee, Teaching in their synagogues and Preaching The Gospel of the Kingdom and Healing all manner of sickness and all manner of disease among the people.
24 And His fame went throughout all Syria. <u>And they brought to Him all sick people that were taken with diverse diseases and torments and those, which were possessed with devils and those, which were lunatic and those that had the palsy and He Healed them</u>.
25 And there followed Him, great multitudes of people; from Galilee and

from Decapolis and from Jerusalem and from Judaea and from beyond Jordan.

Chapter 5

1 And seeing the multitudes, He went up into a mountain and when He was set, His disciples came to Him.

2 And He opened His mouth and Taught them saying,

3 "Blessed are the poor in spirit, for theirs is the Kingdom of Heaven.

4 Blessed are they that mourn, for they shall be Comforted.

5 Blessed are the Meek, for they shall inherit the Earth.

6 Blessed are they, which do Hunger and Thirst after Righteousness, for they shall be Filled.

7 Blessed are the Merciful, for they shall obtain Mercy.

8 Blessed are the Pure in heart, for they shall see God.

9 Blessed are the Peacemakers, for they shall be called the children of God.

10 Blessed are they, which are persecuted for Righteousness' sake, for theirs is the Kingdom of Heaven.

11 Blessed are you, when men shall revile you and persecute you and shall say all manner of evil against you, falsely, for My sake.

12 Rejoice and be exceedingly Glad, for great is your Reward in Heaven. For so persecuted they, the prophets, which were before you.

13 You are the salt of the Earth. But, if the salt has lost his savor, wherewith shall it be salted? It is thenceforth, good for nothing, but to be cast out and to be trodden under foot of men.

14 You are the light of the World. A city that is set on an hill cannot be hid.

15 Neither do men light a candle and put it under a bushel, but on a candlestick and it gives light to all that are in the house.

16 Let your light so shine before men that they may see your good Works and Glorify your Father, which is in Heaven.

17 Think not that I am come to destroy The Law, or the Prophets. I am not come, to destroy, but to Fulfill.

18 For verily, I say to you, "'until Heaven and Earth passes, one jot, or one tittle, shall in no wise, pass from The Law, until all, be Fulfilled.'"

19 Whosoever therefore, shall break one, of these least Commandments and shall teach men so, he shall be called the least in the Kingdom of Heaven. But whosoever, shall Do and Teach them, the same shall be called great in the Kingdom of Heaven.

20 For I say to you that, "except your Righteousness, shall Exceed the righteousness of the scribes and Pharisees, you shall in no case, enter into the Kingdom of Heaven.'"

21 You have heard that it was said of them of old times, "you shall not murder. And whosoever, shall murder, shall be in danger of the Judgment.'"

22 But, I say to you that, "'whosoever is angry with his brother without a cause, shall be in danger of the Judgment. And whosoever, shall say to his brother, "'raca,'" shall be in danger of the council. But whosoever, shall say, "'you fool,'" shall be in danger of Hell fire."'

23 Therefore, if you bring your gift to the altar and there, remember that your brother has anything against you,

24 Leave there, your gift before the altar and go your way. First, be reconciled to your brother and then, come and offer your gift.

25 Agree with your adversary quickly, while you are in the way with him, lest at any time, the adversary delivers you to the judge and the judge delivers you to the officer and you be cast into prison.

26 Verily, I say to you, "you shall by no means come out there, until you have paid the uttermost farthing.'"

27 You have heard that it was said by them of old times, "'you shall not commit adultery.'"

28 But, I say to you that, "'whosoever, looks on a woman to lust after her, has committed adultery with her, already in his heart.'"

29 And if your right eye offends you, pluck it out and cast it from yourself, for it is profitable for you that, one of your members should perish and not that, your whole body should be cast into Hell.

30 And if your right hand offends you, cut it off and cast it from yourself, for it is profitable for you that, one of your members should perish and not that, your whole body should be cast into Hell.

31 It has been said, "'whosoever shall put away his wife, let him give her a writing of

divorcement.'"

32 But, I say to you that, "'whosoever, shall put away his wife, saving for the cause of fornication, causes her to commit adultery. And whosoever, shall marry her that is divorced, commits adultery.'"

33 Again, you have heard that it has been said by them of old times, "'you shall not forswear yourself, but shall Perform to The Lord your oaths.'"
34 But, I say to you, "'swear not at all, neither by Heaven, for it is God's throne,
35 Nor by the Earth, for it is His footstool, neither by Jerusalem, for it is the city of The Great King.
36 Neither shall you swear by your head, because you can not make one hair white, or black.
37 But, let your communication be, "''yea, yea; nay, nay,'"' for whatsoever, is more than these, comes of evil.'"

38 You have heard that it has been said, "'an eye for an eye and a tooth for a tooth.'"
39 But, I say to you that, "'you resist not, evil, but whosoever, shall hit you on your right cheek, turn to him the other, also.'"
40 And if any man will sue you at the Law and take away your coat, let him have your cloak, also.
41 And whosoever, shall compel you to go a mile, go with him two.
42 Give to him that asks you and from him that would borrow of you, turn not yourself, away.

43 You have heard that it has been said, "'you shall love your neighbor and hate your enemy.'"
44 But I say to you, "'love your enemies. Bless them that curse you. Do good to them that hate you and Pray for them, which despitefully use you and persecute you
45 That you may be the children of your Father, which is in Heaven, for He makes His Sun to rise on the evil and on the good and sends rain on the Just and on the unjust.
46 For if you love them, which love you, what reward have you? Do not even, the publicans the same?
47 And if you salute your brothers only, what do you more than others? Do not even, the publicans so?
48 Be you therefore, perfect, even as your Father, which is in Heaven, is Perfect.'"

Chapter 6

1 Take heed that you do not your alms before men, to be seen of them. Otherwise, you have no reward of your Father, which is in Heaven.
2 Therefore, when you do your alms, do not sound a trumpet before yourself, as the hypocrites do in the synagogues and in the streets that they may have glory of men. Verily, I say to you, "'they have their reward.'"
3 But, when you do alms, let not your left hand know what your right hand does
4 That your alms may be in secret and your Father, which sees in secret Himself, shall Reward you openly.

5 And when you Pray, you shall not be as the hypocrites are, for they love to pray standing in the synagogues and in the corners of the streets that they may be seen of men. Verily, I say to you, "'they have their reward.'"
6 But you, when you Pray, enter into your closet and when you have shut your door, Pray to your Father, which is in secret and your Father, which sees in secret, shall reward you openly.
7 But when you Pray, use not, vain repetitions as the heathens do, for they think that they shall be heard for their much speaking.
8 Be not you therefore, like to them, for your Father knows what things you have need of, before you ask Him.
9 After this manner therefore, Pray yourself, 'Our Father, which is in Heaven, Hallowed be Your Name.
10 Your Kingdom come. Your Will be done in Earth, as it is in Heaven.
11 Give us this day, our daily bread.
12 And Forgive us our debts, as we Forgive our debtors.
13 And lead us not into temptation, but Deliver us from evil. For Yours is the Kingdom and the Power and the Glory, for ever. Amen.'

14 For if you Forgive men their trespasses, your Heavenly Father will also, Forgive you.
15 But, if you Forgive not, men their trespasses, neither will your Father Forgive your trespasses.
16 Moreover, when you Fast, be not, as the hypocrites, of a sad countenance. For they disfigure their faces that they may appear to men to fast. Verily, I say to you,

"'they have their reward.'"
17 But you, when you Fast, anoint your head and wash your face
18 That you appear not, to men to Fast, but to your Father, which is in secret and your Father, which sees in secret, shall Reward you openly.

19 Lay not up for yourselves, treasures on Earth, where moth and rust do corrupt and where thieves break through and steal.
20 But, lay up for yourselves, treasures in Heaven, where neither moth, nor rust do corrupt and where thieves do not break through, nor steal.
21 For where your treasure is, there will your heart be, also.
22 The Light of the body is the eye. If therefore, your eye be good, your whole body shall be Full of Light.
23 But, if your eye be evil, your whole body shall be full of Darkness. If therefore, the light that is in you be Darkness, how great is that Darkness!
24 No man can serve two masters. For either, he will hate the one and love the other, or else, he will hold to the one and despise the other. You cannot serve God and mammon.

25 Therefore, I say to you, "'take no thought for your life; what you shall eat, or what you shall drink, nor yet, for your body; what you shall put on. Is not the Life, more than meat and the body, than raiment?
26 Behold the fowls of the air, for they sow not, neither do they reap, nor gather into barns. Yet your Heavenly Father feeds them. Are you not much better than they?
27 Which of you, by taking thought, can add one cubit to his stature?
28 And why take yourself, thought for raiment? Consider the lilies of the field, how they grow. They toil not, neither do they spin.
29 And yet, I say to you that, "'even Solomon in all his glory was not arrayed like one of these.'"
30 Wherefore, if God so clothes the grass of the field, which today is and tomorrow is cast into the oven, shall He not much more clothe you, O you, of little Faith?
31 Therefore, take no thought saying, "'what shall we eat, or what shall we drink, or wherewithal, shall we be clothed?'"
32 For after all these things, do the gentiles seek. For your Heavenly Father knows that you have need of all these things.
33 But, Seek you first, the Kingdom of God and His Righteousness and all these things, shall be added to you.
34 Take therefore, no thought for the morrow, for the morrow shall take thought for the things of itself. Sufficient to the day is the evil, thereof.'"

Chapter 7
1 Judge not that you be not judged,
2 For with what judgement you judge, you shall be judged and with what measure you mete, it shall be measured to you, again.
3 And why behold you the mote that is in your brother's eye, but consider not the beam that is in your own eye?
4 Or, how will you say to your brother, "'let me pull out the mote out of your eye and behold, a beam is in your own eye?'"
5 You hypocrite, first cast out the beam out of your own eye and then, you shall see clearly, to cast out the mote out of your brother's eye.
6 Give not that, which is Holy, to the dogs, neither cast you, your pearls before swine, lest they trample them under their feet and turn, again and rend you.

7 Ask and it shall be Given you. Seek and you shall Find. Knock and it shall be Opened to you.
8 For every one that Asks, Receives and he that Seeks, Finds. And to him that Knocks, it shall be Opened.
9 Or, what man is there of you, whom if his son asks bread, will he give him a stone?
10 Or, if he asks a fish, will he give him a serpent?
11 If you then, being bad, know how to give good gifts to your children, how much more, shall your Father, which is in Heaven Give Good things to them that Ask Him?
12 Therefore, all things, whatsoever you would that men should do to you, do you, even so, to them, for this is The Law and the Prophets.

13 Enter you, in at the strait gate. For wide, is the gate and broad is the way that leads to destruction and many there be, which go in, thereat.
14 Because strait is The Gate and narrow is The Way, which leads to Life and few, there be that find it.
15 Beware of false prophets, which come to you in sheep's clothing, but inwardly, they are ravening wolves.

16 You shall know them by their fruits. Do men gather grapes of thorns, or figs of thistles?
17 Even so, every Good tree, brings forth Good Fruit. But, a corrupt tree brings forth, evil fruit.
18 A Good tree cannot bring forth evil fruit, neither can a corrupt tree bring forth Good Fruit.
19 Every tree that brings not, forth Good Fruit, is hewn down and cast into the fire.
20 Wherefore, by their fruits, you shall know them.

21 Not every one that says to me, "'Lord, Lord,'" shall enter into the Kingdom of Heaven, but he that Does the Will of My Father, which is in Heaven.
22 Many, will say to Me in that day, "'Lord, Lord, have we not prophesied in Your Name and in Your Name, have cast out devils and in Your Name, done many wonderful works?'"
23 And then, will I profess to them, "'I never Knew you. Depart from Me, you that work iniquity.'"
24 Therefore, whosoever Hears these sayings of Mine and Does them, I will liken him to a Wise man, which built his house on a Rock.
25 And the rain descended and the floods came and the winds blew and beat on that house and it fell not, for it was founded on a Rock.
26 And every one that hears these sayings of Mine and does them not, shall be likened to a foolish man, which built his house on the sand
27 And the rain descended and the floods came and the winds blew and beat on that house and it fell and great was the fall of it."

28 And it came to pass, when Jesus had ended these sayings, the people were astonished at His Doctrine.
29 For He Taught them as one having Authority and not as the scribes.

Chapter 8

1 When He was come down from the mountain, great multitudes followed Him.
2 And behold, there came a leper and Worshipped Him saying, "Lord, if You will, You can make me clean."
3 And Jesus put forth His hand and touched him saying, "I will. Be you clean." And immediately, his leprosy was Cleansed.
4 And Jesus said to him, "see you tell no man, but go your way. Show yourself to the priest and offer the gift that Moses commanded, for a Testimony to them."

5 And when Jesus was entered into Capernaum, there came to Him a centurion, beseeching Him
6 And saying, "Lord, my servant lies at home, sick of the palsy, grievously tormented."
7 And Jesus said to him, "I will come and Heal him."
8 The centurion answered and said, "Lord, I am not worthy that You should come under My roof. But, speak the Word, only and my servant shall be Healed.
9 For I am a man under authority; having soldiers under me and I say to this man, "'go'" and he goes and to another, "'come'" and he comes and to my servant, "'do this'" and he does it."
10 When Jesus heard it, He marveled and said to them that followed, "verily, I say to you, I have not found so great Faith; no, not in Israel.
11 And I say to you that, "'many, shall come from the East and West and shall sit down with Abraham and Isaac and Jacob; in the Kingdom of Heaven.
12 But, the children of the kingdom shall be cast out, into outer Darkness. There shall be weeping and gnashing of teeth.'"
13 And Jesus said to the centurion, "go your way and as you have Believed, so be it done to you." And his servant was Healed in the same hour.

14 And when Jesus was come into Peter's house, He saw his wife's, mother, laid and sick of a fever.
15 And He Touched her hand and the fever left her and she rose and ministered to them.
16 When the evening was come, they brought to Him, many that were possessed with devils. And He cast out the spirits, with His Word and Healed all that were sick
17 That it might be Fulfilled, which was spoken by Isaiah, the prophet saying, "HIMSELF, TOOK OUR INFIRMITIES AND BARE OUR SICKENSSES."
18 Now, when Jesus saw great multitudes about Himself, He gave Commandment to depart to the other side.

19 And a certain scribe came and said to Him, "Master, I will follow You, wheresoever, You go."
20 And Jesus said to him, "the foxes have holes and the birds of the air have nests, but The Son of Man has not, where to lay His head."
21 And another of His disciples said to Him, "Lord, suffer me first, to go and bury my father."
22 But, Jesus said to him, "Follow Me and let the Dead bury their dead."
23 And when He was entered into a ship, His disciples followed Him.

24 And behold, there arose a great tempest in the Sea, insomuch that, the ship was covered with the waves, but He was asleep.
25 And His disciples came to Him and woke Him saying, "Lord, save us, we perish!"
26 And He said to them, "why are you fearful, O you of little faith?" Then, He arose and rebuked the winds and the Sea and there was a great calm.
27 But, the men marveled saying, "what manner of Man is this that even the winds and the Sea Obey Him?"

28 And when He was come to the other side, into the country of the Gergesites, there met Him two, possessed with devils coming out of the tombs, exceedingly fierce, so that no man might pass by that way.
29 And behold, they cried out saying, "what have we to do with You, Jesus, You Son of God? Are you come here, to torment us before the time?"
30 And there was a good way off from them, a herd of many swine feeding.
31 So, the devils besought Him saying, "if You cast us out, suffer us to go away into the herd of swine."
32 And He said to them, "go." And when they had come out, they went into the herd of swine and behold, the whole herd of swine ran violently down a steep place, into the Sea and perished in the waters.
33 And they that kept them, fled and went their ways into the city and told every thing and what was befallen to the possessed of the devils.
34 And behold, the whole city came out to meet Jesus and when they saw Him, they besought Him that He would depart out of their coasts.

Chapter 9

1 And He entered into a ship and passed over and came into His own city.
2 And behold, they brought to Him, a man sick of the palsy, lying on a bed. And Jesus, seeing their Faith, said to the sick of the palsy, "son, be of good cheer. Your sins are Forgiven you."
3 And behold, certain of the scribes said within themselves, "this Man blasphemes."
4 And Jesus Knowing their thoughts said, "wherefore, think you evil in your hearts?
5 For whether is easier to say, "'your sins are Forgiven you,'" or to say, "'Arise and walk?'"
6 But that you may know that, The Son of Man has Power on Earth to Forgive sins." Then said He, to the sick of the palsy, "'Arise, take up your bed and go to your house.'"
7 And he arose and departed to his house.
8 But, when the multitudes saw it, they marveled and Glorified God, which had Given such Power to men.
9 And as Jesus passed forth from there, He saw a man named, Matthew, sitting at the receipt of custom and He said to him, "Follow Me." And he arose and Followed Him.

10 And it came to pass, as Jesus sat at meat in the house, behold, many publicans and sinners came and sat down with Him and His disciples.
11 And when the Pharisees saw it, they said to His disciples, "why eats your Master with publicans and sinners?"
12 But, when Jesus heard that, He said to them, "they that be whole, need not a physician, but they that are sick.
13 But, go yourselves and learn what that means. I will have Mercy and not sacrifice, for I am not Come to call the Righteous, but sinners to Repentance."

14 Then came to Him, the disciples of John saying, "why do we and the Pharisees Fast often, but your disciples, Fast not?"
15 And Jesus said to them, "can the children of the bridechamber mourn as long as the Bridegroom is with them? But, the days will come, when the Bridegroom shall be taken from them and then, shall they Fast.
16 No man puts a piece of new cloth to an old garment, for that, which is put in to fill

it up takes from the garment and the rent is made worse.

17 Neither do men put new wine into old bottles else, the bottles break and the wine runs out and the bottles perish. But, they put new wine into new bottles and both are preserved."

18 While He spoke these things to them, behold, there came a certain ruler and Worshipped Him saying, "my daughter is even now, dead. But, come and lay Your hand on her and she shall live."
19 And Jesus arose and followed him and so did His disciples.
20 And behold, a woman, which was diseased with an issue of blood twelve years, came behind Him and touched the hem of His garment.
21 For she said within herself, "if I may but, touch His garment, I shall be whole."
22 But, Jesus turned Himself about and when He saw her, He said, "daughter, be of Good Comfort. Your Faith has made you Whole." And the woman was made Whole from that hour.
23 And when Jesus came into the ruler's house and saw the minstrels and the people making a noise,
24 He said to them, "give place, for the maid is not dead, but sleeps." And they laughed Him, to scorn.
25 But, when the people were put forth, He went in and took her by the hand and the maid arose.
26 And the fame hereof, went abroad into all that land.

27 And when Jesus departed there, two blind men followed Him, crying and saying, "You, son of David, have Mercy on us."
28 And when He was come into the house, the blind men came to Him and Jesus said to them, "Believe you that I am able to Do this?" They said to Him, "yes, Lord."
29 Then touched He, their eyes saying, "according to your Faith, be it to you."
30 And their eyes were opened and Jesus straightly charged them saying, "see that no man knows it."
31 But they, when they were departed, spread abroad His fame in all that country.

32 As they went out, behold, they brought to Him, a dumb man, possessed with a devil.
33 And when the devil was cast out, the dumb spoke and the multitudes marveled saying, "it was never so, seen in Israel."

34 But the Pharisees said, "He casts out devils, through the prince of the devils."
35 And Jesus went about all the cities and villages, Teaching in their synagogues and Preaching The Gospel of the Kingdom and Healing every sickness and every disease among the people.
36 But, when He saw the multitudes, He was moved with Compassion on them, because they fainted and were scattered abroad, as sheep having no shepherd.
37 Then, said He to His disciples, "the harvest truly is plenteous, but the laborers are few.
38 Pray you therefore, The Lord of the harvest that He will send forth laborers into His harvest."

Chapter 10

1 And when He had called to Himself, His twelve disciples, He gave them Power against unclean spirits; to cast them out and to Heal all manner of sickness and all manner of disease.
2 Now, the names of the twelve apostles are these: (the first,) Simeon (who is called Peter) and Andrew, (his brother) James, (the son of Zabdi) and John, (his brother)
3 Philip and Bartholomew, Thomas and Matthew, (the publican) James (the son of Alphaeus) and Lebbaeus, (whose surname, was Thaddaeus)
4 Simeon (the Canaanite) and Judas Iscariot (who also, betrayed Him.)

5 These twelve, Jesus sent forth and Commanded them saying, "go not, into the way of the gentiles and into any city, of the Samaritans; enter you not.
6 But go rather, to the lost sheep of the house of Israel.
7 And as you go, Preach saying, "'the Kingdom of Heaven is at hand.'"
8 Heal the sick, Cleanse the lepers, Raise the dead, Cast Out devils. Freely, you have Received, freely Give.
9 Provide neither gold, nor silver, nor brass in your purses,
10 Nor scrip for your journey, neither two coats, neither shoes, nor yet staves. For the workman is worthy of his meat.
11 And into whatsoever city, or town you shall enter, enquire who in it, is worthy and there abide, until you go there.
12 And when you come into a house, salute it.
13 And if the house be worthy, let your Peace come on it, but if it be not worthy,

let your Peace return to you.

14 And whosoever shall not receive you, nor hear your words, when you depart out of that house, or city, shake off the dust of your feet.

15 Verily, I say to you, "'it shall be more tolerable for the land of Sodom and Gomorrah in The Day of Judgement, than for that city.'"

16 Behold, I send you forth as sheep in the midst of wolves. Be you therefore, wise as serpents and harmless as doves.

17 But beware of men, for they will deliver you up to the councils and they will scourge you in their synagogues.

18 And you shall be brought before governors and kings for my sake, for a Testimony, against them and the gentiles.

19 But, when they deliver you up, take no thought how, or what you shall speak, for it shall be given you in that same hour, what you shall speak.

20 FOR IT IS NOT YOU THAT SPEAKS, BUT THE SPIRIT OF YOUR FATHER, WHICH SPEAKS IN YOU.

21 AND THE BROTHER SHALL DELIVER UP THE BROTHER TO DEATH AND THE FATHER, THE CHILD. AND THE CHILDREN SHALL RISE UP AGAINST THEIR PARENTS AND CAUSE THEM TO BE PUT TO DEATH.

22 AND YOU SHALL BE HATED OF ALL MEN, FOR MY NAME'S SAKE. BUT, HE THAT ENDURES TO THE END SHALL BE SAVED.

23 BUT, WHEN THEY PERSECUTE YOU IN THIS CITY, FLEE YOURSELVES, INTO ANOTHER. For verily, I say to you, "'you shall not have gone over the cities of Israel, until The Son of Man is come.'"

24 The disciple is not above his Master, nor the servant above his Lord.

25 It is enough for the disciple that he be as his Master and the servant as his Lord. If they have called the Master of the house Baalzebub, how much more, shall they call them of His household?

26 Fear them not therefore, for there is nothing covered that shall not be revealed and hid that shall not be known.

27 What I tell you in darkness that speak you in light. And what you Hear in the ear that Preach you on the housetops.

28 And fear not them, which kill the body, but are not able to kill the soul. But rather, Fear Him, which is able to destroy, both soul and body in Hell.

29 Are not two sparrows sold for a farthing? And one of them, shall not fall on the ground without your Father.

30 But, the very hairs of your head are all numbered.

31 Fear you not, therefore. You are of more value, than many sparrows.

32 Whosoever therefore, shall Confess Me before men, him will I Confess also, before My Father, which is in Heaven.

33 But, whosoever shall deny Me before men, him will I also, deny before My Father, which is in Heaven.

34 Think not that I am come to send peace on Earth. I came not, to send peace, but a sword.

35 FOR I AM COME TO SET A MAN AT VARIANCE, AGAINST HIS FATHER AND THE DAUGHTER, AGAINST HER MOTHER AND THE DAUGHTER IN LAW, AGAINST HER MOTHER IN LAW.

36 AND A MAN'S FOES, SHALL BE THEY, OF HIS OWN HOUSEHOLD.

37 He that loves father, or mother more than Me, is not worthy of Me and he that loves son, or daughter more than Me is not worthy of Me.

38 And he that takes not, his cross and Follows after Me, is not worthy of Me.

39 He that finds his life, shall lose it and he that loses his life, for My sake, shall find it.

40 He that receives you, receives Me. And he that receives Me, receives Him that sent Me.

41 He that receives a prophet in the name of a prophet, shall receive a prophet's reward. And he that receives a Righteous man, in the name of a Righteous man, shall receive a Righteous man's reward.

42 And whosoever shall give to drink to one of these little ones, a cup of cold water only, in the name of a disciple, verily, I say to you, "'he shall in no wise, lose his reward.'"

Chapter 11

1 And it came to pass, when Jesus had made an end of Commanding His twelve disciples, He departed there to Teach and to Preach in their cities.

2 Now, when John had heard in the prison, the Works of Christ, he sent two of his disciples

3 And said to Him, "are you He that should come, or do we look for another?"

4 Jesus answered and said to them, "go and show John again, those things, which you do Hear and See:
5 The blind Receive their sight and the lame Walk, the lepers are Cleansed and the deaf Hear, the dead are Raised Up and the poor have The Gospel Preached to them.
6 <u>And Blessed is he, whosoever, shall not, be offended in Me.</u>"

7 And as they departed, Jesus began to say to the multitudes, concerning John, "what went you out into the wilderness to see, a reed shaken with the wind?
8 But, what went you out for to see, a man clothed in soft raiment? Behold, they that wear soft clothing are in kings' houses.
9 But, what went you out for to see, a prophet? Yes, I say to you and more than, a prophet.
10 For this is he, of whom it is written, "'BEHOLD, I SEND MY MESSENGER BEFORE YOUR FACE, WHICH SHALL PREPARE YOUR WAY BEFORE YOU.'"
11 Verily, I say to them that are born of women, there has not risen a greater than John the Baptist. Notwithstanding, he that is least in the Kingdom of Heaven, is greater than he.'"
12 And <u>from the days of John, the Baptist until now, the Kingdom of Heaven suffers violence and the violent take it by force.</u>
13 For all the prophets and The Law, Prophesied until John.
14 And if you will receive it, this is Elijah, which was for to come.
15 He that has ears to hear, let him Hear.

16 But whereunto, shall I liken <u>this generation</u>? It is like to children sitting in the markets and calling to their fellows
17 And saying, "'we have piped to you and you have not danced. We have mourned to you and you have not lamented.'"
18 For John came neither eating, nor drinking and they say, "'he has a devil.'"
19 The Son of Man came eating and drinking and they say, "'behold, a man gluttonous and a winebibber; a friend of publicans and sinners.'" But, Wisdom is Justified of her children."

20 <u>Then began He to upbraid the cities wherein, most of His Mighty Works were done, because they Repented not:</u>
21 "Woe to you, Chorazin! Woe to you, Bethsaida! For if the Mighty Works, which were done in you, had been done in Tyre and Sidon, they would have Repented long ago in sackcloth and ashes.
22 But I say to you, "'it shall be more tolerable for Tyre and Sidon at The Day of Judgement, than for you.'"
23 And you Capernaum, which are exalted to Heaven, shall be brought down to Hell, for if the Mighty Works, which have been done in you, had been done in Sodom, it would have remained until this day.
24 But, I say to you that, "'it shall be more tolerable for the land of Sodom in The Day of Judgement, than for you.'"

25 At that time, Jesus answered and said, "I Thank You, O Father, Lord of Heaven and Earth, because You have hid these things, from the wise and prudent and have revealed them to babes.
26 Even so, Father, for so it seemed Good in Your sight."
27 "All things are Delivered to Me of My Father and no man knows The Son, but The Father. Neither knows any man, The Father, save The Son and he, to whomsoever, The Son will Reveal Himself.
28 Come to Me, all you that labor and are heavy laden and I will give you Rest.
29 Take My yoke on yourself and Learn of Me. For I am Meek and Lowly in heart. And you shall find Rest to your souls.
30 For My yoke is easy and My burden is light."

Chapter 12

1 At that time, Jesus went on the Sabbath Day, through the corn and His disciples were a hungered and began to pluck the ears of corn and to eat.
2 But, when the Pharisees saw it, they said to Him, "behold, Your disciples do that, which is not Lawful to do, on the Sabbath Day."
3 But, He said to them, "have you not read what David did, when he was a hungered and they that were with him,
4 How he entered into the house of God and did eat the showbread, which was not Lawful for him to eat, neither for them, which were with him, but only for the priests?
5 Or, have you not read in The Law, how that on the Sabbath Days, the priests in the temple profane the Sabbath and are blameless?
6 But I say to you that, "'in this place, is One Greater, than the temple.'"
7 But, if you had known what this means,

"'I WILL HAVE MERCY AND NOT SACRIFICE,'" you would not have condemned the guiltless.

8 For The Son of Man is Lord, even of the Sabbath Day."

9 And when He was departed there, He went into their synagogue

10 And behold, there was a man, which had his hand withered. And they asked Him saying, "is it Lawful to Heal on the Sabbath Days?"; that they might accuse Him.

11 And He said to them, "what man shall there be among you that, shall have one sheep and if it falls into a pit on the Sabbath Day, will he not lay hold on it and lift it out?

12 How much then, is a man better than a sheep? Wherefore, it is Lawful to Do Well on the Sabbath Days."

13 Then said He to the man, "stretch forth your hand." And he stretched it forth and it was Restored Whole, like as the other.

14 Then, the Pharisees went out and held a council against Him, how they might destroy Him.

15 But, when Jesus knew it, He withdrew Himself, from there and great multitudes followed Him. And He Healed them all

16 And charged them that, "they should not make Him known"

17 That it might be Fulfilled, which was spoken by Isaiah, the prophet saying,

18 "BEHOLD, MY SERVANT, WHOM I HAVE CHOSEN, MY BELOVED, IN WHOM MY SOUL IS WELL PLEASED. I WILL PUT MY SPIRIT ON HIM AND HE SHALL SHOW JUDGMENT TO THE GENTILES.

19 HE SHALL NOT STRIVE, NOR CRY, NEITHER SHALL ANY MAN HEAR HIS VOICE IN THE STREETS.

20 A BRUISED REED, SHALL HE NOT BREAK AND SMOKING FLAX, SHALL HE NOT QUENCH, UNTIL HE SENDS FORTH JUDGMENT TO VICTORY.

21 AND IN HIS NAME, SHALL THE GENTILES TRUST."

22 Then, was brought to Him, one possessed with a devil; blind and dumb. And He Healed him, insomuch that, the blind and dumb both Spoke and Saw.

23 And all the people were amazed and said, "is not this, the son of David?"

24 But, when the Pharisees Heard it, they said, "this Fellow, does not cast out devils, but by Baalzebub, the prince of the devils."

25 And Jesus Knew their thoughts and said to them, "every kingdom divided against itself, is brought to desolation and every city, or house divided against itself, shall not stand.

26 And if Satan casts out Satan, he is divided against himself. How shall then, his kingdom stand?

27 And if I, by Baalzebub, cast out devils, by whom, do your children cast them out? Therefore, they shall be your judges.

28 But, if I Cast Out devils by The Spirit of God, then the Kingdom of God is Come to you.

29 Or else, how can one enter into a strong man's house and spoil his goods, except he first, bind the strong man and then, he will spoil his house.

30 He that is not with Me, is against Me and he that gathers not, with Me scatters abroad.

31 Wherefore, I say to you, "'all manner of sin and blasphemy, shall be Forgiven to men. But, the blasphemy against The Holy Ghost, shall not be forgiven to men.

32 And whosoever, speaks a word against The Son of Man, it shall be Forgiven him. But, whosoever, speaks against The Holy Ghost, it shall not, be forgiven him; neither in this World, neither in the World to come.'"

33 Either make the tree Good and his Fruit Good, or else, make the tree corrupt and his fruit corrupt. For the tree is known by his fruit.

34 O generation of vipers, how can you being evil, speak Good things? For out of the abundance of the heart, the mouth speaks.

35 A good man out of the good treasure of the heart, brings forth good things and an evil man, out of the evil treasure, brings forth evil things.

36 But, I say to you that, "every idle word that men shall speak, they shall give account thereof, in The Day of Judgement.

37 For by your words, you shall be Justified and by your words, you shall be condemned.'"

38 Then, certain of the scribes and of the Pharisees answered saying, "Master, we would see a Sign from You."

39 But, He answered and said to them, "an evil and adulterous generation seeks after a Sign and there shall no Sign be given to

it, but the Sign of the Prophet Jonah.
40 For as Jonah was three days and three nights in the whale's belly, so shall The Son of Man be three days and three nights in the heart of the Earth.
41 The men of Nineveh, shall rise in Judgment with this generation and shall condemn it, because they Repented at the Preaching of Jonah and behold, a Greater than Jonah is here.
42 The queen of the South shall rise up in the Judgment, with this generation and shall condemn it, for she came from the uttermost parts of the earth to hear the Wisdom of Solomon and behold, a Greater than Solomon is here.
43 When the unclean spirit is gone out of a man, he walks through dry places, seeking rest and finds none.
44 Then he says, "'I will return into my house from whence I came out'" and when he is come, he finds it empty, swept and garnished.
45 Then, goes he and takes with himself, seven other spirits, more wicked than himself and they enter in and dwell there and the last state of that man, is worse than the first. Even so, shall it be also, to this wicked generation."

46 While He yet talked to the people, behold, His mother and His brothers stood without, desiring to speak with Him.
47 Then one said to Him, "behold, your mother and your brothers stand without, desiring to speak with You."
48 But, He answered and said to him that told Him, "who is My mother and who are My brothers?"
49 And He stretched forth His hand toward His disciples and said, "behold, My mother and My brothers!
50 For whosoever, shall Do the Will of My Father, which is in Heaven, the same is My brother and sister and mother."

Chapter 13

1 The same day, went Jesus out of the house and sat by the Sea side.
2 And great multitudes were gathered together to Him, so that He went into a ship and sat. And the whole multitude stood on the shore.
3 And He spoke many things to them in parables saying, "behold, A Sower went forth to Sow.
4 And when He Sowed, some seeds fell by the way side and the fowls came and devoured them up.
5 Some fell on stony places, where they had not much earth and forthwith, they sprang up, because they had no deepness of earth.
6 And when the Sun was up, they were scorched and because they had no root, they withered away.
7 And some fell among thorns and the thorns sprang up and choked them.
8 But, others fell into Good ground and Brought forth Fruit; some one hundredfold, some sixtyfold, some thirtyfold.
9 Who has ears to hear, let him Hear."
10 And the disciples came and said to him, "why speak You, to them in parables?"
11 He answered and said to them, "because it is Given to you to Know the Mysteries of the Kingdom of Heaven, but to them, it is not given.
12 For whosoever has, to him, shall be given and he shall have more abundance. But whosoever has not, from him, shall be taken away; even that he has.
13 Therefore, speak I to them in parables, because THEY SEEING, SEE NOT AND HEARING, THEY HEAR NOT, NEITHER DO THEY UNDERSTAND.
14 And in them is Fulfilled the Prophecy of Isaiah, which says, "'BY HEARING, YOU SHALL HEAR AND SHALL NOT UNDERSTAND AND SEEING, YOU SHALL SEE AND SHALL NOT PERCEIVE.
15 FOR THIS PEOPLE'S HEART IS WAXED GROSS AND THEIR EARS ARE DULL OF HEARING AND THEIR EYES, THEY HAVE CLOSED, LEST AT ANY TIME, THEY SHOULD SEE WITH THEIR EYES AND HEAR WITH THEIR EARS AND SHOULD UNDERSTAND WITH THEIR HEART AND SHOULD BE CONVERTED AND I SHOULD HEAL THEM.'"
16 But Blessed are your eyes, for they See and your ears, for they Hear.
17 For verily, I say to you that, "'many prophets and Righteous men have desired to See those things, which you See and have not seen them and to Hear those things, which you Hear and have not heard them.'"
18 Hear you therefore, the parable of the Sower,
19 When any one Hears The Word of the Kingdom and Understands it not, then comes the wicked one and catches away that, which was Sown in his heart. This is

he, which received Seed by the way side.
20 But, he that received the Seed into stony places, the same is <u>he that, Hears The Word and anon, with joy, receives it,</u>
21 Yet has he <u>no root in himself,</u> but <u>endures for a while, for when tribulation, or persecution arises, because of The Word, by and by, he is offended.</u>
22 He also that received Seed among the thorns, is he that, <u>Hears The Word and the cares of this World and the deceitfulness of riches, choke The Word and he becomes unfruitful.</u>
23 But, he that received Seed into the <u>Good Ground,</u> is he that Hears The Word and Understands it, which also, <u>Bears Fruit</u> and brings forth; some one hundredfold, some sixty, some thirty."

24 Another parable put He forth to them saying, "the Kingdom of Heaven is likened to a Man, which Sowed Good Seed in his field.
25 But, while men slept, his enemy came and sowed <u>tares</u> among the wheat and went his way.
26 But, when the blade was sprung up and Brought forth Fruit, then appeared the tares, also.
27 So, the servants of the householder came and said to him, "'Sir, did not You Sow Good Seed in your field? From whence then, has it tares?'"
28 He said to them, <u>"'an enemy has done this.'"</u> The servants said to him, "'will you then that, we go and gather them up?'"
29 But He said, "'no, lest while you gather up the tares, you root up also, the wheat with them.'"
30 Let both grow together, until the harvest. And in the time of harvest, I will say to the reapers, "'gather yourselves, together first, the tares and bind them in bundles TO BURN THEM. But, gather the wheat into My barn.'"

31 Another parable put He forth to them saying, "the Kingdom of Heaven is like to a grain of mustard Seed, which a Man took and Sowed in His field,
32 Which indeed, is the least of all seeds. But, when it is grown, it is the greatest among herbs and becomes a tree, so that the birds of the air come and lodge in the branches, thereof."
33 Another parable spoke He to them, "the Kingdom of Heaven is like to Leaven, which a woman took and hid in three measures of meal, until the whole was Leavened."
34 All these things, spoke Jesus to the multitude in parables and without a parable, spoke He not to them
35 That it might be Fulfilled, which was spoken by the prophet saying, "I WILL OPEN MY MOUTH IN PARABLES. I WILL UTTER THINGS, WHICH HAVE BEEN KEPT SECRET FROM THE FOUNDATION OF THE WORLD."

36 Then, Jesus sent the multitude away and went into the house. And His disciples came to him saying, "declare to us, the parable of the tares of the field."
37 He answered and said to them, <u>"He that Sows the Good Seed is The Son of Man.</u>
38 The field is the World. <u>The Good Seed, are</u> the children of the Kingdom. But, <u>the tares are the children of the wicked one.</u>
39 <u>The enemy that sowed them, is the Devil.</u> The harvest, is the end of the World and the reapers are the angels.
40 As therefore, the tares are gathered and burned in the fire, so shall it be in the end of this World.
41 <u>The Son of Man, shall send forth His angels and they shall gather out of His Kingdom, all things that offend and them, which do iniquity</u>
42 <u>And shall cast them into a Furnace of Fire. There shall be wailing and gnashing of teeth.</u>
43 Then, shall the Righteous Shine forth as the Sun in the Kingdom of their Father. Who has ears to Hear, let him Hear.

44 Again, the Kingdom of Heaven is like to treasure hid in a field, the which, when a man has found, he hides and for Joy thereof, goes and sells all that He has and buys that field.
45 Again, <u>the Kingdom of Heaven is like</u> to a Merchant Man, <u>seeking goodly pearls</u>
46 Who, when He had found one pearl of great price, <u>went and sold all that He had and bought it.</u>
47 Again, <u>the Kingdom of Heaven is like</u> to a net that was cast into the Sea and gathered of every kind,
48 Which when it was full, they drew to shore and sat down and <u>gathered the good into vessels, but cast the bad away.</u>
49 So, shall it be at the end of the World. <u>The angels shall come forth and sever the wicked from among the Just</u>
50 <u>And shall cast them into the furnace of fire. There shall be wailing and gnashing</u>

of teeth."

51 Jesus said to them, "have you understood all these things?" They said to Him, "yes, Lord."
52 Then, said He to them, "therefore, every scribe, which is Instructed to the Kingdom of Heaven is like to a Man that is a householder, which brings forth out of His treasure, things, new and old."
53 And it came to pass that when Jesus had finished these parables, He departed there.

54 And when He was come into His own country, He Taught them in their synagogue, insomuch that they were astonished and said, "whence has this Man this Wisdom and these Mighty Works?
55 Is not this the Carpenter's Son? Is not His mother called, Mary and His brothers: Jacob and Joseph and Simeon and Judah?
56 And His sisters, are they not all with us? Whence then, has this Man, all these things?"
57 And they were offended in Him. But, Jesus said to them, "a prophet is not without honor, save in His own country and in His own house."
58 And He did not, many Mighty Works there, because of their unbelief.

Chapter 14

1 At that time, Herod the tetrarch heard of the fame of Jesus
2 And said to his servants, "this is John, the Baptist. He is risen from the dead and therefore, Mighty Works do show forth, themselves in Him."
3 For Herod had laid hold on John and bound him and put him in prison for Herodias' sake; his brother, Philip's wife.
4 For John said to him, "it is not Lawful for you to have her."
5 And when he would have put him to death, he feared the multitude, because they counted him as a prophet.

6 But, when Herod's birthday was kept, the daughter of Herodias danced before them and pleased Herod.
7 Whereupon, he promised with an oath to give her whatsoever, she would ask.
8 And she being before, instructed of her mother said, "give me here, John Baptist's head in a charger."

9 And the king was sorry. Nevertheless, for the oath's sake and them, which sat with him at meat, he commanded it to be given her.
10 And he sent and beheaded John in the prison.
11 And his head was brought in a charger and given to the damsel and she brought it to her mother.
12 And his disciples came and took up the body and buried it and went and told Jesus.

13 When Jesus heard of it, He departed there, by ship into a desert place apart and when the people had heard thereof, they followed Him on foot out of the cities.
14 And Jesus went forth and saw a great multitude and was moved with Compassion toward them and He Healed their sicknesses.
15 And when it was evening, His disciples came to him saying, "this is a desert place and the time is now, past. Send the multitude away that they may go into the villages and buy themselves, victuals."
16 But, Jesus said to them, "they need not depart. Give you them to eat."
17 And they said to Him, "we have here, but five loaves and two fish."
18 He said, "bring them here, to Me."
19 And He Commanded the multitude to sit down on the grass and took the five loaves and the two fish and looking up to Heaven, He Blessed and Broke and gave the loaves to His disciples and the disciples to the multitude.
20 And they did all eat and were filled. And they Took Up of the fragments that remained, twelve baskets full.
21 And they that had eaten, were about five thousand men, besides women and children.

22 And straightway, Jesus constrained His disciples to get into a ship and to go before Him, to the other side, while He sent the multitudes away.
23 And when He had sent the multitudes away, He went up into a mountain, apart to Pray. And when the evening was come, He was there, alone.
24 But the ship was now, in the midst of the Sea; tossed with waves, for the wind was contrary.
25 And in the fourth watch of the night, Jesus went to them, walking on the Sea.
26 And when the disciples saw Him

walking on the Sea, they were troubled saying, "it is a spirit" and they cried out for fear.
27 But straightway, Jesus spoke to them saying, "be of good cheer. It is I, be not afraid."

28 And Peter answered Him and said, "Lord, if it be You, bid me come, to You on the water!"
29 And He said, "come!" And when Peter was come down out of the ship, he walked on the water, to go to Jesus.
30 But, when he saw the wind, boisterous, he was afraid and beginning to sink, he cried saying, "Lord, save me!"
31 And immediately, Jesus stretched forth His hand and caught him and said to him, "O you of little faith, wherefore, did you doubt?"
32 And when they had come into the ship, the wind ceased.
33 Then they that were in the ship, came and Worshipped Him saying, "of a Truth, You are The Son of God."

34 And when they were gone over, they came into the land of Chinnereth.
35 And when the men of that place had knowledge of Him, they sent out into all that country, round about and brought to Him, all that were diseased
36 And besought Him that they might only touch the hem of His garment and as many as touched, were made perfectly Whole.

Chapter 15

1 Then came to Jesus, scribes and Pharisees, which were of Jerusalem saying,
2 "Why do Your disciples transgress the tradition of the elders? For they wash not, their hands when they eat bread."
3 But, He answered and said to them, "why do you also, transgress The Commandment of God by your tradition?
4 For God Commanded saying, "'Honor your father and mother and he that curses father, or mother, let him die the death.'"
5 But you say, "'whosoever, shall say to his father, or his mother, ""it is a gift by whatsoever, you might be profited by me
6 And honor not his father, or his mother, he shall be free.'"" Thus, have you made The Commandment of God of none effect, by your tradition.
7 You hypocrites, well did Isaiah Prophesy of you saying,
8 "'THIS PEOPLE DRAWS NEAR TO ME WITH THEIR MOUTH AND HONORS ME WITH THEIR LIPS, BUT THEIR HEART IS FAR FROM ME.
9 BUT IN VAIN, THEY DO WORSHIP ME; TEACHING FOR DOCTRINES, THE COMMANDMENTS OF MEN.'"

10 And He called the multitude and said to them, "Hear and Understand.
11 Not that, which goes into the mouth, defiles a man. But that, which comes out of the mouth, this defiles a man."
12 Then, came His disciples and said to him, "know You that the Pharisees were offended, after they heard this saying?"
13 But, He answered and said, "every plant, which My Heavenly Father has not planted, shall be rooted up.
14 Let them alone. They are blind leaders of the blind. And if the blind leads the blind, both shall fall into the ditch."

15 Then answered Peter and said to Him, "declare to us, this parable."
16 And Jesus said, "are you also, yet without understanding?
17 Do not you yet, Understand that whatsoever, enters in at the mouth, goes into the belly and is cast out into the draught?
18 But those things, which proceed out of the mouth, comes forth from the heart and they defile the man.
19 For out of the heart, proceeds evil thoughts: murders, adulteries, fornications, thefts, false witnesses, blasphemies…
20 These are the things, which defile a man. But, to eat with unwashed hands defiles not a man."

21 Then, Jesus went there and departed into the coasts of Tyre and Sidon.
22 And behold, a woman of Canaan came out of the same coasts and cried to him saying, "have Mercy on me, O Lord, You Son of David. My daughter is grievously vexed with a devil."
23 But, He answered her not a word. And His disciples came and besought Him saying, "send her away, for she cries after us."
24 But, He answered and said, "I am not sent, but to the lost sheep of the house of Israel."
25 Then, came she and Worshipped Him

saying, "Lord, help me."
26 But, He answered and said, "it is not meet to take the children's bread and to cast it to dogs."
27 And she said, "Truth, Lord. Yet, the dogs eat of the crumbs, which fall from their masters' table."
28 Then, Jesus answered and said to her, "O woman, great is your Faith. Be it to you, even as you will." And her daughter was made whole from that very hour.

29 And Jesus departed from there and came near to the Sea of Galilee and went up into a mountain and sat down there.
30 And great multitudes came to Him, having with them, those that were: lame, blind, dumb, maimed and many others and cast them down at Jesus' feet and He Healed them,
31 Insomuch that, the multitude wondered when they saw the dumb to Speak, the maimed to be Whole, the lame to Walk and the blind to See and they Glorified The God of Israel.

32 Then, Jesus called His disciples to Himself and said, "I have Compassion on the multitude, because they continue with Me now, three days and have nothing to eat and I will not send them away fasting, lest they faint in the way."
33 And His disciples said to Him, "where should we have so much bread in the wilderness, as to fill so great a multitude?"
34 And Jesus said to them, "how many loaves have you?" And they said, "seven and a few little fish."
35 And He commanded the multitude to, "sit down on the ground."
36 And He took the seven loaves and the fish and Gave Thanks and broke them and Gave to His disciples and the disciples to the multitude.
37 And they did all eat and were Filled and they Took Up of the broken meat that was left; seven baskets full.
38 And they that did eat, were four thousand men, besides women and children.
39 And He sent away the multitude and took ship and came into the coasts of Magdala.

Chapter 16
1 The Pharisees also, with the Sadducees came and tempting, desired Him that He would show them a Sign from Heaven.
2 He answered and said to them, "when it is evening, you say, "'it will be fair weather, for the sky is red.
3 And in the morning, it will be foul weather today, for the sky is red and lowering.'" O you hypocrites, you can discern the face of the sky. But, can you not discern the Signs of the times?
4 A wicked and adulterous generation seeks after a Sign and there shall no Sign be given to it, but the Sign of the prophet Jonah." And He left them and departed.

5 And when His disciples had come to the other side, they had forgotten to take bread.
6 Then, Jesus said to them, "take Heed and Beware of the leaven of the Pharisees and of the Sadducees."
7 And they reasoned among themselves saying, "it is because we have taken no bread,"
8 Which, when Jesus perceived, He said to them, "O you of little faith. Why reason you among yourselves, because you have brought no bread?
9 Do you not yet understand, neither remember the five loaves of the five thousand and how many baskets you Took Up,
10 Neither the seven loaves of the four thousand and how many baskets you Took Up?
11 How is it that you do not understand that I spoke it not to you, concerning bread that you should Beware of the leaven of the Pharisees and of the Sadducees?"
12 Then Understood they, how that He Commanded them not, beware of the leaven of bread but of, "the doctrine of the Pharisees and of the Sadducees."

13 When Jesus came into the coasts of Caesarea Philippi, He asked His disciples saying, "Whom do men say that I, The Son of Man am?"
14 And they said, "some say that, "'You are John, the Baptist,'" some, "'Elijah'" and others, "'Jeremiah,'" or "'one of the prophets.'"
15 He said to them, "but Whom, say you that I am?"
16 And Simeon Peter answered and said, "You are The Christ, The Son of The Living God."
17 And Jesus answered and said to him, "Blessed are you, Simeon Bar-jona, for flesh and blood has not revealed it to you, but My Father, which is in Heaven.
18 And I say also, to you that, "'you are

Peter and on This Rock, I will build My church and the gates of Hell, shall not prevail against it.

19 And I will Give to you, the keys of the Kingdom of Heaven and whatsoever, you shall bind on Earth, shall be bound in Heaven and whatsoever, you shall loose on Earth, shall be loosed in Heaven.'"

20 Then, charged He, His disciples that they should, "tell no man that He was Jesus, The Christ."

21 From that time forth, began Jesus to Show to His disciples, how that He MUST GO TO JERUSALEM AND SUFFER MANY THINGS OF THE ELDERS AND CHIEF PRIESTS AND SCRIBES AND BE KILLED AND BE RAISED AGAIN, THE THIRD DAY.

22 Then, Peter took Him and began to rebuke Him saying, "be it far from You, Lord. This shall not be to You."

23 But He turned and said to Peter, "get you behind Me, Satan. You are an offence to Me. For you savor not, the things that be of God, but those that be of men."

24 Then, said Jesus to His disciples, "if any man will Come After Me, let him Deny himself and Take Up his cross and Follow Me.

25 For whosoever, will save his life, shall lose it and whosoever, will lose his life for My sake, shall find it.

26 For what is a man profited, if he shall gain the whole World and lose his own soul, or what shall a man give in exchange for his soul?

27 For The Son of Man, shall come in the Glory of His Father, with His angels and then, He shall Reward every man, according to his Works.

28 Verily, I say to you, "'there be some standing here, which shall not taste of death, until they see The Son of Man Coming in His Kingdom.'"

Chapter 17

1 And after six days, Jesus took Peter, James and John (his Brother) and brought them up into a high mountain, apart

2 And was Transfigured before them and His face did Shine as the Sun and His raiment was white as the Light.

3 And behold, there appeared to them, Moses and Elijah talking with Him.

4 Then answered Peter and said to Jesus, "Lord, it is good for us to be here. If You will, let us make here, three Tabernacles: one for You and one for Moses and one for Elijah."

5 While He yet spoke, behold, A Bright Cloud overshadowed them and behold, A Voice out of The Cloud which said, "this is My Beloved Son, in Whom I am Well Pleased. Hear you, Him."

6 And when the disciples heard it, they fell on their faces and were sore afraid.

7 And Jesus came and touched them and said, "arise and be not afraid."

8 And when they had lifted up their eyes, they saw no man, save Jesus only.

9 And as they came down from the mountain, Jesus charged them saying, "tell the Vision to no man, until The Son of Man is Risen again, from the dead."

10 And His disciples asked Him saying, "why then, say the scribes that, "'Elijah must first, come?'"

11 And Jesus answered and said to them, "Elijah truly, shall first, come and restore all things.

12 But I say to you that, "'ELIJAH IS COME, ALREADY and they knew him not, but have done to him, whatsoever they determined. LIKEWISE, SHALL ALSO, THE SON OF MAN SUFFER OF THEM.'"

13 Then, the disciples understood that He spoke to them, of John, the Baptist.

14 And when they had come to the multitude, there came to Him, a certain man Kneeling Down to Him and saying,

15 "Lord, have Mercy on my son, for he is lunatic and sore vexed. For oftentimes, he falls into the fire and often, into the water.

16 And I brought him to Your disciples and they could not cure him."

17 Then, Jesus answered and said, "O Faithless and perverse generation, how long shall I be with you? How long shall I suffer you? Bring him here, to Me."

18 And Jesus rebuked the devil and he departed out of him. And the child was Cured, from that very hour.

19 Then, came the disciples to Jesus, apart and said, "why could not, we Cast him Out?"

20 And Jesus said to them, "because of your unbelief. For verily, I say to you, "'if you have faith as a grain of mustard seed, you shall say to this mountain, "'remove hence, to hitherto place and it shall remove and nothing, shall be impossible to you.

21 Howbeit, this kind, goes not out, but by Prayer and Fasting.'"

22 And while they abode in Galilee, Jesus said to them, "THE SON OF MAN SHALL BE BETRAYED INTO THE HANDS OF MEN
23 AND THEY SHALL KILL HIM AND THE THIRD DAY, HE SHALL BE RAISED AGAIN." And they were exceedingly sorry.

24 And when they had come to Capernaum, they that received tribute money, came to Peter and said, "does not your Master pay tribute?"
25 He said, "yes." And when he was come into the house, Jesus prevented him saying, "what think you, Simeon, of whom do the kings of the Earth take custom, or tribute; of their own children, or of strangers?"
26 Peter said to him, "of strangers." Jesus said to him, "then, are the children free.
27 Notwithstanding, lest we should offend them, go you, to the Sea and cast a hook and take up the fish that first comes up and when you have opened his mouth, you shall Find a piece of money. That, take and give to them, for Me and you."

Chapter 18

1 At the same time, came the disciples to Jesus saying, "who is the greatest in the Kingdom of Heaven?"
2 And Jesus called a little child to Himself and set him in the midst of them,
3 And said, "verily, I say to you, "'except you be Converted and become as little children, you shall not enter into the Kingdom of Heaven.
4 Whosoever therefore, shall Humble himself as this little child, the same is greatest in the Kingdom of Heaven.
5 And whosoever, shall receive one such, little child in My Name Receives Me.
6 But, whosoever shall offend one of these little ones, which Believe in Me, it were better for him that a millstone were hanged about his neck and that he were drowned in the depth of the Sea.
7 Woe to the World, because of offences! For it must needs be that, offences come. But, woe to that man, by whom the offence comes!"
8 Wherefore, if your hand, or your foot offends you, cut them off and cast them from yourself. It is better for you to enter into Life halt, or maimed, rather than having two hands, or two feet, to be cast into everlasting fire.
9 And if your eye offends you, pluck it out and cast it from yourself. It is better for you to enter into Life with one eye, rather than having two eyes, to be cast into Hell fire.
10 Take Heed that, you despise not, one of these little ones. For I say to you that, "'in Heaven, their angels do always, behold the face of My Father, which is in Heaven.'"

11 For The Son of Man is come to Save that, which was lost.
12 How think you? If a Man has one hundred sheep and one of them are gone astray, does He not leave the ninety and nine and go into the mountains and Seek that, which is gone astray?
13 And if so be that, He finds it, verily, I say to you, He Rejoices more of that sheep, than of the ninety and nine, which went not astray.
14 Even so, it is not, the Will of your Father, which is in Heaven that one of these little ones should perish.

15 Moreover, if your brother shall trespass against you, go and tell him his fault, between you and him, alone. If he shall hear you, you have gained your brother.
16 But, if he will not hear you, then take with you one, or two more that in the mouth of two, or three witnesses, every word may be established.
17 And if he shall neglect to hear them, tell it to the church. But, if he neglects to hear the church, let him be to you, as an heathen man and a publican.
18 Verily, I say to you, "'whatsoever, you shall bind on Earth, shall be bound in Heaven and whatsoever, you shall loose on Earth, shall be loosed in Heaven.'"
19 Again, I say to you that, "'if two of you, shall agree on Earth, as touching any thing that they shall ask, it shall be done for them of My Father, which is in Heaven.
20 For where two, or three are gathered together in My Name, there am I, in the midst of them.'"

21 Then, came Peter to Him and said, "Lord, how often, shall my brother sin against me and I Forgive him, until seven times?"
22 Jesus said to him, "I say not to you, "'until seven times, but until, seventy times seven."'
23 Therefore, is the Kingdom of Heaven likened to "'A Certain King,'" which would

take account of His servants.
24 And when He had begun to reckon, one was brought to Him, which owed Him ten thousand talents.
25 But forasmuch, as he had not to pay, his Lord Commanded him to be sold and his wife and children and all that he had and payment to be made.
26 The servant therefore, fell down and Worshipped Him saying, "'Lord, have patience with me and I will pay you all.'"
27 Then, The Lord of that servant, was Moved with Compassion and loosed him and Forgave him the debt.

28 But, the same servant went out and found one of his fellow servants, which owed him one hundred pence and he laid hands on him and took him by the throat saying, "'pay me, that you owe.'"
29 And his fellow servant fell down at his feet and besought him saying, "'have patience with me and I will pay you all.'"
30 And he would not, but went and cast him into prison, until he should pay the debt.
31 So, when his fellow servants saw what was done, they were very sorry and came and told to their Lord all that was done.
32 Then his Lord, after that he had called him, said to him, "'O you wicked servant, I Forgave you All that debt, because you desired Me.
33 Should not you also, have had compassion on your fellow servant, even as I had pity on you?'"
34 And his Lord was wroth and delivered him to the tormentors, until he should pay all that was due to Him.
35 So likewise, shall My Heavenly Father do also, to you, if you, from your hearts forgive not every one, his brother their trespasses."

Chapter 19

1 And it came to pass that when Jesus had finished these sayings, He departed from Galilee and came into the coasts of Judaea, beyond Jordan.
2 And great multitudes followed Him and He Healed them, there.

3 The Pharisees also, came to Him, tempting Him and saying to Him, "is it Lawful for a man to put away his wife, for every cause?"
4 And He answered and said to them, "have you not read that He, which made them at the beginning, '"made them male and female"'
5 And said, "'for this cause, shall a man leave father and mother and shall cleave to his wife and they two, shall be one flesh?'"
6 Wherefore, they are no more two, but one flesh. What therefore, God has joined together, let no man put asunder."

7 They said to Him, "why did Moses then, command to give a writing of divorcement and to put her away?"
8 He said to them, "Moses, because of the hardness of your hearts, suffered you to put away your wives, but from the beginning, it was not so.
9 And I say to you, "whosoever, shall put away his wife, except it be for fornication and shall marry another, commits adultery and whosoever, marries her, which is put away, does commit adultery.'"
10 His disciples said to Him, "if the case of the man be so, with his wife, it is not good to marry."
11 But, He said to them, "all men cannot receive this saying, save they, to whom, it is Given.
12 For there are some eunuchs, which were so born from their mother's womb and there are some eunuchs, which were made eunuchs of men and there be eunuchs, which have made themselves, eunuchs for the Kingdom of Heaven's sake. He that is able to Receive it, let him Receive it."

13 Then, were there brought to Him, little children that He should put His hands on them and Pray. And the disciples rebuked them.
14 But, Jesus said, "suffer little children and forbid them not, to come to Me. For of such, is the Kingdom of Heaven."
15 And He laid His hands on them and departed there.

16 And behold, one came and said to Him, "Good Master, what Good thing shall I do that I may have Eternal Life?"
17 And He said to him, "why call you, Me Good? There is none Good, but One. That is God. But, if you will enter into Life, Keep The Commandments."
18 He said to him, "which?" Jesus said, "you shall do no murder, you shall not commit adultery, you shall not steal, you shall not bear false witness,

19 Honor your father and your mother and you shall love your neighbor as yourself..."
20 The young man said to Him, "all these things, have I Kept from my youth up. What lack I, yet?"
21 Jesus said to him, "if you will be perfect, go and sell that, you have and Give to the poor and you shall have treasure in Heaven and come and Follow Me."
22 But, when the young man heard that saying, he went away sorrowful, for he had great possessions.

23 Then, said Jesus to His disciples, "verily, I say to you that, "'a rich man, shall hardly, enter into the Kingdom of Heaven.'"
24 And again, I say to you, "'it is easier for a camel to go through the eye of a needle, than for a rich man to enter into the Kingdom of God.'"
25 When His disciples heard it, they were exceedingly amazed saying, "who then, can be Saved?"
26 But, Jesus beheld them and said to them, "with men, this is impossible. But, with God, all things are Possible."

27 Then, answered Peter and said to Him, "behold, we have forsaken all and Followed You. What shall we have, therefore?"
28 And Jesus said to them, "verily, I say to you that, "'you, which have Followed Me, in the Regeneration, when The Son of Man shall sit in the throne of His Glory, you also, shall sit on twelve thrones; Judging the twelve tribes of Israel.
29 And every one that has forsaken: houses, or brothers, or sisters, or father, or mother, or wife, or children, or lands, for My Name's sake, shall Receive one hundredfold and shall inherit everlasting Life.
30 But, many that are first, shall be last and the last, shall be first.

Chapter 20

1 For the Kingdom of Heaven is like to a Man that is a householder, which went out early in the morning to hire laborers into His vineyard.
2 And when He had agreed with the laborers for a penny a day, He sent them into His vineyard.
3 And He went out about the third hour and saw others, standing idle in the marketplace
4 And said to them, "'go you also, into the vineyard and whatsoever is right, I will give you.'" And they went their way.
5 Again, He went out about the sixth and ninth hour and did, likewise.
6 And about the eleventh hour, He went out and found others standing idle and said to them, "'why stand you here, all the day idle?'"
7 They said to Him, "'because no man has hired us.'" He said to them, "'go you also, into the vineyard and whatsoever, is right that shall you receive.'"

8 So, when evening was come, The Lord of the vineyard said to His steward, "'call the laborers and give them their hire, beginning from the last to the first.'"
9 And when they came that were hired about the eleventh hour, they received every man a penny.
10 But when the first came, they supposed that they should have received more and they likewise, received every man a penny.
11 And when they had received it, they murmured against The Good Man of the house,
12 Saying, "'these last, have worked, but one hour and You have made them equal to us, which have borne the burden and heat of the day.'"
13 But, He answered one of them and said, "'friend, I do you no wrong. Did not you, agree with Me, for a penny?
14 Take that, yours is and go your way. I will give to this last, even as to you.
15 Is it not Lawful for Me to do what I will with My Own? Is your eye evil, because I am Good?'"
16 So the last, shall be first and the first, last. For many are Called, but few Chosen."

17 And Jesus going up to Jerusalem, took the twelve disciples apart, in the way and said to them,
18 "Behold, we go up to Jerusalem and THE SON OF MAN, SHALL BE BETRAYED TO THE CHIEF PRIESTS AND TO THE SCRIBES AND THEY SHALL CONDEMN HIM TO DEATH
19 AND SHALL DELIVER HIM TO THE GENTILES, TO MOCK AND TO SCOURGE AND TO CRUCIFY HIM AND THE THIRD DAY, HE SHALL RISE, AGAIN."

20 Then came to Him, the mother of Zabdi's children, with her sons;

Worshipping Him and desiring a certain thing of Him.

21 And He said to her, "what will you..?" She said to Him, "grant that these, my two sons may sit, the one, on Your right hand and the other, on the left, in Your kingdom."

22 But, Jesus answered and said, "you know not, what you ask. Are you able to Drink of the Cup that I shall Drink of and to be Baptized with the Baptism that I am Baptized with?" They said to Him, "we are able."

23 And He said to them, "you shall Drink indeed of My Cup and be Baptized with the Baptism that I am Baptized with, but to sit on My right hand and on My left, is not Mine to give, but it shall be given to them, for whom it is prepared of My Father."

24 And when the ten heard it, they were moved with indignation against the two brothers.

25 But Jesus called them to Himself and said, "you know that the princes of the gentiles exercise dominion over them and they that are great, exercise authority on them.

26 But, it shall not be so among you. But, whosoever will be great among you, let him be your minister.

27 And whosoever, will be chief among you, let him be your servant.

28 Even as The Son of Man came not to be ministered to, but to Minister and to give His life a ransom for many."

29 And as they departed from Jericho, a great multitude followed Him.

30 And behold, two blind men sitting by the way side, when they heard that Jesus passed by, cried out saying, "have Mercy on us, O Lord, You son of David."

31 And the multitude rebuked them, because they should hold their peace. But, they cried the more saying, "have Mercy on us, O Lord, You son of David!"

32 And Jesus stood still and called them and said, "what will you that I shall Do to you?"

33 They said to him, "Lord, that our eyes may be Opened."

34 So, Jesus had Compassion on them and Touched their eyes and immediately, their eyes Received Sight and they followed Him.

Chapter 21

1 And when they drew near to Jerusalem and had come to Bethphage, to the Mount of Olives, then sent Jesus two disciples,

2 Saying to them, "go into the village over against yourselves and straightway, you shall find an ass tied and a colt with her. Loose them and bring them to Me.

3 And if any man says anything to you, you shall say, "'The Lord has need of them and straightway, he will send them.'"

4 All this was done that it might be Fulfilled, which was spoken by the prophet saying,

5 "TELL YOU, THE DAUGHTER OF SION, BEHOLD, YOUR KING COMES TO YOU, MEEK AND SITTING ON AN ASS AND A COLT; THE FOAL OF AN ASS."

6 And the disciples went and did as Jesus Commanded them

7 And brought the ass and the colt and put on them, their clothes and they set Him, thereon.

8 And a very great multitude spread their garments in the way. Others cut down branches from the trees and strawed them in the way.

9 And the multitudes that went before and that followed, cried saying, "Hosanna, to The Son of David! Blessed is He that comes in The Name of The Lord! Hosanna in the Highest!"

10 And when He was come into Jerusalem, all the city was moved saying, "Who is this?"

11 And the multitude said, "this is Jesus, The Prophet of Nazareth, of Galilee."

12 And Jesus went into the temple of God and cast out all them that sold and bought in the temple and overthrew the tables of the moneychangers and the seats of them that sold doves

13 And said to them, "it is written, "'My house shall be called the house of Prayer,'" but you have made it a den of thieves!"

14 And the blind and the lame, came to Him in the temple and He Healed them.

15 And when the chief priests and scribes saw the Wonderful things that He did and the children crying in the temple and saying, "Hosanna to The Son of David!," they were sore displeased

16 And said to Him, "hear you, what these say?" And Jesus said to them, "yes, have you never read, "'OUT OF THE MOUTH OF BABES AND SUCKLINGS, YOU HAVE PERFECTED PRAISE?'"

17 And He left them and went out of the city, into Bethany and He lodged there.

18 Now, in the morning, as He returned into the city, He hungered.
19 And when He saw a fig tree in the way, He came to it and found nothing thereon, but leaves only and said to it, "let no fruit grow on you henceforward, for ever." And presently, the fig tree withered away.
20 And when the disciples saw it, they marveled saying, "how soon is the fig tree withered away!"
21 Jesus answered and said to them, "verily, I say to you, "'if you have Faith and doubt not, you shall not only do this, which is done to the fig tree, but also, if you shall say to this mountain, "'be you, removed and be you, cast into the Sea,'"' it shall be done.
22 And all things, whatsoever you shall Ask in Prayer, Believing, you shall Receive.'"

23 And when He was come into the temple, the chief priests and the elders of the people, came to Him as He was Teaching and said, "by what Authority, do You these things and Who gave You this Authority?"
24 And Jesus answered and said to them, "I also, will ask you one thing, which, if you tell Me, I, in like wise, will tell you, by what Authority, I Do these things.
25 The Baptism of John, where was it from, Heaven, or of men?" And they reasoned with themselves saying, "if we shall say, "'from Heaven,'" He will say to us, "'why did you not then, Believe Him?'"
26 But, if we shall say, "'of men,'" we fear the people, for all hold John as a prophet."
27 And they answered Jesus and said, "we cannot tell." And He said to them, "neither tell I you, by what Authority I Do these things.
28 But, what think you? A certain man had two sons and he came to the first and said, "'son, go work today in my vineyard.'"
29 He answered and said, "'I will not,'" but afterward, he Repented and went.
30 And he came to the second and said likewise. And he answered and said, "'I go, Sir'" and went not."
31 Whether of them two, Did the Will of his Father? They said to Him, "the first." Jesus said to them, "verily, I say to you that, "'the publicans and the harlots go into the Kingdom of God, before you."
32 For John came to you in The Way of Righteousness and you believed him not. But, the publicans and the harlots Believed him and you, when you had seen it, repented not, afterward that you might believe him.'"
33 Hear another parable. There was a certain Householder, which planted a vineyard and hedged it, round about and dug a winepress in it and built a tower and let it out to husbandmen and went into a far country.
34 And when the time of the fruit drew near, He sent His servants to the husbandmen that they might Receive the fruits of it.
35 And the husbandmen took His servants and beat one and killed another and stoned another.
36 Again, He sent other servants, more than the first and they did to them, likewise.
37 But last of all, He sent to them, His Son saying, "'they will Reverence My Son.'"
38 But, when the husbandmen saw The Son, they said among themselves, "'this is The Heir. Come, let us kill Him and let us seize on His inheritance.'"
39 And they caught Him and cast Him out of the vineyard and slew Him.
40 When The Lord therefore, of the vineyard comes, what will He do to those husbandmen?"
41 They said to Him, "He will miserably, destroy those wicked men and will let out His vineyard to other husbandmen, which shall render him the fruits in their seasons."

42 Jesus said to them, "did you never read in The Scriptures, "'THE STONE, WHICH THE BUILDERS REJECTED, THE SAME IS BECOME THE HEAD OF THE CORNER, THIS IS THE LORD'S DOING AND IT IS MARVELOUS IN OUR EYES?'"
43 Therefore, say I to you, "'THE KINGDOM OF GOD, SHALL BE TAKEN FROM YOU AND GIVEN TO A NATION BRINGING FORTH THE FRUITS, THEREOF.
44 AND WHOSOEVER, SHALL FALL ON THIS STONE, SHALL BE BROKEN. BUT ON WHOMSOEVER, IT SHALL FALL, IT WILL GRIND HIM TO POWDER.'"
45 And when the chief priests and Pharisees had heard His parables, they perceived that He spoke of them.
46 But, when they sought to lay hands on Him, they feared the multitude, because they took Him for a prophet.

Chapter 22

1 And Jesus answered and spoke to them

again, by parables and said,

2 "The Kingdom of Heaven is like to "'A certain King,'" which made a marriage for His Son

3 And sent forth, His servants to call them that were bidden to the wedding and they would not come.

4 Again, He sent forth other servants saying, "'tell them which are bidden, ""behold, I have prepared My dinner. My oxen and My fatlings are killed and all things are ready. Come to the marriage.""

5 But, they made light of it and went their ways; one to his farm, another to his merchandise.

6 And the remnant took His servants and entreated them spitefully and slew them.

7 But, when The King heard thereof, He was wroth and He sent forth His armies and destroyed those murderers and burned up their city.

8 Then, said He to His servants, "'the wedding is ready, but they, which were bidden, were not worthy.

9 Go you therefore, into the highways and as many as you shall find, bid to the marriage.'"

10 So, those servants went out into the highways and gathered together, all as many as they found; both bad and good and the wedding was furnished with guests.

11 And when The King came in to see the guests, He saw there a man, which had not on a wedding garment.

12 And He said to him, "'friend, how came you in here, not having a wedding garment?'" And he was speechless.

13 Then, said The King to the servants, "'bind him hand and foot and take him away and cast him into Outer Darkness. There shall be weeping and gnashing of teeth.

14 For many are Called, but few are Chosen.'"

15 Then, went the Pharisees and took counsel how they might entangle Him in His talk.

16 And they sent out to Him, their disciples with the Herodians saying, "Master, we know that You are True and Teach The Way of God in Truth, neither care You, for any man, for you regard not the person of men.

17 Tell us therefore, "'what think you, is it Lawful to give tribute to Caesar, or not?'"

18 But, Jesus perceived their wickedness and said, "why tempt you Me, you hypocrites?

19 Show me the tribute money." And they brought to Him a penny.

20 And He said to them, "whose is this image and superscription?"

21 They said to Him, "Caesar's." Then, said He to them, "render therefore, to Caesar the things which are Caesar's and to God, the things that are God's."

22 When they had Heard these words, they marveled and left Him and went their way.

23 The same day, came to Him the Sadducees, which say that, "there is no resurrection" and asked Him

24 Saying, "Master, Moses said, "'if a man dies, having no children, his Brother shall marry his wife and raise up seed to his brother.

25 Now, there were with us, seven brothers and the first, when he had married a wife, deceased and having no issue, left his wife to his brother.

26 Likewise, the second also, and the third, to the seventh.

27 And last of all, the woman died, also.

28 Therefore, in the Resurrection, whose wife shall she be of the seven? For they all had her.'"

29 Jesus answered and said to them, "you do err, not knowing The Scriptures, nor the Power of God.

30 For in the Resurrection, they neither marry, nor are given in marriage, but are as the angels of God in Heaven.

31 But, as touching the Resurrection of the Dead, have you not read that, which was spoken to you by God saying,

32 "'I am The God of Abraham and The God of Isaac and The God of Jacob?'" God is not The God of the dead, but of the Living."

33 And when the multitude heard this, they were astonished at His Doctrine.

34 But, when the Pharisees had heard that He had put the Sadducees to silence, they were gathered together.

35 Then one of them, which was a lawyer, asked Him a question, tempting Him and saying,

36 "Master, which is The Great Commandment in The Law?"

37 Jesus said to him, "'you shall Love The Lord, your God with All your heart and with

All your soul and with All your mind.'"
38 This is the First and Great Commandment.
39 And the Second is like to it, "'you shall Love your neighbor as yourself.'"
40 On these two Commandments, hang All The Law and the Prophets."

41 While the Pharisees were gathered together, Jesus asked them
42 Saying, "what think you of Christ; Whose Son is He?" They said to Him, "The son of David."
43 He said to them, "how then, does David, in Spirit, call Him, "'Lord,'" saying,
44 "'THE LORD SAID TO MY LORD, SIT YOURSELF ON MY RIGHT HAND, UNTIL I MAKE YOUR ENEMIES YOUR FOOTSTOOL?'"
45 If David then, called Him, "'Lord,'" how is He his Son?"
46 And no man was able to answer Him a word, neither did any man from that day forth, ask Him any more questions.

Chapter 23

1 Then, spoke Jesus to the multitude and to His disciples
2 Saying, "the scribes and the Pharisees sit in Moses' seat.
3 All therefore, whatsoever, they bid you, Observe. That, Observe and Do, but do not you, after their works. For they say and do not.
4 For they bind heavy burdens and grievous to be borne and lay them on men's shoulders. But they themselves, will not move them with one of their fingers.
5 But all their works, they do for to be seen of men. They make broad their phylacteries and enlarge the borders of their garments
6 And love the uppermost rooms at feasts and the chief seats in the synagogues
7 And greetings in the markets and to be called of men, "'Rabbi, Rabbi.'"

8 But, be not you called, "'Rabbi,'" for One is Your Master; even Christ and all you, are brothers.
9 And call no man, your Father on the Earth. For One, is your Father, which is in Heaven.
10 Neither be you called Masters, for One is your Master; even Christ.
11 But, he that is greatest among you, shall be your servant.
12 And whosoever, shall exalt himself, shall be abased and he that shall Humble himself, shall be Exalted.

13 But, woe to you, scribes and Pharisees, hypocrites! For you shut up the Kingdom of Heaven, against men. For you neither go in yourselves, neither suffer you them that are entering, to go in.
14 Woe to you, scribes and Pharisees, hypocrites! For you devour widows' houses and for a pretence, make long prayers. Therefore, you shall receive the greater damnation.
15 Woe to you, scribes and Pharisees, hypocrites! For you compass Sea and land to make one proselyte and when he is made, you make him, two times more the child of Hell than yourselves.

16 Woe to you, you blind guides, which say, "'whosoever shall swear by the temple, it is nothing, but whosoever, shall swear by the gold of the temple, he is a debtor!'"
17 You fools and blind, for whether is greater, the gold, or the temple that sanctifies the gold?
18 And Whosoever, shall swear by the altar, it is nothing, but whosoever swears by the gift that is on it, he is guilty.
19 You fools and blind, for whether is greater, the gift, or the altar that sanctifies the gift?
20 Whosoever therefore, shall swear by the altar, swears by it and by all things, thereon.
21 And whosoever, shall swear by the temple, swears by it and by Him that dwells, therein.
22 And he that shall swear by Heaven, swears by The Throne of God and by Him that sits, thereon.

23 Woe to you, scribes and Pharisees, hypocrites! For you pay tithe of mint and anise and cumin and have omitted the weightier matters of The Law: Judgment, Mercy and Faith. These, should you to have done and not to leave the other undone.
24 You blind guides, which strain at a gnat and swallow a camel.
25 Woe to you, scribes and Pharisees, hypocrites! For you make clean, the outside of the cup and of the platter, but within, they are full of extortion and excess.
26 You blind Pharisee, cleanse first that,

which is within the cup and platter that the outside of them, may be clean, also.

27 Woe to you, scribes and Pharisees, hypocrites! For you are like to whited sepulchres, which indeed, appear beautiful outward, but are within, full of dead men's bones and of all uncleanness.

28 Even so you also, outwardly appear righteous to men, but within, you are full of hypocrisy and iniquity.

29 Woe to you, scribes and Pharisees, hypocrites! Because you build the tombs of the prophets and garnish the sepulchres of the Righteous

30 And say, "'if we had been in the days of our fathers, we would not have been partakers with them in the blood of the prophets.'"

31 Wherefore, you are witnesses to yourselves that, you are the children of them, which killed the prophets.

32 Fill you up then, the measure of your fathers.

33 You serpents, you generation of vipers. How can you escape the damnation of Sheol?

34 Wherefore behold, I SEND TO YOU PROPHETS AND WISE MEN AND SCRIBES AND SOME OF THEM, YOU SHALL KILL AND CRUCIFY AND SOME OF THEM, SHALL YOU SCOURGE IN YOUR SYNAGOGUES AND PERSECUTE THEM, FROM CITY TO CITY

35 THAT ON YOU, MAY COME ALL THE RIGHTEOUS BLOOD SHED ON THE EARTH; from the blood of Righteous Abel, to the blood of Zechariah, son of Berechiah, whom you slew between the temple and the altar.

36 Verily, I say to you, "'all these things, shall come on this generation.'"

37 O Jerusalem, Jerusalem, you that kill the prophets and stone them, which are sent to you, how often would I have gathered your children together, even as a hen gathers her chickens under her wings and you would not!

38 Behold, your house is left to you desolate.

39 For I say to you, "'you shall not see Me henceforth, until you shall say, "'"BLESSED IS HE THAT COMES IN THE NAME OF THE LORD."'"

Chapter 24

1 And Jesus went out and departed from the temple. And His disciples came to Him, for to show Him the buildings of the temple.

2 And Jesus said to them, "see you not all these things? Verily, I say to you, "'THERE SHALL NOT BE LEFT HERE, ONE STONE ON ANOTHER THAT SHALL NOT BE THROWN DOWN.'"

3 And as He sat on the Mount of Olives, the disciples came to Him privately saying, "tell us, when shall these things be and what shall be the Sign of Your Coming and of the end of the World."

4 And Jesus answered and said to them, "take Heed that no man, deceives you.

5 For MANY SHALL COME IN MY NAME SAYING, "'I AM CHRIST'" AND SHALL DECEIVE MANY.

6 AND YOU SHALL HEAR OF WARS AND RUMORS OF WARS. See that you be not troubled, for ALL THESE THINGS MUST COME TO PASS, but the end is not yet.

7 FOR NATION SHALL RISE AGAINST NATION AND KINGDOM AGAINST KINGDOM. And THERE SHALL BE FAMINES AND PESTILENCES AND EARTHQUAKES, IN DIVERSE PLACES.

8 ALL THESE, ARE THE BEGINNING OF SORROWS.

9 Then, THEY SHALL DELIVER YOU UP TO BE AFFLICTED AND SHALL KILL YOU. AND YOU SHALL BE HATED OF ALL NATIONS FOR MY NAME'S SAKE.

10 AND THEN, SHALL MANY BE OFFENDED AND SHALL BETRAY ONE ANOTHER AND SHALL HATE ONE ANOTHER.

11 AND MANY FALSE PROPHETS SHALL RISE AND SHALL DECEIVE MANY.

12 AND BECAUSE INIQUITY SHALL ABOUND, THE LOVE OF MANY SHALL WAX COLD.

13 But, he that shall endure to the end, the same shall be Saved.

14 And this Gospel of the Kingdom, shall be Preached in all the World for a witness to all nations and then, shall the end come.

15 When you therefore, shall see the Abomination of Desolation, spoken of by Daniel, the prophet stand in the Holy place (whosoever reads, let him Understand)

16 Then let them, which be in Judaea, flee into the mountains.

17 Let him, which is on the housetop not come down to take any thing, out of his

house.
18 Neither let him, which is in the field, return back to take his clothes.
19 And woe to them that are with child and to them that give suck in those days!
20 But, Pray yourselves that your flight be not in the winter, neither on the Sabbath Day.
21 For then, shall be great tribulation, such as was not since the beginning of the World to this time; no, nor ever shall be.
22 And except those days should be shortened, there should no flesh be saved. But, for the elect's sake, those days, shall be shortened.

23 Then, if any man shall say to you, "'lo, here is Christ,'" or "'there…,'" believe it not.
24 For there shall arise false christs and false prophets and shall show great signs and wonders, insomuch that, if it were possible, they shall deceive, the very elect.
25 Behold, I have told you before.
26 Wherefore, if they shall say to you, "behold, He is in the desert,'" go not, forth, "behold, He is in the secret chambers,'" believe it not.
27 For as the lightning comes out of the East and shines, even to the West, so shall also, the Coming of The Son of Man be.
28 For wheresoever, the carcass is, there will the eagles be gathered, together.

29 Immediately, after the tribulation of those days, shall the Sun be darkened and the Moon shall not give her light and the stars, shall fall from Heaven and the powers of the heavens, shall be shaken
30 And then, shall appear, the Sign of The Son of Man in Heaven. And then, shall all the tribes of the Earth mourn and they shall see The Son of Man Coming in The Clouds of Heaven with Power and Great Glory.
31 And He shall send His angels with a great sound of a trumpet and they shall gather together His elect from the four winds; from one end of Heaven to the other.

32 Now, learn a parable of the fig tree, "'when his branch is yet tender and puts forth leaves, you know that summer is near.
33 So likewise, you, when you shall see all these things, Know that it is near; even at the doors.'"
34 Verily, I say to you, "'this generation shall not pass, until all these things, be Fulfilled.'"
35 Heaven and Earth shall pass away, but My Words shall not pass away.
36 But, of that day and hour, knows no man; no, not the angels of Heaven, but My Father, only.

37 But, as the days of Noah were, so shall also, the Coming of The Son of Man be.
38 For as in the days that were before the flood, they were eating and drinking, marrying and giving in marriage, until the day that Noah entered into the Ark
39 And knew not, until the flood came and took them all away. So shall also, the Coming of The Son of Man be.
40 Then, shall two be in the field; the one, shall be Taken and the other, left.
41 Two women shall be grinding at the mill; the one, shall be Taken and the other, left.
42 Watch therefore, for you know not, what hour your Lord does Come.
43 But know this that, if The Good Man of the house had known in what watch the thief would come, he would have watched and would not have suffered his house to be broken up.
44 Therefore, be you also ready, for in such an hour as you think not, The Son of Man Comes.

45 Who then, is a Faithful and Wise servant, whom his Lord has made ruler over His household, to give them meat in due season?
46 Blessed is that servant, whom his Lord, when He Comes, shall find so, Doing.
47 Verily, I say to you that, "'He shall make him ruler over all His goods.'"
48 But and if that evil servant shall say in his heart, "'my Lord delays His Coming'"
49 And shall begin to hit his fellow servants and to eat and drink with the drunken,
50 The Lord of that servant, shall Come in a day, when he looks not for Him and in an hour that he is not aware of
51 And shall cut him asunder and appoint him his portion with the hypocrites. There shall be weeping and gnashing of teeth.

Chapter 25

1 Then, shall the Kingdom of Heaven be likened to ten virgins, which took their lamps and went forth to meet the Bridegroom.
2 And five of them, were Wise and five,

were foolish.

3 They that were foolish, took their lamps and took no Oil with themselves.

4 But the Wise, took Oil in their vessels with their lamps.

5 While the Bridegroom tarried, they all slumbered and slept.

6 And at midnight, there was a cry made, "'behold, the Bridegroom Comes! Go yourselves, out to meet Him!'"

7 Then, all those virgins arose and trimmed their lamps.

8 And the foolish said to the Wise, "'give us of your Oil, for our lamps are gone out.'"

9 But the wise, answered saying, "'not so, lest there be not enough for us and you. But, go you rather, to them that sell and buy for yourselves.'"

10 And while they went to buy, the Bridegroom came and they that were ready, went in with Him to the marriage and the door was shut.

11 Afterward, came also, the other virgins saying, "'Lord, Lord, open to us.'"

12 But, He answered and said, "'verily, I say to you, "'I know you not.'"'"

13 Watch therefore, for you know neither, the day, nor the hour, wherein The Son of Man comes.

14 For the Kingdom of Heaven is as a Man travelling into a far country, who Called His own servants and delivered to them, His goods.

15 And to one, He gave five talents, to another, two and to another, one; to every man, according to his several ability and straightway, took His journey.

16 Then, he that had received the five talents, went and traded with the same and made them other, five talents.

17 And likewise, he that had received two, he also, gained other, two.

18 But, he that had received one, went and dug in the earth and hid his Lord's money.

19 <u>After a long time</u>, The Lord of those servants came and reckoned with them.

20 And so, he that had received five talents, came and brought other five talents saying, "'Lord, You delivered to me five talents. Behold, I have gained besides them, five talents more.'"

21 His Lord said to him, "'well done, you good and Faithful servant. You have been Faithful over a few things. I will make you ruler over many things. Enter you, into the Joy of your Lord.'"

22 He also that had received two talents, came and said, "'Lord, You delivered to me two talents. Behold, I have gained two other talents, besides them.'"

23 His Lord said to him, "'well done, good and Faithful servant. You have been Faithful over a few things. I will make you ruler over many things. Enter you, into the Joy of your Lord.'"

24 Then, he which had received the one talent, came and said, "'Lord, I knew You that You are a hard man; reaping where You have not Sown and gathering where You have not strawed

25 And I was afraid and went and hid Your talent in the earth. Lo, there You have that is Yours.'"

26 His Lord answered and said to him, "'you wicked and slothful servant, you knew that I reap where I sowed not and gather where I have not strawed.

27 You ought therefore, to have put My money to the exchangers and then, at My Coming, I should have received My own, with usury.

28 Take therefore, the talent from him and give it to him, which has ten talents.'"

29 <u>For to every one that has, shall be given and he shall have abundance. But from him that has not, shall be taken away; even that, which he has.</u>

30 And cast you, the unprofitable servant, into Outer Darkness. There shall be weeping and gnashing of teeth.

31 When The Son of Man shall Come in His Glory and all the Holy angels with Him, then, shall He sit on the Throne of His Glory.

32 And before Him, shall be gathered all nations and He shall separate them, one from another; as a Shepherd divides His sheep from the goats.

33 And He shall set the sheep on His right hand, but the goats, on the left.

34 Then, shall The King say to them on His right hand "'come you Blessed of My Father, inherit the Kingdom, prepared for you from the foundation of the World,

35 For I was a hungered and you gave Me meat. I was thirsty and you gave Me drink. I was a stranger and you took Me in,

36 Naked and you clothed Me. I was sick and you visited Me. I was in prison and you came to Me.'"

37 Then, shall the Righteous answer Him

saying, "'Lord, when saw we, You a hungered and fed You, or thirsty and gave You drink?
38 When saw we, You a stranger and took You in, or naked and clothed You?
39 Or, when saw we, You sick, or in prison and came to You?'"
40 And The King shall answer and say to them, "'verily, I say to you, ""in as much as you have done it to one of the least of these, My brothers, you have done it to Me.'""

41 Then shall He say also, to them on the left hand, ""depart from Me, you cursed, into everlasting fire, prepared for the Devil and his angels,
42 For I was a hungered and you gave Me no meat. I was thirsty and you gave Me no drink.
43 I was a stranger and you took Me not in; naked and you clothed Me not; sick and in prison and you visited Me not.'"
44 Then, shall they also, answer Him saying, "'Lord, when saw we, You a hungered, or athirst, or a stranger, or naked, or sick, or in prison and did not minister to You?'"
45 Then, shall He answer them saying, "'verily, I say to you, ""in as much as you did it not, to one of the least of these, you did it not, to Me.'""
46 And these, shall go away into everlasting punishment, but the Righteous, into Life Eternal."

Chapter 26

1 And it came to pass, when Jesus had finished all these sayings, He said to His disciples,
2 "You know that after two days, is The Feast of The Passover and THE SON OF MAN IS BETRAYED TO BE CRUCIFIED."
3 Then assembled together, the chief priests and the scribes and the elders of the people, to the palace of the high priest, who was called Caiaphas
4 And consulted that they might take Jesus by subtlety and kill Him.
5 But they said, "not on the feast day, lest there be an uproar among the people."

6 Now, when Jesus was in Bethany, in the house of Simeon, the leper,
7 There came to Him, a woman having an alabaster box of very precious ointment and poured it on His head, as He sat at meat.

8 But when His disciples saw it, they had indignation saying, "to what purpose is this waste?
9 For this ointment might have been sold for much and given to the poor."
10 When Jesus understood it, He said to them, "why trouble you, the woman? For she has Worked a Good Work on Me.
11 For you have the poor always with you. But Me, you have not, always.
12 For in that, she has poured this ointment on My Body, she did it for My burial.
13 Verily, I say to you, "'wheresoever, This Gospel shall be Preached in the whole World, there shall also, this that this woman has done, be told for a memorial of her.'"

14 Then, one of the twelve, called Judas Iscariot, went to the chief priests
15 And said to them, "what will you give me and I will deliver Him to you?" And THEY COVENANTED WITH HIM, FOR THIRTY PIECES OF SILVER.
16 And from that time, he sought opportunity to betray Him.

17 Now, the first day of The Feast of Unleavened Bread, the disciples came to Jesus saying to Him, "where will You that we prepare for You to eat the Passover?"
18 And He said, "go into the city to such a man and say to him, "'The Master said, ""My time is at hand. I will Keep The Passover at your house with My disciples.'""
19 And the disciples did as Jesus had appointed them and they made ready, The Passover.

20 Now, when the evening was come, He sat down with the twelve.
21 And as they did eat, He said, "verily, I say to you that, one of you, shall betray Me."
22 And they were exceedingly sorrowful and began, every one of them, to say to Him, "Lord, is it I?"
23 And He answered and said, "he that dips his hand with Me in the dish, the same shall betray Me.
24 The Son of Man goes as it is written of Him, but woe to that man, by whom, The Son of Man is betrayed! It had been good for that man, if he had not been born."
25 Then Judas, which betrayed Him, answered and said, "Master, is it I?" He

said to him, "you have said."

26 And as they were eating, Jesus took bread and Blessed it and broke it and gave it to the disciples and said, "take, eat. This is My Body."

27 And He took the cup and Gave Thanks and gave it to them saying, "drink yourselves, all of it."

28 For this is My Blood of The New Testament, which is shed for many, for the Remission of sins.

29 But I say to you, "'I will not drink henceforth, of this fruit of the vine, until that day, when I drink it new with you in My Father's kingdom.'"

30 And when they had sung a hymn, they went out into the Mount of Olives.

31 Then said Jesus to them, "ALL YOU, SHALL BE OFFENDED, BECAUSE OF ME THIS NIGHT, for it is written, "'I WILL SLAY THE SHEPHERD AND THE SHEEP OF THE FLOCK, SHALL BE SCATTERED ABROAD.'"

32 BUT, AFTER I AM RISEN AGAIN, I WILL GO BEFORE YOU, INTO GALILEE."

33 Peter answered and said to Him, "though all men shall be offended because of You, yet will I never, be offended."

34 Jesus said to him, "verily, I say to you that, "'THIS NIGHT, BEFORE THE COCK CROWS, YOU SHALL DENY ME, THRICE.'"

35 Peter said to Him, "though I should die with You, yet will I not deny You." Likewise also, said all the disciples.

36 Then, came Jesus with them, to a place called Gethsemane and said to the disciples, "sit yourselves here, while I go and Pray there."

37 And He took with Himself, Peter and the two sons of Zabdi and began to be sorrowful and very heavy.

38 Then, said He to them, "My soul is exceedingly sorrowful, even to death. Tarry yourselves, here and watch with Me."

39 And He went a little further and fell on His face and Prayed saying, "O My Father, if it be possible, let this Cup pass from Me, nevertheless, not as I will, but as You Will."

40 And He came to the disciples and found them asleep and said to Peter, "what, could you not watch with Me, one hour?

41 Watch and Pray that you enter not into temptation. The spirit indeed, is willing, but the flesh is weak."

42 He went away again, the second time and Prayed saying, "O My Father, if this Cup may not pass away from Me, except I Drink it, Your Will be Done."

43 And He came and found them asleep again, for their eyes were heavy.

44 And He left them and went away, again and Prayed the third time, saying the same words.

45 Then came He, to His disciples and said to them, "sleep on now and take your rest. Behold, the hour is at hand and The Son of Man is betrayed into the hands of sinners.

46 Rise, let us be going. Behold, he is at hand that does betray Me."

47 And while He yet spoke, lo, Judas, one of the twelve, came and with him, a great multitude with swords and staves; from the chief priests and elders of the people.

48 Now he that betrayed Him, gave them a sign saying, "Whomsoever, I shall kiss that same, is He. Hold Him fast."

49 And forthwith, he came to Jesus and said, "hail, Master" and he KISSED HIM.

50 And Jesus said to him, "friend, wherefore are you come?" Then, came they and laid hands on Jesus and took Him.

51 And behold, one of them, which were with Jesus stretched out his hand and drew his sword and struck a servant of the high priest's and cut off his ear.

52 Then, said Jesus to him, "put up again, your sword into his place. For all they that take the sword, shall perish with the sword.

53 Think you that I cannot now, Pray to My Father and He shall presently, Give Me more than twelve legions of angels?

54 But how then, shall The Scriptures be Fulfilled that thus, it must be?"

55 In that same hour said Jesus to the multitudes, "are you come out as against a thief with swords and staves for to take Me? I sat daily, with you Teaching in the temple and you laid no hold on Me.

56 But, all this was done that The Scriptures of the Prophets, might be Fulfilled." Then, ALL THE DISCIPLES FORSOOK HIM AND FLED.

57 And they that had laid hold on Jesus, led Him away to Caiaphas, (the high priest) where the scribes and the elders

were assembled.
58 But, Peter followed Him afar off, to the high priest's palace and went in and sat with the servants, to see the end.

59 Now, the chief priests and elders and all the council, sought false witness against Jesus; to put Him to death,
60 But found none. Yes, though many false witnesses came, yet found they none. At the last, came two false witnesses
61 And said, "this Fellow said, "'I am able to destroy the temple of God and to build it in three days.'"
62 And the high priest rose and said to Him, "answer you nothing? What is it, which these witness against You?"
63 But, Jesus held His peace. And the high priest answered and said to Him, "I adjure You, by The Living God that you tell us, whether You are the Christ, The Son of God."
64 Jesus said to him, "you have said, nevertheless I say to you, "'hereafter, you shall see The Son of Man sitting on the right hand of Power and coming in The Clouds of Heaven.'"
65 Then, the high priest rent his clothes saying, "He has spoken blasphemy! What further need, have we of witnesses? Behold now, you have heard His blasphemy!"
66 What think you? They answered and said, "He is guilty of death!"
67 Then, DID THEY SPIT ON HIS FACE AND BUFFETED HIM AND OTHERS, SLAPPED HIM WITH THE PALMS OF THEIR HANDS
68 Saying, "PROPHESY TO US, YOU CHRIST. WHO IS HE THAT STUNG YOU?"

69 Now, Peter sat without, in the palace and a damsel came to him saying, "you also, were with Jesus of Galilee."
70 But, he denied before them all saying, "I KNOW NOT, WHAT YOU SAY."
71 And when he was gone out into the porch, another maid saw him and said to them that were there, "this fellow was also, with Jesus of Nazareth."
72 And again, he denied with an oath, "I DO NOT KNOW, THE MAN."
73 And after a while, came to him, they that stood by and said to Peter, "surely, you also, are one of them, for your speech betrays you."
74 Then, began he to curse and to swear saying, "I KNOW NOT, THE MAN" and immediately, the cock crew.
75 And Peter remembered the Word of Jesus, which said to him, "BEFORE THE COCK CROWS, YOU SHALL DENY ME, THRICE." And he went out and wept bitterly.

Chapter 27

1 When the morning was come, all the chief priests and elders of the people, took counsel against Jesus; to put Him to death.
2 And when they had bound Him, they led Him away and delivered Him to Pontius Pilate, the Governor.

3 Then Judas, which had betrayed Him, when he saw that He was condemned, repented himself and brought again, the thirty pieces of silver, to the chief priests and elders
4 Saying, "I have sinned, in that I have betrayed the Innocent Blood." And they said, "what is that to us? See yourself, to that."
5 And he cast down the pieces of silver in the temple and departed and went and hanged himself.

6 And the chief priests, took the silver pieces and said, "it is not Lawful, for to put them into the treasury, because it is the price of blood."
7 And they took counsel and BOUGHT WITH THEM, THE POTTER'S FIELD, to bury strangers in.
8 Wherefore, that field was called, "the Field of Blood" to this day.
9 Then was Fulfilled that, which was spoken by Jeremiah, the prophet saying …AND THEY TOOK THE THIRTY PIECES OF SILVER; THE PRICE OF HIM THAT WAS VALUED, WHOM THEY OF THE CHILDREN OF ISRAEL, DID VALUE
10 AND GAVE THEM FOR THE POTTER'S FIELD, AS THE LORD APPOINTED ME.

11 And Jesus stood before the governor. And the governor asked him saying, "are You, The King of the Jews?" And Jesus said to him, "You said."
12 And when He was accused of the chief priests and elders, HE ANSWERED NOTHING.
13 Then, said Pilate to Him, "hear You not, how many things, they witness against You?"

14 And HE ANSWERED HIM, TO NEVER A WORD, insomuch that, the governor marveled greatly.

15 Now at that feast, the governor was wont to release to the people a prisoner, whom they would.
16 And they had then, a notable prisoner, called Barabbas.
17 Therefore, when they were gathered together, Pilate said to them, "whom will you that I release to you, Barabbas, or Jesus, which is called, Christ?"
18 For he knew that, for envy, they had delivered Him.
19 When he was set down on the judgement seat, his wife sent to him saying, "have you nothing, to do with that Just Man, for I have suffered many things this day, in a Dream because of Him."

20 But, the chief priests and elders persuaded the multitude that they should ask Barabbas and destroy Jesus.
21 The governor answered and said to them, "whether of the two, will you that I release to you?" They said, "Barabbas."
22 Pilate said to them, "what shall I do then with Jesus, which is called, Christ?" They all said to him, "let Him be crucified!"
23 And the governor said, "why, what evil has He done?" But, they cried out the more saying, "let Him be crucified!"
24 When Pilate saw that he could prevail nothing, but that rather, a tumult was made, he took water and washed his hands before the multitude saying, "I am innocent of The Blood of this Just Person. See yourselves, to it."
25 Then answered all the people and said, "HIS BLOOD BE ON US AND ON OUR CHILDREN."
26 Then released he, Barabbas to them. And when he had scourged Jesus, he delivered Him, to be crucified.

27 Then, the soldiers of the governor took Jesus into the common hall and gathered to Him, the whole band of soldiers.
28 And THEY STRIPPED HIM AND PUT ON HIM, A SCARLET ROBE.
29 AND WHEN THEY HAD PLATTED A CROWN OF THORNS, THEY PUT IT ON HIS HEAD AND A REED IN HIS RIGHT HAND AND THEY BOWED THE KNEE BEFORE HIM AND MOCKED HIM saying, "HAIL, KING OF THE JEWS!"
30 AND THEY SPIT ON HIM AND TOOK THE REED AND BEAT HIM ON THE HEAD.
31 And after that, they had mocked Him, they took the robe off from Him and put His own raiment on Him and led Him away to crucify Him.
32 And as they came out, they found a man of Cyrene, Simeon by name. Him, they compelled to bear His cross.
33 And when they had come to a place called, Golgotha, that is to say, A Place of a Skull,
34 THEY GAVE HIM VINEGAR TO DRINK, MINGLED WITH GALL. And when He had tasted thereof, He would not drink.
35 And THEY CRUCIFIED HIM AND PARTED HIS GARMENTS, CASTING LOTS that it might be Fulfilled, which was spoken by the prophet, "THEY PARTED MY GARMENTS AMONG THEMSELVES AND ON MY VESTURE, DID THEY CAST LOTS."

36 And sitting down, they watched Him, there
37 And set up over His head, His accusation written, "This is Jesus, The King of the Jews."
38 Then were there two thieves crucified with Him; one, on the right hand and another, on the left.
39 And they that passed by, REVILED HIM; WAGGING THEIR HEADS
40 And saying, "YOU, THAT DESTROY THE TEMPLE AND BUILD IT IN THREE DAYS, SAVE YOURSELF. IF YOU ARE THE SON OF GOD, COME DOWN FROM THE CROSS."

41 Likewise also, the chief priests, mocking Him, with the scribes and elders said,
42 "HE SAVED OTHERS. HIMSELF, HE CANNOT SAVE. IF HE IS THE KING OF ISRAEL, LET HIM NOW, COME DOWN FROM THE CROSS AND WE WILL BELIEVE HIM.
43 HE TRUSTED IN GOD. LET HIM DELIVER HIMSELF NOW, IF HE WILL HAVE HIM, FOR HE SAID,"'I AM, THE SON OF GOD.'"
44 The thieves also, which were crucified with Him, cast the same in his teeth.

45 Now, from the sixth hour, there was darkness over all the land, to the ninth hour.
46 And about the ninth hour, Jesus cried with a loud voice saying, "ELI, ELI, LAMA SABACHTHANI?!" that is to say, "MY

GOD, MY GOD, WHY HAVE YOU FORSAKEN ME?!"

47 Some of them that stood there, when they heard that said, "this Man, calls for Elijah."
48 And straightway, one of them ran and TOOK A SPONGE AND FILLED IT WITH VINEGAR AND PUT IT ON A REED AND GAVE HIM TO DRINK.
49 The rest said, "let be, let us see whether Elijah will come to save Him."
50 Jesus, when He had cried again, with a loud voice, yielded up The Ghost.

51 And behold, the veil of the temple was rent in two; from the top, to the bottom and the earth did quake and the rocks rent.
52 AND THE GRAVES WERE OPENED AND MANY BODIES OF THE SAINTS, WHICH SLEPT, AROSE
53 AND CAME OUT OF THE GRAVES AFTER HIS RESURRECTION AND WENT INTO THE HOLY CITY AND APPEARED TO MANY.
54 Now, when the centurion and they that were with him, watching Jesus, saw the earthquake and those things that were done, they Feared greatly saying, "Truly, this was The Son of God."
55 And many women were there beholding afar off, which Followed Jesus from Galilee, Ministering to Him,
56 Among which, was Mary Magdalene and Mary, the mother of James and Joseph and the mother of Zabdi's children.

57 When the evening was come, there came a rich man, of Arimathaea, named Joseph, who also, himself was Jesus' disciple.
58 He went to Pilate and begged the Body of Jesus. Then, Pilate commanded the Body to be delivered.
59 And when Joseph had taken the Body, he wrapped it in a clean linen cloth
60 And laid it in his own new tomb, which he had hewn out in the rock. And he rolled a great stone to the door of the sepulchre and departed.
61 And there, was Mary Magdalene and the other Mary, sitting over against the sepulchre.

62 Now, the next day that followed the day of the preparation, the chief priests and Pharisees came together, to Pilate
63 Saying, "Sir, we remember that that deceiver said, while He was yet alive, "'AFTER THREE DAYS, I WILL RISE AGAIN.'"
64 Command therefore that, the sepulchre be made sure, until the third day, lest His disciples come by night and steal Him away and say to the people, "'He is Risen from the dead, so the last error, shall be worse, than the first.'"
65 Pilate said to them, "you have a watch. Go your way. Make it as sure as you can."
66 So, they went and made the sepulchre sure; sealing the stone and setting a watch.

Chapter 28

1 In the end of the Sabbath, as it began to dawn toward the first day of the week, came Mary Magdalene and the other Mary to see the sepulchre.
2 And behold, there was a great earthquake, for the angel of The Lord descended from Heaven and came and rolled back the stone from the door and sat on it.
3 His countenance was like lightning and his raiment, white as snow.
4 And for fear of him, the keepers did shake and became as dead men.

5 And the angel answered and said to the women, "fear not yourselves, for I know that you seek Jesus, which was crucified.
6 He is not here, for HE IS RISEN," as he said, "come, see the place where The Lord laid
7 And go quickly and tell His disciples that, HE IS RISEN FROM THE DEAD. And behold, He goes before you into Galilee. There, you shall see Him. Lo, I have told you."
8 And they departed quickly, from the sepulchre with Fear and Great Joy and did run to bring His disciples word.
9 And as they went to tell His disciples, behold, Jesus met them saying, "all hail." And they came and held Him by the feet and Worshipped Him.
10 Then, said Jesus to them, "be not afraid. Go tell My brothers that, "'they go into Galilee and there, shall they see Me.'"

11 Now, when they were going, behold, some of the watch came into the city and showed to the chief priests all the things that were done.
12 And when they were assembled with the elders and had taken counsel, they gave large money to the soldiers
13 Saying, "say yourselves, "'His disciples came by night and stole Him away while

we slept.'"
14 And if this comes to the governor's ears, we will persuade him and secure you."
15 So, they took the money and did as they were Taught. And this saying is commonly reported among the Jews, until this day.

16 Then, the eleven disciples went away into Galilee; into a mountain, where Jesus had appointed them.
17 And when they saw Him, they Worshipped Him, but some doubted.
18 And Jesus came and spoke to them saying, "All Power is Given to Me in Heaven and in Earth.
19 Go yourselves, therefore and Teach all nations; Baptizing them in The Name of The Father and of The Son and of The Holy Ghost;
20 Teaching them to Observe All things, whatsoever I have Commanded you and lo, I am with you always; even to the end of the World. Amen."

Mark

Chapter 1

1 The beginning of The Gospel of Jesus Christ, The Son of God.
2 As it is written in the Prophets, BEHOLD, I SEND MY MESSENGER BEFORE YOUR FACE, WHICH SHALL PREPARE YOUR WAY BEFROE YOU.
3 THE VOICE OF ONE CRYING IN THE WILDERNESS, PREPARE YOU, THE WAY OF THE LORD. MAKE HIS PATHS STRAIGHT.
4 John did Baptize in the wilderness and Preach the Baptism of Repentance for the Remission of sins.
5 And there went out to him, all the land of Judaea and they of Jerusalem and were all Baptized of him in the river of Jordan, Confessing their sins.
6 And John was clothed with camel's hair and with a girdle of a skin about his loins. And he did eat locusts and wild honey
7 And Preached saying, "there comes One Mightier than I, after me, the latchet of Whose shoes, I am not worthy to stoop down and unloose.
8 I indeed, have Baptized you with water, but He shall Baptize you with The Holy Ghost."

9 And it came to pass, in those days that JESUS CAME FROM NAZARETH of Galilee and was Baptized of John in Jordan.
10 And straightway, coming up out of the water, He saw the heavens opened and The Spirit, like a dove descending on Himself.
11 And there came A Voice from Heaven saying, "You are My beloved Son, in Whom I am well Pleased."
12 And immediately, The Spirit drove Him into the wilderness.
13 And He was there in the wilderness, forty days; tempted of Satan and was with the wild beasts. And the angels ministered to Him.

14 Now, after that John was put in prison, Jesus came into Galilee, Preaching The Gospel of the Kingdom of God
15 And saying, "the time is Fulfilled and the Kingdom of God is at hand. Repent you and Believe The Gospel."
16 Now, as He walked by the Sea of Galilee, He saw Simeon and Andrew, his brother casting a net into the Sea, for they were fishers.
17 And Jesus said to them, "come you, after Me and I will make you to become fishers of men."
18 And straightway, they forsook their nets and Followed Him.
19 And when He had gone a little further there, He saw James, the son of Zabdi and John, his brother, who also, were in the ship mending their nets.
20 And straightway, He called them and they left their father, Zabdi in the ship with the hired servants and went after Him.

21 And they went into Capernaum and straightway, on the Sabbath Day, He entered into the synagogue and Taught.
22 And they were astonished at His Doctrine, for He Taught them as one that had Authority and not as the scribes.
23 And there was in their synagogue, a man with an unclean spirit and he cried out
24 Saying, "let us alone! What have we to do with You, You Jesus of Nazareth?! Are You come to destroy us?! I know You, who You are, The Holy One of God!"
25 And Jesus rebuked him saying, "hold your peace and come out of him."

26 And when the unclean spirit had torn him and cried with a loud voice, he came out of him.
27 And they were all amazed, insomuch that, they questioned among themselves saying, "what thing is this? What New Doctrine is this? For with Authority Commands He, even the unclean spirits and they do Obey Him."
28 And immediately, His fame spread abroad, throughout all the region round about, Galilee.

29 And forthwith, when they had come out of the synagogue, they entered into the house of Simeon and Andrew, with James and John.
30 But Simeon's wife's, mother laid sick of a fever and anon, they told Him of her.
31 And He came and took her by the hand and lifted her up and immediately, the fever left her and she ministered to them.

32 And at evening, when the Sun did set, they brought to Him all that were diseased and them that were possessed with devils.
33 And all the city was gathered together at the door.
34 And He Healed many that were sick of diverse diseases and cast out many devils and suffered not the devils to speak, because they knew Him.

35 And in the morning, rising up, a great while before day, He went out and departed into a solitary place and there, Prayed.
36 And Simeon and they that were with Him, followed after Him.
37 And when they had found Him, they said to Him, "all men Seek for You."
38 And He said to them, "let us go into the next towns that I may Preach there also, for therefore, came I forth."
39 And He Preached in their synagogues, throughout all Galilee and Cast Out devils.

40 And there came a leper to Him, beseeching Him and kneeling down to Him and saying to Him, "if You will, You can make me Clean."
41 And Jesus, Moved with Compassion, put forth His hand and Touched him and said to him, "I will. Be you, Clean."
42 And as soon as He had spoken, immediately, the leprosy departed from him and he was Cleansed.
43 And He straightly charged him and forthwith, sent him away

44 And said to him, "see you say nothing to any man, but go your way. Show yourself to the priest and offer for your Cleansing, those things, which Moses commanded, for a Testimony to them."
45 But, he went out and began to publish it much and to blaze abroad the matter, insomuch that Jesus could no more, openly enter into the city, but was without in desert places and they came to Him from every quarter.

Chapter 2

1 And again, He entered into Capernaum after some days and it was noised that He was in the house.
2 And straightway, many were gathered together, insomuch that, there was no room to receive them; no, not so much as about the door and He Preached The Word to them.
3 And they came to Him, bringing one, sick of the palsy, which was borne of four.
4 And when they could not come near to Him for the press, they uncovered the roof where He was and when they had broken it up, they let down the bed wherein, the sick of the palsy laid.
5 When Jesus saw their Faith, He said to the sick of the palsy, "son, your sins be Forgiven you."

6 But, there was certain of the scribes sitting there and reasoning in their hearts,
7 "Why does this Man thus, speak blasphemies? Who can Forgive sins, but God, only?"
8 And immediately, when Jesus perceived in His Spirit that they so reasoned within themselves, He said to them, "why reason yourselves, these things in your hearts?
9 Whether is it easier to say to the sick of the palsy, "'your sins be Forgiven you,'" or to say, "'Arise and take up your bed and walk?'"
10 But that you may know that, The Son of Man has Power on Earth to Forgive sins, (he said to the sick of the palsy)
11 I say to you, "'Arise and take up your bed and go your way into your house.'"
12 And immediately, he arose, took up the bed and went forth before them all, insomuch that, they were all amazed and Glorified God saying, "we never saw it on this fashion."

13 And He went forth again, by the Sea side and all the multitude resorted to Him and He Taught them.

14 And as He passed by, He saw Levi, the son of Alphaeus sitting at the receipt of custom and said to him, "Follow Me" and he arose and Followed Him.

15 And it came to pass that, as Jesus sat at meat in his house, many publicans and sinners sat also, together with Jesus and His disciples, for there were many and they Followed Him.

16 And when the scribes and Pharisees saw Him eat with publicans and sinners, they said to His disciples, "how is it that, He eats and drinks with publicans and sinners?"

17 When Jesus heard it, He said to them, "they that are whole, have no need of the physician, but they that are sick. I came not to call the Righteous, but sinners to Repentance."

18 And the disciples of John and of the Pharisees used to Fast. And they came and said to Him, "why do the disciples of John and of the Pharisees Fast, but Your disciples Fast not?"

19 And Jesus said to them, "can the children of the bridechamber Fast, while the Bridegroom is with them? As long as they have the Bridegroom with them, they cannot Fast.

20 But the days will come, when the Bridegroom shall be taken away from them and then, shall they Fast in those days.

21 No man also, sews a piece of new cloth on an old garment, else the new piece that filled it up, takes away from the old and the rent is made worse.

22 And no man puts new wine into old bottles, else the new wine does burst the bottles and the wine is spilled and the bottles will be marred. But, new wine must be put into new bottles."

23 And it came to pass that, He went through the corn fields on the Sabbath Day and His disciples began as they went, to pluck the ears of corn.

24 And the Pharisees said to Him, "behold, why do they on the Sabbath Day that, which is not Lawful?"

25 And He said to them, "have you never read what David did, when he had need and was a hungered; he and they that were with him,

26 How he went into the house of God in the days of Abiathar, the high priest and did eat the showbread, which is not Lawful to eat, but for the priests and gave also, to them, which were with him?"

27 And He said to them, "the Sabbath was made for man and not man, for the Sabbath.

28 Therefore, The Son of Man is Lord also, of the Sabbath."

Chapter 3

1 And He entered again, into the synagogue and there was a man there, which had a withered hand.

2 And they watched Him, whether He would Heal him on the Sabbath Day that they might accuse Him.

3 And He said to the man, which had the withered hand, "stand forth."

4 And He said to them, "is it Lawful to Do Good on the Sabbath Days, or to do evil; to save life, or to kill?" But, they held their peace.

5 And when He had looked, round about on them with anger, being grieved for the hardness of their hearts, He said to the man, "stretch forth your hand." And he stretched it out and his hand was Restored Whole, as the other.

6 And the Pharisees went forth and straightway, took counsel with the Herodians against Him, how they might destroy Him.

7 But Jesus withdrew Himself, with His disciples to the Sea. And a great multitude from Galilee, followed Him and from Judaea

8 And from Jerusalem and from Idumaea and from beyond Jordan and they about Tyre and Sidon; a great multitude, when they had heard what great things He Did, came to Him.

9 And He spoke to His disciples that a small ship should wait on Him, because of the multitude, lest they should throng Him.

10 For He had Healed many, insomuch that, they pressed on Him for to touch Him, as many as had plagues.

11 And unclean spirits, when they saw Him, fell down before Him and cried saying, "You are The Son of God!"

12 And He straightly, charged them that they, "should not make Him known."

13 And He went up into a mountain and called to Himself, whom He would and they came to Him.

14 And He Ordained twelve that they should be with Him and that He might send them forth to Preach

15 And to have Power to Heal sicknesses and to Cast Out devils:
16 (And Simeon, He surnamed,) Peter
17 And James (the son of Zabdi) and John (the brother of James and He surnamed them, Boanerges, which is, the Sons of Thunder)
18 And Andrew and Philip and Bartholomew and Matthew and Thomas and James (the son of Alphaeus) and Thaddaeus and Simeon (the Canaanite)
19 And Judas Iscariot, which also, betrayed Him. And they went into a house

20 And the multitude came together again, so that they could not so much as eat bread.
21 And when His friends heard of it, they went out to lay hold on Him, for they said, "He is beside Himself."
22 And the scribes, which came down from Jerusalem said, "He has Baalzebub and by the prince of the devils, casts He out devils."
23 And He called them to Himself and said to them in parables, "how can Satan cast out Satan?
24 And if a kingdom is divided against itself that kingdom cannot stand.
25 And if a house is divided against itself that house cannot stand.
26 And if Satan rises up against himself and is divided, he cannot stand, but has an end.
27 No man can enter into a strong man's house and spoil his goods, except he will first, bind the strong man and then, he will spoil his house.
28 Verily, I say to you, "'all sins shall be Forgiven to the sons of men and blasphemies wherewith, whatsoever they shall blaspheme.
29 But, he that shall blaspheme against The Holy Ghost has never forgiveness, but is in danger of eternal damnation.'"
30 Because they said, "He has an unclean spirit."

31 There came then, His brothers and His mother and standing without, sent to Him, calling Him.
32 And the multitude sat about Him and they said to Him, "behold, your mother and your brothers without, seek for You."
33 And He answered them saying, "who is My mother, or My brothers?"
34 And He looked, round about on them, which sat about Him and said, "behold, My mother and My brothers!
35 For whosoever shall Do The Will of God, the same is My brother and My sister and mother."

Chapter 4

1 And He began again, to Teach by the Sea side. And there was gathered to Himself, a great multitude, so that He entered into a ship and sat in the Sea. And the whole multitude was by the Sea on the land.
2 And He Taught them many things by parables and said to them in His Doctrine,
3 "Hearken! Behold, there went out a Sower to Sow.
4 And it came to pass, as He Sowed, some fell by the way side and the fowls of the air came and devoured it up.
5 And some fell on stony ground, where it had not much earth and immediately, it sprang up, because it had no depth of earth.
6 But when the Sun was up, it was scorched and because it had no root, it withered away.
7 And some fell among thorns. And the thorns grew up and choked it and it yielded no fruit.
8 And others fell on Good Ground and did yield Fruit that sprang up and increased and brought forth; some thirty and some sixty and some, one hundred."
9 And He said to them, "he that has ears to hear, let him Hear."

10 And when He was alone, they that were about Him with the twelve, asked of Him the parable.
11 And He said to them, "to you, it is Given to Know the Mystery of the Kingdom of God. But, to them that are without, all these things are done in parables
12 That, "'SEEING, THEY MAY SEE AND NOT PERCEIVE AND HEAR AND NOT UNDERSTAND, LEST AT ANY TIME, THEY SHOULD BE CONVERTED AND THEIR SINS SHOULD BE FORGIVEN THEM.'"

13 And He said to them, "Know you not this parable? And how then, will you Know all parables?
14 The Sower, Sows The Word.
15 And these are they, by the way side where The Word is Sown, but when they have Heard, Satan comes, immediately and takes away The Word that was Sown

in their hearts.

16 And these are they likewise, which are Sown on stony ground, who when they have Heard The Word, immediately Receive it with Gladness

17 And have no root in themselves and so endure, but for a time. Afterward, when affliction, or persecution arises, for The Word's sake, immediately, they are offended.

18 And these are they, which are Sown among thorns, such as Hear The Word

19 And the cares of this World and the deceitfulness of riches and the lusts of other things entering in, choke The Word and it becomes unfruitful.

20 And these are they, which are Sown on Good Ground, such as Hear The Word and Receive it and bring forth Fruit; some thirty times, some sixty and some one hundred."

21 And He said to them, "is a candle brought to be put under a bushel, or under a bed and not to be set on a candlestick?

22 For there is nothing hid, which shall not be manifested, neither was any thing kept secret, but that it should come abroad.

23 If any man has ears to hear, let him Hear."

24 And He said to them, "take Heed, what you hear. With what measure you mete, it shall be measured to you and to you that Hear, shall more be Given.

25 For he that has, to him shall be Given and he that has not, from him, shall be taken; even that which he has."

26 And He said, "so is the Kingdom of God, as if a Man should Cast Seed into the Ground

27 And should sleep and rise night and day and the seed should spring and grow up, he knows not how.

28 For the earth brings forth fruit of herself; first, the blade, then the ear, after that, the full corn in the ear.

29 But, when the fruit is brought forth, immediately, He puts in the sickle, because the harvest is come."

30 And He said, "Whereunto, shall we liken the Kingdom of God, or with what comparison, shall we compare it?:

31 It is like a grain of mustard seed, which when it is Sown in the earth, is less than all the seeds that be in the earth,

32 But when it is sown, it Grows up and becomes greater than all herbs and shoots out great branches, so that the fowls of the air may lodge under the shadow of it."

33 And with many such parables, spoke He The Word to them, as they were able to Hear it.

34 But without a parable, spoke He not to them. And when they were alone, He expounded all things to His disciples.

35 And the same day, when the evening was come, He said to them, "let us pass over to the other side."

36 And when they had sent away the multitude, they took Him even as He was in the ship. And there were also, with Him, other little ships.

37 And there arose a great storm of wind. And the waves beat into the ship, so that it was now, full.

38 And He was in the hinder part of the ship, asleep on a pillow. And they awoke Him and said to Him, "Master, care you not that we perish?"

39 And He arose and rebuked the wind and said to the Sea, "peace. Be still." And the wind Ceased and there was a great calm.

40 And He said to them, "why are you so fearful? How is it that, you have no Faith?"

41 And they Feared exceedingly and said one to another, "what manner of Man is this that even the wind and the Sea Obey Him?"

Chapter 5

1 And they came over to the other side of the Sea, into the country of the Gadarenes.

2 And when He was come out of the ship, immediately there met Him out of the tombs, a man with an unclean spirit,

3 Who had his dwelling among the tombs and no man could bind him; no, not with chains,

4 Because that he had been often bound with fetters and chains. And the chains had been plucked asunder, by him and the fetters broken in pieces. Neither could any man tame him.

5 And always, night and day, he was in the mountains and in the tombs, crying and cutting himself with stones.

6 But when he saw Jesus afar off, he ran and Worshipped Him,

7 And cried with a loud voice and said, "what have I to do with You, Jesus, You Son of The Most High God?! I adjure You

by God that You torment me not!"
8 For He said to him, "come out of the man, you unclean spirit."
9 And He asked him, "what is your name?" And he answered saying, "my name is Legion, for we are many."
10 And he besought Him much that, 'He would not send them away out of the country.'

11 Now, there was there, near to the mountains, a great herd of swine feeding.
12 And all the devils besought Him saying, "send us into the swine that we may enter into them."
13 And forthwith, Jesus gave them leave. And the unclean spirits went out and entered into the swine and the herd ran violently down a steep place into the Sea (they were about two thousand) and were choked in the Sea.
14 And they that fed the swine, fled and told it in the city and in the country. And they went out to see what it was that was done.
15 And they came to Jesus and saw him that was possessed with the devil and had the legion, sitting and clothed and in his right mind and they were afraid.
16 And they that saw it, told them how it befell to him that was possessed with the devil and also, concerning the swine.
17 And they began to pray Him to depart out of their coasts.

18 And when He was come into the ship, he that had been possessed with the devil, prayed Him that he might be with Him.
19 Howbeit, Jesus suffered him not, but said to him, "go home to your friends and tell them how Great things The Lord has done for you and has had Compassion on you."
20 And He departed and began to publish in Decapolis, how Great things Jesus had done for him and all men did marvel.
21 And when Jesus was passed over again, by ship to the other side, much people gathered to Him and He was near to the Sea.

22 And behold, there came one of the rulers of the synagogue, Jair, by name and when he saw Him, he fell at His feet
23 And besought Him greatly saying, "my little daughter lies at the point of death. I pray You, come and lay your hands on her that she may be Healed and she shall live."

24 And Jesus went with him and much people followed Him and thronged Him.

25 And a certain woman, which had an issue of blood, twelve years
26 And had suffered many things of many physicians and had spent all that she had and was nothing bettered, but rather grew worse,
27 When she had heard of Jesus, came in the press behind and touched His garment.
28 For she said, "if I may touch, but His clothes, I shall be Whole."
29 And straightway, the fountain of her blood was dried up and she felt in her body that she was Healed of that plague.

30 And Jesus, immediately knowing in Himself that Power had gone out of Himself, turned Himself about, in the press and said, "who touched My clothes?"
31 And His disciples said to Him, "You see the multitude thronging You and say You, "who touched Me?"
32 And He looked, round about to see her that had done this thing.
33 But the woman Fearing and Trembling, knowing what was done in her, came and fell down before Him and told Him all the truth.
34 And He said to her, "daughter, your Faith has made you Whole. Go in Peace and be Whole of your plague."

35 While He yet spoke, there came from the ruler of the synagogue's house, certain, which said, "your daughter is dead. Why trouble you, The Master any further?"
36 As soon as Jesus heard the word that was spoken, He said to the ruler of the synagogue, "be not afraid. Only Believe."
37 And He suffered no man to follow Him, save Peter and James and John, the brother of James.

38 And He came to the house of the ruler of the synagogue and saw the tumult and them that wept and wailed greatly.
39 And when He was come in, He said to them, "why make you, this ado and weep? The damsel is not dead, but sleeps."
40 And they laughed Him to scorn. But, when He had put them all out, He took the father and the mother of the damsel and them that were with Him and entered in, where the damsel was lying.
41 And He took the damsel by the hand

and said to her, "talitha cumi," which is, being interpreted, "damsel, I say to you, Arise."
42 And straightway, the damsel Arose and Walked, for she was of the age of twelve years. And they were astonished with a great astonishment.
43 And He charged them straightly that no man should know it and commanded that, "something should be given her, to eat."

Chapter 6
1 And He went out from there and came into His own country and His disciples followed Him.
2 And when the Sabbath Day was come, He began to Teach in the synagogue. And many Hearing Him, were astonished saying, "from whence, has this man, these things and what Wisdom is this, which is Given to Him that even such Mighty Works are Wrought by His hands?
3 Is not this the carpenter, The Son of Mary, the Brother of James and Joseph and of Judah and Simeon and are not His sisters here with us?" And they were offended at Him.
4 But Jesus said to them, "a prophet is not without Honor, but in His own country and among His own kin and in His own house."
5 And He could there, do no Mighty Work, save that He laid His hands on a few sick folks and Healed them.
6 And He marveled, because of their unbelief. And He went, round about the villages Teaching.

7 And He called to Himself, the twelve and began to send them forth, by two and two and gave them Power over unclean spirits
8 And Commanded them that they should take nothing for their journey, save a staff only; no scrip, no bread, no money in their purse,
9 But be shod with sandals and not, put on two coats.
10 And He said to them, "in what place wheresoever, you enter into a house, there abide, until you depart from that place.
11 And whosoever, shall not receive you, nor hear you, when you depart there, shake off the dust under your feet for a Testimony against them. Verily, I say to you, "'it shall be more tolerable for Sodom and Gomorrah in the Day of Judgement, than for that city.'"
12 And they went out and Preached that, "men should Repent."
13 And they Cast Out many devils and Anointed with oil, many that were sick and Healed them.

14 And King Herod, heard of Him (for His Name was spread abroad) and he said that, "John, the Baptist was risen from the dead and therefore, Mighty Works do show forth themselves, in Him."
15 Others said that, "it is Elijah" and others said that, "it is a prophet," or as, "one of the prophets."
16 But when Herod heard thereof, he said, "it is John, whom I beheaded. He is risen from the dead."
17 For Herod himself, had sent forth and laid hold on John and bound him in prison, for Herodias' sake, his brother, Philip's wife, for he had married her.
18 For John had said to Herod, "it is not Lawful for you to have your brother's wife."
19 Therefore, Herodias had a quarrel against him and would have killed him, but she could not.
20 For Herod feared John, knowing that he was a Just man and a Holy and observed him. And when he heard him, he did many things and heard him, gladly.

21 And when a convenient day was come that Herod, on his birthday made a supper to his lords, high captains and chief estates of Galilee
22 And when the daughter of the said Herodias, came in and danced and pleased Herod and them that sat with him, the king said to the damsel, "ask of me whatsoever, you will and I will give it you."
23 And he swore to her, "whatsoever, you shall ask of me, I will give it you, to the half of my kingdom."
24 And she went forth and said to her mother, "what shall I ask?" And she said, "the head of John, the Baptist."
25 And she came in straightway, with haste to the king and asked saying, "I will that you give me, by and by in a charger, the head of John, the Baptist."
26 And the king was exceedingly sorry. Yet, for his oath's sake and for their sakes, which sat with him, he would not reject her.
27 And immediately, the king sent an executioner and commanded his head to be brought. And he went and beheaded him in the prison
28 And brought his head in a charger and gave it to the damsel and the damsel gave it to her mother.
29 And when his disciples heard of it, they

came and took up his corpse and laid it in a tomb.

30 And the apostles gathered themselves together, to Jesus and told Him all things; both what they had Done and what they had Taught.
31 And He said to them, "come you, yourselves apart into a desert place and rest a while." For there were many, coming and going and they had no leisure, so much as to eat.
32 And they departed into a desert place by ship, privately.
33 And the people saw them departing and many knew Him and ran afoot there, out of all cities. And out went they and came together to Him.

34 And Jesus, when he came out, saw much people and was Moved with Compassion toward them, because they were as sheep not having a shepherd. And He began to Teach them many things.
35 And when the day was now, far spent, His disciples came to Him and said, "this is a desert place and now, the time is far passed.
36 Send them away that they may go into the country, round about and into the villages and buy themselves bread. For they have nothing to eat."
37 He answered and said to them, "Give you, them to eat." And they said to Him, "shall we go and buy two hundred pennyworth of bread and give them to eat?"
38 He said to them, "how many loaves have you? Go and see." And when they knew, they said, "five and two fish."
39 And He Commanded them to, "make all sit down by companies, on the green grass."
40 And they sat down in ranks; by hundreds and by fifties.
41 And when He had taken the five loaves and the two fish, He looked up to Heaven and Blessed and Broke the loaves and Gave them to His disciples to set before themselves. And the two fish, Divided He among them all.
42 And they did all eat and were Filled.
43 And they took up twelve baskets full of the fragments and of the fish.
44 And they that did eat of the loaves, were about five thousand men.
45 And straightway, He constrained His disciples to get into the ship and to go to the other side; before to Bethsaida, while He sent away the people.
46 And when He had sent them away, He departed into a mountain to Pray.
47 And when evening was come, the ship was in the midst of the Sea and He alone, on the land.
48 And He saw them toiling in rowing, for the wind was contrary to them. And about the fourth watch of the night, He came to them, Walking on the Sea and would have passed by them.
49 But when they saw Him Walking on the Sea, they supposed it had been a spirit and cried out,
50 For they all saw Him and were troubled. And immediately, He talked with them and said to them, "be of good cheer. It is I, be not afraid."
51 And He went up to them into the ship and the wind ceased and they were sore amazed in themselves, beyond measure and wondered.
52 For they considered not the Miracle of the loaves, for their heart was hardened.

53 And when they had passed over, they came into the land of Chinnereth and drew to the shore.
54 And when they had come out of the ship, straightway they knew Him
55 And ran through that whole region, round about and began to carry about in beds, those that were sick, where they heard He was.
56 And wheresoever, He entered into villages, or cities, or country, they laid the sick in the streets and besought Him that they might touch if it were, but the border of His garment. And as many as touched Him, were Made Whole.

Chapter 7

1 Then, came together to Him, the Pharisees and certain of the scribes, which came from Jerusalem.
2 And when they saw some of His disciples eat bread with defiled (that is to say, with unwashed) hands, they found fault.
3 For the Pharisees and all the Jews, except they wash their hands often, eat not, holding the tradition of the elders.
4 And when they came from the market, except they wash, they eat not. And many other things there be, which they have received to hold, as the washing of cups and pots; brazen vessels and of tables.)
5 Then, the Pharisees and scribes asked

Him, "why walk not, Your disciples, according to the tradition of the elders, but eat bread with unwashed hands?"

6 He answered and said to them, "well, has Isaiah Prophesied of you hypocrites, as it is written, "'THIS PEOPLE HONORS ME WITH THEIR LIPS, BUT THEIR HEART IS FAR FROM ME.

7 HOWBEIT, IN VAIN DO THEY WORSHIP ME, TEACHING FOR DOCTRINES, THE COMMANDMENTS OF MEN.'"

8 For laying aside The Commandment of God, you hold the tradition of men, as the washing of pots and cups and many other such like things, you do."

9 And He said to them, "full well, you reject The Commandment of God that you may keep your own tradition.

10 For Moses said, "'Honor your father and your mother and whosoever, curses father, or mother let him die the death,'"

11 But you say, "'if a man shall say to his father, or mother, "'it is Corban (that is to say, a gift) by whatsoever, you might be profited by me, he shall be free.'"

12 And you suffer him no more, to do anything, for his father, or his mother,

13 Making The Word of God of none effect through your tradition, which you have delivered and many such like things, do you."

14 And when He had called all the people to Himself, He said to them, "Hearken to Me, every one of you and Understand.

15 There is nothing from without a man that entering into him, can defile him. But, the things which come out of him, those are they, that defile the man.

16 If any man has ears to Hear, let him Hear."

17 And when He was entered into the house from the people, His disciples asked Him, concerning the parable.

18 And He said to them, "are you so, without understanding, also? Do you not perceive that whatsoever thing from without enters into the man, it cannot defile him?

19 Because it enters not into his heart, but into the belly and goes out into the draught, purging all meats."

20 And He said, "that which comes out of the man, that defiles the man.

21 For from within, out of the heart of men, proceed evil thoughts: adulteries, fornications, murders,

22 Thefts, covetousness, wickedness, deceit, lasciviousness, an evil eye, blasphemy, pride, foolishness.

23 All these evil things, come from within and defile the man."

24 And from there, He arose and went into the borders of Tyre and Sidon and entered into a house and would have no man know it, but He could not be hid.

25 For a certain woman, whose young daughter had an unclean spirit, heard of Him and came and fell at His feet.

26 The woman was a Greek, a Syrophenician by nation. And she besought Him that, He would Cast Forth the devil Out of her daughter.

27 But Jesus said to her, "let the children first, be filled. For it is not meet to take the children's bread and to cast it to the dogs."

28 And she answered and said to Him, "yes Lord, yet the dogs under the table eat of the children's crumbs."

29 And He said to her, "for this saying, go your way, the devil is gone out of your daughter."

30 And when she had come to her house, she found the devil gone out and her daughter laid on the bed.

31 And again, departing from the coasts of Tyre and Sidon, He came to the Sea of Galilee; through the midst of the coasts of Decapolis.

32 And they brought to Him, one that was deaf and had an impediment in his speech. And they beseeched Him to put His hand on him.

33 And He took him aside from the multitude and put His fingers into his ears and He spit and Touched his tongue

34 And looking up to Heaven, He sighed and said to him, "Ephphasa," that is, "be Opened."

35 And straightway, his ears were Opened and the string of his tongue was Loosed and he Spoke Plainly.

36 And He charged them that, "they should tell no man." But, the more He charged them, so much the more, a great deal they published it

37 And were beyond measure astonished saying, "He has Done all things well. He Makes both the deaf to Hear and the dumb to Speak."

Chapter 8

1 In those days, the multitude being very

great and having nothing to eat, Jesus called His disciples to Himself and said to them,

2 "I have Compassion on the multitude, because they have now been with Me three days and have nothing to eat

3 And if I send them away fasting to their own houses, they will faint by the way, for some of them came from far."

4 And His disciples answered Him, "from whence can a man satisfy these men with bread here, in the wilderness?"

5 And He asked them, "how many loaves have you?" And they said, "seven."

6 And He commanded the people to sit down on the ground and He took the seven loaves and Gave Thanks and Broke and Gave to His disciples to set before them and they did set them before the people.

7 And they had a few small fish and He Blessed and commanded to set them also, before them.

8 So, they did eat and were Filled and they took up of the broken meat that was left, seven baskets.

9 And they that had eaten, were about four thousand and He sent them away.

10 And straightway, He entered into a ship with His disciples and came into the parts of Dalmanutha.

11 And the Pharisees came forth and began to question with Him, seeking of Him a Sign from Heaven, tempting Him.

12 And He sighed deeply in His Spirit and said, "why does this generation seek after a Sign? Verily, I say to you, "'there shall no Sign be given to this generation.'"

13 And He left them and entering into the ship again, departed to the other side.

14 Now, the disciples had forgotten to take bread, neither had they in the ship with them, more than one loaf.

15 And He charged them saying, "take heed. Beware of the leaven of the Pharisees and of the leaven of Herod."

16 And they reasoned among themselves saying, "it is because we have no bread."

17 And when Jesus knew it, He said to them, "why reason you, because you have no bread? Perceive yourselves not, yet neither understand? Have you, your hearts, yet hardened,

18 Having eyes, see you not and having ears, hear you not and do you not remember,

19 When I broke the five loaves among five thousand how many baskets full of fragments took you up?" They said to Him, "twelve."

20 "And when the seven among four thousand, how many baskets full of fragments took you up?" And they said, "seven."

21 And He said to them, "how is it that you do not understand?"

22 And He came to Bethsaida and they brought a blind man to Him and besought Him to Touch him.

23 And He took the blind man by the hand and led him out of the town. And when He had spit on his eyes and put His hands on him, He asked him if he saw anything.

24 And He looked up and said, "I see men as trees, walking."

25 After that, He put His hands again, on his eyes and made him look up and he was restored and Saw every man, Clearly.

26 And He sent him away to his house saying, "neither go into the town, nor tell it to any, in the town."

27 And Jesus went out and His disciples, into the towns of Caesarea Philippi. And by the way, He asked His disciples, saying to them, "Whom do men say that I am?"

28 And they answered, "John, the Baptist, but some say, "'Elijah'" and others, "'one of the prophets.'"

29 And He said to them, "but Whom say you that I am?" And Peter answered and said to Him, "You are The Christ."

30 And He charged them that, "they should tell no man of Himself."

31 And He began to Teach them that, "THE SON OF MAN MUST SUFFER MANY THINGS AND BE REJECTED OF THE ELDERS AND OF THE CHIEF PRIESTS AND SCRIBES AND BE KILLED AND AFTER THREE DAYS, RISE AGAIN."

32 And He spoke that saying openly. And Peter took Him and began to rebuke Him.

33 But, when He had turned about and looked on His disciples, He rebuked Peter saying, "get you behind Me Satan, for you savor not, the things that be of God, but the things that be of men."

34 And when He had called the people to Himself, with His disciples also, He said to them, "whosoever will come after Me, let him deny himself and Take Up his Cross and Follow Me.

35 For whosoever will save his life, shall lose it. But, whosoever shall lose his life, for My sake and The Gospel's, the same shall save it.
36 For what shall it profit a man, if he shall gain the whole World and lose his own soul?
37 Or, what shall a man give in exchange for his soul?
38 Whosoever therefore, shall be ashamed of Me and of My Words in this adulterous and sinful generation, of him also, shall The Son of Man be ashamed, when He comes in the Glory of His Father with the Holy angels."

Chapter 9

1 And He said to them, "verily, I say to you that, "'THERE BE SOME OF THEM THAT STAND HERE, WHICH SHALL NOT TASTE OF DEATH, UNTIL THEY HAVE SEEN THE KINGDOM OF GOD COME WITH POWER.'"

2 And after six days, Jesus took with Himself, Peter and James and John and led them up into a high mountain apart, by themselves and He was Transfigured before them.
3 And His raiment became Shining; exceedingly white as snow, so as no fuller on Earth can white them.
4 And there appeared to them, Elijah with Moses and they were talking with Jesus.
5 And Peter answered and said to Jesus, "Master, it is good for us to be here and let us make three tabernacles: one for You and one for Moses and one for Elijah."
6 For he knew not what to say, for they were sore afraid.
7 And there was A Cloud that overshadowed them and A Voice came out of The Cloud saying, "this is My beloved Son. Hear Him."
8 And suddenly, when they had looked round about, they saw no man any more, save Jesus only, with themselves.
9 And as they came down from the mountain, He charged them that they, "should tell no man what things they had seen, until THE SON OF MAN WERE RISEN FROM THE DEAD."
10 And they kept that saying with themselves, questioning one with another what, "the Rising from the dead" should mean.
11 And they asked Him saying, "why say the scribes that Elijah must first, come?"
12 And He answered and told them, "ELIJAH, VERILY COMES FIRST AND RESTORES ALL THINGS and how it is written of The Son of Man that, "'HE MUST SUFFER MANY THINGS AND BE SET AT NOUGHT.'"
13 But, I say to you that, "'ELIJAH IS INDEED, COME AND THEY HAVE DONE TO HIM, WHATSOEVER THEY DETERMINED, AS IT IS WRITTEN OF HIM.'"

14 And when He came to His disciples, He saw a great multitude about them and the scribes questioning with them.
15 And straightway, all the people, when they beheld Him, were greatly amazed and running to Him, saluted Him.
16 And He asked the scribes, "what question you with them?"
17 And one of the multitude answered and said, "Master, I have brought to You my son, which has a dumb spirit.
18 And wheresoever, he takes him, he tears him and he foams and gnashes with his teeth and pines away. And I spoke to Your disciples that, "they should Cast him Out" and they could not.
19 He answered him and said, "O Faithless generation, how long shall I be with you? How long shall I suffer you? Bring him to Me."
20 And they brought him to Him and when He saw him, straightway, the spirit tore him and he fell on the ground and wallowed, foaming.
21 And He asked his father, "how long is it, ago since this came to him?" And he said, "of a child.
22 And oftentimes, it has cast him into the fire and into the waters, to destroy him. But, if You can do any thing, have Compassion on us and help us."
23 Jesus said to him, "if you can Believe, All things are Possible to him that Believes."
24 And straightway, the father of the child cried out and said with tears, "Lord, I Believe. Help you, my unbelief!"
25 When Jesus saw that the people came running together, He rebuked the foul spirit saying to him, "you dumb and deaf spirit, I charge you, come out of him and enter no more into him."
26 And the spirit cried and rent him sore and came out of him. And he was as one dead, insomuch that, many said, "he is dead."

27 But, Jesus took him by the hand and lifted him up and he arose.
28 And when He was come into the house, His disciples asked Him privately, "why could not, we Cast him Out?"
29 And He said to them, "this kind can come forth by nothing, but by Prayer and Fasting."
30 And they departed there and passed through Galilee and He would not that any man should know it.
31 For He Taught His disciples and said to them, "THE SON OF MAN IS DELIVERED INTO THE HANDS OF MEN AND THEY SHALL KILL HIM AND AFTER THAT, HE IS KILLED, HE SHALL RISE, THE THIRD DAY."
32 But, they understood not that saying and were afraid to ask Him.
33 And He came to Capernaum and being in the house, He asked them, "what was it that you disputed among yourselves, by the way?"
34 But, they held their peace, for by the way, they had disputed among themselves, who should be the greatest.
35 And He sat down and called the twelve and said to them, "if any man, desires to be first, the same shall be last of all and servant of all."
36 And He took a child and set him in the midst of them. And when He had taken him in his arms, He said to them,
37 "Whosoever shall receive one of such children in My Name, Receives Me and whosoever, shall Receive Me, receives not Me, but Him that sent Me."

38 And John answered Him saying, "Master, we saw one Casting Out devils in Your Name and he follows not us. And we forbade him, because he follows not us.
39 But, Jesus said, "forbid him not, for there is no man, which shall Do a Miracle in My Name that can lightly speak evil of Me.
40 For he that is not against us is on our part.
41 For whosoever, shall give you a cup of water to drink in My Name, because you belong to Christ, verily I say to you, he shall not lose his reward.
42 And whosoever, shall offend one of these little ones that Believe in Me, it is better for him that a millstone were hanged about his neck and he were cast into the Sea.

43 And if your hand offends you, cut it off. It is better for you to enter into Life maimed, than having two hands to go into Sheol; into the fire that never shall be quenched,
44 Where "'THEIR WORM DIES NOT AND THE FIRE IS NOT QUENCHCED.'"
45 And if your foot offends you, cut it off. It is better for you to enter halt into Life, than having two feet, to be cast into Sheol; into the fire, that never, shall be quenched,
46 Where, "'THEIR WORM DIES NOT AND THE FIRE IS NOT QUENCHED.'"
47 And if your eye offends you, pluck it out. It is better for you to enter into the Kingdom of God with one eye, than having two eyes to be cast into Sheol fire,
48 Where "'THEIR WORM DIES NOT AND THE FIRE IS NOT QUENCHED.'"
49 For every one, shall be salted with fire and every sacrifice, shall be salted with salt.
50 Salt is good, but if the salt has lost his saltines, wherewith will you season it? Have salt in yourselves and have Peace, one with another."

Chapter 10

1 And He rose from there and came into the coasts of Judaea, by the further side of Jordan and the people resorted to Him again. And as He was accustomed, He Taught them, again.
2 And the Pharisees came to Him and asked Him, "is it Lawful for a man to put away his wife?," tempting Him.
3 And He answered and said to them, "what did Moses command you?"
4 And they said, "Moses suffered to write a bill of divorcement and to put her away."
5 And Jesus answered and said to them, "for the hardness of your heart, he wrote you this precept.
6 But, from the beginning of the Creation God, "'made them male and female.
7 For this cause, shall a man leave his father and mother and cleave to his wife
8 And they two, shall be one flesh,'" so then, they are no more two, but one flesh.
9 What therefore, God has joined together, let not man put asunder."

10 And in the house, His disciples asked Him again, of the same matter.
11 And He said to them, "whosoever, shall put away His wife and marry another, commits adultery, against her.
12 And if a woman shall put away her husband and be married to another, she

commits adultery."

13 And they brought young children to Him that He should touch them. And His disciples rebuked those that brought them.
14 But, when Jesus saw it, He was much displeased and said to them, "suffer the little children to come to Me and forbid them not, for of such, is the Kingdom of God.
15 Verily, I say to you, "'whosoever, shall not receive the Kingdom of God as a little child, he shall not enter, therein.'"
16 And He took them up in His arms, put His hands on them and Blessed them.

17 And when He was gone forth into the way, there came one running and kneeled to Him and asked Him, "Good Master, what shall I Do, that I may inherit Eternal Life?"
18 And Jesus said to him, "why call you, Me Good? There is none Good, but One, that is God.
19 You know The Commandments: do not commit adultery, do not murder, do not steal, do not bear false witness, defraud not, Honor your father and mother…"
20 And he answered and said to Him, "Master, all these, have I Observed from my youth."
21 Then, Jesus beholding him, Loved him and said to him, "one thing you lack, go your way, sell whatsoever you have and Give to the poor and you shall have treasure in Heaven and come, Take Up the Cross and Follow Me."
22 And he was sad at that saying and went away grieved, for he had great possessions.
23 And Jesus looked, round about and said to His disciples, "how hardly, shall they that have riches, enter into the Kingdom of God."

24 And the disciples were astonished at His Words. But, Jesus answered again, and said to them, "children, how hard is it, for them that trust in riches, to enter into the Kingdom of God?
25 It is easier for a camel to go through the eye of a needle, than for a rich man, to enter into the Kingdom of God."
26 And they were astonished out of measure saying among themselves, "who then, can be Saved?"
27 And Jesus looking on them said, "with men, it is impossible, but not with God. For with God, All things are Possible."

28 Then, Peter began to say to Him, "lo, we have left all and have Followed You."
29 And Jesus answered and said, "verily, I say to you, "'there is no man that has left: house, or brothers, or sisters, or father, or mother, or wife, or children, or lands, for My sake and The Gospel's,
30 But he shall Receive one hundredfold now, in this time: houses and brothers and sisters and mothers and children and lands, with persecutions and in the World to come, Eternal Life.
31 But, many that are first, shall be last and the last, first.'"

32 And they were in the way, going up to Jerusalem and Jesus went before them and they were amazed. And as they followed, they were afraid. And He took again, the twelve and began to tell them what things should happen to Himself,
33 Saying, "behold, we go up to Jerusalem and THE SON OF MAN SHALL BE DELIVERED TO THE CHIEF PRIESTS AND TO THE SCRIBES. AND THEY SHALL CONDEMN HIM TO DEATH AND SHALL DELIVER HIM TO THE GENTILES
34 AND THEY SHALL MOCK HIM AND SHALL SCOURGE HIM AND SHALL SPIT ON HIM AND SHALL KILL HIM. AND THE THIRD DAY, HE SHALL RISE AGAIN."

35 And James and John, (the sons of Zabdi) came to Him saying, "Master, we would that You should do for us, whatsoever we shall desire."
36 And He said to them, "what would you that I should do for you?"
37 They said to Him, "grant to us that we may sit, one on Your right hand and the other, on Your left hand in Your Glory."
38 But, Jesus said to them, "you know not, what you ask. Can you Drink of the Cup that I Drink of and be Baptized with the Baptism that I am Baptized with?"
39 And they said to Him, "we can." And Jesus said to them, "you shall indeed, Drink of the Cup that I Drink of and with the Baptism that I am Baptized withal, shall you be Baptized.
40 But, to sit on My right hand and on My left hand, is not Mine to give. But, it shall be Given to them, for whom it is prepared."

41 And when the ten heard it, they began to be much displeased with James and John.

42 But, Jesus called them to Himself and said to them, "you know that, they which are accounted to rule over the gentiles, exercise lordship over them and their great ones, exercise authority on them.
43 But, so shall it not be, among you. But whosoever, will be great among you, shall be your minister.
44 And whosoever of you, will be the chiefest, shall be servant of all.
45 For even The Son of Man came not, to be ministered to, but to minister and to Give His life a ransom for many."

46 And they came to Jericho. And as He went out of Jericho, with His disciples and a great numbers of people, blind Bartimaeus, the son of Timaeus, sat by the highway side, begging.
47 And when he heard that it was Jesus, of Nazareth he began to cry out and say, "Jesus, you son of David, have Mercy on me!"
48 And many charged him that he should, "hold his peace." But, he cried the more a great deal, "You son of David, have Mercy on me!"
49 And Jesus stood still and Commanded him to be called. And they called the blind man saying to him, "be of Good Comfort. Rise, He calls you."
50 And he, casting away his garment, rose and came to Jesus.
51 And Jesus answered and said to him, "what will you that I should Do to you?" The blind man said to Him, "Lord, that I might Receive my Sight."
52 And Jesus said to him, "go your way. Your Faith has made you Whole." And immediately, he Received his Sight and followed Jesus in the way.

Chapter 11

1 And when they came near to Jerusalem, to Bethphage and Bethany, at the Mount of Olives, He sent forth, two of His disciples
2 And said to them, "go your way, into the village, over against yourselves and as soon as you are entered into it, you shall find a colt tied, whereon never man sat. Loose him and bring him.
3 And if any man says to you, "'why do you this?,'" say you that, "'The Lord has need of him'" and straightway, he will send him here."
4 And they went their way and found the colt tied by the door without, in a place where two ways met and they loosed him.

5 And certain of them that stood there, said to them, "what do you, loosing the colt?"
6 And they said to them, even as Jesus had Commanded and they let them go.
7 And they brought the colt to Jesus and cast their garments on him and He sat on him.
8 And many spread their garments in the way and others cut down branches off the trees and strawed them in the way.
9 And they that went before and they that followed, cried saying, "HOSANNA! BLESSED IS HE THAT COMES IN THE NAME OF THE LORD!
10 BLESSED BE THE KINGDOM OF OUR FATHER, DAVID THAT COMES IN THE NAME OF THE LORD! HOSANNA IN THE HIGHEST!"

11 And Jesus entered into Jerusalem and into the temple. And when He had looked round about, on all things and now, the evening was come, He went out to Bethany with the twelve.
12 And on the morrow, when they had come from Bethany, He was hungry.
13 And seeing a fig tree afar off having leaves, He came, if haply, He might find any thing, thereon. And when He came to it, He found nothing, but leaves, for the time of figs, was not yet.
14 And Jesus answered and said to it, "no man eat fruit of you hereafter, for ever." And His disciples heard it.

15 And they come to Jerusalem and Jesus went into the temple and began to cast out them that sold and bought in the temple and overthrew the tables of the moneychangers and the seats of them that sold doves
16 And would not suffer that any man, should carry any vessel through the temple.
17 And He Taught saying to them, "is it not written, "'My house shall be called of all nations, the House of Prayer?'" But, you have made it a den of thieves!"
18 And the scribes and chief priests heard it and sought how they might destroy Him, for they feared Him, because all the people were astonished at His Doctrine.
19 And when evening was come, He went out of the city.

20 And in the morning, as they passed by, they saw the fig tree dried up from the roots.

21 And Peter calling to remembrance, said to Him, "Master behold, the fig tree, which You cursed is withered away."
22 And Jesus answering, said to them, "have Faith in God.
23 For verily, I say to you that, "'whosoever, shall say to this mountain, "'be you, removed and be you, cast into the Sea and shall not doubt in his heart, but shall Believe that those things, which he said, shall come to pass, he shall have whatsoever, he says.'"
24 Therefore, I say to you, "'whatsoever things you desire, when you Pray, Believe that you Receive them and you shall have them.'"
25 And when you stand Praying, Forgive, if you have anything against any that your Father also, which is in Heaven, may Forgive you, your trespasses.
26 But, if you do not forgive, neither will your Father, which is in Heaven, forgive your trespasses."

27 And they came again, to Jerusalem and as He was walking in the temple, there came to Him, the chief priests and the scribes and the elders
28 And said to Him, "by what Authority Do You, these things and Who Gave You this Authority to Do these things?"
29 And Jesus answered and said to them, "I will also, ask of you one question and answer me. And I will tell you, by what Authority I Do these things;
30 The Baptism of John, was it from Heaven, or of men? Answer Me."
31 And they reasoned with themselves saying, "if we shall say, "'from Heaven,'" He will say, "'why then, did you not believe Him?'"
32 But, if we shall say, "'of men…'" (they feared the people, for all men counted John that he was a prophet, indeed.)
33 And they answered and said to Jesus, "we cannot tell." And Jesus answering said to them, "neither do I tell you, by what Authority I Do these things."

Chapter 12

1 And He began to speak to them by parables, "a certain Man planted a vineyard and set a hedge about it and dug a place for the winefat and built a tower and let it out to husbandmen and went into a far country.
2 And at the season, He sent to the husbandmen, a servant that He might receive from the husbandmen of the fruit of the vineyard.
3 And they caught him and beat him and sent him away, empty.
4 And again, He sent to them, another servant. And at him, they cast stones and wounded him in the head and sent him away, shamefully handled.
5 And again, He sent another. And him, they killed and many others, beating some and killing some.
6 Having yet therefore, one Son; His well beloved, He sent Him also, last to them saying, "'they will reverence My Son.'"
7 But those husbandmen said among themselves, "'this is the heir. Come, let us kill Him and the inheritance, shall be ours.'"
8 And they took Him and killed Him and cast Him out of the vineyard.
9 What shall therefore, The Lord of the vineyard do? He will come and destroy the husbandmen and will give the vineyard to others.
10 And have you not read this Scripture, "'THE STONE, WHICH THE BUILDERS REJECTED, IS BECOME THE HEAD OF THE CORNER,
11 THIS WAS THE LORD'S DOING AND IT IS MARVELOUS IN OUR EYES?'"
12 And they sought to lay hold on Him, but feared the people, for they knew that He had spoken the parable against them and they left Him and went their way.
13 And they sent to Him, certain of the Pharisees and of the Herodians, to catch Him in His Words.
14 And when they had come, they said to Him, "Master, we know that You are True and care for no man, for You regard not, the person of men, but Teach The Way of God in Truth. Is it Lawful to give tribute to Caesar, or not,
15 Shall we give, or shall we not give?" But He, knowing their hypocrisy, said to them, "why tempt you, me? Bring Me a penny that I may see it."
16 And they brought it. And He said to them, "whose is this image and superscription?" And they said to Him, "Caesar's."
17 And Jesus answering, said to them, "render to Caesar, the things that are Caesar's and to God, the things that are God's." And they marveled at Him.

18 Then came to Him, the Sadducees, which say "there is no Resurrection" and they asked Him saying,
19 "Master, Moses wrote to us, "'if a man's brother dies and leaves his wife behind himself and leaves no children that his brother should take his wife and raise up seed to his brother.'"
20 Now, there were seven brothers and the first, took a wife and dying, left no seed.
21 And the second, took her and died, neither left he, any seed and the third, likewise.
22 And the seven had her and left no seed. Last of all, the woman died, also.
23 In the Resurrection therefore, when they shall Rise, whose wife shall she be of them? For the seven had her to wife."
24 And Jesus answering said to them, "do you not, therefore err, because you know not, The Scriptures, neither the Power of God?
25 For when they shall Rise from the dead, they neither marry, nor are given in marriage, but are as the angels, which are in Heaven.
26 And as touching the dead that they Rise, have you not read in the scroll of Moses, how in the bush, God spoke to him saying, "'I am The God of Abraham and The God of Isaac and The God of Jacob?'"
27 He is not The God of the dead, but The God of the Living. You therefore, do greatly err."

28 And one of the scribes came and having heard them reasoning, together and perceiving that He had answered them well, asked Him, "which, is The First Commandment of all?"
29 And Jesus answered him, "The first, of all The Commandments is, "'Hear O Israel, The Lord our God is One Lord
30 And you shall Love The Lord your God with All your heart and with All your soul and with All your mind and with All your strength.'" This is The first Commandment.
31 And the second, is like, namely this, "'you shall Love your neighbor as yourself.'" There is none other, Commandment greater than these."
32 And the scribe said to Him, "well Master, You have said The Truth, for there is One God and there is none other, but He.
33 And to Love Him with All the heart and with All the Understanding and with All the soul and with All the strength and to Love his neighbor as himself, is more than all, whole burnt offerings and sacrifices."
34 And when Jesus saw that he answered discreetly, He said to him, "you are not far from the Kingdom of God." And no man after that, did ask Him any question.

35 And Jesus answered and said, while He Taught in the temple, "how say the scribes that, "'Christ is The Son of David?'"
36 For David himself, said by The Holy Ghost, "'THE LORD SAID TO MY LORD, ""SIT YOURSELF, ON MY RIGHT HAND, UNTIL I MAKE YOUR ENEMIES, YOUR FOOTSTOOL.""'
37 David therefore, himself calls Him Lord and where is He then, his Son?" And the common people Heard Him Gladly.

38 And He said to them in His Doctrine, "Beware of the scribes, which love to go in long clothing and love salutations in the marketplaces
39 And the chief seats in the synagogues and the uppermost rooms at feasts,
40 Which devour widows' houses and for a pretence, make long prayers. These, shall receive greater damnation."

41 And Jesus sat over against the treasury and beheld how the people cast money into the treasury. And many that were rich, cast in much.
42 And there came a certain poor widow and she threw in two mites, which make a farthing.
43 And He called to Himself, His disciples and said to them, "verily, I say to you that, "'this poor widow, has cast more in, than all they, which have cast into the treasury.
44 For all they, did cast in of their abundance. But, she of her want, did cast in All that she had; even all her living.'"

Chapter 13
1 And as He went out of the temple, one of His disciples said to Him, "Master, see what manner of stones and what buildings are here!"
2 And Jesus answering, said to him, "SEE YOU, THESE GREAT BUILDINGS? THERE SHALL NOT BE LEFT, ONE STONE ON ANOTHER THAT SHALL NOT BE THROWN DOWN."
3 And as He sat on the Mount of Olives over against the temple, Peter and James and John and Andrew asked Him privately,

4 "Tell us, when shall these things be and what, shall be the Sign, when all these things shall be fulfilled?"

5 And Jesus answering them, began to say, "take Heed, lest any man deceive you.
6 For MANY SHALL COME IN MY NAME SAYING, "'I AM CHRIST'" AND SHALL DECEIVE MANY.
7 AND WHEN YOU SHALL HEAR OF WARS AND RUMORS OF WARS, be you, not troubled. FOR SUCH THINGS MUST NEEDS BE, but the end shall not be yet.
8 FOR NATION SHALL RISE AGAINST NATION AND KINGDOM AGAINST KINGDOM and THERE SHALL BE EARTHQUAKES IN DIVERSE PLACES AND THERE SHALL BE FAMINES AND TROUBLES. These are the Beginnings of Sorrows.
9 But, take Heed to yourselves, for THEY SHALL DELIVER YOU UP TO COUNCILS AND IN THE SYNAGOGUES. YOU SHALL BE BEATEN AND YOU SHALL BE BROUGHT BEFORE RULERS AND KINGS, FOR MY SAKE, for a Testimony against them.
10 And The Gospel must first, be published among all nations.
11 But, WHEN THEY SHALL LEAD YOU AND DELIVER YOU UP, take no thought beforehand, what you shall speak, neither do you premeditate. But whatsoever, shall be Given you in that hour, that speak yourselves, for it is not you that speaks, but The Holy Ghost.
12 Now, the brother shall betray the brother to death and the father, the son. And children shall rise up against their parents and shall cause them to be put to death.
13 And YOU SHALL BE HATED OF ALL MEN, FOR MY NAME'S SAKE. But, he that shall endure to the end, the same, shall be Saved.

14 But, when you shall see the Abomination of Desolation, spoken of by Daniel, the prophet, standing where it should not, (let him that reads Understand) then let them that be in Judaea, flee to the mountains.
15 And let him that is on the housetop, not go down into the house, neither enter therein, to take any thing out of his house.
16 And let him that is in the field, not turn back again, for to take up his garment.
17 But, woe to them that are with child and to them that give suck in those days!
18 And Pray yourselves that your flight be not in the winter.
19 For IN THOSE DAYS, SHALL BE AFFLICTION, such as was not from the beginning of the creation; which God Created to this time, neither shall be.
20 And except that The Lord had shortened those days, no flesh should be saved. But, for the elect's sake, whom He has Chosen, He has shortened the days.

21 And then, if any man shall say to you, "'lo, here is Christ,'" or "'lo, he is there,'" believe him not.
22 For FALSE CHRISTS AND FALSE PROPHETS SHALL RISE AND SHALL SHOW SIGNS AND WONDERS TO SEDUCE, IF IT WERE POSSIBLE, EVEN THE ELECT.
23 But, take yourselves Heed. Behold, I have foretold you all things.

24 But, in those days, after that tribulation, the Sun shall be darkened and the Moon shall not give her light
25 And the stars of Heaven shall fall and the powers that are in heaven shall be shaken.
26 And then, shall they see The Son of Man Coming in The Clouds with Great Power and Glory.
27 And then, shall He send His angels and shall gather together, His elect, from the four winds, from the uttermost parts of the Earth to the uttermost parts of Heaven.

28 Now, Learn a parable of the fig tree. When her branch is yet, tender and puts forth leaves, you know that Summer is near.
29 So you, in like manner, when you shall see these things come to pass, know that it is near; even at the doors.
30 Verily, I say to you that, "'this generation shall not pass, until all these things, be done.
31 Heaven and Earth shall pass away, but My Words shall not pass away.
32 But, of that day and that hour, knows no man; no, not the angels, which are in Heaven, neither The Son, but the Father.
33 Take yourselves Heed. Watch and Pray, for you know not, when the time is.'"

34 For The Son of Man is as a Man taking a far journey, who left His house and gave Authority to His servants and to every

man, his Work and Commanded the porter to watch.
35 Watch yourselves therefore, for you know not, when The Master of the house Comes; at evening, or at midnight, or at the cock crowing, or in the morning,
36 Lest coming suddenly, He finds you sleeping.
37 And what I say to you, I say to all, "'Watch.'"

Chapter 14

1 After two days, was The Feast of The Passover and of Unleavened Bread. And the chief priests and the scribes, sought how they might take Him by craft and put Him to death.
2 But they said, "not on the feast day, lest there be an uproar of the people."

3 And being in Bethany, in the house of Simeon, the leper as He sat at meat, there came a woman having an alabaster box of ointment of spikenard, very precious and she broke the box and poured it on His head.
4 And there were some that had indignation within themselves and said, "why was this waste of the ointment made?
5 For it might have been sold for more than three hundred pence and have been given to the poor." And they murmured against her.
6 And Jesus said, "let her alone, why trouble you, her? She has Worked a Good Work on Me.
7 For you have the poor with you always and when, soever you will, you may Do them Good. But, Me you have not, always.
8 She has Done what she could. She has come beforehand, to Anoint My Body to the burying.
9 Verily, I say to you, "'WHERESOEVER, THIS GOSPEL, SHALL BE PREACHED THROUGHOUT THE WHOLE WORLD. THIS, ALSO THAT SHE HAS DONE, SHALL BE SPOKEN OF FOR A MEMORIAL OF HER.'"

10 And Judas Iscariot, one of the twelve, went to the chief priests, to betray Him, to them.
11 And when they heard it, they were glad and promised to give him money. And he sought how he might conveniently betray Him.

12 And the first day of Unleavened Bread, when they killed the Passover, His disciples said to Him, "where will You that we go and prepare that You may eat the Passover?"
13 And He sent forth, two of His disciples and said to them, "go yourselves, into the city and there, shall meet you a man bearing a pitcher of water, follow him.
14 And wheresoever, he shall go in, say you to the good man of the house, "'The Master said, "'where is the guest chamber, where I shall eat the Passover with My disciples?'"'
15 And he will show you a large upper room furnished. And prepared there. Make ready for us."
16 And His disciples went forth and came into the city and found as He had said to them and they made ready the Passover.

17 And in the evening, He came with the twelve.
18 And as they sat and did eat, Jesus said, "verily, I say to you, "'ONE OF YOU, WHICH EATS WITH ME, SHALL BETRAY ME.'"
19 And they began to be sorrowful and to say to Him, one by one, "is it I?" And another said, "is it I?"
20 And He answered and said to them, "it is one of the twelve that dips with Me in the dish.
21 The Son of Man, indeed goes as it is written of Him, but woe to that man, by whom The Son of Man is betrayed! Good were it, for that man, if he had never been born."

22 And as they did eat, Jesus took bread and Blessed and broke it and gave to them and said, "take, eat. This is My Body."
23 And He took the cup and when He had Given Thanks, He gave it to them and they all drank of it.
24 And He said to them, "this is My Blood of The New Testament, which is shed for many.
25 Verily, I say to you, "'I will drink no more, of the fruit of the vine, until that day that I drink it new in the Kingdom of God.'"
26 And when they had sung a hymn, they went out into the Mount of Olives.

27 And Jesus said to them, "ALL YOU, SHALL BE OFFENDED, BECAUSE OF ME THIS NIGHT, for it is written, "'I WILL

SLAY THE SHEPHERD AND THE SHEEP SHALL BE SCATTERED.'"
28 But, after that I am Risen, I will go before you into Galilee."
29 But Peter said to Him, "although all shall be offended, yet will not I."
30 And Jesus said to him, "verily, I say to you that, "'THIS DAY, EVEN IN THIS NIGHT, BEFORE THE COCK CROWS TWICE, YOU SHALL DENY ME THRICE.'"
31 But, He spoke the more vehemently, "if I should die with You, I will not deny You, in any wise." Likewise also, said they all.

32 And they came to a place, which was named, Gethsemane and He said to His disciples, "sit yourselves here, while I shall Pray."
33 And He took with Himself, Peter and James and John and began to be sore amazed and to be very heavy
34 And said to them, "My soul is exceedingly sorrowful to death. Tarry yourselves, here and watch."
35 And He went forward a little and fell on the ground and Prayed that, if it were possible, the hour might pass from Himself.
36 And He said, "Abba Father, All things are Possible to You. Take away this Cup from Me, nevertheless not, what I will, but what You Will."

37 And He came and found them sleeping and said to Peter, "Simeon, you sleep? Could not, you watch one hour?
38 Watch yourself and Pray, lest you enter into temptation. The spirit truly is ready, but the flesh is weak."
39 And again, He went away and Prayed and spoke the same words.
40 And when He returned, He found them asleep again, (for their eyes were heavy) neither knew they, what to answer Him.
41 And He came the third time and said to them, "Sleep on now and take your rest. It is enough. The hour is come. Behold, THE SON OF MAN IS BETRAYED INTO THE HANDS OF SINNERS.
42 Rise up, let us go. Lo, he that betrays Me is at hand."

43 And immediately, while He yet spoke, came Judas; one of the twelve and with him, a great multitude with swords and staves, from the chief priests and the scribes and the elders.
44 And he that betrayed Him, had given them a token saying, "Whomsoever I shall kiss, that same, is He. Take Him and lead Him away, safely."
45 And as soon as he was come, he went straightway to Him and said, "MASTER, MASTER" AND KISSED HIM.
46 And they laid their hands on Him and took Him.

47 And one of them that stood by, drew a sword and struck a servant of the high priest and cut off his ear.
48 And Jesus answered and said to them, "are you come out as against a thief with swords and with staves to take Me?
49 I was daily with you, in the temple, Teaching and you took Me not. But, The Scriptures must be Fulfilled."
50 And THEY ALL FORSOOK HIM AND FLED.

51 And there followed him, a certain young man, having a linen cloth, cast about his naked body. And the young men laid hold on him
52 And he left the linen cloth and fled from them naked.
53 AND THEY LED JESUS AWAY TO THE HIGH PRIEST AND WITH HIM, WERE ASSEMBLED, ALL THE CHIEF PRIESTS AND THE ELDERS AND THE SCRIBES.
54 And Peter followed Him afar off; even into the palace of the high priest and he sat with the servants and warmed himself at the fire.

55 And the chief priests and all the council sought for witness against Jesus, to put Him to death and found none.
56 For many bare false witness against Him, but their witness agreed not, together.
57 And there arose certain and BARE FALSE WITNESS AGAINST HIM saying,
58 "We heard him say, "'I will destroy this temple that is made with hands and within three days, I will build another, made without hands.'"
59 But, neither so, did their witness agree, together.

60 And the high priest stood up in the midst and asked Jesus saying, "answer You nothing? What is it, which these witness against You?"
61 But, HE HELD HIS PEACE AND ANSWERED NOTHING. Again, the high priest asked Him and said to Him, "are

You, The Christ, The Son of the Blessed?"
62 And Jesus said, "I am and you shall see The Son of Man sitting on the right hand of Power and coming in The Clouds of Heaven."
63 Then, the high priest rent his clothes and said, "what need we, any further witnesses?
64 You have heard the blasphemy. What think you?" And they all condemned Him to be guilty of death.
65 And SOME BEGAN TO SPIT ON HIM AND TO COVER HIS FACE AND TO BUFFET HIM AND TO SAY TO HIM, "PROPHESY." AND THE SERVANTS DID STRIKE HIM WITH THE PALMS OF THEIR HANDS.

66 And as Peter was beneath, in the palace, there came one of the maids of the high priest.
67 And when she saw Peter warming himself, she looked on him and said, "...and you also, were with Jesus of Nazareth."
68 But, HE DENIED SAYING, "I KNOWNOT, NEITHER UNDERSTAND I, WHAT
YOU SAY." And he went out into the porch and THE COCK CREW.
69 And a maid saw him, again and began to say to them that stood by, "this is one of them."
70 And HE DENIED IT, again. And a little after, they that stood by, said again, to Peter, "surely, you are one of them, for you are a Galilaean and your speech agrees, thereto."
71 But, he began to curse and to swear saying, "I KNOW NOT THIS MAN OF WHOM, YOU SPEAK!"
72 And THE SECOND TIME, THE COCK CREW. And Peter called to mind, the Word that Jesus said to him, "BEFORE THE COCK CROWS TWICE, YOU SHALL DENY ME, THRICE." And when he thought thereon, he wept.

Chapter 15

1 And straightway in the morning, the chief priests held a consultation with the elders and scribes and the whole council and bound Jesus and carried Him away and delivered Him to Pilate.
2 And Pilate asked Him, "are You The King of the Jews?" And He answering, said to them, "you said it."
3 And the chief priests accused Him of many things, but HE ANSWERED NOTHING.
4 And Pilate asked Him again saying, "answer You nothing? Behold, how many things they witness against You."
5 But Jesus, yet answered nothing, so that Pilate marveled.

6 Now at that feast, he released to them one prisoner, whomsoever, they desired.
7 And there was one named, Barabbas, which laid bound with them that had made insurrection with him; who had committed murder in the insurrection.
8 And the multitude crying aloud, began to desire him to do as he had ever done, to them.
9 But Pilate answered them saying, "will you that I release to you, The King of the Jews?"
10 For he knew that the chief priests had delivered Him, for envy.

11 But, the chief priests moved the people that he should rather release Barabbas to them.
12 And Pilate answered and said again to them, "what will you then that I shall do to Him, Whom you call, The King of the Jews?"
13 And they cried out again, "Crucify Him!"
14 Then Pilate said to them, "why, what evil has He done?" And they cried out the more exceedingly, "Crucify Him!"
15 And so Pilate, willing to content the people, released Barabbas to them and delivered Jesus, when he had scourged Him, to be crucified.

16 And the soldiers led Him away into the hall, called Praetorium and they called together, the whole band.
17 And THEY CLOTHED HIM WITH PURPLE AND PLATTED A CROWN OF THORNS AND PUT IT ABOUT HIS HEAD
18 AND BEGAN TO SALUTE HIM, "HAIL, KING OF THE JEWS!"
19 AND THEY BEAT HIM ON THE HEAD WITH A REED AND DID SPIT ON HIM AND BOWING THEIR KNEES, WORSHIPPED HIM.
20 AND WHEN THEY HAD MOCKED HIM, THEY TOOK OFF THE PURPLE FROM HIM AND PUT HIS OWN CLOTHES ON HIM AND LED HIM OUT TO CRUCIFY HIM.

21 And they compelled one, Simon, a Cyrenian, who passed by, coming out of the country, the father of Alexander and

Rufus, to bear His cross.

22 And they brought Him to the place, Golgotha, which is being interpreted, the Place of a Skull.

23 And THEY GAVE HIM TO DRINK WINE, MINGLED WITH MYRRH. BUT,

HE RECEIVED IT NOT.

24 AND WHEN THEY HAD CRUCIFIED HIM, THEY PARTED HIS GARMENTS; CASTING LOTS ON THEM, WHAT EVERY MAN SHOULD TAKE.

25 And it was the third hour and THEY CRUCIFIED HIM.

26 And the superscription of His accusation was written over, "The King of the Jews."

27 And with Him, THEY CRUCIFIED TWO THIEVES; the one, on his right hand and the other, on his left.

28 And The Scripture was Fulfilled, which says "…AND HE WAS NUMBERED WITH THE TRANSGRESSORS."

29 AND THEY THAT PASSED BY, RAILED ON HIM; WAGGING THEIR HEADS AND SAYING, "AH, YOU THAT DESTROY THE TEMPLE AND BUILD IT IN THREE DAYS,

30 SAVE YOURSELF AND COME DOWN FROM THE CROSS."

31 Likewise also, THE CHIEF PRIESTS, MOCKING, SAID AMONG THEMSELVES, WITH THE SCRIBES, "HE SAVED OTHERS. HIMSELF, HE CANNOT SAVE.

32 LET CHRIST, THE KING OF ISRAEL DESCEND NOW, FROM THE CROSS THAT WE MAY SEE AND BELIEVE." And they that were crucified with him reviled Him.

33 And when the sixth hour was come, there was darkness over the whole land, until the ninth hour.

34 And at the ninth hour, Jesus cried with a loud voice saying, "ELOI, ELOI, LAMA SABACHTHANI?" which is, being interpreted, "MY GOD, MY GOD, WHY HAVE YOU FORSAKEN ME?!"

35 And some of them that stood by, when they heard it said, "behold, He calls Elijah."

36 And one ran and FILLED A SPONGE FULL OF VINEGAR AND PUT IT ON A REED AND GAVE HIM TO DRINK saying, "let alone, let us see whether Elijah will come to take Him down."

37 And Jesus cried with a loud voice and gave up The Ghost.

38 And the veil of the temple was rent in two, from the top to the bottom.

39 And when the centurion, which stood over against Him, saw that He so cried out and gave up The Ghost, he said, "Truly, this Man was The Son of God."

40 There were also, women looking on afar off; among whom, were Mary Magdalene and Mary, the mother of James, the younger and of Joseph and Salome

41 (Who also, when He was in Galilee, Followed Him and Ministered to Him) and many other women, which came up with Him to Jerusalem.

42 And now, when the evening was come, because it was the preparation that is, the day before the Sabbath,

43 Joseph, of Arimathaea, an Honorable counselor, which also, waited for the Kingdom of God, came and went in boldly, to Pilate and craved the Body of Jesus.

44 And Pilate marveled, if He were already dead and calling to Him, the centurion, he asked him whether, "He had been any while dead."

45 And when he knew it of the centurion, he gave the Body to Joseph.

46 And he bought fine linen and took Him down and wrapped Him in the linen and laid Him in a sepulchre, which was hewn out of a rock and rolled a stone to the door of the sepulchre.

47 And Mary Magdalene and Mary, the mother of Joseph, beheld where He was laid.

Chapter 16

1 And when the Sabbath was past, Mary Magdalene and Mary, the mother of James and Salome, had bought sweet spices that they might come and Anoint Him.

2 And very early in the morning, the first day of the week, they came to the sepulchre at the rising of the Sun.

3 And they said among themselves, "who shall roll us away the stone from the door of the sepulchre?"

4 And when they looked, they saw that the stone was rolled away, for it was very great.

5 And entering into the sepulchre, they saw a young man sitting on the right side, clothed in a long white garment and they

were affrighted.

6 And he said to them, "be not affrighted. You seek Jesus, of Nazareth, which was crucified. He is Risen. He is not here. Behold, the place where they laid Him.

7 But, go your way. Tell His disciples and Peter that He goes before you, into Galilee. There, shall you see Him, as He said to you."

8 And they went out quickly and fled from the sepulchre, for they trembled and were amazed. Neither said they any thing to any man, for they were afraid.

9 Now, when Jesus was Risen early the first day of the week, He appeared first, to Mary Magdalene; Out of whom, He had Cast seven devils.

10 And she went and told them that had been with Him, as they mourned and wept.

11 And they, when they had heard that He was alive and had been seen of her, believed not.

12 After that, He appeared in Another Form to two of them, as they walked and went into the country.

13 And they went and told it to the residue. Neither believed they them.

14 Afterward, He appeared to the eleven as they sat at meat and upbraided them, with their unbelief and hardness of heart, because they believed not them, which had seen Him, after He was Risen.

15 And He said to them, "go you, into all the World and Preach The Gospel to every creature.

16 He that Believes and is Baptized shall be Saved, but he that believes not, shall be damned.

17 And these Signs shall follow them that Believe: IN MY NAME, THEY SHALL CAST OUT DEVILS, THEY SHALL SPEAK WITH NEW TONGUES,

18 THEY SHALL TAKE UP SERPENTS AND IF THEY DRINK ANY DEADLY THING, IT SHALL NOT HURT THEM. THEY SHALL LAY HANDS ON THE SICK AND THEY SHALL RECOVER."

19 So then, after The Lord had spoken to them, He was received up into Heaven and sat on the right hand of God.

20 And they went forth and Preached every where; The Lord Working with them and Confirming, The Word, with Signs following. Amen.

Luke

Chapter 1

1 Forasmuch as many have taken in hand to set forth in order a declaration of those things, which are most surely, Believed among us,

2 Even as they delivered them to us, which from the beginning, were eyewitnesses and ministers of The Word,

3 It seemed good to me also, having had perfect understanding of all things, from the very first, to write to you in order, most excellent Theophilus

4 That you might know the certainty of those things, wherein you have been instructed.

5 There was in the days of Herod, the king of Judaea, a certain priest named Zechariah, of the course of Abia and his wife was of the daughters of Aaron and her name was Elisheba.

6 And they were both Righteous before God; Walking in All The Commandments and Ordinances of The Lord, blameless.

7 And they had no child, because that Elisheba was barren and they both were now, well stricken in years.

8 And it came to pass that, while he executed the priest's office before God in the order of his course,

9 According to the custom of the priest's office, his lot was to burn incense when he went into the temple of The Lord.

10 And the whole multitude of the people were Praying without, at the time of incense.

11 And there appeared to him an angel of The Lord, standing on the right side of the altar of incense.

12 And when Zechariah saw him, he was troubled and fear fell on him.

13 But, the angel said to him, "FEAR NOT, ZECHARIAH, FOR YOUR PRAYER IS HEARD AND YOUR WIFE, ELISHEBA, SHALL BEAR YOU A SON AND YOU SHALL CALL HIS NAME, JOHN.

14 And you shall have Joy and Gladness and many shall Rejoice at his birth.

15 For he shall be great in the sight of The Lord and shall drink neither wine, nor strong drink and HE SHALL BE FILLED

WITH THE HOLY GHOST; EVEN FROM HIS MOTHER'S WOMB.

16 And MANY OF THE CHILDREN OF ISRAEL, SHALL HE TURN TO THE LORD, THEIR GOD.

17 And he shall go before Him in The Spirit and Power of Elijah, to TURN THE HEARTS OF THE FATHERS TO THE CHILDREN AND THE DISOBEDIENT, TO THE WISDOM OF THE JUST, TO MAKE READY A PEOPLE PREPARED FOR THE LORD."

18 And Zechariah said to the angel, "whereby, shall I know this? For I am an old man and my wife, well stricken in years."

19 And the angel answering said to him, "I am Gabriel that stands in the presence of God and am sent to speak to you and to show you these Glad tidings.

20 And behold, you shall be dumb and not able to speak, until the day that these things shall be performed, because you believed not my words, which shall be Fulfilled in their season."

21 And the people waited for Zechariah and marveled that he tarried so long, in the temple.

22 And when he came out, he could not speak to them and they perceived that he had seen a Vision in the temple, for he beckoned to them and remained speechless.

23 And it came to pass that, as soon as the days of his ministration were accomplished, he departed to his own house.

24 And after those days, his wife Elisheba, conceived and hid herself five months saying,

25 "Thus, has The Lord dealt with me in the days wherein, He looked on me, to take away my reproach among men."

26 And in the sixth month, the Angel, Gabriel, was sent from God to a city of Galilee, named, Nazareth

27 To a virgin espoused to a man, whose name was Joseph, of the house of David. And the virgin's name was, Mary.

28 And the angel came in to her and said, "hail you that are highly favored, The Lord is with you. Blessed are you among women."

29 And when she saw him, she was troubled at his saying and cast in her mind what manner of salutation this should be.

30 And the angel said to her, "fear not, Mary, for you have found favor with God.

31 And behold, YOU SHALL CONCEIVE IN YOUR WOMB AND BRING FORTH A SON AND SHALL CALL HIS NAME, JESUS.

32 HE SHALL BE GREAT AND SHALL BE CALLED, THE SON OF THE HIGHEST. AND THE LORD, God shall Give to Him, the throne of His, father, David.

33 And He shall Reign over the house of Jacob, for ever and of His Kingdom, there shall be no end."

34 Then said Mary to the angel, "how shall this be, seeing I know not a man?"

35 And THE ANGEL ANSWERED AND SAID TO HER, "THE HOLY GHOST, SHALL COME ON YOU AND THE POWER OF THE HIGHEST, SHALL OVERSHADOW YOU. THEREFORE, ALSO THAT HOLY THING, WHICH SHALL BE BORN OF YOU, SHALL BE CALLED, THE SON OF GOD.

36 And behold, your cousin, Elisheba, she has also, conceived a son in her old age and this is the sixth month with her, who was called barren.

37 For with God, nothing shall be impossible."

38 And Mary said, "behold, the handmaid of The Lord. Be it to me, according to your word." And the angel departed from her.

39 And Mary arose in those days and went into the hill country with haste into a city of Judah

40 And entered into the house of Zechariah and saluted Elisheba.

41 And it came to pass that, when Elisheba heard the salutation of Mary, the babe leaped in her womb and Elisheba was Filled with The Holy Ghost.

42 And she spoke out with a loud voice and said, "Blessed are you among women and Blessed is the Fruit of your womb!

43 And where is this to me that the mother of my Lord, should come to me?!

44 For lo, as soon as the voice of your salutation sounded in my ears, the babe leaped in my womb for Joy.

45 And Blessed is she that Believed, for there shall be a performance of those things, which were told her, from The Lord."

46 And Mary said, "my soul does Magnify The Lord,

47 And my spirit has Rejoiced in God, my Savior.

48 For he has regarded the low estate of his handmaiden. For behold, from henceforth, all generations shall call me Blessed.
49 For He that is Mighty, has done to me, Great Things and Holy is His Name.
50 And His Mercy is on them that Fear Him; from generation to generation.
51 He has shown strength with His arm. He has scattered the proud in the imagination of their hearts.
52 He has put down the mighty from their seats and exalted them of low degree.
53 He has filled the hungry with Good things and the rich, He has sent empty away.
54 He has helped His servant, Israel in remembrance of His Mercy.
55 As He spoke to our fathers; to Abraham and to his seed, for ever."
56 And Mary abode with her about three months and returned to her own house.

57 Now, Elisheba's full time came that she should be delivered and SHE BROUGHT FORTH A SON.
58 And her neighbors and her cousins heard how The Lord had shown Great Mercy on her and they Rejoiced with her.
59 And it came to pass that on the eighth day, they came to circumcise the child. And they called him, Zechariah, after the name of his father.
60 And his mother answered and said, "not so, but he shall be called, John."
61 And they said to her, "there is none of your kindred that is called by this name."

62 And they made signs to his father, how he would have him called.
63 And he asked for a writing table and wrote saying, "his name is John." And they marveled, all.
64 And his mouth was opened, immediately and his tongue Loosed and he spoke and Praised God.
65 And Fear came on all that dwelled, round about them. And all these sayings, were noised abroad, throughout all the hill country of Judaea.
66 And all they that heard them, laid them up in their hearts saying, "what manner of child, shall this be!" And the hand of The Lord was with him.

67 And his father, Zechariah was Filled With The Holy Ghost and Prophesied saying,

68 "BLESSED BE THE LORD, GOD OF ISRAEL, FOR HE HAS VISITED AND REDEEMED HIS PEOPLE
69 AND HAS RAISED UP A HORN OF SALVATION FOR US IN THE HOUSE OF HIS SERVANT, DAVID,"
70 As He spoke by the mouth of His Holy prophets, which have been, since the World began
71 That, "WE SHOULD BE SAVED, FROM OUR ENEMIES AND FROM THE HAND OF ALL THAT HATE US,
72 TO PERFORM THE MERCY PROMISED TO OUR FATHERS AND TO REMEMBER HIS HOLY COVENANT,
73 THE OATH, WHICH HE SWORE TO OUR FATHER, ABRAHAM
74 THAT HE WOULD GRANT TO US THAT WE BEING DELIVERED OUT OF THE HAND OF OUR ENEMIES, MIGHT SERVE HIM WITHOUT FEAR,
75 IN HOLINESS AND RIGHTEOUSNESS BEFORE HIM, ALL THE DAYS OF OUR LIVES.

76 AND YOU CHILD, SHALL BE CALLED, THE PROPHET OF THE HIGHEST, FOR YOU SHALL GO BEFROE THE FACE OF THE LORD, TO PREPARE HIS WAYS,
77 TO GIVE KNOWLEDGE OF SALVATION TO HIS PEOPLE, BY THE REMISSION OF THEIR SINS,
78 THROUGH THE TENDER MERCY OF OUR GOD, WHEREBY, THE DAYSPRING FROM ON HIGH HAS VISITED US,
79 TO GIVE LIGHT TO THEM THAT SIT IN DARKNESS AND IN THE SHADOW OF DEATH, TO GUIDE OUR FEET INTO THE WAY OF PEACE."
80 And the child grew and waxed strong in Spirit and was in the deserts until the day of his showing, to Israel.

Chapter 2

1 And it came to pass, in those days that there went out a decree from Caesar Augustus that all the World should be taxed.
2 (And this taxing was first made when Cyrenius was governor of Syria.)
3 And all went to be taxed; every one, into his own city.
4 And Joseph also, went up from Galilee, OUT OF THE CITY OF NAZARETH, into Judaea; to the City of David, which is called Bethlehem (because he was of the house and lineage of David)

5 To be taxed with Mary, his espoused wife, being great with child.
6 And so it was that, while they were there, the days were accomplished that she should be delivered.
7 And SHE BROUGHT FORTH HER FIRSTBORN SON and wrapped him in swaddling clothes and laid Him in a manger, because there was no room for them in the inn.

8 And there were in the same country, shepherds abiding in the field, keeping watch over their flock by night.
9 And lo, the angel of The Lord came on them and the Glory of The Lord shone, round about them and they were sore afraid.
10 And the angel said to them, "fear not, for behold, I bring you Good tidings of Great Joy, which shall be to all people.
11 For to you is born this day, in the City of David, a Savior, which is Christ, The Lord."
12 And this shall be a Sign to you: you shall find the babe wrapped in swaddling clothes, lying in a manger.
13 And suddenly, there was with the angel, a multitude of the Heavenly Host, Praising God and saying,
14 "Glory to God in the Highest and on Earth; Peace, Good Will, toward men."

15 And it came to pass, as the angels were gone away from them into Heaven, the shepherds said one to another, "let us now, go even to Bethlehem and see this thing, which is come to pass, which The Lord has made known to us."
16 And they came with haste and found Mary and Joseph and the Babe, lying in a manger.
17 And when they had seen it, they made known abroad the saying, which was told them, concerning this Child.
18 And all they that heard it, wondered at those things, which were told them, by the shepherds.
19 But, Mary kept all these things and pondered them in her heart.
20 And the shepherds returned, Glorifying and Praising God, for all the things that they had Heard and Seen, as it was told to them.

21 And when eight days were accomplished, for the circumcising of the Child, His Name was called, Jesus, which was so named of the angel before He was Conceived in the womb.

22 And when the days of her purification, according to the Law of Moses were accomplished, they brought Him to Jerusalem, to present Him to The Lord
23 (As it is written in The Law of The Lord, "every male that opens the womb, shall be called Holy, to The Lord")
24 And to offer a sacrifice, according to that, which is said in the Law of The Lord, "a pair of turtledoves, or two young pigeons."

25 And behold, there was a man in Jerusalem, whose name was Simeon and the same man was Just and Devout, waiting for the consolation of Israel and The Holy Ghost was on him.
26 And it was revealed to him by The Holy Ghost that he should not see death, before he had seen The Lord's, Christ.
27 And he came by The Spirit, into the temple and when the parents brought in the Child, Jesus, to do for Him, after the Custom of the Law,
28 Then took he Him up in his arms and Blessed God and said,
29 "Lord, now let me, Your servant depart in Peace, according to Your Word,

30 For my eyes have seen Your Salvation,
31 Which You have prepared before the face of all people;
32 A LIGHT TO LIGHTEN THE GENTILES AND THE GLORY OF YOUR PEOPLE, ISRAEL."

33 And Joseph and His mother, marveled at those things, which were spoken of him.
34 And Simeon Blessed them and said to Mary, His mother, "BEHOLD, THIS CHILD IS SET FOR THE FALL AND RISING AGAIN, OF MANY IN ISRAEL AND FOR A SIGN, WHICH SHALL BE SPOKEN AGAINST;
35 YES, A SWORD SHALL PIERCE THROUGH YOUR OWN SOUL, ALSO THAT THE THOUGHTS OF MANY HEARTS MAY BE REVEALED."

36 And there was one, Hannah, a prophetess, the daughter of Penuel, of the tribe of Asher. She was of a great age and had lived with a husband, seven years from her virginity.
37 And she was a widow of about eighty and four years, which departed not, from the temple, but Served God with Fastings and Prayers, night and day.
38 And she coming in that instant, Gave

Thanks, likewise to The Lord and spoke of Him to all them that looked for Redemption in Jerusalem.

39 And when they had performed all things, according to the Law of The Lord, they returned into Galilee, to their own city, Nazareth.

40 And the Child grew and waxed Strong in Spirit; Filled with Wisdom and the Grace of God was on Him.

41 Now, His parents went to Jerusalem, every year at the feast of The Passover.

42 And when He was twelve years old, they went up to Jerusalem, after the custom of the Feast.

43 And when they had fulfilled the days, as they returned, The Child, Jesus tarried behind in Jerusalem and Joseph and his mother knew not of it.

44 But they, supposing Him to have been in the company, went a day's journey and they sought Him among their kinsfolk and acquaintances.

45 And when they found Him not, they turned back again, to Jerusalem seeking Him.

46 And it came to pass that, after three days, they found Him in the temple, sitting in the midst of the doctors; both hearing them and asking them questions.

47 And all that Heard Him, were astonished at His Understanding and Answers.

48 And when they saw Him, they were amazed. And His mother said to Him, "Son, why have You thus, dealt with us? Behold, your father and I, have sought You, sorrowing."

49 And He said to them, "how is it that you sought Me? Knew you not that I must be about My Father's Business?"

50 And they understood not, the saying which He spoke to them.

51 And He went down with them and came to Nazareth and was subject to them. But, His mother kept all these sayings in her heart.

52 And Jesus Increased in Wisdom and Stature and in Favor with God and man.

Chapter 3

1 Now, in the fifteenth year of the reign of Tiberius Caesar, (Pontius Pilate, being governor of Judaea and Herod, being tetrarch of Galilee and his brother, Philip, tetrarch of Ituraea and of the region of Trachonitis and Lysanias, the tetrarch of Abilene,

2 Annas and Caiaphas, being the high priests) The Word of God came to John (the son of Zechariah) in the wilderness.

3 And he came into all the country, about Jordan, Preaching the Baptism of Repentance, for the Remission of sins

4 As it is written in the scroll of the words of Isaiah, the prophet saying, "THE VOICE OF ONE CRYING IN THE WILDERNESS, PREPARE YOU, THE WAY OF THE LORD. MAKE HIS PATHS STRAIGHT.

5 EVERY VALLEY SHALL BE FILLED AND EVERY MOUNTAIN AND HILL, SHALL BE BROUGHT LOW AND THE CROOKED, SHALL BE MADE STRAIGHT AND THE ROUGH WAYS, SHALL BE MADE SMOOTH

6 AND ALL FLESH SHALL SEE THE SALVATION OF GOD."

7 Then, said he to the multitude that came forth to be Baptized of him, "O generation of vipers, who has Warned you to flee from the wrath to come?

8 Bring forth therefore, Fruits Worthy of Repentance and begin not, to say within yourselves, "'we have Abraham, to our father,'" for I say to you that, "'God is able of these stones, to raise up children to Abraham.'"

9 And now also, the axe is laid to the root of the trees. Every tree therefore, which brings not, forth Good Fruit, is hewn down and cast into the fire."

10 And the people asked him saying, "what shall we do, then?"

11 He answered and said to them, "he that has two coats, let him impart to him that has none and he that has meat, let him do, likewise."

12 Then came also, publicans to be Baptized and said to him, "Master, what shall we do?"

13 And he said to them, "exact no more, than that, which is appointed you."

14 And the soldiers likewise, demanded of him saying, "and what shall we do?" And he said to them, "do violence to no man, neither accuse any, falsely and be content with your wages."

15 And as the people were in expectation and all men mused in their hearts of John, whether he were the Christ, or not,

16 John answered saying to them all, "I indeed, Baptize you with water, but One Mightier than I, comes; the latchet of Whose shoes I am not worthy, to unloose.

He shall Baptize you with The Holy Ghost and with Fire,

17 Whose fan is in His hand and He will throughly, Purge His floor and will gather the wheat into His garner. But, the chaff, He will burn with fire, unquenchable."

18 And many other things in his exhortation, Preached he, to the people.

19 (But Herod the tetrarch, being reproved by him, for Herodias, his brother, Philip's wife and for all the evils, which Herod had done,

20 Added yet this above all that, he shut up John in prison.)

21 Now, when all the people were Baptized, it came to pass that, Jesus also, being Baptized and Praying, the Heaven was opened

22 And The Holy Ghost descended in a bodily shape, like a dove on Him and A Voice came from Heaven, which said, "You are My beloved Son. In You, I am Well Pleased."

23 And Jesus Himself, began to be about thirty years of age: being (as was supposed) the son of Joseph, which was the son of Eli,

24 Which was the son of Matthat, which was the son of Levi, which was the son of Melchi, which was the son of Janna, which was the son of Joseph,

25 Which was the son of Mattathah, which was the son of Amos, which was the son of Nahum, which was the son of Elioenai, which was the son of Nogah,

26 Which was the son of Maath, which was the son of Mattathijah, which was the son of Shimei, which was the son of Joseph, which was the son of Judah,

27 Which was the son of Joanna, which was the son of Rhesa, which was the son of Zerubbabel, which was the son of Shealtiel, which was the son of Nerijah,

28 Which was the son of Melchi, which was the son of Addi, which was the son of Cosam, which was the son of Elmodam, which was the son of Er,

29 Which was the son of Jose, which was the son of Eliezer, which was the son of Jorim, which was the son of Matthithiah, which was the son of Levi,

30 Which was the son of Simeon, which was the son of Judah, which was the son of Joseph, which was the son of Jonan, which was the son of Eliakim,

31 Which was the son of Melea, which was the son of Menan, which was the son of Mattithjah, which was the son of Nathan, which was the son of David,

32 Which was the son of Jesse, which was the son of Obed, which was the son of Boaz, which was the son of Salmon, which was the son of Nahshon,

33 Which was the son of Amminadab, which was the son of Aram, which was the son of Hezron, which was the son of Pharez, which was the son of Judah,

34 Which was the son of Jacob, which was the son of Isaac, which was the son of Abraham, which was the son of Terah, which was the son of Nahor,

35 Which was the son of Serug, which was the son of Reu, which was the son of Peleg, which was the son of Eber, which was the son of Salah,

36 Which was the son of Cainan, which was the son of Arphaxad, which was the son of Shem, which was the son of Noah, which was the son of Lamech,

37 Which was the son of Methuselah, which was the son of Enoch, which was the son of Jared, which was the son of Mahalaleel, which was the son of Cainan,

38 Which was the son of Enos, which was the son of Seth, which was the son of Adam, which was the son of God.

Chapter 4

1 And Jesus being Full of The Holy Ghost, returned from Jordan and was led by The Spirit, into the wilderness,

2 Being forty days, tempted of the Devil. And in those days, He did eat nothing and when they were ended, He afterward hungered.

3 And the Devil said to Him, "if You are The Son of God, Command this stone that it be made bread."

4 And Jesus answered him saying, "it is written that, "'man shall not Live by bread alone, but by every Word of God.'"

5 And the Devil, taking Him up into a high mountain, showed to Him all the kingdoms of the World, in a moment of time.

6 And the Devil said to Him, "all this power, will I give You and the glory of them, for that is delivered to me and to whomsoever, I will give it.

7 If You therefore, will worship me, all shall be Yours."

8 And Jesus answered and said to him, "get you behind Me, Satan, for it is written, you shall Worship The Lord, your God and Him only, shall you Serve."

9 And he brought Him to Jerusalem and set Him on a pinnacle of the temple and said to Him, "if You are The Son of God, cast Yourself down from hence,
10 For it is written, He shall give His angels charge over you, to keep you.
11 And in their hands, they shall bear you up, lest at any time, you dash your foot against a stone."
12 And Jesus answering said to him, "it is said, "'you shall not tempt The Lord your God.'"
13 And when the Devil had ended all the temptations, he departed from Him for a season.

14 And Jesus returned in The Power of The Spirit, into Galilee and there went out a fame of Him through all the region, round about.
15 And He Taught in their synagogues, being Glorified of all.
16 And He came to Nazareth, where He had been brought up and as His custom was, He went into the synagogue on the Sabbath Day and stood up, for to read.
17 And there was delivered to Him, the scroll of the prophet, Isaiah. And when He had opened the scroll, He found the place where it was written,
18 "THE SPIRIT OF THE LORD IS ON ME, BECAUSE HE HAS ANOINTED ME TO PREACH THE GOSPEL TO THE POOR. HE HAS SENT ME TO HEAL THE BROKENHEARTED, TO PREACH DELIVERANCE TO THE CAPTIVES AND RECOVERING OF SIGHT TO THE BLIND, TO SET AT LIBERTY THEM THAT ARE BRUISED,
19 TO PREACH THE ACCEPTABLE YEAR OF THE LORD."
20 And He furled the scroll and He gave it again, to the Minister and sat down. And the eyes of all them that were in the synagogue were fastened on Him.
21 And He began to say to them, "this day, is this scripture Fulfilled in your ears."
22 And all bare Him witness and wondered at the Gracious Words, which proceeded out of His mouth. And they said, "is not this Joseph's Son?"
23 And He said to them, "you will surely, say to Me this proverb: "'PHYSICIAN, HEAL YOURSELF. WHATSOEVER, WE HAVE HEARD DONE IN CAPERNAUM, DO ALSO, HERE IN OUR COUNTRY.'"
24 And He said, "verily, I say to you, "'no prophet is accepted in His own country.'"
25 But, I tell you of a Truth, "'many widows were in Israel in the days of Elijah, when the heaven was shut up three years and six months, when great famine was throughout all the land
26 But, to none of them was Elijah sent, save to Zarephath, a city of Sidon; to a woman that was a widow.
27 And many lepers were in Israel in the time of Elisha, the prophet and none of them were cleansed, saving Naaman, the Syrian.'"

28 And all they in the synagogue, when they heard these things, were filled with wrath
29 And rose up and thrust Him out of the city and led Him to the brow of the hill, whereon, their city was built that they might cast Him down, headlong.
30 But He, passing through the midst of them, went His way
31 And came down to Capernaum, a city of Galilee and Taught them on the Sabbath Days.
32 And they were astonished at His Doctrine, for His Word was with Power.

33 And in the synagogue, there was a man, which had a spirit of an unclean devil and cried out with a loud voice
34 Saying, "let us alone! What have we to do with You, You Jesus, of Nazareth?! Are You come to destroy us?! I know You, Who You are, The Holy One of God!"
35 And Jesus rebuked him saying, "hold your peace and come out of him." And when the devil had thrown him in the midst, he came out of him and hurt him not.
36 And they were all amazed and spoke among themselves saying, "what A Word is this? For with Authority and Power, He Commands the unclean spirits and they come out."
37 And the fame of Him went out into every place of the country, round about.

38 And He arose out of the synagogue and entered into Simeon's house. And Simeon's wife's, mother was taken with a great fever and they besought Him for her.
39 And He stood over her and rebuked the fever and it left her and immediately, she arose and ministered to them.

40 Now, when the Sun was setting, all they that had any sick with diverse diseases, brought them to Him and He laid His hands on every one of them and Healed

them.
41 And devils also, came out of many, crying out and saying, "You are Christ, The Son of God!" And He rebuking them, suffered them not, to speak. For they knew that He was Christ.
42 And when it was day, He departed and went into a desert place and the people sought Him and came to Him and stayed Him that He should not depart from them.
43 And He said to them, "I must Preach the Kingdom of God to other cities also, for therefore, am I sent."
44 And He Preached in the synagogues of Galilee.

Chapter 5

1 And it came to pass that, as the people pressed on Him to Hear The Word of God, He stood by the Lake of Chinnereth
2 And saw two ships standing by the lake. But, the fishermen were gone out of them and were washing their nets.
3 And He entered into one of the ships, which was Simeon's and prayed him that he would thrust out a little from the land. And He sat down and Taught the people out of the ship.
4 Now, when He had left speaking, He said to Simeon, "launch out into the deep and let down your nets for a haul."
5 And Simeon answering said to Him, "Master, we have toiled all the night and have taken nothing, nevertheless, at Your Word, I will let down the net."
6 And when they had this done, they enclosed a great multitude of fish and their net broke.
7 And they beckoned to their partners, which were in the other ship that they should come and help them. And they came and filled both the ships, so that they began to sink.
8 When Simeon Peter saw it, he fell down at Jesus' knees saying, "depart from me, for I am a sinful man, O Lord."
9 For he was astonished and all that were with him, at the haul of the fish, which they had taken
10 And so was also, James and John, the sons of Zabdi, which were partners with Simeon. And Jesus said to Simeon, "fear not, FROM HENCEFORTH, YOU SHALL CATCH MEN."
11 And when they had brought their ships to land, they forsook all and Followed Him.

12 And it came to pass, when He was in a certain city, behold, a man full of leprosy who seeing Jesus, fell on his face and besought Him saying, "Lord, if you will, you can make me Clean."
13 And He put forth His hand and touched him saying, "I will. Be you Clean." And immediately, the leprosy Departed from him.
14 And He charged him to, "tell no man, but go and show yourself, to the priest and offer for your Cleansing, according as Moses commanded, for a Testimony to them."
15 But, so much the more, went there a fame abroad of Him and great multitudes came together, to Hear and to be Healed by Him of their infirmities.
16 And He withdrew Himself, into the wilderness and Prayed.

17 And it came to pass on a certain day, as He was Teaching that there were Pharisees and doctors of the Law sitting by, which had come out of every town of Galilee and Judaea and Jerusalem and The Power of The Lord was present to Heal them.
18 And behold, men brought in a bed, a man which was taken with a palsy and they sought means to bring him in and to lay him before Him.
19 And when they could not find by what way they might bring him in, because of the multitude, they went on the housetop and let him down through the tiling with his couch into the midst before Jesus.
20 And when He saw their Faith, He said to him, "man, your sins are Forgiven you."
21 And the scribes and the Pharisees began to reason saying, "Who is this, which speaks blasphemies? Who can Forgive sins, but God, alone?"
22 But, when Jesus perceived their thoughts, He answering, said to them, "what reason yourselves in your hearts?
23 Whether is easier to say, "'your sins are Forgiven you,'" or to say, "'Rise up and walk?'"
24 But that you may know that, The Son of Man has Power on Earth to Forgive sins." He said to the sick of the palsy, "I say to you, Rise and take up your bed and go into your house."
25 And immediately, he Rose up before them and took up that, whereon he laid and departed to his own house, Glorifying God.
26 And they were all amazed and they Glorified God and were filled with Fear

saying, "we have seen strange things today."

27 And after these things, He went forth and saw a publican, named, Levi sitting at the receipt of custom and He said to him, "Follow Me."
28 And he left all, rose up and Followed Him.
29 And Levi made him a great feast in His own house and there was a great company of publicans and of others that sat down with them.

30 But, their scribes and Pharisees murmured against His disciples saying, "why do you eat and drink with publicans and sinners?"
31 And Jesus answering, said to them, "they that are whole, need not a physician, but they that are sick.
32 I came not to call the Righteous, but sinners to Repentance."
33 And they said to Him, "why do the disciples of John, Fast often and make Prayers and likewise, the disciples of the Pharisees, but yours eat and drink?"
34 And He said to them, "can you make the children of the bridechamber Fast, while the Bridegroom is with them?
35 But the days will come, when the Bridegroom shall be taken away from them and then, shall they Fast in those days."

36 And He spoke also, a parable to them, "no man puts a piece of a new garment on an old. If otherwise, then both the new makes a rent and the piece that was taken out of the new, agrees not with the old.
37 And no man puts new wine into old bottles, else the new wine will burst the bottles and be spilled and the bottles shall perish.
38 But new wine, must be put into new bottles and both are preserved.
39 No man also, having drunk old wine, straightway desires new, for he says, "'the old is better.'"

Chapter 6

1 And it came to pass on the second Sabbath, after the first that He went through the corn fields and His disciples plucked the ears of corn and did eat; rubbing them in their hands.
2 And certain of the Pharisees said to them, "why do You that, which is not Lawful to do on the Sabbath Days?"
3 And Jesus answering them said, "have you not read so much as this, what David did, when himself, was a hungered and they, which were with him,
4 How he went into the house of God and did take and eat the showbread and gave also, to them that were with him, which it is not Lawful to eat, but for the priests, alone?"
5 And He said to them that, "The Son of Man is Lord also, of the Sabbath."

6 And it came to pass also, on another Sabbath that He entered into the synagogue and Taught and there was a man whose right hand was withered.
7 And the scribes and Pharisees watched Him, whether He would Heal on the Sabbath Day that they might find an accusation against Him.
8 But He knew their thoughts and said to the man, which had the withered hand, "rise up and stand forth in the midst." And he rose and stood forth.
9 Then said Jesus to them, "I will ask you one thing, "'is it Lawful on the Sabbath Days to Do Good, or to do evil; to save life, or to destroy it?'"
10 And looking round about on them all, He said to the man, "stretch forth your hand." And he did so and his hand was Restored Whole as the other.
11 And they were filled with madness and communed, one with another, what they might do to Jesus.

12 And it came to pass, in those days that He went out into a mountain to Pray and continued all night in Prayer to God.
13 And when it was day, He called to Himself, His disciples and of them, He Chose twelve, whom also, He named apostles:
14 (Simeon whom He also, named) Peter and Andrew, (his brother) James and John, Philip and Bartholomew,
15 Matthew and Thomas, James (the son of Cheleph) and Simeon (called Zealot)
16 And Judah (the brother of James) and Judas Iscariot (which also, was the traitor.)
17 And He came down with them and stood in the plain and the company of His disciples and a great multitude of people, out of all Judaea and Jerusalem and from the Sea coast of Tyre and Sidon, which came to hear Him and to be Healed of their diseases

18 And they that were vexed with unclean spirits and they were Healed.
19 And the whole multitude, sought to touch Him, for there went Power out of Him and Healed them all.

20 And He lifted up His eyes on His disciples and said, "Blessed be you poor, for yours is the Kingdom of God.
21 Blessed are you that hunger now, for you shall be filled. Blessed are you that weep now, for you shall laugh.
22 Blessed are you when men shall hate you and when they shall separate you from their company and shall reproach you and cast out your name as evil for The Son of Man's sake.
23 Rejoice yourselves in that day and leap for Joy, for behold, your reward is great in Heaven. For in the like manner, did their fathers to the prophets.
24 But woe to you that are rich, for you have received your consolation.
25 Woe to you that are full, for you shall hunger. Woe to you that laugh now, for you shall mourn and weep.

26 Woe to you, when all men shall speak well of you, for so did their fathers to the false prophets.
27 But I say to you which Hear, "'Love your enemies. Do Good to them, which hate you,
28 Bless them that curse you and Pray for them, which despitefully use you.
29 And to him that strikes you on the one cheek, offer also, the other. And him that takes away your cloak, forbid not to take your coat, also.
30 Give to every man that asks of you and of him that takes away your goods, ask them not again.
31 And as you would that men should do to you, do you also, to them, likewise.
32 For if you love them, which love you, what thanks have you? For sinners also, love those that love themselves.
33 And if you do good to them, which do good to you, what thanks have you? For sinners also, do even the same.
34 And if you lend to them, of whom you hope to receive, what thanks have you? For sinners also, lend to sinners, to receive as much again.
35 But Love you, your enemies and Do Good and lend; hoping for nothing, again and your Reward shall be great and you shall be the children of The Highest, for He is Kind to the unthankful and to the evil.

36 Be you therefore, merciful, as your Father also, is Merciful.'"
37 Judge not and you shall not be judged. Condemn not and you shall not be condemned. Forgive and you shall be Forgiven.
38 Give and it shall be Given to you; Good Measure, pressed down and shaken, together and running over, shall men Give into your bosom. For with the same measure that you mete withal, it shall be measured to you, again."

39 And He spoke a parable to them, "can the blind lead the blind? Shall they not both fall into the ditch?
40 The disciple is not above his Master, but every one that is perfect, shall be as his Master.
41 And why behold you the mote that is in your brother's eye, but perceive not, the beam that is in your own eye?
42 Either, how can you say to your brother, "'brother, let me pull out the mote that is in your eye,'" when you yourself, behold not the beam that is in your own eye? You hypocrite, cast out first, the beam out of your own eye and then, shall you see clearly to pull out the mote that is in your brothers eye.
43 For a good tree brings not, forth corrupt fruit. Neither does a corrupt tree, bring forth Good Fruit.
44 For every tree is known by his own fruit. For of thorns, men do not gather figs, nor of a bramble bush, gather they grapes.
45 A good man, out of the good treasure of his heart, brings forth that, which is good. And an evil man, out of the evil treasure of his heart, brings forth that, which is evil. For of the abundance of the heart, his mouth speaks.
46 And why call you me, "'Lord, Lord'" and do not, the things, which I say?

47 Whosoever, comes to Me and Hears My sayings and Does them, I will show you to whom he is like:
48 He is like a man, which built a house and dug deep and laid the foundation on a Rock and when the flood arose, the stream beat vehemently on that house and could not shake it, for it was founded on a Rock.
49 But, he that Hears and does not, is like a man that without a foundation, built a house on the earth against which, the stream did beat vehemently and immediately, it fell and the ruin of that

house was great."

Chapter 7

1 Now, when He had ended all His sayings in the audience of the people, He entered into Capernaum.
2 And a certain centurion's servant, who was dear to Him, was sick and ready to die.
3 And when He heard of Jesus, he sent to Him, the elders of the Jews, beseeching Him that He would come and Heal his servant.
4 And when they came to Jesus, they besought Him instantly saying that, "he was worthy for whom, He should do this
5 For he loves our nation and he has built us a synagogue."

6 Then, Jesus went with them. And when He was now, not far from the house, the centurion sent friends to Him, saying to Him, "Lord, trouble not Yourself, for I am not worthy that You should enter under my roof.
7 Wherefore, neither thought I myself worthy to come to You, but say in a Word and my servant shall be Healed.
8 For I also, am a man set under authority; having under me, soldiers and I say to one, "'go'" and he goes and to another, "'come'" and he comes and to my servant, "'do this'" and he does it.
9 When Jesus heard these things, He marveled at him and turned Himself, about and said to the people that followed Him, "I say to you, "'I have not found so great Faith; no, not in Israel.'"
10 And they that were sent, returning to the house, found the servant Whole that had been sick.

11 And it came to pass, the day after that He went into a city, called, Nain and many of His disciples went with Him and much people.
12 Now, when He came near to the gate of the city, behold, there was a dead man carried out, the only son of his mother and she was a widow. And much people of the city was with her.
13 And when The Lord saw her, He had Compassion on her and said to her, "weep not."
14 And He came and touched the bier and they that bare him, stood still. And He said, "young man, I say to you, "'Rise.'"
15 And he that was dead, Sat Up and began to speak. And He delivered him to his mother.
16 And there came a Fear on all and they Glorified God saying that, "a Great Prophet is risen up among us and that God has visited His people."
17 And this rumor of Him, went forth, throughout all Judaea and throughout all the region, round about.
18 And the disciples of John showed Him of all these things.

19 And John, calling to himself, two of his disciples, sent them to Jesus saying, "are You He that should come, or look we for another?"
20 When the men had come to Him they said, "John Baptist, has sent us to You saying, "'are You He that should come, or look we for another?'"
21 And in that same hour, He Cured many of their infirmities and plagues and of evil spirits. And to many that were blind, He Gave Sight.
22 Then, Jesus answering said to them, "go your way and tell John what things you have Seen and Heard, how that, the blind See, the lame Walk, the lepers are Cleansed, the deaf Hear, the dead are Raised, to the poor, The Gospel is Preached.
23 And Blessed is he, whosoever, shall not be offended in Me."

24 And when the messengers of John were departed, He began to speak to the people concerning John, "what went you out into the wilderness for to see, a reed shaken with the wind?
25 But what went you out for to see, a man clothed in soft raiment? Behold, they which are gorgeously appareled and live delicately, are in kings' courts.
26 But, what went you out for to see, a prophet? Yes, I say to you and much more, than a prophet.
27 This is he, of whom it is written, "'BEHOLD, I SEND MY MESSENGER BEFORE YOUR FACE, WHICH SHALL PREPARE YOUR WAY BEFORE YOU.'"
28 For I say to you, "'among those that are born of women, there is not a greater prophet, than John, the Baptist. But, he that is least in the Kingdom of God is greater than he.'"
29 And all the people that heard Him and the publicans, Justified God, being Baptized with the Baptism of John.
30 But, the Pharisees and lawyers rejected the Counsel of God against themselves,

being not Baptized of him.

31 And The Lord said, "whereunto then, shall I liken the men of this generation and to what, are they like?
32 They are like to children sitting in the marketplace and calling one to another and saying, "'we have piped to you and you have not danced. We have mourned to you and you have not wept.'"
33 For John, the Baptist came neither eating bread, nor drinking wine and you say, "'he has a devil.'"
34 The Son of Man is come, eating and drinking and you say, "'behold, a gluttonous man and a winebibber; a friend of publicans and sinners!'"
35 But, Wisdom is Justified of all her children."

36 And one of the Pharisees desired Him that He would eat with him. And He went into the Pharisee's house and sat down to meat.
37 And behold, a woman in the city, which was a sinner, when she knew that Jesus sat at meat in the Pharisee's house, brought an alabaster box of ointment
38 And stood at His feet behind Him, weeping and began to wash His feet with tears and did wipe them with the hairs of her head and kissed His feet and Anointed them, with the ointment.
39 Now, when the Pharisee, which had bidden Him saw it, He spoke within himself saying, "this Man, if He were a prophet, would have known who and what manner of woman this is that touches Him, for she is a sinner."

40 And Jesus answering said to him, "Simeon, I have somewhat to say to you." And he said, "Master, say on."
41 "There was a certain Creditor, which had two debtors: the one, owed five hundred pence and the other, fifty.
42 And when they had nothing to pay, he frankly Forgave them both. Tell Me therefore, which of them will Love Him most?"
43 Simeon answered and said, I suppose that, he to whom He Forgave most. And He said to him, "You have rightly Judged."
44 And He turned to the woman and said to Simeon, "see you, this woman? I entered into your house. You gave Me no water for my feet, but she has washed My feet with tears and wiped them with the hairs of her head.
45 You gave Me no kiss. But, this woman, since the time I came in, has not ceased to kiss My feet.
46 My head, with oil, you did not anoint. But, this woman has Anointed My feet with ointment.
47 Wherefore, I say to you, "'her sins, which are many, are Forgiven. For she Loved much, but to whom little is Forgiven, the same Loves little.'"
48 And He said to her, "your sins are Forgiven."
49 And they that sat at meat with Him, began to say within themselves, "Who is this, that Forgives sins, also?"
50 And He said to the woman, "your Faith has Saved you. Go in peace."

Chapter 8

1 And it came to pass, afterwards that He went throughout every city and village, Preaching and showing the Glad Tidings of the Kingdom of God. And the twelve were with Him
2 And certain women, which had been Healed of evil spirits and infirmities: Mary, called Magdalene (out of whom, went seven devils)
3 And Joanna (the wife of Chuza, Herod's steward) and Susanna and many others, which Ministered to Him of their substance.
4 And when much people were gathered together and had come to Him out of every city, He spoke by a parable,
5 "A Sower went out to Sow His Seed. And as He Sowed, some fell by the way side and it was trodden down and the fowls of the air devoured it.
6 And some fell on a rock. And as soon as it was sprung up, it withered away, because it lacked moisture.
7 And some fell among thorns. And the thorns sprang up with it and choked it.
8 And others fell on Good Ground and sprang up and Bare Fruit, one hundredfold." And when He had said these things, He cried, "he that has ears to hear, let him Hear!"

9 And His disciples asked him saying, "what might this parable be?"
10 And He said, "to you, it is Given to Know the Mysteries of the Kingdom of God, but to others, in parables that, "'SEEING, THEY MIGHT NOT SEE AND HEARING, THEY MIGHT NOT UNDERSTAND.'"
11 Now, the parable is this: The Seed, is

The Word of God.

12 Those by the way side, are they that Hear. Then, comes the Devil and takes away The Word out of their hearts, lest they should Believe and be Saved.

13 They on the rock, are they which, when they Hear, Receive The Word with Joy and these have no root, which for a while, Believe and in time of temptation, fall away.

14 And that, which fell among thorns, are they which, when they have Heard, go forth and are choked with cares and riches and pleasures of this life and bring no fruit to perfection.

15 But that on the Good Ground, are they, which in an Honest and good heart, having Heard The Word, Keep it and bring forth Fruit with patience.

16 No man, when he has lighted a candle, covers it with a vessel, or puts it under a bed, but sets it on a candlestick that they which enter in, may see the light.

17 For nothing, is secret that shall not be made manifest. Neither any thing, hid that shall not be known and comes abroad.

18 Take Heed therefore, how you Hear. For whosoever has, to him shall be Given and whosoever has not, from him shall be taken; even that, which he seems to have."

19 Then came to Him, His mother and His brothers and could not come at Him for the press.

20 And it was told Him, by certain, which said, "Your mother and Your brothers stand without, desiring to see You."

21 And He answered and said to them, "My mother and My brothers are these, which Hear The Word of God and Do it."

22 Now it came to pass, on a certain day that He went into a ship with His disciples and He said to them, "let us go over to the other side of the lake." And they launched forth.

23 But as they sailed, He fell asleep. And there came down a storm of wind on the lake and they were filled with water and were in jeopardy.

24 And they came to Him and woke Him saying, "Master, Master, we perish!" Then, He rose and rebuked the wind and the raging of the water and they Ceased and there was a calm.

25 And He said to them, "where is your Faith?" And they being afraid, wondered, saying one to another, "what manner of Man is this? For He Commands even the winds and water and they Obey Him."

26 And they arrived at the country of the Gadarenes, which is over against Galilee.

27 And when He went forth to land, there met Him out of the city a certain man, which had devils long time and wore no clothes, neither abode in any house, but in the tombs.

28 When he saw Jesus, he cried out and fell down before Him and with a loud voice said, "what have I to do with You, Jesus, You Son of God, Most High?! I beseech You, torment me not!"

29 (For He had Commanded the unclean spirit to come out of the man. For oftentimes, it had caught him and he was kept bound with chains and in fetters and he broke the bands and was driven of the devil into the wilderness.)

30 And Jesus asked him saying, "what is your name?" And he said, "Legion," because many devils were entered into him.

31 And they besought Him that, "He would not Command them to go out into the deep."

32 And there was there, a herd of many swine feeding on the mountain and they besought Him that, "He would suffer them to enter into them." And He suffered them.

33 Then, went the devils Out of the man and entered into the swine. And the herd ran violently down a steep place into the lake and were drowned.

34 When they that fed them, saw what was done, they fled and went and told it in the city and in the country.

35 Then, they went out to see what was done and came to Jesus and found the man, Out of whom, the devils were Departed, sitting at the feet of Jesus, clothed and in his right mind and they were afraid.

36 They also, which saw it, told them by what means he that was possessed of the devils was Healed.

37 Then, the whole multitude of the country of the Gadarenes round about, besought Him to depart from them, for they were taken with great fear. And He went up into the ship and returned back, again.

38 Now the man out of whom, the devils were departed, besought Him that He might be with Him. But, Jesus sent him away saying,

39 "Return to your own house and show how Great things, God has Done to you." And he went his way and published throughout the whole city, how Great things Jesus had Done to him.

40 And it came to pass that, when Jesus was returned, the people Gladly Received Him, for they were all waiting for Him.
41 And behold, there came a man named, Jair and he was a ruler of the synagogue and he Fell Down at Jesus' feet and besought Him that He would come into his house.
42 For he had one only daughter; about twelve years of age and she laid a dying. But as He went, the people thronged Him.
43 And a woman having an issue of blood twelve years, which had spent all her living on physicians, neither could be healed of any,
44 Came behind Him and touched the border of His garment and immediately, her issue of blood stanched.

45 And Jesus said, "who touched Me?" When all denied, Peter and they that were with Him said, "Master, the multitude throngs You and press You and say You, "who touched Me?"
46 And Jesus said, "somebody has touched Me, for I perceive that Power is gone out of Me."
47 And when the woman saw that she was not hid, she came Trembling and Falling Down before Him, she declared to Him before all the people for what cause she had touched Him and how she was Healed, immediately.
48 And He said to her, "daughter, be of Good Comfort. Your Faith has made you Whole. Go in Peace."

49 While He yet spoke, there came one, from the ruler of the synagogue's house saying to him, "your daughter is dead, trouble not the Master."
50 But when Jesus heard it, He answered him saying, "fear not. Believe only and she shall be Made Whole."
51 And when He came into the house, He suffered no man to go in, save Peter and James and John and the father and the mother of the maiden.
52 And all wept and bewailed her. But He said, "weep not. She is not dead, but sleeps."
53 And they laughed Him to scorn, knowing that she was dead.

54 And He put them all out and took her by the hand and called saying, "maid, Rise."
55 And her spirit came again and she Rose straightway and He Commanded to, "give her meat."
56 And her parents were astonished. But, He charged them that, "they should tell no man what was done."

Chapter 9

1 Then, He called His twelve disciples together and Gave them Power and Authority over All devils and to Cure diseases.
2 And He sent them to Preach the Kingdom of God and to Heal the sick.
3 And He said to them, "take nothing for your journey; neither staves, nor scrip, neither bread, neither money, neither have two coats, apiece.
4 And whatsoever house you enter into, there abide and there, depart.
5 And whosoever will not receive you, when you go out of that city, shake off the very dust from your feet for a Testimony against them."
6 And they departed and went through the towns, Preaching The Gospel and Healing, every where.

7 Now Herod the tetrarch, heard of all that was done by Him and he was perplexed, because that it was said of some that, "John was risen from the dead"
8 And of some that, "Elijah had appeared" and of others that, "one of the old prophets was risen, again."
9 And Herod said, "John, have I beheaded, but Who is this, of Whom, I hear such things?" And he desired to see Him.
10 And the apostles, when they were returned, told Him all that they had Done. And He took them and went aside, privately into a desert place belonging to the city called, Bethsaida.

11 And the people, when they knew it, followed Him and He received them and spoke to them of the Kingdom of God and Healed them that had need of Healing.
12 And when the day began to wear away, then came the twelve and said to Him, "send the multitude away that they may go into the towns and country, round about and lodge and get victuals. For we are here in a desert place."
13 But, He said to them, "Give you, them to eat." And they said, "we have no more,

but five loaves and two fish, except we should go and buy meat for all this people."

14 For they were about five thousand men. And He said to His disciples, "make them sit down, by fifties in a company."

15 And they did so and made them all sit down.

16 Then, He took the five loaves and the two fish and looking up to Heaven, He Blessed them and Broke and Gave to the disciples to set before the multitude.

17 And they did eat and were all Filled and there was taken up of fragments that remained to them, twelve baskets.

18 And it came to pass, as He was alone Praying, His disciples were with Him and He asked them saying, "Whom say the people that I am?"

19 They answering said, "John, the Baptist," but some say, "Elijah" and others say that, "one of the old prophets is risen, again."

20 He said to them, "but Whom say you that I am?" Peter answering said, "The Christ of God."

21 And He straightly, charged them and Commanded them to, "tell no man that thing"

22 Saying, "THE SON OF MAN MUST SUFFER MANY THINGS AND BE REJECTED OF THE ELDERS AND CHIEF PRIESTS AND SCRIBES AND BE SLAIN AND BE RAISED, THE THIRD DAY."

23 And He said to them all, "if any man will Come After Me, let him Deny himself and Take Up his Cross, daily and Follow Me.

24 For whosoever will save his life, shall lose it. But, whosoever will lose his life, for My sake, the same shall save it.

25 For what is a man advantaged, if he gains the whole World and loses himself, or be cast away?

26 For whosoever shall be ashamed of Me and of My Words, of him, shall The Son of Man be ashamed, when He shall come in His Own Glory and in His Father's and of the Holy angels.

27 But, I tell you of a Truth, "'there be some standing here, which shall not taste of death, until THEY SEE THE KINGDOM OF GOD.'"

28 And it came to pass, about an eight days after these sayings, He took Peter and John and James and went up into a mountain to Pray.

29 And as He Prayed, the fashion of His countenance was Altered and His raiment was white and glistering.

30 And behold, there talked with Him, two men, which were Moses and Elijah,

31 Who appeared in Glory and spoke of His decease, which He should accomplish at Jerusalem.

32 But Peter and they that were with Him, were heavy with sleep. And when they were awake, they saw His Glory and the two men that stood with Him.

33 And it came to pass, as they departed from Him, Peter said to Jesus, "Master, it is good for us to be here and let us make three tabernacles: one for You and one for Moses and one for Elijah," not knowing what He said.

34 While he thus spoke, there came A Cloud and overshadowed them and they Feared as they entered into The Cloud.

35 And there came A Voice out of The Cloud saying, "this is My Beloved Son. Hear Him."

36 And when The Voice was past, Jesus was found alone. And they kept it close and told no man in those days, any of those things which they had Seen.

37 And it came to pass that on the next day, when they had come down from the hill, much people met Him.

38 And behold, a man of the company cried out saying, "Master, I beseech You, look on my son, for he is my only child!

39 And lo, a spirit takes him and he suddenly cries out and it tears him that he foams, again and bruising him hardly, departs from him!

40 And I besought Your disciples to cast him out and they could not!"

41 And Jesus answering said, "O faithless and perverse generation, how long shall I be with you and suffer you? Bring your son here."

42 And as He was yet a coming, the devil threw him down and tore him. And Jesus rebuked the unclean spirit and Healed the child and delivered him again, to his father.

43 And they were all amazed at The Mighty Power of God. But, while they wondered, every one, at all things, which Jesus did, He said to His disciples,

44 "Let these sayings sink down into your ears, for THE SON OF MAN SHALL BE DELIVERED INTO THE HANDS OF MEN."

45 But they understood not this saying and it was hid from them that they perceived it not. And they feared to ask Him of that saying.

46 Then, there rose a reasoning among them, which of them should be greatest.
47 And Jesus, perceiving the thought of their hearts, took a child and set him by Himself
48 And said to them, "whosoever shall Receive this child in My Name, Receives Me and whosoever, shall Receive Me, Receives Him that sent Me. For he that is least among you all, the same shall be great."

49 And John answered and said, "Master, we saw one Casting Out devils in Your Name and we forbade him, because he Follows not with us."
50 And Jesus said to him, "forbid him not, for he that is not against us is for us."

51 And it came to pass, when the time was come that He should be received up, He steadfastly, set His face to go to Jerusalem
52 And sent messengers before His face. And they went and entered into a village of the Samaritans, to make ready for Him.
53 And they did not receive Him, because His face was as though He would go to Jerusalem.
54 And when His disciples, James and John saw this, they said, "Lord will You that we command fire to come down from Heaven and consume them, even as Elijah did?"
55 But, He turned and rebuked them and said, "you know not, what manner of spirit you are of,
56 For The Son of Man is not come to destroy men's lives, but to Save them." And they went to another village.
57 And it came to pass that, as they went in the way, a certain man said to Him, "Lord, I will follow You wheresoever, you go."
58 And Jesus said to him, "foxes have holes and birds of the air, have nests, but The Son of Man has not, where to lay His head."
59 And He said to another, "Follow Me." But, he said, "Lord, suffer me first, to go and bury my father."
60 Jesus said to him, "let the Dead bury their dead. But, go you and Preach the Kingdom of God."

61 And another, also said, "Lord, I will follow You, but let me first, go bid them farewell, which are at home at my house."
62 And Jesus said to him, "no man, having put his hand to the plough and looking back, is fit for the Kingdom of God."

Chapter 10

1 After these things, The Lord appointed other seventy, also and sent them two and two, before His face into every city and place, where He Himself, would come.
2 Therefore, said He to them, "the harvest truly is great, but the laborers are few. Pray you therefore, The Lord of the harvest that, He would send forth laborers into His harvest.
3 Go your ways. Behold, I send you forth, as lambs among wolves.
4 Carry neither purse, nor scrip, nor shoes and salute no man, by the way.

5 And into whatsoever house you enter, first say, "'Peace be to this house.'"
6 And if The Son of Peace be there, your Peace shall rest on it. If not, it shall turn to you, again.
7 And in the same house remain, eating and drinking such things as they give, for the laborer is worthy of his hire. Go not from house to house.
8 And into whatsoever city, you enter and they receive you, eat such things as are set before you
9 And Heal the sick that are, therein and say to them, "'The Kingdom of God is come near to you.'"

10 But, into whatsoever city you enter and they receive you not, go your ways out into the streets of the same and say,
11 "'Even the very dust of your city, which cleaves on us, we do wipe off against you. Notwithstanding, be you sure of this that, the Kingdom of God is come near to you.'"
12 But I say to you that, "'it shall be more tolerable in that day for Sodom, than for that city.

13 Woe to you, Chorazin! Woe to you, Bethsaida! For if the Mighty Works had been done in Tyre and Sidon, which have been Done in you, they had a great while ago, Repented, sitting in sackcloth and ashes.
14 But, it shall be more tolerable for Tyre and Sidon at the Judgment, than for you.
15 And you, Capernaum, which are

exalted to Heaven, shall be thrust down to Hell.
16 He that hears you, Hears Me and he that despises you, despises Me and he that despises Me despises Him, that sent Me.'"

17 And the seventy returned again, with Joy, saying, "Lord, even the devils are subject to us through Your Name."
18 And He said to them, "I beheld Satan, as lightning fall from Heaven.
19 Behold, I Give to you Power to tread on serpents and scorpions and over all the power of the enemy and nothing, shall by any means hurt you.
20 Notwithstanding, in this, rejoice not that the spirits are subject to you, but rather, Rejoice because your names are written in Heaven."

21 In that hour, Jesus Rejoiced in Spirit and said, "I Thank You, O Father, Lord of Heaven and Earth that You have hid these things from the wise and prudent and have Revealed them to babes. Even so, Father, for so it seemed Good in Your sight."

22 "All things are Delivered to Me of My Father and no man knows Who The Son is, but the Father and Who The Father is, but The Son and He to whom, The Son will Reveal Himself."
23 And He turned Himself, to His disciples and said privately, "Blessed are the eyes which See the things that you See.
24 For I tell you that, '"many prophets and kings have desired to See those things, which you See and have not seen them and to Hear those things, which you Hear and have not heard them."'

25 And behold, a certain lawyer stood up and tempted Him saying, "Master, what shall I do to inherit Eternal Life?"
26 He said to him, "what is written in The Law, how read you?"
27 And he answering said, "you shall Love The Lord, your God with All your heart and with All your soul and with All your strength and with All your mind and your neighbor, as yourself."
28 And He said to him, "you have answered Right. This Do and you shall Live."
29 But he, willing to justify himself, said to Jesus, "and who is my neighbor?"
30 And Jesus answering said, "a certain man went down from Jerusalem, to Jericho and fell among thieves, which stripped him of his raiment and wounded him and departed, leaving him half dead.
31 And by chance, there came down a certain priest that way and when he saw him, he passed by on the other side.
32 And likewise, a Levite, when he was at the place, came and looked on him and passed by on the other side.
33 But a certain Samaritan, as he journeyed, came where he was. And when he saw him, he had Compassion on him
34 And went to him and bound up his wounds, pouring in oil and wine and set him on his own beast and brought him to an inn and took care of him.
35 And on the morrow, when he departed, he took out two pence and gave them to the host and said to him, "'take care of him and whatsoever, you spend more, when I come again, I will repay you.'"
36 Which now, of these three, think you was neighbor, to him that fell among the thieves?"
37 And he said, "he that showed Mercy on him." Then, said Jesus to him, "go and Do you, Likewise."

38 Now it came to pass, as they went that He entered into a certain village. And a certain woman named Martha, received Him into her house.
39 And she had a sister, called Mary, which also, sat at Jesus' feet and Heard His Word.
40 But, Martha was cumbered about much serving and came to Him and said, "Lord, do you not care that my sister has left me to serve alone? Bid her, therefore that she help me."
41 And Jesus answered and said to her, "Martha, Martha, you are careful and troubled about many things.
42 But, one thing is needful and Mary has chosen that Good part, which shall not be taken away from her."

Chapter 11

1 And it came to pass that, as He was Praying in a certain place, when He ceased, one of His disciples said to Him, "Lord, Teach us to Pray as John also, Taught his disciples."
2 And He said to them, "when you Pray say, "'Our Father, which is in Heaven, Hallowed be Your Name. Your Kingdom come. Your will be done, as in Heaven, so on Earth.

3 Give us, day by day, our daily bread.
4 And Forgive us our sins, for we also, Forgive every one that is indebted to us. And lead us not into temptation, but deliver us from evil.'"

5 And He said to them, "which of you, shall have a friend and shall go to him at midnight and say to him, "'friend, lend me three loaves.
6 For a friend of mine in his journey, is come to me and I have nothing to set before him'"
7 And he from within, shall answer and say, "'trouble me not. The door is now, shut and my children are with me in bed. I cannot rise and give you?'"
8 I say to you, "'though he will not rise and give him, because he is his friend, yet because of his importunity, he will rise and give him as many as he needs.'"
9 And I say to you, "'Ask and it shall be Given you. Seek and you shall Find. Knock and it shall be Opened to you.
10 For every one that Asks, Receives and he that Seeks, Finds and to him that Knocks, it shall be Opened.
11 If a son shall ask bread of any of you that is a father, will he give him a stone, or if he asks a fish, will he for a fish, give him a serpent?
12 Or, if he shall ask an egg, will he offer him a scorpion?
13 If you then, being evil, know how to give good gifts to your children, how much more, shall your Heavenly Father, Give The Holy Spirit, to them that ask Him?'"

14 And He was Casting Out a devil and it was dumb. And it came to pass, when the devil was Gone Out, the dumb spoke and the people wondered.
15 But some of them said, "He Casts Out devils, through Baalzebub, the chief of the devils."

16 And others, tempting Him, sought of Him a Sign from Heaven.
17 But He knowing their thoughts, said to them, "every kingdom, divided against itself, is brought to desolation and a house divided, against a house falls.
18 If Satan also, be divided against himself, how shall his kingdom stand? Because you say that, "'I Cast Out devils through Baalzebub.'"
19 And if I, by Baalzebub, Cast Out devils, by whom do your sons cast them out? Therefore, they shall be your Judges.
20 But if I, with the finger of God, Cast Out devils, no doubt, the Kingdom of God is come on you.
21 When a strong man armed, keeps his palace, his goods are in Peace.
22 But, when a stronger than he, shall come on him and overcome him, he takes from him, all his armor, wherein he trusted and divides his spoils.
23 He that is not with Me is against Me and he that gathers not, with Me, scatters.
24 When the unclean spirit is Gone Out of a man, he walks through dry places, seeking rest and finding none, he says, "'I will return to my house, whence I Came Out.'"
25 And when he comes, he finds it swept and garnished.
26 Then he goes and takes to himself, seven other spirits, more wicked than himself and they enter in and dwell there and the last state of that man, is worse than the first."

27 And it came to pass, as He spoke these things, a certain woman of the company lifted up her voice and said to Him, "Blessed is the womb that bare You and the paps, which You have sucked."
28 But He said, "yes rather, Blessed are they that Hear The Word of God and Keep it."
29 And when the people were gathered thick together, He began to say, "this is an evil generation. They seek a Sign and there shall no Sign be given it, but the Sign of Jonah, the prophet.
30 For as Jonah was a Sign to the Ninevites, so shall also, The Son of Man be to this generation.
31 The queen of the South, shall rise up in the Judgment with the men of this generation and condemn them, for she came from the utmost parts of the earth to Hear the Wisdom of Solomon and behold, a Greater, than Solomon is here.
32 The men of Nineveh shall rise up in the Judgment with this generation and shall condemn it, for they Repented at the Preaching of Jonah and behold, a Greater, than Jonah is here.
33 No man, when he has Lighted a candle, puts it in a secret place, neither under a bushel, but on a candlestick that they which come in, may see the Light.
34 The Light of the body is the eye. Therefore, when your eye is good, your

whole body also, is Full of Light. But, when your eye is evil, your body also, is full of Darkness.

35 Take Heed, therefore that the light, which is in you, is not Darkness.

36 If your whole body therefore, be Full of Light, having no part Dark, the whole shall be Full of Light; as when the Bright Shining of a candle does give you Light."

37 And as He spoke, a certain Pharisee besought Him to dine with him. And He went in and sat down to meat.

38 And when the Pharisee saw it, he marveled that He had not first, washed before dinner.

39 And The Lord said to him, "now, do you Pharisees make clean the outside of the cup and the platter. But, your inward part is full of ravening and wickedness.

40 You fools, did not He that made that, which is without, make that, which is within, also?

41 But, rather give alms of such things as you have and behold, all things are clean to you.

42 But, woe to you, Pharisees! For you tithe mint and rue and all manner of herbs and pass over Judgment and the Love of God. These ought, you to have done and not to leave the other undone.

43 Woe to you, Pharisees! For you love the uppermost seats in the synagogues and greetings in the markets.

44 Woe to you, scribes and Pharisees, hypocrites! For you are as graves, which appear not. And the men that walk over them are not aware of them."

45 Then, answered one of the lawyers and said to Him, "Master, thus saying, you reproach us, also."

46 And He said, "woe to you also, you lawyers! For you lade men with burdens, grievous to be borne and you yourselves, touch not the burdens, with one of your fingers.

47 Woe to you! For you build the sepulchres of the prophets and your fathers killed them.

48 Truly, you bear witness s that you allow the deeds of your fathers, for they indeed, killed them and you build their sepulchres.

49 Therefore also, said the Wisdom of God, "'I WILL SEND THEM PROPHETS AND APOSTLES AND SOME OF THEM, THEY SHALL SLAY AND PERSECUTE

50 That the blood of all the prophets, which was shed from the foundation of the World, may be required of this generation;

51 From the blood of Abel, to the blood of Zechariah, which perished between the altar and the temple.'" Verily, I say to you, "'it shall be required of this generation."

52 Woe to you, lawyers! For you have taken away the Key of Knowledge. You entered not in, yourselves and them that were entering in, you hindered.'"

53 And as He said these things to them, the scribes and the Pharisees began to urge Him, vehemently and to provoke Him to speak of many things,

54 Laying wait for Him and seeking to catch something out of His mouth that they might accuse Him.

Chapter 12

1 In the mean time, when there were gathered together an innumerable multitude of people, insomuch that they trod, one on another, He began to say to His disciples, "first of all, Beware yourselves of the leaven of the Pharisees, which is hypocrisy.

2 For there is nothing covered that shall not be revealed, neither hid that shall not be known.

3 Therefore whatsoever, you have spoken in darkness, shall be heard in the light and that, which you have spoken in the ear, in closets, shall be proclaimed on the housetops.

4 And I say to you My friends, "'be not afraid of them that kill the body and after that, have no more that they can do.

5 But, I will Forewarn you, Whom you shall Fear. Fear Him, which after He has killed, has Power to cast into Sheol. Yes, I say to you, "'Fear Him!'"

6 Are not five sparrows, sold for two farthings and not one of them, is forgotten before God?

7 But, even the very hairs of your head, are all numbered. Fear not, therefore, you are of more value, than many sparrows.

8 Also, I say to you, "'whosoever, shall Confess Me before men, him shall The Son of Man also, Confess before the angels of God.

9 But, he that denies Me before men, shall be denied before the angels of God.

10 And whosoever, shall speak a word against The Son of Man, it shall be Forgiven him. But to him that blasphemes

against The Holy Ghost, it shall not, be forgiven.'"
11 And when they bring you to the synagogues and to magistrates and powers, take yourselves, no thought how, or what thing, you shall answer, or what you shall say,
12 For The Holy Ghost shall Teach you in the same hour, what you ought to say."

13 And one of the company said to Him, "Master, speak to my brother that he divides the inheritance with me."
14 And He said to him, "man, who made Me a judge, or a divider over you?"
15 And He said to them, "take Heed and Beware of covetousness, for a man's life consists not, in the abundance of the things, which he possesses."

16 And He spoke a parable to them saying, "the ground of a certain rich man, brought forth plentifully.
17 And he thought within himself saying, "'what shall I do, because I have no room, where to bestow my fruits?"
18 And he said, "'this, will I do. I will pull down my barns and build greater and there, will I bestow all my fruits and my goods.
19 And I will say to my soul, ""'soul, you have much goods laid up for many years. Take your ease; eat, drink and be merry.'"
20 But God said to him, "'you fool, this night, your soul shall be required of you. Then, whose shall those things be, which you have provided?'"
21 So is he that lays up treasure for himself and is not rich, toward God."

22 And He said to His disciples, "therefore, I say to you, "'take no thought for your life; what you shall eat, neither for the body, what you shall put on.
23 The Life is more than meat and the body is more than raiment.
24 Consider the ravens, for they neither sow, nor reap, which neither have storehouse, nor barn and God feeds them. How much more, are you, better than the fowls?"
25 And which of you with taking thought can add to his stature, one cubit?
26 If you then, be not able to do that thing, which is least, why take yourselves, thought for the rest?
27 Consider the lilies, how they grow. They toil not, they spin not and yet, I say to you that, "'Solomon, in all his glory, was not arrayed like one of these.'"
28 If then, God so clothes the grass, which is today in the field and tomorrow, is cast into the oven, how much more will He clothe you, O you, of little faith?
29 And seek not yourselves, what you shall eat, or what you shall drink, neither be you of doubtful mind.
30 For all these things, do the nations of the World seek after and your Father knows that you have need of these things.
31 But rather, Seek yourselves, the Kingdom of God and all these things, shall be added to you.
32 Fear not, little flock, for it is your Father's Good Pleasure to Give you the Kingdom.
33 Sell that you have and give alms. Provide yourselves bags, which wax not old; a treasure in the Heavens that fails not; where no thief approaches, neither moth corrupts.
34 For where your treasure is, there will your heart be, also.

35 Let your loins be girded about and your Lights Burning
36 And you yourselves, like to men that Wait for their Lord, when He will return from the wedding that when He comes and knocks, they may open to Him, immediately.
37 Blessed are those servants, whom The Lord, when He Comes, shall find Watching. Verily, I say to you that, "'he shall gird himself and make them to sit down to meat and will come forth and serve them.
38 And if He shall come in the second watch, or come in the third watch and find them so, Blessed are those servants.
39 And this know that, if the good man of the house had known what hour the thief would come, he would have watched and not have suffered his house to be broken through.
40 Be yourselves therefore, Ready also, for The Son of Man comes at an hour when you think not.'"

41 Then, Peter said to Him, "Lord, speak You, this parable to us, or even to all?"
42 And The Lord said, "who then, is that Faithful and Wise steward, whom his Lord shall make ruler over His household; to give them their portion of meat in due season?
43 Blessed is that servant, whom his Lord, when He Comes, shall find so, Doing.

44 Of a Truth, I say to you that, "'He will make him ruler over all that He has.'"
45 But and if that servant says in his heart, "'my Lord delays His Coming'" and shall begin to beat the menservants and maidens and to eat and drink and to be drunken,
46 The Lord of that servant, will come in a day, when he looks not for Him and at an hour, when he is not aware and will cut him in sunder and will appoint him his portion with the unbelievers.
47 And that servant, which Knew his Lord's Will and prepared not himself, neither Did according to His Will, shall be beaten with many stripes.
48 But, he that knew not and did commit things worthy of stripes, shall be beaten with few stripes. For to whomsoever, much is Given, of him, shall be much Required. And to whom, men have committed much, of him, they will ask the more.

49 I am come to send Fire on the Earth. And what will I, if it be already, kindled?
50 But, I have a Baptism to be Baptized with and how am I straitened until it be accomplished!
51 Suppose you that I am come to give peace on Earth? I tell you, "'no, but rather, division.'"
52 For from henceforth, there shall be five in one house divided; three against two and two against three.
53 The father shall be divided against the son and the son, against the father; the mother against the daughter and the daughter against the mother; the mother in law against her daughter in law and the daughter in law, against her mother in law.

54 And He said also, to the people, "'when you see a cloud rise out of the West, straightway you say, "'there comes a shower'" and so, it is.
55 And when you see the South wind blow, you say, "'there will be heat'" and it comes to pass.
56 You hypocrites, you can discern the face of the sky and of the earth. But, how is it that you do not discern this time?
57 Yes and why even of yourselves, Judge you not what is Right?
58 When you go with your adversary to the magistrate, as you are in the way, give diligence that you may be delivered from him, lest he hales you to the judge and the judge delivers you to the officer and the officer casts you into prison.

59 I tell you, you shall not depart there, until you have paid the very last mite."

Chapter 13

1 There were present at that season, some that told Him of the Galilaeans, whose blood Pilate had mingled with their sacrifices.
2 And Jesus answering said to them, "suppose you that these Galilaeans were sinners above all the Galilaeans, because they suffered such things?
3 I tell you, "'no, but except you Repent, you shall all likewise perish.'"
4 Or, those eighteen, on whom the tower in Siloam fell and slew them, think you that they were sinners above all men that dwelled in Jerusalem?
5 I tell you, "'no, but except you Repent, you shall all likewise perish.'"

6 He spoke also, this parable, "a certain Man, had a fig tree planted in His vineyard. And He came and sought Fruit, thereon and found none.
7 Then said He, to the dresser of His vineyard, "'behold, these three years, I came seeking Fruit on this fig tree and find none. Cut it down. Why cumbers it the ground?'"
8 And he answering, said to Him, "'Lord, let it alone, this year also, until I shall dig about it and dung it
9 And if it Bears Fruit, well. And if not, then after that, you shall cut it down.'"

10 And He was Teaching in one of the synagogues on the Sabbath.
11 And behold, there was a woman, which had a spirit of infirmity, eighteen years and was bowed together and could in no wise, lift up herself.
12 And when Jesus saw her, He called her to Himself and said to her, "woman, you are Loosed from your infirmity."
13 And He laid His hands on her and immediately, she was Made Straight and Glorified God.
14 And the ruler of the synagogue answered with indignation, because that Jesus had Healed on the Sabbath Day and said to the people, "there are six days, in which men, ought to work. In them therefore, come and be Healed and not on the Sabbath Day."
15 The Lord then answered him and said, "you hypocrite, does not each one of you, on the Sabbath loose his ox, or his ass

from the stall and lead him away to watering?
16 And ought not this woman, being a daughter of Abraham, whom Satan has bound, lo, these eighteen years, be Loosed from this bond on the Sabbath Day?"
17 And when He had said these things, all His adversaries were ashamed. And all the people Rejoiced for all the Glorious things that were Done by Him.

18 Then said He, "to what is the Kingdom of God like and whereunto, shall I resemble it?:
19 It is like a grain of mustard seed, which a Man took and cast into His garden and it grew and waxed a great tree. And the fowls of the air lodged in the branches of it."
20 And again, He said, "whereunto, shall I liken the Kingdom of God?:
21 It is like leaven, which a woman took and hid in three measures of meal, until the whole was leavened."
22 And He went through the cities and villages, Teaching and journeying, toward Jerusalem.

23 Then said one to Him, "Lord, are there few that be Saved?" And He said to them,
24 "Strive to enter in at the Strait Gate. For many, I say to you, will seek to enter in and shall not be able.
25 When once The Master of the house is risen up and has shut to the door and you begin to stand without and to knock at The Door saying, "'Lord, Lord, open to us'" and He shall answer and say to you, "'I know you not, who you are.'"
26 Then, you shall begin to say, "'we have eaten and drunk in Your Presence and You have Taught in our streets.'"
27 But, He shall say, "'I tell you, I know you not, who you are. Depart from me, all you workers of iniquity.'"
28 There shall be weeping and gnashing of teeth, when you shall see Abraham and Isaac and Jacob and all the prophets, in the Kingdom of God and you yourselves, thrust out.
29 And they shall come from the East and from the West and from the North and from the South and shall sit down in the Kingdom of God.
30 And behold, there are last, which shall be first. And there are first, which shall be last."

31 The same day, there came certain of the Pharisees saying to Him, "get Yourself out and depart hence, for Herod will kill You."
32 And He said to them, "go, yourselves and tell that fox, "'behold, I Cast Out devils and I do Cures, today and tomorrow and the third day, I shall be Perfected.
33 Nevertheless, I must walk today and tomorrow and the day following, for it cannot be that a prophet perishes out of Jerusalem.'"
34 O Jerusalem, Jerusalem, which kills the prophets and stones them that are sent to you. How often, would I have gathered your children together, as a hen does gather her brood under her wings and you would not!
35 Behold, your house is left to you desolate and verily, I say to you, "'you shall not see Me, until the time comes, when you shall say, "'Blessed is he that comes in The Name of The Lord.'''"

Chapter 14

1 And it came to pass, as He went into the house of one of the chief Pharisees to eat bread on the Sabbath Day that they watched Him.
2 And behold, there was a certain man before Him, which had the dropsy.
3 And Jesus answering, spoke to the lawyers and Pharisees saying, "is it Lawful to Heal on the Sabbath Day?"
4 And they held their peace. And He took him and Healed him and let him go
5 And answered them saying, "which of you, shall have an ass, or an ox fallen into a pit and will not straightway, pull him out on the Sabbath Day?"
6 And they could not answer Him again, to these things.

7 And He put forth a parable to those, which were bidden, when He marked how they chose out the chief rooms saying to them,
8 "When you are bidden of any man to a wedding, sit not down in the highest room, lest a more honorable man than you, is bidden of him
9 And he that commanded you and he comes and says to you, "'give this man place and you begin with shame, to take the lowest room.'"
10 But, when you are bidden, go and sit down in the lowest room that when he that

commanded you comes, he may say to you, "'friend, go up higher.'" Then, you shall have dignity in the presence of them that sit at meat with you.
11 For whosoever exalts himself, shall be abased and he that Humbles himself, shall be exalted."

12 Then He said also, to him that commanded Him, "when you make a dinner, or a supper, call not your friends, nor your brothers, neither your kinsmen, nor your rich neighbors, lest they also, bid you again and a recompense be made you.
13 But, when you make a feast, call the poor, the maimed, the lame, the blind.
14 And you shall be Blessed, for they cannot recompense you, for you shall be Recompensed at the Resurrection of the Just."
15 And when one of them that sat at meat with Him, Heard these things, He said to him, "Blessed is he that shall eat bread in the Kingdom of God."

16 Then, He said to him, "a certain Man made a great supper and commanded many.
17 And sent His servant at supper time to say to them that were bidden, "'come, for all things are now, ready.'"
18 And they all, with one consent began to make excuses. The first said to Him, "'I have bought a piece of ground and I must needs go and see it. I pray You, have me excused.'"
19 And another said, "'I have bought five yoke of oxen and I go to prove them. I pray You, have me excused.'"
20 And another said, "'I have married a wife and therefore, I cannot come.'"

21 So that servant came and showed his Lord these things. Then, The Master of the house, being angry said to His servant, "'go out quickly, into the streets and lanes of the city and bring in here, the poor and the maimed and the halt and the blind.'"
22 And the servant said, "'Lord, it is done as You have Commanded and yet, there is room.'"
23 And The Lord said to the servant, "'go out into the highways and hedges and compel them to come in that My house may be filled.'"
24 For I say to you that, "'none of those men, which were bidden, shall taste of My supper.'"

25 And there went great multitudes with Him and He turned and said to them,
26 "If any man, comes to Me and hates not his father and mother and wife and children and brothers and sisters; yes and his own life also, he cannot be My disciple.
27 And whosoever, does not bear his cross and come after Me, cannot be My disciple.
28 For which of you, intending to build a tower, sits not down first and counts the cost; whether he has sufficient to finish it?
29 Lest haply, after he has laid the foundation and is not able to finish it, all that behold it, begin to mock him
30 Saying, "'this man began to build and was not able to finish.'"
31 Or, what king, going to make war against another king, sits not down, first and consults whether he is able with ten thousand to meet him that comes against him, with twenty thousand?
32 Or else, while the other is yet a great way off, he sends an ambassador and desires conditions of peace.
33 So likewise, whosoever he be of you that Forsakes not All that he has, he cannot be My disciple.
34 Salt is good, but if the salt has lost his savor, wherewith shall it be seasoned?
35 It is neither fit for the land, nor yet, for the dunghill, but men cast it out. He that has ears to Hear, let him Hear."

Chapter 15

1 Then, drew near to Him, all the publicans and sinners for to Hear Him.
2 And the Pharisees and scribes murmured saying, "this man receives sinners and eats with them."
3 And He spoke this parable to them saying,
4 "What man of you, having a hundred sheep, if he loses one of them, does not leave the ninety and nine in the wilderness and goes after that, which is lost, until he finds it?
5 And when he has found it, he lays it on his shoulders, rejoicing.
6 And when he comes home, he calls together, his friends and neighbors saying to them, "'rejoice with me, for I have found my sheep, which was lost.
7 I say to you that likewise, Joy shall be in Heaven, over one sinner that Repents, more than over ninety and nine Just persons, which need no Repentance.
8 Either, what woman having ten pieces of

silver, if she loses one piece, does not light a candle and sweep the house and seek diligently, until she finds it?

9 And when she has found it, she calls her friends and her neighbors together saying, "'rejoice with me, for I have found the piece, which I had lost.'"

10 Likewise, I say to you, "there is Joy in the presence of the angels of God over one sinner that Repents.'"

11 **And He said,** "a certain Man had two sons.

12 And the younger of them, said to his Father, "'Father, give me the portion of goods that falls to me.'" And he divided to them his living.

13 And not many days after, the younger son gathered all together and took his journey into a far country and there, wasted his substance with riotous living.

14 And when he had spent all, there arose a mighty famine in that land and he began to be in want.

15 And he went and joined himself to a citizen of that country and he sent him into his fields to feed swine.

16 And he would fain, have filled his belly with the husks that the swine did eat and no man gave to him.

17 And when he came to himself, he said, "'how many hired servants of my Father's have bread enough and to spare and I perish with hunger?!

18 I will rise and go to my Father and will say to him, "'Father, I have sinned against Heaven and before You

19 And am no more worthy, to be called Your son. Make me, as one of Your hired servants.''"

20 And he arose and came to his Father. But, when he was yet a great way off, his Father saw him and had compassion and ran and fell on his neck and kissed him.

21 And the son said to him, "'Father, I have sinned against Heaven and in Your sight and am no more, worthy to be called Your son.'"

22 But, the Father said to his servants, "'bring forth, the best robe and put it on him and put a ring on his hand and shoes on his feet

23 And bring here, the fatted calf and kill it and let us eat and be Merry.

24 For this My son, was Dead and is Alive, again. He was lost and is Found.'" And they began to be Merry.

25 Now, His elder son, was in the field and as he came and drew near to the house, he heard music and dancing.

26 And he called one of the servants and asked what these things meant.

27 And he said to him, "'your brother is come and your Father has killed the fatted calf, because He has received him safe and sound.'"

28 And he was angry and would not go in. Therefore, came his Father out and entreated him.

29 And he answering, said to his Father, "'lo, these many years do I serve You, neither transgressed I at any time, Your Commandments and yet, You never gave me a kid that I might make Merry with my friends.

30 But, as soon as this, Your son was come, which has devoured Your living with harlots, You have killed for him, the fatted calf.'"

31 And He said to him, "'son, you are ever with Me and all that I have is yours.

32 It was meet that we should make Merry and be Glad, for this your brother, was Dead and is Alive, again and was lost and is Found.'"

Chapter 16

1 And He said also, to His disciples, "there was a certain Rich Man, which had a steward and the same was accused to Him that he had wasted His goods.

2 And He called him and said to him, "'how is it that, I hear this of you? Give an account of your stewardship, for you may be, no longer steward.

3 Then, the steward said within himself, "'what shall I do? For my Lord takes away from me, the stewardship. I cannot dig. To beg, I am ashamed.

4 I am resolved what to do that when I am put out of the stewardship, they may receive me into their houses.'"

5 So, he called every one of his Lord's debtors to himself and said to the first, "'how much owe you to my Lord?'"

6 And he said, "'one hundred measures of oil.'" And he said to him, "'take your bill and sit down quickly and write fifty.'"

7 Then, he said to another "'and how much owe you?'" And he said, "'one hundred measures of wheat.'" And he said to him, "'take your bill and write eighty.'"

8 And The Lord commended the unjust steward, because he had, "'done wisely,'" for the children of this World are in their

generation, wiser than the children of Light.

9 And I say to you, "'make to yourselves, friends of the mammon of unrighteousness that when you fail, they may receive you into everlasting habitations.'"

10 He that is Faithful in that, which is least, is Faithful also, in much and he that is unjust, in the least, is unjust also, in much.

11 If therefore, you have not been Faithful in the unrighteous mammon, who will commit to your Trust, the True Riches?

12 And if you have not been faithful in that, which is another man's, who shall give you that, which is your own?

13 No servant can serve two masters. For either, he will hate the one and love the other, or else, he will hold to the one and despise the other. You cannot serve God and mammon."

14 And the Pharisees also, who were covetous heard all these things and they derided Him.

15 And He said to them, "you are they, which justify yourselves before men. But, God knows your hearts. For that, which is highly esteemed among men, is abomination in the Sight of God.

16 The Law and the prophets were until John. Since that time, the Kingdom of God is Preached and every man presses into it.

17 And it is easier for Heaven and Earth to pass, than one tittle of The Law to fail.

18 Whosoever, puts away his wife and marries another, commits adultery and whosoever marries her that is put away from her husband, commits adultery.

19 There was a certain rich man, which was clothed in purple and fine linen and fared sumptuously, every day.

20 And there was a certain beggar named Lazarus, which was laid at his gate; full of sores

21 And desiring to be fed with the crumbs, which fell from the rich man's table. Moreover, the dogs came and licked his sores.

22 And it came to pass that, the beggar died and was carried by the angels into Abraham's bosom. The rich man also, died and was buried.

23 And in Sheol, he lifted up his eyes; being in torments and saw Abraham afar off and Lazarus in his bosom.

24 And he cried and said, "'father Abraham, have Mercy on me and send Lazarus that he may dip the tip of his finger in water and cool my tongue, for I am tormented in this flame!'"

25 But Abraham said, "'son, remember that you, in your lifetime, received your Good things and likewise, Lazarus, evil things. But now, he is Comforted and you are tormented.

26 And besides, all this, between us and you, there is a great gulf fixed, so that, they which would pass from hence, to you cannot. Neither can they pass to us that would come from there.'"

27 Then he said, "'I pray you therefore, father that you would send him to my father's house.

28 For I have five brothers that he may testify to them, lest they also, come into this place of torment.'"

29 Abraham said to him, "'they have Moses and the prophets. Let them hear them.'"

30 And he said, "'no father Abraham, but if one went to them from the dead, they will Repent.'"

31 And he said to him, "'if they hear not, Moses and the prophets, neither will they be persuaded, though one rose from the dead.'"

Chapter 17

1 Then He said to the disciples, "it is impossible, but that offences will come, but woe to him, through whom, they come!

2 It were better for him that a millstone were hanged about his neck and he cast into the Sea, than that, he should offend one of these little ones.

3 Take heed to yourselves. If your brother trespasses against you, Rebuke him and if he Repents, Forgive him.

4 And if he trespasses against you seven times in a day and seven times in a day, turns again, to you saying, "'I Repent.'" You shall Forgive him."

5 And the apostles said to The Lord, "Increase our Faith."

6 And The Lord said, "if you had Faith as a grain of mustard seed, you might say to this sycamore tree, "'be you plucked up by the roots and be you planted in the Sea and it should Obey you.

7 But which of you, having a servant plowing, or feeding cattle, will say to him by and by, when he is come from the field, "'go and sit down to meat?'"

8 And will not rather say to him, "'make ready wherewith, I may sup. And gird

yourself and serve me, until I have eaten and drunken. And afterward, you shall eat and drink?'"

9 Does he thank that servant, because he did the things that were Commanded him? I think not.

10 So likewise, you, when you shall have Done all those things, which are Commanded you, say, "'we are unprofitable servants. We have Done that, which was our duty to Do.'"

11 And it came to pass, as He went to Jerusalem that He passed through the midst of Samaria and Galilee.

12 And as He entered into a certain village, there met Him, ten men that were lepers, which stood afar off.

13 And they lifted up their voices and said, "Jesus, Master, have Mercy on us!"

14 And when He saw them, He said to them, "go show yourselves to the priests." And it came to pass that, as they went, they were Cleansed.

15 And one of them, when he saw that he was Healed, turned back and with a loud voice Glorified God,

16 And Fell Down on his face at His feet; Giving Him Thanks (and he was a Samaritan.)

17 And Jesus answering said, "were there not, ten Cleansed? But, where are the nine?

18 There are not found that returned to Give Glory to God, save this stranger."

19 And He said to him, "arise. Go your way. Your Faith has made you Whole."

20 And when He was demanded of the Pharisees, when the Kingdom of God should come, He answered them and said, "the Kingdom of God comes not with observation.

21 Neither shall they say, "'lo here, or lo there!'" For, behold, the Kingdom of God is within you."

22 And he said to the disciples, "THE DAYS WILL COME, WHEN YOU SHALL DESIRE TO SEE ONE OF THE DAYS OF THE SON OF MAN AND YOU SHALL NOT SEE IT.

23 And THEY SHALL SAY TO YOU, "'SEE HERE…,'" or "'SEE THERE…,'" go not after them, nor follow them.

24 For as the lightning that lightens out of the one part under heaven, shines to the other part under heaven, so shall also, The Son of Man be in His Day.

25 But first, MUST HE SUFFER MANY THINGS AND BE REJECTED OF THIS GENERATION.

26 And as it was in the days of Noah, so shall it be also, in the days of The Son of Man:

27 They did eat, they drank, they married wives, they were given in marriage, until the day that Noah entered into the Ark and the flood came and destroyed them all.

28 Likewise also, as it was in the days of Lot: they did eat, they drank, they bought, they sold, they planted, they built…

29 But, the same day that Lot went out of Sodom, it rained fire and brimstone from heaven and destroyed them all.

30 Even thus, shall it be in the day when The Son of Man is Revealed.

31 In that day, he which shall be on the housetop and his stuff in the house, let him not, come down to take it away and he that is in the field, let him likewise not, return back.

32 Remember Lot's wife:

33 Whosoever, shall seek to save his life, shall lose it and whosoever, shall lose his life, shall preserve it.

34 I tell you, in that night, there shall be two men in one bed; the one, shall be taken and the other, shall be left.

35 Two women shall be grinding together; the one, shall be taken and the other, left.

36 Two men shall be in the field; the one, shall be taken and the other, left."

37 And they answered and said to Him, "where, Lord?" And He said to them, "wheresoever, the body is, there will the eagles be gathered, together."

Chapter 18

1 And He spoke a parable to them to this end that, "men, ought always, to Pray and not to faint"

2 Saying, "there was in a city, a judge, which feared not, God, neither regarded man.

3 And there was a widow in that city. And she came to him saying, "'avenge me, of my adversary.'"

4 And he would not, for a while, but afterwards, he said within himself, "'though I fear not, God, nor regard man,

5 Yet because this widow troubles me, I will avenge her, lest by her continual coming, she wearies me.'"

6 And The Lord said, "Hear what the unjust

judge said,

7 "'…and shall not God avenge His own elect, which cry day and night to Him, though He bears long with them?'"

8 I tell you that, "'He will avenge them, speedily. Nevertheless, when The Son of Man comes, shall He find Faith on the Earth?'"

9 And He spoke this parable to certain, which trusted in themselves that they were righteous and despised others,

10 "Two men went up into the temple to pray; the one, a Pharisee and the other, a publican.

11 The Pharisee stood and prayed thus, with himself, "'God, I thank You that I am not as other men are: extortioners, unjust, adulterers, or even, as this publican.

12 I fast twice in the week, I give tithes of all that I possess.'"

13 And the publican, standing afar off, would not lift up, so much as his eyes to Heaven, but beat on his breast saying, "'God be Merciful to me a sinner.'"

14 I tell you, "'this man went down to his house Justified, rather than the other. For every one that exalts himself, shall be abased and he that Humbles himself, shall be exalted.'"

15 And they brought to Him also, infants that He would touch them. But, when His disciples saw it, they rebuked them.

16 But, Jesus called them to Himself and said, "suffer little children to come to Me and forbid them not, for of such, is the Kingdom of God.

17 Verily, I say to you, "'whosoever, shall not receive the Kingdom of God as a little child, shall in no wise, enter therein.'"

18 And a certain ruler asked Him saying, "Good Master, what shall I do to inherit Eternal Life?"

19 And Jesus said to him, "why call you, Me Good? None is Good, save One. That is, God.

20 You know The Commandments: do not commit adultery, do not murder, do not steal, do not bear false witness, Honor your father and your Mother…"

21 And he said, "all these, have I Kept from my youth up."

22 Now, when Jesus heard these things, He said to him, "yet, lack you one thing, sell all that you have and distribute to the poor and you shall have treasure in Heaven and come, Follow Me."

23 And when he heard this, he was very sorrowful, for he was very rich.

24 And when Jesus saw that he was very sorrowful, He said, "how hardly, shall they that have riches, enter into the Kingdom of God!

25 For it is easier for a camel to go through a needle's eye, than for a rich man, to enter into the Kingdom of God."

26 And they that heard it said, "who then, can be Saved?"

27 And He said, "the things which are impossible with men, are Possible with God."

28 Then Peter said, "lo, we have left all and Followed You."

29 And He said to them, "verily, I say to you, "'there is no man that has left: house, or parents, or brothers, or wife, or children, for the Kingdom of God's sake,

30 Who shall not Receive manifold more, in this present time and in the World to come, Life everlasting.'"

31 Then, He took to Himself, the twelve and said to them, "behold, we go up to Jerusalem and all things that are written by the prophets, concerning the Son of Man, shall be Accomplished,

32 FOR HE SHALL BE DELIVERED TO THE GENTILES AND SHALL BE MOCKED AND SPITEFULLY ENTREATED AND SPIT ON.

33 AND THEY SHALL SCOURGE HIM AND PUT HIM TO DEATH AND THE THIRD DAY, HE SHALL RISE AGAIN."

34 And they understood none of these things. And this saying, was hid from them, neither knew they, the things which were spoken.

35 And it came to pass that, as He was come near to Jericho, a certain blind man sat by the way side begging.

36 And hearing the multitude pass by, He asked what it meant.

37 And they told Him that, Jesus of Nazareth passes by.

38 And he cried saying, "Jesus, you son of David, have Mercy on me!"

39 And they, which went before, rebuked him that he should hold his peace. But, he cried so much the more, "You son of David, have Mercy on me!"

40 And Jesus stood and Commanded him to be brought to Himself. And when he was come near, He asked him

41 Saying, "what will you that I shall Do to you?" And he said, "Lord, that I may Receive my Sight."
42 And Jesus said to him, "Receive your Sight. Your Faith has Saved you."
43 And immediately, he Received his sight and followed Him, Glorifying God and all the people, when they saw it, gave Praise to God.

Chapter 19

1 And Jesus entered and passed through Jericho.
2 And behold, there was a man named Zacchaeus, which was the chief among the publicans and he was rich.
3 And he sought to see Jesus, Who He was and could not, for the press, because he was little of stature.
4 And he ran before and climbed up into a sycamore tree to see Him, for He was to pass that way.
5 And when Jesus came to the place, He looked up and saw him and said to him, "Zacchaeus, make haste and come down, for today, I must abide at your house."
6 And he made haste and came down and received Him, Joyfully.

7 And when they saw it, they all murmured saying that, "He was gone to be guest with a man, that is a sinner."
8 And Zacchaeus stood and said to The Lord, "behold, Lord, the half of my goods, I Give to the poor and if I have taken any thing, from any man by false accusation, I restore him four times."
9 And Jesus said to him, "this day, is Salvation come to this house, forsomuch as he also, is a son of Abraham.
10 For The Son of Man is come to seek and to Save that, which was lost."

11 And as they heard these things, He added and spoke a parable, because He was near to Jerusalem and because they thought that the Kingdom of God should immediately, appear.
12 He said therefore, "a certain Nobleman, went into a far country to receive for Himself, a Kingdom and to return.
13 And He called His ten servants and delivered them ten pounds and said to them, "'occupy until I come.'"
14 But, His citizens hated him and sent a message after Him saying, "'we will not have this man, to Reign over us.'"
15 And it came to pass that, when He was returned, having received the Kingdom, then He Commanded these servants to be called to Himself, to whom He had given the money that He might know how much every man had gained by trading.

16 Then came the first saying, "'Lord, Your pound has gained ten pounds.'"
17 And He said to him, "'well, you good servant, because you have been Faithful in a very little, you have Authority over ten cities.'"
18 And the second came saying, "'Lord, Your pound has gained five pounds.'"
19 And He said likewise to him, "'you are also, over five cities.'"
20 And another came saying, "'Lord behold, here is Your pound, which I have kept laid up in a napkin.
21 For I feared You, because You are an austere Man. You take up that You lay not down and reap that, you did not sow.'"
22 And He said to him, "'out of your own mouth, will I Judge you, you wicked servant. You knew that I was an austere Man; taking up that, I laid not down and reaping that, I did not sow.
23 Wherefore then, you gave not, My money into the bank that at My coming, I might have required My Own, with usury?'"
24 And He said to them that stood by, "'take from him, the pound and give it to him that has ten pounds.'"
25 (And they said to Him, "'Lord, he has ten pounds.'")
26 For I say to you that, "'to every one, which has, shall be given and from him that has not, even that he has, shall be taken away from him.'"
27 But, those my enemies, which would not that, I should Reign over them, bring here and slay them before Me."
28 And when He had thus spoken, He went before, ascending up to Jerusalem.

29 And it came to pass, when He was come near to Bethphage and Bethany, at the mount called the Mount of Olives, He sent two of His disciples,
30 Saying, "go you, into the village over against yourselves in the which, at your entering, you shall find a colt tied, whereon yet never man sat. Loose him and bring him here.
31 And if any man asks you, "'why do you loose him?'" Thus, you shall say to him, "'because The Lord has need of him.'"
32 And they that were sent, went their way

and found even as He had said to them.
33 And as they were loosing the colt, the owners thereof, said to them, "why loose you the colt?"
34 And they said, "The Lord has need of him."

35 And they brought him to Jesus and they cast their garments on the colt and they set Jesus, thereon.
36 And as He went, they spread their clothes in the way.
37 And when He was come near, even now, at the descent of the Mount of Olives, the whole multitude of the disciples began to Rejoice and Praise God with a loud voice, for all the Mighty Works that they had Seen
38 Saying, "BLESSED BE THE KING THAT COMES IN THE NAME OF THE LORD, PEACE IN HEAVEN AND GLORY IN THE HIGHEST!"

39 And some of the Pharisees from among the multitude said to Him, "Master, rebuke Your disciples."
40 And He answered and said to them, "I tell you that, "'if these, should hold their peace, the stones would immediately, cry out.'"
41 And when He was come near, He beheld the city and wept over it
42 Saying, "IF YOU HAVE KNOWN, EVEN YOU, AT LEAST IN THIS YOUR DAY, THE THINGS WHICH BELONG TO YOUR PEACE! BUT NOW, THEY ARE HID FROM YOUR EYES.
43 FOR THE DAYS SHALL COME ON YOU THAT YOUR ENEMIES SHALL CAST A TRENCH ABOUT YOU AND COMPASS YOU, ROUND AND KEEP YOU IN ON EVERY SIDE,
44 AND SHALL LAY YOU EVEN, WITH THE GROUND AND YOUR CHILDREN WITHIN YOU. AND THEY SHALL NOT LEAVE IN YOU, ONE STONE, ON ANOTHER, BECAUSE YOU KNEW NOT THE TIME OF YOUR VISITATION."

45 And He went into the temple and began to cast out them that sold, therein and them that bought
46 Saying to them, "it is written, "'My house is the House of Prayer,'" but you have made it a den of thieves."
47 And He Taught daily, in the temple. But, the chief priests and the scribes and the chief of the people sought to destroy him
48 And could not find what they might do, for all the people were very attentive to Hear Him.

Chapter 20

1 And it came to pass that, on one of those days, as He Taught the people in the temple and Preached The Gospel, the chief priests and the scribes came on Him with the elders
2 And spoke to Him saying, "tell us, by what Authority, Do You these things, or Who is He that Gave You this Authority?"
3 And He answered and said to them, "I will also, ask you one thing and answer Me.
4 The Baptism of John, was it from Heaven, or of men?"
5 And they reasoned with themselves saying, "if we shall say, "'from Heaven,'" He will say, "'why then, believed you, Him not?'"
6 But and if we say, "'of men,'" all the people will stone us, for they be persuaded that John was a prophet."
7 And they answered that they, "could not tell where it was."
8 And Jesus said to them, "neither tell I you, by what Authority I Do these things."

9 Then, began He to speak to the people this parable, "a certain Man planted a vineyard and let it forth to husbandmen and went into a far country for a long time.
10 And at the season, He sent a servant to the husbandmen that they should give him of the fruit of the vineyard. But, the husbandmen beat him and sent him away empty.
11 And again, He sent another servant and they beat him, also and entreated him shamefully and sent him away empty.
12 And again, He sent a third and they wounded him, also and cast him out.
13 Then, said The Lord of the vineyard, "'what shall I do? I will send My Beloved Son. It may be, they will Reverence Him, when they see Him.'"
14 But, when the husbandmen saw Him, they reasoned among themselves saying, "'this is the heir. Come, let us kill Him that the inheritance may be ours.'"
15 So, they cast Him out of the vineyard and killed Him. What therefore, shall The Lord of the vineyard do to them?
16 He shall come and destroy these husbandmen and shall give the vineyard to others." And when they heard it, they said, "God forbid."

17 And He beheld them and said, "what is this then that is written, "'THE STONE, WHICH THE BUILDERS REJECTED, THE SAME IS BECOME THE HEAD OF THE CORNER?'"
18 Whosoever, shall fall on that Stone, shall be broken. But on whomsoever, it shall fall, it will grind him to powder."

19 And the chief priests and the scribes the same hour, sought to lay hands on Him. And they feared the people, for they perceived that He had spoken this parable against them.
20 And they watched Him and sent forth spies, which should feign themselves, just men that they might take hold of His Words that so they might deliver Him to the power and authority of the governor.
21 And they asked Him saying, "Master, we know that You Say and Teach Rightly, neither accept You, the person of any, but Teach The Way of God, Truly.
22 Is it Lawful for us to give tribute to Caesar, or no?"
23 But, He perceived their craftiness and said to them, "why tempt you, Me?
24 Show Me a penny. Whose image and superscription has it?" They answered and said, "Caesar's."
25 And He said to them, "render therefore, to Caesar the things, which are Caesar's and to God the things, which are God's."
26 And they could not take hold of His Words before the people. And they marveled at His answer and held their peace.

27 Then came to Him, certain of the Sadducees, which deny that, there is any Resurrection and they asked Him,
28 Saying, "Master, Moses wrote to us, "'if any man's brother dies, having a wife and he dies without children that, his brother should take his wife and raise up seed to his brother.
29 There were therefore, seven brothers and the first took a wife and died without children.
30 And the second took her to wife and he died childless.
31 And the third took her and in like manner, the seven, also and they left no children and died.
32 Last of all, the woman died, also.
33 Therefore, in the Resurrection, whose wife of them, is she? For seven had her to wife."

34 And Jesus answering, said to them, "the children of this World, marry and are given in marriage.
35 But they, which shall be accounted worthy to obtain that World and the Resurrection from the dead, neither marry, nor are given in marriage.
36 Neither can they die any more, for they are equal to the angels and are the children of God; being the children of the Resurrection.
37 Now that the dead are Raised, even Moses showed at the bush, when he called The Lord, "'The God of Abraham and The God of Isaac and The God of Jacob,'"
38 For He is not, a God of the dead, but of the Living; for all Live to Him."
39 Then, certain of the scribes answering said, "Master, you have well said."
40 And after that, they did not ask Him any question at all.

41 And He said to them, "How say they that, "'Christ, is David's Son?'"
42 And David himself, said in the scroll of Psalms, "'THE LORD SAID TO MY LORD, SIT YOURSELF ON MY RIGHT HAND
43 UNTIL I MAKE YOUR ENEMIES, YOUR FOOTSTOOL.'"
44 David therefore, calls Him Lord. How is He then, his Son?"

45 Then, in the audience of all the people, He said to His disciples,
46 "Beware of the scribes, which desire to walk in long robes and love greetings in the markets and the highest seats in the synagogues and the chief rooms at feasts,
47 Which devour widows' houses and for a show, make long prayers. The same, shall receive greater damnation."

Chapter 21

1 And He looked up and saw the rich men casting their gifts into the treasury.
2 And He saw also, a certain poor widow casting in there, two mites.
3 And He said, "of a Truth, I say to you that, "'this poor widow, has cast in more, than they all.
4 For all these, have of their abundance, cast in to the offerings of God. But, she of her penury, has cast in All the living that she had.'"

5 And as some spoke of the temple, how it

was adorned with goodly stones and gifts, He said,

6 "As for these things, which you behold, THE DAYS WILL COME, IN THE WHICH, THERE SHALL NOT BE LEFT, ONE STONE ON ANOTHER THAT SHALL NOT BE THROWN DOWN."

7 And they asked Him saying, "Master, but when shall these things be and what Sign will there be, when these things shall come to pass?"

8 And He said, "take Heed that you be not deceived, for MANY SHALL COME IN MY NAME SAYING, "'I AM CHRIST AND THE TIME DRAWS NEAR.'" Go yourselves not, therefore after them.

9 BUT, WHEN YOU SHALL HEAR OF WARS AND COMMOTIONS, BE NOT TERRIFIED, FOR THESE THINGS MUST FIRST, COME TO PASS. But the end, is not, by and by."

10 Then, said He to them, "NATION SHALL RISE AGAINST NATION AND KINGDOM AGAINST KINGDOM.

11 AND GREAT EARTHQUAKES SHALL BE IN DIVERSE PLACES AND FAMINES AND PESTILENCES AND FEARFUL SIGHTS AND GREAT SIGNS, SHALL THERE BE, FROM HEAVEN.

12 But, before all these, THEY SHALL LAY THEIR HANDS ON YOU AND PERSECUTE YOU; DELIVERING YOU UP TO THE SYNAGOGUES AND INTO PRISONS, BEING BROUGHT BEFORE KINGS AND RULERS FOR MY NAME'S SAKE.

13 AND IT SHALL TURN TO YOU FOR A TESTIMONY.

14 Settle it therefore, in your hearts, not to meditate before, what you shall answer.

15 For I will Give you a mouth and Wisdom, which all your adversaries shall not be able to gainsay, nor resist.

16 AND YOU SHALL BE BETRAYED, BOTH BY PARENTS AND BROTHERS AND KINSFOLK AND FRIENDS. AND SOME OF YOU, SHALL THEY CAUSE TO BE PUT TO DEATH.

17 AND YOU SHALL BE HATED OF ALL MEN, FOR MY NAME'S SAKE.

18 But, there shall not a hair of your head perish.

19 In your patience, possess yourself, your souls.

20 And when you shall see Jerusalem compassed with armies, then know that, the desolation thereof, is near.

21 Then, let them which are in Judaea, flee to the mountains and let them, which are in the midst of it, depart out and let not, them that are in the countries, enter there into.

22 For these be the days of vengeance that all things which are written, may be Fulfilled.

23 But, woe to them that are with child and to them that give suck in those days! For there shall be great distress in the land and wrath on this people.

24 And they shall fall by the edge of the sword and shall be led away captive, into all nations. AND JERUSALEM SHALL BE TRODDEN DOWN OF THE GENTILES, UNTIL THE TIMES OF THE GENTILES, BE FULFILLED.

25 AND THERE SHALL BE SIGNS IN THE SUN AND IN THE MOON AND IN THE STARS AND ON THE EARTH; DISTRESS OF NATIONS, WITH PERPLEXITY, THE SEA AND THE WAVES ROARING,

26 Men's hearts failing them for fear and for looking after those things, which are coming on the Earth. FOR THE POWERS OF HEAVEN SHALL BE SHAKEN.

27 And then, shall they see The Son of Man coming in A Cloud with Power and Great Glory.

28 And when these things begin to come to pass, then look up and lift up your heads, for your redemption draws near."

29 And He spoke to them a parable, "behold, the fig tree and all the trees.

30 When they now, shoot forth, you see and know of your own selves that Summer is now, near at hand.

31 So likewise, you, when you see these things come to pass, Know yourselves that the Kingdom of God is near at hand.

32 Verily, I say to you, "'this generation shall not pass away, until all be fulfilled.

33 Heaven and Earth shall pass away, but My Words shall not pass away.

34 And take Heed to yourselves, lest at any time, your hearts be overcharged with surfeiting and drunkenness and cares of this life and so that day comes on you, unawares.

35 For as a snare, shall it come on all them that dwell on the face of the whole Earth.

36 Watch yourselves, therefore and Pray always that you may be accounted worthy to escape all these things that shall come

to pass and to stand before The Son of Man.'"

37 And in the day time, He was Teaching in the temple and at night, He went out and abode in the mount that is called the Mount of Olives.
38 And all the people came early in the morning to Him in the temple, for to hear Him.

Chapter 22

1 Now, The Feast of Unleavened Bread drew near, which is called The Passover.
2 And the chief priests and scribes sought how they might kill Him, for they feared the people.
3 Then entered Satan, into Judas, surnamed Iscariot; being of the number of the twelve.
4 And he went his way and communed with the chief priests and captains, how he might betray Him to them.
5 And they were glad and covenanted to give him money.
6 And he promised and sought opportunity to betray Him to them in the absence of the multitude.

7 Then, came the day of Unleavened Bread, when the Passover must be killed.
8 And He sent Peter and John saying, "go and prepare us, The Passover that we may eat."
9 And they said to Him, "where will You that we prepare?"
10 And He said to them, "behold, when you are entered into the city, there shall a man meet you, bearing a pitcher of water. Follow him into the house where he enters in.
11 And you shall say to the good man of the house, "'The Master asks you, "''where is the guest chamber, where I shall eat the Passover with My disciples?'"'
12 And he shall show you a large upper room, furnished. There, make ready."

13 And they went and found as He had said to them and they made ready, The Passover.
14 And when the hour was come, He sat down and the twelve apostles with Him.
15 And He said to them, "with desire, I have desired to eat this Passover with you before I suffer.
16 For I say to you, "'I will not any more, eat thereof, until it be Fulfilled in the Kingdom of God.'"
17 And He took the cup and Gave Thanks and said, "take this and divide it among yourselves.
18 For I say to you, "'I will not drink of the fruit of the vine, until the Kingdom of God shall come.'"
19 And He took bread and Gave Thanks and broke it and gave to them saying, "this is My Body, which is Given For you. This Do in Remembrance of Me";
20 Likewise also, the cup after supper saying, "this cup is The New Testament in My Blood, which is Shed For you.

21 But behold, the hand of him that betrays Me is with Me on the table.
22 And Truly, The Son of Man goes, as it was determined, but Woe to that man, by whom He is betrayed."
23 And they began to enquire among themselves, which of them it was that should do this thing.

24 And there was also, a strife among them, which of them should be accounted the greatest.
25 And He said to them, "the kings of the gentiles, exercise lordship over them and they that exercise authority on them, are called benefactors.
26 But, you shall not be so. But he that is greatest among you, let him be as the younger and he that is chief, as he that does serve.
27 For whether is greater, he that sits at meat, or he that serves? Is not he that sits at meat? But, I am among you, as He that Serves.

28 You are they, which have continued with Me in My temptations.
29 And I appoint to you a Kingdom, as My Father has appointed to Me.
30 That you may eat and drink at My table in My Kingdom and sit on thrones, Judging the twelve tribes of Israel."

31 And The Lord said, "Simeon, Simeon, behold, Satan has desired to have you that he may sift you as wheat.
32 But, I have Prayed for you that your Faith, fails not and when you are Converted, strengthen your brothers."
33 And he said to Him, "Lord, I am ready to go with both, into prison and to death."
34 And He said, "I tell you Peter, THE COCK SHALL NOT CROW THIS DAY,

BEFORE THAT, YOU SHALL THRICE, DENY THAT YOU KNOW ME."

35 And He said to them, "when I sent you without purse and scrip and shoes, lacked you, any thing?" And they said, "nothing."
36 Then, He said to them, "but now, he that has a purse, let him take it and likewise, his scrip. And he that has no sword, let him sell his garment and buy one.
37 For I say to you that, "'this that is written, must yet be Accomplished in Me and ""HE WAS RECKONED AMONG THE TRANSGRESSORS,'"" for the things concerning Me have an end."
38 And they said, "Lord, behold, here are two swords." And He said to them, "it is enough."

39 And He came out and went as He was wont, to the Mount of Olives and His disciples also, followed Him.
40 And when He was at the place, He said to them, "Pray that you enter not, into temptation."
41 And He was withdrawn from them, about a stone's cast and Kneeled Down and Prayed
42 Saying, "Father, if you are willing, remove this Cup from Me. Nevertheless, not My will, but Yours, be Done."
43 And there appeared an angel to Him from Heaven, strengthening Him.
44 And being in an agony, He Prayed more earnestly and His sweat was as it were, great drops of blood, falling down to the ground.
45 And when He rose up from Prayer and was come to His disciples, He found them sleeping for sorrow
46 And said to them, "why sleep you? Rise and Pray, lest you enter into temptation."

47 And while He yet spoke, behold, a multitude and he that was called Judas; one of the twelve, went before them and drew near to Jesus to kiss Him.
48 But, Jesus said to him, "Judas, YOU BETRAY THE SON OF MAN WITH A KISS?"
49 When they, which were about Him, saw what would follow, they said to Him, "Lord, shall we slay with the sword?"
50 And one of them struck the servant of the high priest and cut off his right ear.
51 And Jesus answered and said, "suffer you thus far." And He touched his ear and Healed him.
52 Then, Jesus said to the chief priests and captains of the temple and the elders, which had come to Him, "are you come out, as against a thief, with swords and staves?
53 When I was daily with you in the temple, you stretched forth, no hands against Me. But, this is your hour and the power of Darkness."

54 Then, took they Him and led Him and brought Him into the high priest's house. And Peter followed afar off.
55 And when they had kindled a fire in the midst of the hall and were set down together, Peter sat down among them.
56 But a certain maid beheld him as he sat by the fire and earnestly looked on him and said, "this man was also, with Him."
57 And he DENIED Him saying, "woman, I KNOW HIM NOT."
58 And after a little while, another saw him and said, "you are also, of them." And Peter said, "MAN, I AM NOT."
59 And about the space of one hour, after another confidently affirmed saying, "of a truth, this fellow also, was with Him, for he is a Galilaean."
60 And Peter said, "MAN, I KNOW NOT, WHAT YOU SAY." And immediately, while he yet spoke, THE COCK CREW.
61 And The Lord turned and looked on Peter. And Peter remembered the Word of The Lord, how He had said to him, "BEFORE THE COCK CROWS, YOU SHALL DENY ME THRICE."
62 And Peter went out and wept bitterly.

63 And THE MEN THAT HELD JESUS, MOCKED HIM AND BEAT HIM.
64 AND WHEN THEY HAD BLINDFOLDED HIM, THEY STRUCK HIM ON THE FACE AND ASKED HIM SAYING, "PROPHESY. WHO IS IT THAT HIT YOU?"
65 AND MANY OTHER THINGS, BLASPHEMOUSLY, SPOKE THEY AGAINST HIM.

66 And as soon as it was day, the elders of the people and the chief priests and the scribes came together and led Him into their council saying,
67 "Are You the Christ? Tell us." And He said to them, "if I tell you, you will not believe
68 And if I also, ask you, you will not answer Me, nor let Me go.
69 HEREAFTER, SHALL THE SON OF MAN SIT ON THE RIGHT HAND OF THE

POWER OF GOD."

70 Then said they all, "are You then, The Son of God?" And He said to them, "you say that, I am."

71 And they said, "what need we, any further, witness? For we ourselves, have heard of His Own mouth."

Chapter 23

1 And the whole multitude of them, rose and led Him to Pilate.

2 AND THEY BEGAN TO ACCUSE HIM SAYING, "WE FOUND THIS FELLOW PERVERTING THE NATION AND FORBIDDING TO GIVE TRIBUTE TO CAESAR SAYING THAT, "'HE HIMSELF, IS CHRIST, A KING.'"

3 And Pilate asked him saying, "are You The King of the Jews?" And He answered him and said, "you said it."

4 Then said Pilate to the chief priests and to the people, "I find no fault in this man."

5 And they were the more fierce saying, "HE STIRS UP THE PEOPLE; TEACHING THROUGHOUT ALL JEWRY; BEGINNING FROM GALILEE, TO THIS PLACE!"

6 When Pilate heard of Galilee, he asked whether, The Man, were a Galilaean.

7 And as soon as he knew that, He belonged to Herod's jurisdiction, he sent Him to Herod, who himself also, was at Jerusalem, at that time.

8 And when Herod saw Jesus, he was exceedingly glad, for he was desirous to see Him of a long season, because he had heard many things of Him and he hoped to have seen some Miracle done by Him.

9 Then, he questioned with Him in many words, but HE ANSWERED HIM NOTHING.

10 And the chief priests and scribes, stood and vehemently accused Him.

11 And Herod with his men of war, SET HIM AT NOUGHT AND MOCKED HIM AND ARRAYED HIM IN A GORGEOUS ROBE and sent Him again, to Pilate.

12 And the same day, Pilate and Herod were made friends together, for before, they were at enmity between, themselves.

13 And Pilate, when he had called together, the chief priests and the rulers and the people,

14 Said to them, "you have brought this Man to me, as one that perverts the people. And behold, I, having examined Him before you, have found no fault in this Man, touching those things whereof, you accuse Him.

15 No, nor yet Herod, for I sent you to him and lo, nothing worthy of death is done to Him.

16 I WILL THEREFORE, CHASTISE HIM and release Him."

17 (For of necessity, He must release one to them, at the feast.)

18 And they cried out all at once saying, "away with this Man and release to us, Barabbas!"

19 (Who for a certain sedition, made in the city and for murder, was cast into prison.)

20 Pilate therefore, willing to release Jesus, spoke again, to them.

21 But they cried saying, "crucify Him! Crucify Him!"

22 And he said to them the third time, "why, what evil has He done? I have found no cause of death in Him. I will therefore, chastise Him and let Him go."

23 And they were instant, with loud voices, requiring that He might be crucified. And the voices of them and of the chief priests, prevailed.

24 And Pilate gave sentence that it should be as they required.

25 And he released to them, him that for sedition and murder, was cast into prison, whom they had desired. But, he delivered Jesus to their will.

26 And as they led Him away, they laid hold on one, Simeon, a Cyrenian coming out of the country and on him, they laid the cross that He might bear it after Jesus.

27 And there followed Him, a great company of people and of women, which also, bewailed and lamented Him.

28 But Jesus turning to them said, "daughters of Jerusalem, weep not for Me, but weep for yourselves and for your children.

29 For behold, the days are coming, in the which, they shall say, "'BLESSED ARE THE BARREN AND THE WOMBS THAT NEVER BARE AND THE PAPS, WHICH NEVER GAVE SUCK.'"

30 THEN, SHALL THEY BEGIN TO SAY TO THE MOUNTAINS, "'FALL ON US AND TO THE HILLS, COVER US.'"

31 For if they do these things in a green tree, what shall be done in the dry?"

32 And there were also, two other, malefactors, led with Him to be put to death.
33 And when they had come to the place, which is called Calvary, there, THEY CRUCIFIED HIM AND THE MALEFACTORS; one, on the right hand and the other, on the left.

34 Then said Jesus, "Father, Forgive them, for they know not what they do." AND THEY PARTED HIS RAIMENT AND CAST LOTS.
35 And the people stood beholding. And the rulers also, with them derided Him saying, "HE SAVED OTHERS. LET HIM SAVE HIMSELF, IF HE IS CHRIST, THE CHOSEN OF GOD."
36 And the soldiers also, mocked Him, coming to Him and OFFERING HIM VINEGAR
37 And saying, "if You are The King of the Jews, save Yourself."
38 And a superscription also, was written over Him in letters of Greek and Latin and Hebrew, "This is The King of the Jews."

39 And one of the malefactors, which were hanged, railed on Him saying, "if You are Christ, save Yourself and us."
40 But the other answering, rebuked him saying, "do not, you Fear God, seeing you are in the same condemnation?
41 And we indeed, justly, for we receive the due reward of our deeds, but this Man has done nothing amiss."
42 And he said to Jesus, "Lord, remember me when You come into Your Kingdom."
43 And Jesus said to him, "verily, I say to you, "'today, you shall be with Me in Paradise.'"

44 And it was about the sixth hour and there was a darkness over all the Earth, until the ninth hour.
45 And the Sun was darkened and the veil of the temple was rent in the midst.
46 And when Jesus had cried with a loud voice, He said, "Father, into Your hands, I commend My Spirit!" And having said thus, He gave up The Ghost.
47 Now, when the centurion saw what was done, he Glorified God saying, "certainly, this was a RIGHTEOUS Man."
48 And all the people that came together to that sight, beholding the things which were done, beat their breasts and returned.
49 And all His acquaintances and the women that followed Him from Galilee, stood afar off, beholding these things.

50 And behold, there was a man named, Joseph, a counselor and he was a good man and a Just
51 (The same had not consented to the counsel and deed of them.) He was of Arimathaea, a city of the Jews who also, himself Waited for the Kingdom of God.
52 This man went to Pilate and begged the Body of Jesus.
53 And he took it down and wrapped it in linen and laid it in a sepulchre that was hewn in stone, wherein never man before, was laid.
54 And that day, was the preparation and the Sabbath drew on.
55 And the women also, which came with Him from Galilee, followed after and beheld the sepulchre and how His Body was laid.
56 And they returned and prepared spices and ointments and rested the Sabbath Day, according to The Commandment.

Chapter 24

1 Now, on the first day of the week, very early in the morning, they came to the sepulchre, bringing the spices which they had prepared and certain others with them.
2 And they found the stone rolled away from the sepulchre.
3 And they entered in and found not the Body of The Lord, Jesus.
4 And it came to pass, as they were much perplexed thereabout, behold, two men stood by them in shining garments
5 And as they were afraid and bowed down their faces to the earth, they said to them, "why seek you, the Living among the dead?
6 He is not here, but is Risen. Remember how He spoke to you, when He was yet, in Galilee
7 Saying, "'THE SON OF MAN MUST BE DELIVERED INTO THE HANDS OF SINFUL MEN AND BE CRUCIFIED AND THE THIRD DAY, RISE AGAIN?'"

8 And they remembered His Words
9 And returned from the sepulchre and told all these things to the eleven and to all the rest.
10 It was Mary Magdalene and Joanna and Mary, the mother of James and other women that were with them, which told

these things to the apostles.
11 And their words seemed to them, as idle tales and they believed them not.
12 Then, rose Peter and ran to the sepulchre and stooping down, he beheld the linen clothes laid by themselves and departed, wondering in himself at that, which was come to pass.
13 And behold, two of them went that same day to a village called, Emmaus, which was from Jerusalem, about sixty furlongs.
14 And they talked together, of all these things, which had happened.

15 And it came to pass that, while they communed together and reasoned, Jesus Himself, drew near and went with them.
16 But, their eyes were held that they should not know Him.
17 And He said to them, "what manner of communications are these that you have one to another, as you walk and are sad?"
18 And the one of them, whose name was, Cleopas, answering said to Him, "are You only a stranger in Jerusalem and have not known the things, which are come to pass there in these days?"
19 And He said to them, "what things?" And they said to Him, "concerning Jesus, of Nazareth, which was a prophet; Mighty in Deed and Word before God and all the people
20 And how the chief priests and our rulers delivered Him to be condemned to death and have crucified Him.
21 But, we Trusted that it had been He, which should have redeemed Israel and besides all this, today is the third day, since these things were done.

22 Yes and certain women also, of our company made us astonished, which were early at the sepulchre
23 And when they found not His Body, they came saying that, they had also, "'seen a Vision of angels,'" which said that, "'He was alive.'"
24 And certain of them, which were with us went to the sepulchre and found it even so, as the women had said, but Him, they saw not."
25 Then He said to them, "O fools and slow of heart to Believe, all that the prophets have spoken.
26 Ought not, Christ to have suffered these things and to enter into His Glory?"
27 And beginning at Moses and all the prophets, He expounded to them, in all The Scriptures, the things concerning Himself.

28 And they drew near to the village, where they went and He made as though He would have gone further.
29 But they constrained Him saying, "abide with us, for it is toward evening and the day is far spent." And He went in, to tarry with them.
30 And it came to pass, as He sat at meat with them, He took bread and Blessed it and broke and gave to them.
31 And their eyes were Opened and they Knew Him and He Vanished out of their sight.
32 And they said one to another, "did not our heart burn within us, while He talked with us by the way and while He opened to us, The Scriptures?"
33 And they rose up the same hour and returned to Jerusalem and found the eleven gathered together and them that were with them
34 Saying, "The Lord is Risen, indeed and has appeared to Simeon!"
35 And they told what things were done in the way and how He was Known of them in breaking of bread.
36 And as they thus spoke, Jesus Himself, stood in the midst of them and said to them, "Peace be to you."
37 But they were terrified and affrighted and supposed that they had seen a spirit.
38 And He said to them, "why are you troubled and why do thoughts arise in your hearts?
39 Behold, My hands and My feet that it is I, Myself. Handle Me and see, for a spirit has not flesh and bones, as you see Me have."
40 And when He had thus spoken, He showed them His hands and His feet.
41 And while they yet believed not, for joy and wondered, He said to them, "have you here, any meat?"
42 And they gave Him a piece of a broiled fish and of a honeycomb.
43 And He took it and did eat before them.

44 And He said to them, "these are the Words, which I spoke to you, while I was yet with you that, ALL THINGS MUST BE FULFILLED, WHICH WERE WRITTEN IN THE LAW OF MOSES AND IN THE PROPHETS AND IN THE PSALMS, CONCERNING ME."
45 Then opened He, their Understanding

that, they might Understand The Scriptures
46 And said to them, "thus, it is written and thus, it behooved Christ TO SUFFER AND TO RISE FROM THE DEAD THE THIRD DAY
47 AND THAT REPENTANCE AND REMISSION OF SINS, SHOULD BE PREACHED IN HIS NAME AMONG ALL NATIONS, BEGINNING AT JERUSALEM.
48 And you are witnesses of these things.
49 And behold, I SEND THE PROMISE OF MY FATHER ON YOU. But, tarry yourselves in the city of Jerusalem, UNTIL YOU ARE ENDUED WITH POWER FROM ON HIGH."
50 And He led them out as far as to Bethany and He lifted up His hands and Blessed them.
51 And it came to pass, while He Blessed them, He was parted from them and Carried Up into Heaven.
52 And they Worshipped Him and returned to Jerusalem with great Joy
53 And were continually, in the temple, Praising and Blessing God. Amen.

John

Chapter 1

1 In the beginning, was The Word. And The Word was with God and The Word, was God.
2 The Same was in the beginning, with God.
3 All things were made by Him. And without Him, was not, any thing made that was made.
4 In Him, was Life. And the Life, was the Light of men.
5 And The Light Shines in Darkness. And the Darkness, comprehended it not.

6 There was a man sent from God, whose name was John. 7 The same, came for a witness; to bear witness, of The Light that all men through him, might Believe.
8 He was not, That Light, but was sent to Bear Witness, of That Light.
9 That was The True Light, which Lights every man that comes into the World.
10 He was in the World. And the World was made by Him. And the World knew Him not.
11 He came to His own and His own, received Him not.

12 But, as many as Received Him, to them, Gave He, Power to become the sons of God; even to them that Believe on His Name,
13 Which were born, not of blood, nor of the will of the flesh, nor of the will of man, but of God.
14 And The Word was made flesh and dwelled among us; (and we beheld His Glory; The Glory, as of The Only Begotten of The Father) full of Grace and Truth.

15 John Bare Witness of Him and cried saying, "this was He, of Whom I spoke! He that comes after me, is Preferred before me, for He was before me!"
16 And of His Fullness, have all we Received and Grace for Grace.
17 For the Law was given by Moses, but Grace and Truth, came by Jesus Christ.
18 No man has seen God at any time. The Only Begotten Son, which is in the bosom of The Father, He has declared Him.

19 And this is the record of John, when the Jews sent priests and Levites from Jerusalem to ask him, "who are you?"
20 And he confessed and denied not, but confessed, "I am not, the Christ."
21 And they asked him, "what then, are you, Elijah?" And he said, "I am not." "Are you that prophet?" And he answered, "no."
22 Then, said they to him, "who are you that we may give an answer to them that sent us? What say you, of yourself?"
23 He said, "I am, "'THE VOICE OF ONE CRYING IN THE WILDERNESS. MAKE STRAIGHT, THE WAY OF THE LORD,'" as said the Prophet Isaiah.

24 And they which were sent, were of the Pharisees.
25 And they asked him and said to him, "why Baptize you then, if you are not that Christ, nor Elijah, neither that prophet?"
26 John answered them saying, "I Baptize with water, but there stands One among you, whom you know not.
27 He it is, Who coming after me, is Preferred before me, whose shoe's latchet, I am not worthy to unloose."
28 These things were done in Bethabara, beyond Jordan, where John was Baptizing.

29 The next day, John saw Jesus coming to him and said, "behold, <u>The Lamb of God, which takes away the sin of the World</u>.
30 This is He of Whom, I said, "'after me, comes a Man, which is Preferred before me, for <u>He was before me</u>.'"
31 And I knew him not, but that He should be made manifest to Israel. Therefore, am I come Baptizing with water.

32 And John bare record saying, "I saw The Spirit descending from Heaven like a dove and it abode on Him."
33 And I knew Him not, but He that sent me to Baptize with water, the same said to me, "on Whom, you shall see The Spirit descending and remaining on Him, the same is He, which Baptizes with The Holy Ghost."
34 And I saw and bare record that this is, <u>The Son of God</u>.

35 Again, the next day after, John stood and two of his disciples
36 And looking on Jesus as He walked, he said, "behold, The Lamb of God!"
37 And the two disciples heard him speak and they followed Jesus.
38 Then, Jesus turned and saw them following and asked them, "what Seek you?" They said to Him, "Rabbi, (which is to say, being interpreted, Master) where dwell You?"
39 He said to them, "come and see." They came and saw where He dwelled and abode with Him that day, for it was about the tenth hour.
40 One of the two, which heard John speak and followed Him, was Andrew, Simeon Peter's brother.
41 He first found his own brother, Simeon and said to him, "we have found The Messiah," (which is, being interpreted, The Christ.)
42 And he brought him to Jesus. And when Jesus beheld him, He said, "you are Simeon, the son of Jonah. You shall be called Cephas" (which is by interpretation, a stone.)

43 The day following, Jesus would go forth into Galilee and found Philip and said to him, "Follow Me."
44 Now Philip, was of Bethsaida; the city of Andrew and Peter.
45 Philip found Nathanael and said to him, "we have found Him, of Whom, Moses, in The Law and the Prophets did write; Jesus of Nazareth, the son of Joseph."
46 And Nathanael said to him, "can there, any good thing, come out of Nazareth?" Philip said to him, "come and see."
47 Jesus saw Nathanael coming to Him and said of him, "behold, an Israelite indeed, in Whom is no guile!"
48 Nathanael asked Him, "whence Know You me?" Jesus answered and said to him, "before that Philip called you, when you were under the fig tree, I saw you."
49 Nathanael answered and said to him, "Rabbi, You are The Son of God. You are The King of Israel."
50 Jesus answered and said to him, "because I said to you, "'I saw you under the fig tree,'" Believe you? You shall see Greater things than these."
51 And He said to him, "verily, verily, I say to you, "'hereafter, you shall see Heaven open and the angels of God ascending and descending on The Son of Man.'"

Chapter 2

1 And the third day, there was a marriage in Cana, of Galilee and the mother of Jesus was there.
2 And both Jesus was called and His disciples, to the marriage.
3 And when they wanted wine, the mother of Jesus said to Him, "they have no wine."
4 Jesus asked her, "woman, what have I to do with you? My hour is not yet come."
5 His mother said to the servants, "whatsoever, He says to you, do it."

6 And there were set there, six water pots of stone; after the manner of the purifying of the Jews, containing two or three firkins, apiece.
7 Jesus said to them, "fill the water pots with water." And they filled them up to the brim.
8 And He said to them, "Draw Out now and bear to the governor of the feast." And they bare it.
9 When the ruler of the feast had tasted the water that was made wine and knew not, where it was, (But the servants which drew the water knew) the governor of the feast called the bridegroom
10 And said to him, "every man, at the beginning, does set forth good wine and when men have well drunk, then that, which is worse, but you have kept the good wine until now."
11 This beginning of Miracles, did Jesus in Cana, of Galilee and manifested forth His

Glory and His disciples Believed on Him.

12 After this, He went down to Capernaum; He and His mother and His brothers and His disciples and they continued there, not many days.
13 And the Jews' Passover was at hand and Jesus went up to Jerusalem
14 And found in the temple, those that sold oxen and sheep and doves and the changers of money, sitting.
15 And when He had made a scourge of small cords, He drove them all out of the temple and the sheep and the oxen and poured out the changers' money and overthrew the tables
16 And said to them that sold doves, "take these things, hence. Make not My Father's house a house of merchandise."
17 And His disciples remembered that it was written, "THE ZEAL OF YOUR HOUSE HAS EATEN ME UP."

18 Then, answered the Jews and said to Him, "what Sign show you to us, seeing that you do these things?"
19 Jesus answered and said to them, "destroy this Temple and in three days, I will Raise it Up."
20 Then said the Jews, "forty and six years, was this temple in building. And will You rear it up in three days?"
21 But He spoke of the Temple of His Body.
22 (When therefore, He was Risen from the dead, His disciples remembered that He had said this to them and they Believed The Scripture and The Word, which Jesus had said.)

23 Now, when He was in Jerusalem, at The Passover; in the feast day, many Believed in His Name, when they saw the Miracles which He Did.
24 But, Jesus did not commit Himself to them, because He Knew all men
25 And needed not that any should testify of man, for He knew what was in man.

Chapter 3
1 There was a man of the Pharisees named, Nicodemus; a ruler of the Jews.
2 The same, came to Jesus by night and said to Him, "Rabbi, we know that You are a Teacher come from God, for no man, can Do these Miracles that You Do, except God be with Him."
3 Jesus answered and said to him, "verily, verily, I say to you, "'except a man be Born Again, he cannot see the Kingdom of God.'"
4 Nicodemus said to him, "how can a man be born when he is old? Can he enter the second time, into his mother's womb and be born?"
5 Jesus answered, "verily, verily, I say to you, "'except a man be born of water and of The Spirit, he cannot enter into the Kingdom of God.
6 That, which is born of the flesh is flesh and that, which is born of The Spirit is spirit.'"
7 Marvel not that I said to you, "'you must be Born Again.'"
8 The wind blows where it lists and you hear the sound thereof, but can not tell where it comes and where it goes. So is every one, that is born of The Spirit."
9 Nicodemus answered and said to Him, "how can these things be?"
10 Jesus answered and said to him, "are you a master of Israel and know not, these things?
11 Verily, verily, I say to you, "'we speak that, we do know and testify that, we have seen and you receive not our witness.
12 If I have told you earthly things and you believe not, how shall you Believe, if I tell you of Heavenly things?
13 And no man has ascended up to Heaven, but He that came down from Heaven; even The Son of Man, which is in Heaven.
14 And as Moses lifted up the serpent in the wilderness, even so, must The Son of Man be Lifted Up
15 That whosoever, Believes in Him, should not perish, but have Eternal Life.
16 For God so loved the World that He gave His only, begotten Son that whosoever, Believes in Him should not perish, but have everlasting Life.
17 For God sent not, His Son into the World to condemn the World, but that the World through Him, might be Saved.
18 He that Believes on Him, is not condemned, but he that believes not, is condemned already, because he has not, believed in The Name of The Only Begotten Son of God.

19 And this is the condemnation that: Light is come into the World and men loved Darkness, rather than Light, because their deeds were evil.

20 For every one that does evil, hates The Light, neither comes to The Light, lest his deeds should be Reproved.
21 But he that Does Truth, comes to The Light that His deeds may be made manifest that they are worked in God.'"

22 After these things, came Jesus and His disciples into the land of Judaea and there, He tarried with them and Baptized.
23 And John also, was Baptizing in Aenon, near to Salim, because there was much water there and they came and were Baptized.
24 For John was not yet, cast into prison.
25 Then, there arose a question between some of John's disciples and the Jews about purifying.
26 And they came to John and said to him, "Rabbi, He that was with you beyond Jordan, to Whom you bare witness, behold, the same Baptizes and all men come to Him."
27 John answered and said, "a man can receive nothing, except it be Given him, from Heaven.
28 You yourselves bear me witness that I said, "'I am not, The Christ, but that I am sent before Him.'"
29 He that has the bride is the Bridegroom, but the friend of the Bridegroom, which stands and Hears Him, Rejoices greatly, because of the Bridegroom's voice. This, my Joy therefore, is fulfilled.
30 He must Increase, but I must decrease.
31 He that comes from Above is above all. He that is of the Earth is earthly and speaks of the Earth. He that comes from Heaven is above all.
32 And what He has seen and heard, that He Testifies and no man Receives His Testimony.
33 He that has Received His Testimony, has set to His seal that God is True.
34 For He, Whom God has sent, speaks The Words of God, for God gives not The Spirit by measure to Him.
35 The Father Loves The Son and has Given All things, into His hand.
36 He that Believes on The Son, has everlasting Life and he that believes not, The Son, shall not see Life, but the wrath of God abides on Him."

Chapter 4

1 When therefore, The Lord knew how the Pharisees had heard that Jesus made and Baptized more disciples than John,
2 (Though Jesus Himself Baptized not, but His disciples)
3 He left Judaea and departed again, into Galilee.
4 And He must needs go through Samaria.
5 Then came He, to a city of Samaria, which is called Sychar; near to the parcel of ground that Jacob gave to his son, Joseph.
6 Now, Jacob's well was there. Jesus therefore, being wearied with His journey, sat thus, on the well and it was about the sixth hour.
7 There, came a woman of Samaria to draw water. Jesus said to her, "give Me to drink"
8 (For His disciples were gone away, to the city to buy meat.)
9 Then, said the woman of Samaria to Him, "how is it that You, being a Jew ask drink of me, which am a woman of Samaria? For the Jews have no dealings with the Samaritans."
10 Jesus answered and said to her, "if you Knew The Gift of God and Who it is that asks you, "'give Me to drink,'" you would have asked of Him and He would have Given you Living Water."
11 The woman said to Him, "Sir, You have nothing to draw with and the well is deep. From whence then, have You that Living Water?
12 Are You greater than our father, Jacob, which gave us the well and drank thereof, himself and his children and his cattle?"
13 Jesus answered and said to her, "whosoever, drinks of this water, shall thirst again,
14 But whosoever, Drinks of The Water that I shall Give him, shall never thirst. But, The Water that I shall Give him, shall be in him, a Well of Water springing up into everlasting Life."
15 The woman said to Him, "Sir, Give me this Water that I thirst not, neither come here to draw."

16 Jesus said to her, "go call your husband and come here."
17 The woman answered and said, "I have no husband." Jesus said to her, "you have well said, "'I have no husband.'"
18 For you have had five husbands and he, whom you now have, is not your husband. In that, you said, truly."
19 The woman said to Him, "Sir, I perceive that, You are a prophet."

20 Our fathers Worshipped in this mountain and You say that, "in Jerusalem, is the place where men ought to Worship."
21 Jesus said to her, "woman, Believe Me, the hour comes, when you shall neither in this mountain, nor yet at Jerusalem, Worship The Father.
22 You Worship, you know not what. We know, what we Worship, for Salvation is of the Jews.
23 But, THE HOUR COMES AND NOW IS, WHEN THE TRUE WORSHIPPERS, SHALL WORSHIP THE FATHER IN SPIRIT AND IN TRUTH, for The Father seeks such, to Worship Him.
24 God is a Spirit and they that Worship Him, must Worship Him in Spirit and in Truth.
25 The woman said to Him, "I know that Messiah comes, which is called, Christ. When He is come, He will tell us all things."
26 Jesus said to her, "I, that speak to you, am He."
27 And on this, came His disciples and marveled that He talked with the woman. Yet, no man said, "what seek You, or "why talk You with her?"
28 The woman then left her water pot and went her way into the city and said to the men,
29 "Come, see a Man, which told me all things that ever, I did. Is not, this The Christ?"
30 Then, they went out of the city and came to Him.
31 In the mean while, His disciples prayed Him saying, "Master, eat."
32 But, He said to them, "I have meat to eat that you know not of."
33 Therefore, said the disciples, one to another, "has any man brought Him anything to eat?"
34 Jesus said to them, "My meat, is to Do The Will of Him that sent Me and to Finish His Work.
35 Say you not, "'there are yet, four months and then, comes harvest?'" Behold, I say to you, "'lift up your eyes and look on the fields, for they are white, already to harvest.
36 And he that reaps, receives wages and gathers Fruit to Life Eternal that both he that sows and he that reaps, may rejoice, together.
37 And herein, is that saying true, ""one sows and another reaps.""
38 I sent you to reap that whereon, you bestowed no labor. Other men labored and you are entered into their labors."
39 And many of the Samaritans of that city, Believed on Him, for the saying of the woman, which Testified, "He told me all that ever, I did."
40 So, when the Samaritans had come to Him, they besought Him that He would tarry with them. And He abode there, two days.
41 And many more Believed, because of His Own Words
42 And said to the woman, "now, we Believe, not because of your saying, for we have Heard Him ourselves and Know that, this is indeed, The Christ; The Savior of the World."
43 Now after two days, He departed there and went into Galilee.
44 For Jesus Himself, Testified that, "a prophet has no honor in His own country."
45 Then, when He was come into Galilee, the Galilaeans Received Him, having Seen all the things that He Did at Jerusalem, at the feast, for they also, went to the feast.
46 So, Jesus came again, into Cana, of Galilee, where He made the water, wine. And there was a certain nobleman, whose son was sick at Capernaum.
47 When he heard that, Jesus was come out of Judaea, into Galilee he went to Him and besought Him that He would come down and Heal his son, for he was at the point of death.
48 Then, said Jesus to him, "except you see Signs and Wonders, you will not believe."
49 The nobleman said to him, "Sir, come down ere, my child dies."
50 Jesus said to him, "go your way, your son lives." And the man Believed The Word that Jesus had spoken to him and he went his way.
51 And as he was now going down, his servants met him and told him saying, "your son lives."
52 Then, enquired he of them, the hour when he began to Amend. And they said to him, "yesterday, at the seventh hour, the fever left him."
53 So, the father knew that it was at the same hour, in the which, Jesus said to him, "your son lives" and himself Believed and his whole house.
54 This is again, the second Miracle that Jesus did, when He was come out of

Judaea, into Galilee.

Chapter 5

1 After this, there was a feast of the Jews and Jesus went up to Jerusalem.
2 Now, there is at Jerusalem, by the sheep market, a pool, which is called in the Hebrew tongue, Bethesda; having five porches.
3 In these, lay a great multitude of impotent folks of blind, halt, withered; waiting for the moving of the water.
4 For an angel went down at a certain season, into the pool and troubled the water. Whosoever then first, after the troubling of the water, stepped in was made whole of whatsoever, disease he had.
5 And a certain man was there, which had an infirmity, thirty and eight years.

6 When Jesus saw him lie and knew that he had been now, a long time in that case, He asked him, "will you be Made Whole?"
7 The impotent man answered him, "Sir, I have no man, when the water is troubled, to put me into the pool. But while I am coming, another steps down before me."
8 Jesus said to him, "Rise, take up your bed and Walk."
9 And immediately, the man was Made Whole and took up his bed and Walked and on the same day, was the Sabbath.

10 The Jews therefore, said to Him that was Cured, "it is the Sabbath Day. It is not Lawful for you to carry your bed."
11 He answered them, "He that Made me Whole, the same said to me, "'Take Up your bed and Walk.'"
12 Then asked they him, "what Man is that, which said to you, "'Take Up your bed and Walk?'"
13 And he that was Healed knew not, Who it was, for Jesus had conveyed Himself away; a multitude being in that place.

14 Afterward, Jesus found him in the temple and said to him, "behold, you are Made Whole. Sin no more, lest a worse thing come to you."
15 The man departed and told the Jews that, it was Jesus, which had Made him Whole.
16 And therefore, did the Jews persecute Jesus and sought to slay Him, because He had Done these things on the Sabbath Day.

17 But, Jesus answered them, "My Father Works, hereto and I Work."
18 Therefore, the Jews sought the more, to kill Him, because He not only, had broken the Sabbath, but said also that, "God was His Father," making Himself Equal with God.
19 Then, answered Jesus and said to them, "verily, verily, I say to you, "'The Son can Do nothing of Himself, but what He sees The Father Do, for what things soever He Does, these also, Does The Son, likewise.
20 For The Father Loves The Son and Shows Him all things that Himself Does and He will Show Him Greater Works than these that you may marvel.
21 For as The Father Raises Up the dead and Quickens them, even so, The Son Quickens, whom He Will.
22 For The Father judges no man, but has committed all Judgment, to The Son
23 That all men, should Honor The Son, even as they Honor The Father. He that honors not, The Son, honors not, The Father, which has sent Him.

24 Verily, verily, I say to you, "'he that Hears My Word and Believes on Him that sent Me, has everlasting Life and shall not come into condemnation, but is passed from Death, to Life.'"
25 Verily, verily, I say to you, "'the hour is coming and now is, when the dead shall Hear the Voice of The Son of God and they that Hear, shall Live.
26 For as The Father has Life in Himself, so has He Given to The Son to have Life in Himself.
27 And has Given Him Authority to execute Judgment also, because He is The Son of Man.
28 Marvel not at this, FOR THE HOUR IS COMING, IN THE WHICH, ALL THAT ARE IN THE GRAVES, SHALL HEAR HIS VOICE,
29 And shall come forth; they, that have Done good, to the Resurrection of Life and they that have done evil, to the Resurrection of Damnation.'"

30 I can of My Own Self, do nothing. As I Hear, I Judge and My Judgment is Just, because I Seek not, My Own Will, but The Will of The Father, which has sent Me.
31 If I bear witness of Myself, My witness is not true.
32 There is Another that Bears Witness of

Me and I know that, The Witness, which He Witnesses of Me, is True.
33 You sent to John and he Bares Witness to The Truth.
34 But I receive not, testimony from man, but these things I say that, you might be Saved.
35 He was a Burning and a Shining Light and you were willing for a season to Rejoice in His Light.

36 But, I have Greater Witnesses than that of John, for the Works, which The Father has Given Me to Finish, the same Works that I Do, Bear Witness of Me that The Father has sent Me.
37 And The Father Himself, which has sent Me, has borne witness of Me. You have neither Heard His Voice at any time, nor seen His shape.
38 And you have not, His Word abiding in you, for Whom He has sent, Him you believe not.
39 Search The Scriptures. For in them, you think you have Eternal Life and they are they, which Testify of Me.
40 And you will not come to Me that you might have Life.

41 I receive not honor from men.
42 But I know you that you have not the Love of God in you.
43 I am come in My Father's Name and you receive Me not. If another shall come in his own name, him, you will receive.
44 How can you believe, which receive honor, one of another and seek not, the Honor that comes from God, only?

45 Do not think that I will accuse you to The Father. There is One that accuses you; even Moses, in whom you trust.
46 For had you believed Moses, you would have Believed Me, for he wrote of Me.
47 But, if you believe not, his writings, how shall you Believe My Words?"

Chapter 6

1 After these things, Jesus went over the Sea of Galilee, which is the Sea of Tiberias.
2 And a great multitudes followed Him, because they Saw His Miracles, which He did on them that were diseased.
3 And Jesus went up into a mountain and there, He sat with His disciples.
4 And The Passover; a feast of the Jews, was near.

5 When Jesus then, lifted up His eyes and saw a great company come to Him, He asked to Philip, "where shall we buy bread that these may eat?"
6 And this, He said to Prove him, for He Himself, Knew what He would Do.
7 Philip answered Him, "two hundred pennyworth of bread is not sufficient for them that every one of them may take a little."
8 One of His disciples, Andrew (Simeon Peter's brother) asked Him,
9 "There is a lad here, which has five barley loaves and two small fish, but what are they among so many?"
10 And Jesus said, "make the men sit down." Now, there was much grass in the place. So, the men sat down in numbers, about five thousand.

11 And Jesus took the loaves and when He had Given Thanks, He distributed to the disciples and the disciples to them that were set down and likewise, of the fish as much as they would.
12 When they were filled, He said to His disciples, "gather up the fragments that remain that nothing be lost."
13 Therefore, they gathered them together and filled twelve baskets with the fragments of the five barley loaves, which remained over and above to them that had eaten.
14 Then those men, when they had Seen the Miracle that Jesus Did said, "this is of a Truth, that prophet that should come into the World."
15 When Jesus therefore, perceived that they would come and take Him by force, to make him a king, He departed again, into a mountain Himself, alone.

16 And when evening was now come, His disciples went down to the Sea
17 And entered into a ship and went over the Sea, toward Capernaum. And it was now, dark and Jesus was not come to them.
18 And the Sea arose by reason of a great wind that blew.
19 So, when they had rowed about five and twenty, or thirty furlongs, they saw Jesus Walking On the Sea and drawing near to the ship and they were afraid.
20 But He said to them, "it is I. Be not afraid."
21 Then, they willingly received Him into the ship and immediately, the ship was at

the land where they went.

22 The day following, when the people which stood on the other side of the Sea, saw that there was none other boat there, save that one where into, His disciples were entered and that Jesus went not, with his disciples into the boat, but that his disciples were gone away alone

23 (Howbeit, there came other boats from Tiberias, near to the place where they did eat bread after that, The Lord had Given Thanks.)

24 When the people therefore, saw that Jesus was not there, neither His disciples, they also, took shipping and came to Capernaum, seeking for Jesus.

25 And when they had found Him on the other side of the Sea, they said to Him, "Rabbi, when came you here?"

26 Jesus answered them and said, "verily, verily, I say to you, "'you seek Me not, because you Saw the Miracles, but because you did eat of the loaves and were Filled.

27 Labor not for the meat which perishes, but for that meat, which endures to everlasting Life, which The Son of Man shall Give to you, for Him, has God, The Father Sealed.'"

28 Then they said to Him, "what shall we Do that we might Work the Works of God?"

29 Jesus answered and said to them, "this is the Work of God that, you Believe on Him, whom He has sent."

30 They said therefore, to Him, "what Sign show You then that we may See and Believe You? What do You Work?

31 Our fathers did eat manna in the desert as it is written, "He gave them bread from Heaven to eat."

32 Then, Jesus said to them, "verily, verily, I say to you, "'Moses gave you not that bread from Heaven, but My Father Gives you The True Bread from Heaven.

33 For The Bread of God is: He, which comes down from Heaven and Gives Life to the World.'"

34 Then said they to Him, "Lord, evermore, Give us This Bread."

35 And Jesus said to them, "I am The Bread of Life. He that Comes To Me shall never hunger and he that Believes on Me, shall never thirst.

36 But, I said to you that, "'you also, have Seen Me and believe not.

37 All that The Father Gives Me, shall come to Me and him that Comes To Me, I will in no wise, cast out.

38 For I came down from Heaven, not to do My Own will, but The Will of Him that sent Me.

39 And this is, The Father's Will, which has sent Me that of all, which He has Given Me, I should lose nothing, but should Raise it Up again, at the last day.

40 And this is The Will of Him that sent Me: that every one, which Sees The Son and Believes on Him, may have everlasting Life and I will Raise him Up at the last day.'"

41 The Jews then murmured at Him, because He said, "I am The Bread, which came down from Heaven."

42 And they said, "is not this Jesus, the son of Joseph, Whose father and mother we know? How is it then that He says, "'I came down from Heaven?'"

43 Jesus therefore, answered and said to them, "murmur not, among yourselves.

44 No man can Come To Me, except The Father, which has sent Me, Draws Him and I will Raise him Up at the last day.

45 It is written in the Prophets, "'...AND THEY SHALL BE ALL TAUGHT OF GOD...'" Every man therefore that has Heard and has Learned of The Father, Comes To Me;

46 Not that any man has seen The Father, save He, which is of God. He, has seen The Father.

47 Verily, verily, I say to you, "'he that Believes on Me, has everlasting Life.

48 I am that Bread of Life.

49 Your fathers did eat manna in the wilderness and are dead.

50 This is The Bread, which comes down from Heaven that a man may Eat, thereof and not Die.

51 I am The Living Bread, which came down from Heaven. If any man, Eats of this Bread, he shall Live for ever and The Bread that I will Give, is My Flesh, which I will Give, for the life of the World.'"

52 The Jews therefore, strove among themselves saying, "how can this Man, give us His Flesh to eat?"

53 Then Jesus said to them, "verily, verily, I say to you, "'except you Eat The Flesh of The Son of Man and Drink His Blood, you have no Life in you.

54 Whosoever, Eats My Flesh and Drinks My Blood, has Eternal Life and I will Raise him Up at the last day.

55 For My Flesh is Meat, indeed and My Blood is Drink, indeed.
56 He that Eats My Flesh and Drinks My Blood, Dwells in Me and I, in him.
57 As the Living Father has sent Me and I Live by The Father, so He that Eats Me, even he shall Live by Me.
58 This is that Bread, which came down from Heaven; not as your fathers did eat manna and are dead. He that Eats of this Bread, shall Live, for ever.'"

59 These things, He said in the synagogue, as He Taught in Capernaum.
60 Many therefore, of His disciples, when they had Heard this said, "this is a hard saying. Who can Hear it?"
61 When Jesus Knew in Himself that His disciples murmured at it, He said to them, "does this offend you?
62 What and if you shall see The Son of Man ascend up, where He was before?
63 It is The Spirit that Quickens. The flesh profits nothing. The Words that I speak to you, they are Spirit and they are Life.
64 But, there are some of you that believe not." For Jesus Knew from the beginning, who they were that believed not and who should betray Him.
65 And He said, "therefore, I said to you that, "'no man, can Come To Me, except it were Given to him of My Father.'"

66 From that time, many of His disciples went back and walked no more, with Him.
67 Then said Jesus, to the twelve, "will you also, go away?"
68 Then, Simeon Peter answered Him, "Lord, to whom shall we go? You have The Words of Eternal Life.
69 And we Believe and are sure that, You are that Christ; The Son of The Living God."
70 Jesus answered them, "have I not, Chosen you twelve and one of you is a devil?"
71 He spoke of Judas Iscariot, the son of Simeon, for he it was that should betray Him; being one of the twelve.

Chapter 7

1 After these things, Jesus walked in Galilee for He would not walk in Jewry, because the Jews sought to kill Him.
2 Now, the Jews' Feast of Tabernacles was at hand.
3 His brothers therefore, said to Him, "depart, hence and go into Judaea that Your disciples also, may see the Works that You Do.
4 For there is no man that does any thing, in secret and he himself, seeks to be known openly. If you Do these things, show Yourself to the World."
5 For neither did his brothers Believe in Him.
6 Then Jesus said to them, "My time is not yet come. But, your time is always ready.
7 The World cannot hate you. But Me, it hates, because I Testify of it that the works thereof, are evil.
8 Go yourselves up to this feast. I go not up yet, to this feast, for My time is not yet, fully come."
9 When He had said these words to them, He abode still, in Galilee.
10 But, when His brothers were gone up, then He went also, up to the feast; not openly, but as it were, in secret.

11 Then, the Jews sought Him at the feast and said, "where is He?"
12 And there was much murmuring among the people concerning Him, for some said, "He is a Good Man." Others said, "no, but He deceives the people."
13 Howbeit, no man spoke openly of Him, for fear of the Jews.
14 Now, about the midst of the feast, Jesus went up into the temple and Taught.
15 And the Jews marveled saying, "how Knows this Man letters, having never learned?"

16 Jesus answered them and said, "My Doctrine is not Mine, but His that sent Me.
17 If any man will Do His Will, he shall Know of The Doctrine, whether it be of God, or whether I speak of Myself.
18 He that speaks of himself, seeks his own glory, but He that seeks His Glory that sent Him, the same is True and no unrighteousness is in Him.
19 Did not Moses give you The Law and yet, none of you Keeps The Law? Why go you about to kill Me?"
20 The people answered and said, "You have a devil. Who goes about to kill You?"
21 Jesus answered and said to them, "I have done one Work and you all marvel.
22 Moses therefore, gave to you, circumcision (not because it is of Moses, but of The Father's) and you, on the Sabbath Day, circumcise a man.
23 If a man on the Sabbath Day, receives circumcision that the Law of Moses should

not be broken, are you angry at Me, because I have Made a man every whit, Whole on the Sabbath Day?
24 Judge not according to the appearance, but Judge Righteous Judgment."

25 Then said some of them of Jerusalem, "is not this He, Whom they seek to kill?
26 But lo, He speaks boldly and they say nothing, to Him. Do the rulers know indeed that this is The Very Christ?
27 Howbeit, we know this man, whence He is, but when Christ comes, no man knows where He is."
28 Then, cried Jesus in the temple as He Taught saying, "you both know Me and you know whence I am and I am not come of Myself, but He that sent Me is True, Whom you know not.
29 But, I Know Him, for I am from Him and He has sent Me."

30 Then they sought to take Him, but no man laid hands on Him, because His hour was not yet, come.
31 And many of the people Believed on Him and said, "when Christ comes, will He do more Miracles than these, which this Man has Done?"
32 The Pharisees heard that the people murmured such things, concerning Him and the Pharisees and the chief priests sent officers to take Him.
33 Then, Jesus said to them, "yet a little while, am I with you and then, I go to Him that sent Me.
34 You shall seek Me and shall not find Me and where I am, there, you cannot come."
35 Then, said the Jews among themselves, "where will He go that we shall not find Him? Will He go to the dispersed among the gentiles and Teach the gentiles?"
36 What manner of saying is this that He said, "you shall seek Me and shall not find Me and where I am, there you cannot come?"

37 In the last day, that great day of the feast, Jesus stood and cried saying, "if any man thirsts, let Him Come To Me and Drink.
38 HE THAT BELIEVES ON ME, as The Scripture has said, "'OUT OF HIS BELLY, SHALL FLOW RIVERS OF LIVING WATER.'"
39 But, this spoke He of The Spirit, which they that Believe on Him, should Receive, for The Holy Ghost was not yet, Given, because that, Jesus was not yet, Glorified.
40 Many of the people therefore, when they Heard this saying said, "of a Truth, this is THE PROPHET."
41 Others said, "this is THE CHRIST." But, some said, "SHALL CHRIST COME OUT OF GALILEE?"
42 Has not The Scripture said that, CHIRST COMES OF THE SEED OF DAVID AND OUT OF THE TOWN OF BETHLEHEN, WHERE DAVID WAS?"
43 So, there was a division among the people, because of Him.
44 And some of them would have taken Him, but no man, laid hands on Him.

45 Then, came the officers to the chief priests and Pharisees and they said to them, "why have you not brought Him?"
46 The officers answered, "never, man spoke like this Man."
47 Then answered them the Pharisees, "are you also, deceived?
48 Have any of the rulers, or of the Pharisees believed on Him?
49 But this people, who knows not, the Law are cursed."
50 Nicodemus said to them, (he that came to Jesus by night, being one of them)
51 "Does our Law Judge any man, before it hears him and knows what he does?"
52 They answered and said to him, "are you also, of Galilee? Search and look, for out of Galilee, arises no prophet."
53 And every man went to his own house.

Chapter 8

1 Jesus went to the Mount of Olives.
2 And early in the morning, He came again, into the temple and all the people came to Him and He sat down and Taught them.
3 And the scribes and Pharisees brought to Him, a woman taken in adultery and when they had set her in the midst,
4 They said to Him, "Master, this woman was taken in adultery, in the very act.
5 Now, Moses in the law commanded us that, such should be stoned. But, what say you?"
6 This they said, tempting Him that they might have to accuse Him. But, Jesus stooped down and with his finger, wrote on the ground, as though He heard them not.
7 So, when they continued asking Him, He lifted up Himself and said to them, "he that is without sin among you, let him first, cast a stone at her."

8 And again, He stooped down and wrote on the ground.
9 And they which heard it, being convicted by their own conscience, went out one by one, beginning at the eldest, even to the last. And Jesus was left alone and the woman standing, in the midst.
10 When Jesus had lifted up Himself and saw none, but the woman, He said to her, "woman, where are those, your accusers? Has no man condemned you?"
11 She said, "no man, Lord." And Jesus said to her, "neither do I condemn you. Go and sin, no more."

12 Then spoke Jesus again, to them saying, "I am The Light of the World. He that Follows Me, shall not walk in Darkness, but shall have The Light of Life."
13 The Pharisees therefore, said to Him, "You bear record of Yourself. Your Record, is not True."
14 Jesus answered and said to them, "though I Bear Record of Myself, yet My Record is True, for I know whence I came and where I go. But, you cannot tell whence I come and where I go.
15 You judge after the flesh. I judge no man.
16 And yet, if I Judge, My Judgment is True, for I am not alone, but I and The Father that sent Me.
17 It is also, written in your Law that the Testimony of two men is True.
18 I am One that Bears Witness of Myself and The Father that sent Me, Bears Witness of Me."

19 Then said they to Him, "where is Your Father?" Jesus answered, "you neither know Me, nor My Father. If you had Known Me, you should have Known My Father, also."
20 These Words spoke Jesus in the treasury, as He Taught in the temple and no man laid hands on Him, for his hour was not yet, come.
21 Then said Jesus again, to them, "I go My way and you shall seek Me and shall Die in your sins. Where I go, you cannot come."
22 Then said the Jews, "will He kill Himself?," because He said, "where I go, you cannot come."
23 And He said to them, "you are from beneath. I am from Above. You are of this World. I am not of this World.
24 I said therefore, to you that, "'you shall Die in your sins,'" for if you believe not that I am He, you shall Die in your sins.
25 Then, said they to Him, "Who are You?" And Jesus said to them, "even the same that I said to you from the beginning.
26 I have many things to say and to Judge of you, but He that sent Me is True and I speak to the World those things, which I have Heard of Him."
27 They understood not that He spoke to them of The Father.
28 Then said Jesus to them, "when you have Lifted Up The Son of Man, then you shall Know that I am He and that I Do nothing of Myself. But as My Father has Taught Me, I speak these things.
29 And He that sent Me, is with Me. The Father has not, left Me alone, for I Do Always, those things that Please Him."
30 As He spoke these Words, many Believed on Him.
31 Then said Jesus to those Jews, which Believed on Him, "if you Continue in My Word then, are you My disciples, indeed
32 And you shall Know The Truth and The Truth, shall make you Free."
33 They answered Him, "we are Abraham's seed and were never in bondage to any man. How say You, "you shall be made Free?"
34 Jesus answered them, "verily, verily, I say to you, "'whosoever, continues sinning, is the servant of sin.'"
35 And the servant abides not, in the house, for ever. But, The Son Abides, ever.
36 If The Son therefore, shall make you Free, you shall be Free indeed.
37 I know that you are Abraham's seed, but you seek to kill Me, because My Word has no place in you.
38 I speak that, which I have seen with My Father and you do that, which you have seen with your father."
39 They answered and said to Him, Abraham is our father. Jesus said to them, "if you were Abraham's children, you would do the Works of Abraham.
40 But now, you seek to kill Me; A Man that has told you The Truth, which I have Heard of God. This did not Abraham.
41 You do the deeds of your father." Then, they said to Him, "we are not born of fornication. We have one Father, even God."
42 Jesus said to them, "if God were your

Father, you would Love Me, for I proceeded forth and came from God. Neither came I, of Myself, but He sent Me.
43 Why do you not understand My speech? Even because, you cannot Hear My Word.
44 You are of your father, the Devil and the lusts of your father you will do. He was a murderer from the beginning and abode not in The Truth, because there is no Truth in him. When he speaks a lie, he speaks of his own, for he is a liar and the father of it.
45 And because I tell you The Truth, you believe Me not.
46 Which of you convicts Me of sin and if I say The Truth, why do you not believe Me?
47 He that is of God, Hears God's Words. You therefore, hear them not, because you are not of God."

48 Then, answered the Jews and said to Him, "say we not well that you are a Samaritan and have a devil?"
49 Jesus answered, "I have not a devil. But, I Honor My Father and you, do dishonor Me.
50 And I seek not, My Own Glory. There is One that Seeks and Judges.
51 Verily, verily, I say to you, "'if a man Keeps My Saying, he shall never see Death.'"
52 Then, the Jews said to Him, "now, we know that, You have a devil. Abraham is dead and the prophets and You say, "'if a man Keeps My Saying, he shall never taste of Death.'"
53 Are you Greater than our father, Abraham, which is dead and the prophets are dead? Whom make You, Yourself?

54 Jesus answered, "if I Honor Myself, My Honor is nothing. It is My Father that Honors Me, of Whom, you say that, He is your God,
55 Yet you have not known Him. But, I Know Him and if I should say, "'I know Him not,'" I shall be a liar like to you. But, I Know Him and Keep His Saying.
56 Your father, Abraham, Rejoiced to see My Day and he saw it and was Glad."
57 Then the Jews said to Him, "You are not yet, fifty years old. And have You seen Abraham?"
58 Jesus said to them, "verily, verily, I say to you, "'before Abraham was, I Am.'"
59 Then took they up stones to cast at Him, but Jesus hid Himself and went out of the temple; going through the midst of them and so, passed by.

Chapter 9

1 And as Jesus passed by, He saw a man which was blind from his birth.
2 And His disciples asked Him saying, "Master, who did sin; this man, or his parents that he was born blind?"
3 Jesus answered, "neither has this man sinned, nor his parents, but that the Works of God should be made manifest in him.
4 I must Work the Works of Him that sent me, while it is day. The night comes, when no man can Work.
5 As long as I am in the World, I am The Light of the World."
6 When He had thus spoken, He spat on the ground and made clay of the spit. And He anointed the eyes of the blind man with the clay,
7 And said to him, "go, wash in the pool of Siloam" (which is by interpretation, Sent.) He went his way, therefore and washed and came seeing."

8 The neighbors, therefore and they which before, had seen him that he was blind said, "is not this he that sat and begged?"
9 Some said, "this is he." Others said, "he is like him." But he said, "I am he."
10 Therefore, said they to him, "how were your eyes Opened?"
11 He answered and said, "A Man that is called, Jesus, made clay and anointed my eyes and said to me, "'go to the pool of Siloam and wash'" and I went and washed and I Received Sight."
12 Then they said to him, "where is He?" He said, "I know not."
13 They brought to the Pharisees, him that beforetime, was blind.
14 And it was the Sabbath Day, when Jesus made the clay and Opened his eyes.

15 Then again, the Pharisees also, asked him how he had Received his Sight. He said to them, "He put clay on my eyes and I washed and do See."
16 Therefore, some of the Pharisees said, "this Man is not of God, because He keeps not, the Sabbath Day." Others said, "how can a Man that is a sinner, do such Miracles?" And there was a division among them.
17 They said to the blind man again, "what say you, of Him that He has Opened your

eyes?" He said, "He is a Prophet."

18 But the Jews did not believe concerning Him that, he had been blind and Received his Sight, until they called the parents of him that had Received his Sight.

19 And they asked them saying, "is this your son, who you say was born blind? How then, does he now, See?"

20 His parents answered them and said, "we know that this is our son and that he was born blind,

21 But by what means he now sees, we know not, or Who has Opened his eyes, we know not. He is of age, ask him. He shall speak for himself."

22 These words spoke his parents, because they feared the Jews, for the Jews had agreed already that if any man did Confess that, He was Christ, he should be put out of the synagogue.

23 Therefore, his parents said, "he is of age, ask him."

24 Then again, they called the man that was blind and said to him, "Give God the Praise. We know that this Man is a sinner."

25 He answered and said, "whether He is a sinner or no, I know not. One thing I know that, whereas I was blind, now I See."

26 Then, they said to Him again, "what did He, to you? How Opened He your eyes?"

27 He answered them, "I have told you, already and you did not hear. Wherefore, would you hear it, again? Will you also, be His disciples?"

28 Then, they reviled him and said, "you are His disciple. But, we are Moses' disciples.

29 We know that God spoke to Moses. As for this Fellow, we know not, from whence He is."

30 The man answered and said to them, "why herein, is a marvelous thing that you know not, from whence He is and yet, He has Opened my eyes.

31 Now, we know that God hears not sinners, but if any man be a Worshipper of God and Does His Will, him He Hears.

32 Since the World began, was it not heard that, any man Opened the eyes of one that was born blind.

33 If this man were not of God, He could do nothing."

34 They answered and said to him, "you were altogether, born in sins and do you Teach us?" And they cast him out.

35 Jesus heard that they had cast him out. And when He had found him, He said to him, "do you Believe on The Son of God?"

36 He answered and said, "Who is He, Lord that I might Believe on Him?"

37 And Jesus said to him, "you have both Seen Him and it is He that talks with you."

38 And he said, "Lord, I Believe." And he Worshipped Him.

39 And Jesus said, "for Judgment, I am come into this World that they, which see not, might See and that they, which See, might be made blind."

40 And some of the Pharisees, which were with Him, heard these Words and said to Him, "are we blind, also?"

41 Jesus said to them, "if you were blind, you should have no sin. But now, you say, "'we See,'" therefore, your sin remains.

Chapter 10

1 Verily, verily, I say to you, "'He that enters not, by The Door into the sheepfold, but climbs up some other way, the same is a thief and a robber.

2 But He that enters in by The Door, is The Shepherd of the sheep.

3 To Him, The Porter opens and the sheep Hear His Voice and He calls His Own sheep by name and leads them out.

4 And when He puts forth, His Own sheep, He goes before them and the sheep Follow Him, for they Know His Voice.

5 And a stranger, will they not follow, but will flee from him, for they know not, the voice of strangers.'"

6 This parable, spoke Jesus to them, but they understood not, what things they were, which He spoke to them.

7 Then said Jesus to them again, "verily, verily, I say to you, "'I am The Door of the sheep.

8 All, that ever came before Me, are thieves and robbers, but the sheep did not hear them.

9 I am The Door. By Me, if any man enters in, he shall be Saved and shall go in and out and find pasture.

10 The thief comes not, but for to steal and to kill and to destroy. I am come that they might have Life and that, they might have it more abundantly.

11 I am The Good Shepherd. The Good Shepherd Gives His Life for the sheep.

12 But, he that is a hireling and not, The Shepherd, Whose Own, the sheep are not,

sees the wolf coming and leaves the sheep and flees. And the wolf catches them and scatters the sheep.
13 The hireling flees, because he is a hireling and Cares not for the sheep.
14 I am The Good Shepherd and Know My sheep and am Known of Mine.
15 As The Father Knows Me, even so, Know I, The Father and I lay down My Life for the sheep.
16 And other sheep I have, which are not of this fold. Them also, I must bring and they shall Hear My Voice and there shall be one fold and one Shepherd.
17 Therefore, does My Father Love Me, because I lay down My Life that I might take it, again.
18 No man, takes it from Me, but I lay it down of Myself. I have Power to lay it down and I have Power to take it again. This Commandment have I received of My Father.'"
19 There was a division therefore again, among the Jews for these sayings.
20 And many of them said, "He has a devil and is mad. Why Hear you, Him?"
21 Others said, "these are not The Words of him that has a devil. Can a devil Open the eyes of the blind?"

22 And it was at Jerusalem, The Feast of the Dedication and it was Winter.
23 And Jesus walked in the temple, in Solomon's porch.
24 Then, came the Jews, round about Him and said to Him, "how long do You make us to doubt? If you are The Christ, tell us plainly."
25 Jesus answered them, "I told you and you believed not. The Works that I Do, In My Father's Name, they Bear Witness of Me.
26 But, you believe not, because you are not of My sheep, as I said to you.
27 My sheep Hear My Voice and I Know them and they Follow Me
28 And I Give to them Eternal Life and they shall never perish, neither shall any man, pluck them out of My hand.
29 My Father, which Gave them Me, is Greater than all. And no man, is able to pluck them out of My Father's hand.
30 I and My Father are One."
31 Then, the Jews took up stones again, to stone Him.

32 Jesus answered them, "many Good Works, have I shown you from My Father. For which of those Works, do you stone Me?"
33 The Jews answered Him saying, "for a Good Work, we stone You not, but for blasphemy and because that, You, being a Man, make Yourself, God."
34 Jesus answered them, "is it not written in your law, I said, "'you are gods?'"
35 If He called them gods, to whom, The Word of God came and The Scripture cannot be broken,
36 Say yourselves of Him, Whom The Father has Sanctified and sent into the World, "'You blaspheme,'" because I said, "'I am The Son of God?'"
37 If I do not, the Works of My Father, believe Me not.
38 But if I do, though you believe not Me, Believe the Works that, you may Know and Believe that The Father is in Me and I in Him."
39 Therefore, they sought again, to take Him, but He escaped out of their hand
40 And went away again, beyond Jordan, into the place where John, at first Baptized and there, He abode.
41 And many resorted to Him and said, "John did no Miracle, but all things that John spoke of this Man were True."
42 And many Believed on Him there.

Chapter 11

1 Now, a certain man was sick named, Lazarus, of Bethany; the town of Mary and her sister, Martha
2 (It was that Mary, which Anointed The Lord with ointment and wiped His feet with her hair, whose brother, Lazarus was sick.)
3 Therefore, his sisters sent to Him saying, "Lord behold, he whom You love is sick."
4 When Jesus heard that, He said, "this sickness is not to death, but for the Glory of God that The Son of God, might be Glorified, thereby."

5 Now, Jesus loved Martha and her sister and Lazarus.
6 When He had heard therefore that he was sick, He abode two days, still in the same place, where He was.
7 Then after that, He said to His disciples, "let us go into Judaea, again."
8 His disciples said to Him, "Master, the Jews of late, sought to stone You and You go there, again?"
9 Jesus answered, "are there not twelve hours in the day? If any man walks in the

day, he stumbles not, because he sees the light of this World.
10 But, if a man walks in the Night, he stumbles, because there is no light in himself."

11 These things, said He and after that, He said to them, "our friend, Lazarus sleeps. But I go that I may wake him out of sleep."
12 Then, His disciples said, "Lord, if he sleeps, he shall do well."
13 Howbeit, Jesus spoke of his death. But they thought that He had spoken of taking of rest, in sleep.
14 Then Jesus said to them plainly, "Lazarus is dead.
15 And I am glad for your sakes that I was not there, to the intent, you may Believe. Nevertheless, let us go to him."
16 Then Thomas said, which is called, Didymus, to his fellow disciples, "let us also, go that we may die with him."
17 Then when Jesus came, He found that, he had laid in the grave, four days, already.

18 Now, Bethany was near to Jerusalem, about fifteen furlongs off.
19 And many of the Jews came to Martha and Mary, to comfort them, concerning their brother.
20 Then Martha, as soon as she heard that Jesus was coming, went and met Him. But Mary sat still, in the house.
21 Then said Martha to Jesus, "Lord, if You had been here, my brother had not died.
22 But I know that even now, whatsoever, You will ask of God, God will Give it You."

23 Jesus said to her, "your brother, shall Rise again."
24 Martha said to Him, "I know that he shall Rise again, in the Resurrection at the last day."
25 Jesus said to her, "I am The Resurrection and The Life. He that Believes in Me, though he were dead, yet he shall Live
26 And whosoever, Lives and Believes in Me, shall never Die. You Believe this?"
27 She said to Him, "yes, Lord. I Believe that You are The Christ; The Son of God, which should come into the World."
28 And when she had so said, she went her way and called Mary, her sister secretly saying, "The Master is come and calls for you."
29 As soon as she heard that, she arose quickly and came to Him.
30 Now, Jesus was not yet come into the town, but was in that place, where Martha met Him.
31 The Jews then, which were with her in the house and comforted her, when they saw Mary that she rose up hastily and went out, followed her saying, "she goes to the grave to weep there."
32 Then, when Mary was come where Jesus was and saw Him, she fell down at His feet saying to Him, "Lord, if You had been here, my brother had not died."
33 When Jesus therefore, saw her weeping and the Jews also, weeping which came with her, He groaned in The Spirit and was troubled.
34 And said, "where have you laid him?" They said to Him, "Lord, come and see."35 Jesus wept.

36 Then said the Jews, "behold, how He loved him!"
37 And some of them said, "could not this Man, which Opened the eyes of the blind, have caused that, even this man, should not have died?"
38 Jesus therefore again, groaning in Himself, came to the grave. It was a cave and a stone laid on it.
39 Jesus said, "take you away the stone." Martha, the sister of him that was dead, said to Him, "Lord, by this time, he stinks. For he has been dead four days."
40 Jesus asked her, "said I not to you that, if you would Believe, you should see the Glory of God?"

41 Then they took away the stone from the place, where the dead was laid. And Jesus lifted up His eyes and said, "Father, I Thank You that You have Heard Me.
42 And I knew that You Hear Me always, but because of the people which stand by, I said it that they may Believe that, You have sent Me."
43 And when He thus, had spoken, He cried with a loud voice, "Lazarus, come forth!"
44 And He that was dead, came forth; bound hand and foot, with grave clothes and his face was bound about, with a napkin. Jesus said to them, "loose him and let him go."
45 Then, many of the Jews, which came to Mary and had seen the things which Jesus Did, Believed on Him.
46 But some of them went their ways to the

Pharisees and told them what things Jesus had Done.

47 Then, gathered the chief priests and the Pharisees a council and said, "what do we..? For this Man Does many Miracles.
48 <u>If we let Him thus alone, all men will Believe on Him and the Romans, shall come and take away, both our place and nation."</u>
49 And one of them, named Caiaphas, being the high priest that same year said to them, "you know nothing at all,
50 Nor consider that, it is expedient for us that one Man should die for the people and that, the whole nation perish not."
51 And this he spoke not of himself, but being high priest that year, he Prophesied that, JESUS SHOULD DIE FOR THAT NATION
52 AND NOT FOR THAT NATION ONLY, BUT THAT ALSO, HE SHOULD GATHER TOGETHER IN ONE, THE CHILDREN OF GOD THAT WERE SCATTERED ABROAD.
53 Then, from that day forth, they took counsel together, for to put Him to death.
54 Jesus therefore, walked no more, openly among the Jews, but went there, to a country near to the wilderness; into a city called, Ephraim and there, continued with His disciples.

55 And the Jews' Passover was near at hand. And many went out of the country, up to Jerusalem before The Passover, to purify themselves.
56 Then, sought they for Jesus and spoke among themselves, as they stood in the temple, "what think you that He will not come to the feast?"
57 Now, both the chief priests and the Pharisees had given a commandment that, if any man knew where He were, he should show it that they might take Him.

Chapter 12

1 Then Jesus, six days before The Passover, came to Bethany, where Lazarus was, which had been dead; whom He Raised from the dead.
2 There, they made Him a supper and Martha Served, but Lazarus was one of them that sat at the table with Him.

3 Then, Mary took a pound of ointment of spikenard, very costly and Anointed the feet of Jesus and wiped His feet with her hair and the house was filled with the odor of the ointment.
4 Then asked one of His disciples, Judas Iscariot, (Simeon's son; which should betray Him)
5 "Why was not, this ointment sold for three hundred pence and given to the poor?"
6 (This he said not that he cared for the poor, but because he was a thief and had the bag and bare what was put, therein.)

7 Then said Jesus, "let her alone. Against the day of My burying, has she kept this.
8 For the poor always, you have with you, but Me, you have not always."
9 Much people of the Jews therefore, knew that He was there and they came not, for Jesus' sake only, but that they might see Lazarus also, whom He had Raised from the dead.
10 But the chief priests consulted that, <u>they might put Lazarus also, to death</u>,
11 Because that, by reason of him, many of the Jews went away and Believed on Jesus.

12 On the next day, much people that had come to the feast, when they heard that Jesus was coming to Jerusalem,
13 Took branches of palm trees and went forth, to meet Him and cried, "HOSANNA, BLESSED IS THE KING OF ISRAEL THAT COMES IN THE NAME OF THE LORD!"
14 And Jesus, when He had found a young ass, sat thereon, as it is written,
15 "FEAR NOT, DAUGHTER OF SION. BEHOLD, YOUR KING COMES, SITTING ON AN ASS'S COLT."
16 These things, understood not, His disciples at the first, but when Jesus was Glorified, then remembered they that these things were written of Him and that they had done these things to Him.

17 The people, therefore that were with Him, when He called Lazarus out of his grave and Raised him from the dead, bare record.
18 For this cause, the people also, met Him, for that they heard that, He had Done this Miracle.
19 The Pharisees therefore, said among themselves, "perceive you, how you prevail nothing? Behold, the World is gone after Him."
20 And there were certain Greeks among them that came up to Worship at the feast.
21 The same came therefore, to Philip,

which was of Bethsaida, of Galilee and desired him saying, "Sir, we would see Jesus."
22 Philip came and told Andrew and again, Andrew and Philip, told Jesus.

23 And Jesus answered them saying, "the hour is come that The Son of Man should be Glorified.
24 Verily, verily, I say to you, "'except a corn of wheat falls into the ground and dies, it abides alone. But, if it dies, it brings forth much fruit.'"
25 He that loves his life, shall lose it and he that hates his life, in this World, shall Keep it to Life Eternal.
26 If any man Serves Me, let him Follow Me and where I am, there shall also, My servant be. If any man Serves Me, him will My Father Honor.

27 Now, is My soul troubled. And what shall I say? Father, save Me from this hour. But, for this cause, I came to this hour.
28 Father, Glorify Your Name." Then, came there A Voice from Heaven saying, "I have both Glorified it and will Glorify it, again."
29 The people therefore that stood by and Heard it said that, "it thundered." Others said, "an angel spoke to Him."
30 Jesus answered and said, "this Voice came not, because of Me, but for your sakes.
31 Now, is the Judgment of this World. Now, shall the prince of this World be cast out.
32 And I, if I be Lifted Up from the Earth, will Draw all men to Myself."
33 This He said, signifying what death He should die.
34 The people answered Him, "we have heard out of The Law that Christ abides, for ever. And how say you, "'The Son of Man must be Lifted Up?'" Who is this, Son of Man?"

35 Then, Jesus said to them, "yet a little while, is The Light with you. Walk while you have The Light, lest Darkness comes on you. For he that walks in Darkness knows not where he goes.
36 While you have Light, Believe in The Light that you may be the children of Light." These things, spoke Jesus and departed and did hide Himself from them.
37 BUT, THOUGH HE HAD DONE SO MANY MIRACLES BEFORE THEM, YET THEY BELIEVED NOT, ON HIM,
38 That the saying of Isaiah, the prophet might be Fulfilled, which he spoke, "LORD, WHO HAS BELIEVED OUR REPORT AND TO WHOM, HAS THE ARM OF THE LORD BEEN REVEALED?"
39 Therefore, they could not believe, because that Isaiah said again,
40 "HE HAS BLINDED THEIR EYES AND HARDENED THEIR HEART THAT THEY SHOULD NOT SEE WITH THEIR EYES, NOR UNDERSTAND WITH THEIR HEART AND BE CONVERTED AND I SHOULD HEAL THEM."
41 These things, said Isaiah, when he saw His Glory and spoke of Him.
42 Nevertheless, among the chief rulers also, many Believed on Him, but because of the Pharisees, they did not Confess Him, lest they should be put out of the synagogue,
43 For they loved the praise of men, more than the Praise of God.

44 Jesus cried and said, "he that Believes on Me, Believes not, on Me, but on Him that sent Me!
45 And he that Sees Me, Sees Him that sent Me!
46 I am Come, A Light into the World that whosoever, Believes on Me, should not abide in Darkness!
47 And if any man Hears My Words and believes not, I judge him not, for I came not to judge the World, but to Save the World.
48 He that rejects Me and receives not, My Words, has One that Judges him: The Word that I have spoken. The same, shall Judge him in the last day.
49 For I have not spoken of Myself, but The Father, which sent Me. He Gave Me a Commandment; what I should say and what I should speak.
50 And I know that, His Commandment is Life everlasting. Whatsoever, I speak therefore, even as The Father said to Me, so I speak."

Chapter 13

1 Now, before the feast of The Passover, when Jesus knew that His hour was come that He should depart out of this World to The Father; having Loved His Own, which were in the World, He Loved them to the end.
2 And supper being ended, the Devil having now, put into the heart of Judas Iscariot (Simeon's son) to betray Him,

3 Jesus knowing that, The Father had Given All things, into His hands and that He was come from God and went to God,
4 He rose from supper and laid aside His garments and took a towel and girded Himself.
5 After that, He poured water into a basin and began to wash the disciples' feet and to wipe them with the towel wherewith, He was girded.
6 Then came He, to Simeon Peter and Peter asked Him, "Lord, do you wash my feet?"
7 Jesus answered and said to him, "what I do, you know not now, but you shall know, hereafter."
8 Peter said to Him, "You shall never, wash my feet." Jesus answered him, "if I wash you not, you have no part with Me."
9 Simeon Peter said to Him, "Lord, not my feet only, but also, my hands and my head."
10 Jesus said to him, "he that is washed needs not, save to wash his feet, but is clean every whit and you are clean, but not all."
11 For He Knew who should betray Him. Therefore, He said, "you are not all clean."

12 So, after He had washed their feet and had taken His garments and was set down again, He said to them, "know you what I have done to you?
13 You call Me Master and Lord and you say well, for so I am.
14 If I then, your Lord and Master, have washed your feet, you also, ought to wash one another's feet.
15 For I have given you an example that you should do as I have done to you.
16 Verily, verily, I say to you, "'the servant is not greater than his Lord. Neither He that is sent, Greater than He that sent Him.'"
17 If you know these things, happy are you, if you do them.

18 I speak not of you all. I Know whom I have Chosen, but that The Scripture may be Fulfilled, "'HE THAT EATS BREAD WITH ME, HAS LIFTED UP HIS HEEL AGAINST ME.'"
19 Now, I tell you before it comes that when it is come to pass, you may Believe that I am He.
20 Verily, verily, I say to you, "'he that receives whomsoever, I send, Receives Me and He that Receives Me, Receives Him that sent Me.'"
21 When Jesus had thus said, He was troubled in Spirit and Testified and said, "verily, verily, I say to you that one of you, shall betray Me."
22 Then, the disciples looked one on another, doubting of whom He spoke.
23 Now, there was leaning on Jesus' bosom, one of his disciples, whom Jesus loved.
24 Simeon Peter therefore, beckoned to Him that He should ask who it should be of whom, He spoke.
25 He then lying on Jesus' breast asked Him, "Lord, who is it?"
26 Jesus answered, "he it is, to whom I shall give a sop, when I have dipped it." And when He had dipped the sop, He gave it to Judas Iscariot (the son of Simeon.)
27 And after the sop, Satan entered into him. Then Jesus said to him, "that you do, do quickly."

28 Now, no man at the table, knew for what intent He spoke this to him.
29 For some of them thought, because Judas had the bag that Jesus had said to him, 'buy those things that we have need of against the feast,' or that, 'he should give something to the poor.'
30 He then having received the sop, went immediately, out and it was night.

31 Therefore, when he was gone out, Jesus said, "now, is The Son of Man Glorified and God is Glorified in Him.
32 If God be Glorified in Him, God shall also, Glorify Him in Himself and shall straightway, Glorify Him.
33 Little children, yet a little while, I am with you. You shall Seek Me and as I said to the Jews, "'where I go, you cannot come,'" so now, I say to you.
34 A New Commandment I Give to you that, "'you Love one another, as I have Loved you that you also, Love one another.'"
35 By this, shall all men Know that you are My disciples; if you have Love, one to another."
36 Simeon Peter said to Him, "Lord, where go You?" Jesus answered him, "where I go, you can not follow Me now, but you shall follow Me, afterwards."
37 Peter said to Him, "Lord, why cannot I follow You, now? I will lay down my life for Your sake."
38 Jesus answered him, "will you lay down

your life for My sake? Verily, verily, I say to you, "'THE COCK SHALL NOT CROW, UNTIL YOU HAVE DENIED ME THRICE.'"

Chapter 14

1 Let not your hearts be troubled. You Believe in God. Believe also, in Me.
2 In My Father's house are many mansions. If it were not so, I would have told you. I go to prepare a place for you.
3 And if I go and prepare a place for you, I will come again and Receive you to Myself that where I am, there you may be, also.
4 And where I go, you Know and The Way you Know."
5 Thomas asked Him, "Lord, we know not, where you go. And how can we Know The Way?"

6 Jesus said to him, "I am The Way, The Truth and The Life. No man, Comes to The Father, but by Me.
7 If you had Known Me, you should have Known My Father, also. And from henceforth, you Know Him and have seen Him."
8 Philip said to him, "Lord, show us The Father and it suffices us."
9 Jesus asked him, "have I been so long time with you and yet, have you not known Me, Philip? He that has seen Me, has seen The Father. And how say you then, "'show us The Father?'"
10 Believe you not that I am in The Father and The Father in Me? The Words that I speak to you, I speak not of Myself, but The Father that dwells in Me. He Does the Works.
11 Believe Me that, I am in The Father and The Father in Me, or else, Believe Me, for the very Works' sake.

12 Verily, verily, I say to you, "he that Believes on Me, the Works that I Do, he shall Do, also and Greater Works than these, he shall Do, because I go to My Father.
13 And whatsoever, you shall Ask In My Name, that will I Do that The Father may be Glorified in The Son.
14 If you shall ask any thing, in My Name, I will Do it.
15 If you Love Me, Keep My Commandments
16 And I will Pray The Father and He shall Give you another Comforter that He may Abide with you, for ever;

17 Even The Spirit of Truth, Whom the World cannot receive, because it sees Him not, neither knows Him, but you Know Him, for He Dwells with you and shall be in you.

18 I will not leave you comfortless. I will come to you.
19 Yet a little while and the World sees Me, no more. But, you see Me. Because I Live, you shall Live, also.
20 At that day, you shall Know that I am in My Father and you, in Me and I, in you.
21 He that Has My Commandments and Keeps them, he it is, that Loves Me. And he that Loves Me, shall be Loved of My Father and I will Love him and will Manifest Myself, to him."
22 Judah asked Him (not Iscariot) "Lord, how is it that, You will Manifest Yourself to us and not to the World?"

23 Jesus answered and said to him, "if a man Loves Me, he will Keep My Words. And My Father will Love him. And We will come to him and make Our abode with him.
24 He that loves Me not, keeps not, My Sayings. And The Word, which you Hear is not Mine, but The Father's, which sent Me.
25 These things, have I spoken to you; being yet, present with you.
26 But, The Comforter, which is The Holy Ghost, Whom The Father will send in My Name, He shall Teach you all things and bring all things, to your remembrance, whatsoever I have said to you.
27 Peace I leave with you. My Peace, I Give to you, not as the World gives, I Give to you. Let not your hearts be troubled, neither let it be afraid.

28 You have heard how, I said to you, "'I go away and come again, to you.'" If you Loved Me, you would Rejoice, because I said, "'I go to The Father, for My Father is Greater, than I.'"
29 And now, I have told you before it comes to pass that, when it is comes to pass, you might Believe.
30 Hereafter, I will not talk much with you, for the prince of this World comes and has nothing in Me.
31 But that the World may know that, I Love The Father. And as The Father Gave Me Commandment, even so, I Do. Arise, let us go, hence.

Chapter 15

1 I am The True Vine and My Father is The Husbandman.
2 Every branch in Me that bears not fruit, He takes away and every branch that Bears Fruit, He Purges it that it may Bring Forth More Fruit.
3 Now, you are Clean through The Word, which I have spoken to you.
4 Abide in Me and I in you. As the branch cannot bear fruit of itself, except it Abides in The Vine, no more can you, except you abide in Me.
5 I am The Vine. You are the branches. He that Abides in Me and I in him, the same Brings Forth Much Fruit, for without Me, you can do nothing.
6 If a man abides not, in Me, he is cast forth, as a branch and is withered and men gather them and cast them into the fire and they are burned.
7 If you Abide in Me and My Words Abide in you, you shall Ask what you will and it shall be Done to you.
8 Herein, is My Father Glorified that you Bear Much Fruit, so you shall be My disciples.
9 As The Father has Loved Me, so have I Loved you. Continue yourselves, in My Love.
10 If you Keep My Commandments, you shall Abide in My Love, even as I have Kept My Father's Commandments and Abide in His Love.
11 These things, have I spoken to you that My Joy might remain in you and that, your Joy might be Full.
12 This is My Commandment that: you Love one another, as I have Loved you.
13 Greater Love has no man than this that, a Man lays down his life for his friends.
14 You are My friends, if you Do Whatsoever, I Command you.
15 Henceforth, I call you not, servants. For the servant knows not, what his Lord does, but I have called you friends, for all things that I have Heard of My Father, I have made Known to you.
16 You have not, Chosen Me, but I have Chosen you and Ordained you that you should go and Bring Forth Fruit and that your Fruit should remain that whatsoever, you shall Ask of The Father in My Name, He may Give it you.
17 These things, I Command you that, you Love one another.
18 If the World hates you, you know that it hated Me, before it hated you.
19 If you were of the World, the World would love his own, but because you are not, of the World, but I have Chosen you, out of the World. Therefore, the World hates you.
20 Remember The Word that I said to you, "'the servant is not greater than his Lord.'" If they have persecuted Me, they will also, persecute you. If they have Kept My sayings, they will keep yours, also.
21 But all these things, will they do to you, for My Name's sake, because they know not, Him that sent Me.
22 If I had not come and spoken to them, they had not had sin. But now, they have no cloak for their sin.
23 He that hates Me, hates My Father, also.
24 If I had not done among them, the Works which none other man did, they had not had sin. But now, have they both seen and hated both Me and My Father.
25 But this comes to pass that The Word might be Fulfilled that is written in their Law, "'THEY HATED ME WITHOUT A CAUSE.'"
26 BUT, WHEN THE COMFORTER IS COME, WHOM I WILL SEND TO YOU, FROM THE FATHER; EVEN THE SPIRIT OF TRUTH, WHICH PROCEEDS FROM THE FATHER, HE SHALL TESTIFY OF ME.
27 And you also, shall bear witness, because you have been with Me, from the beginning.

Chapter 16

1 These things, have I spoken to you that you should not be offended.
2 THEY SHALL PUT YOU OUT OF THE SYNAGOGUES. YES, THE TIME COMES THAT WHOSOEVER KILLS YOU, WILL THINK THAT HE DOES GOD SERVICE.
3 And these things, will they do to you, because they have not known The Father, nor Me.
4 But these things, have I told you that when the time shall come, you may remember that I told you of them. And these things, I said not to you, at the beginning, because I was with you.
5 But now, I go My Way to Him that sent Me and none of you asks me, "'where go You?'"

6 But, because I have said these things to you, sorrow has filled your heart.

7 Nevertheless, I tell you The Truth. It is expedient for you that I go away, for if I go not away, <u>The Comforter</u> will not come to you. But if I depart, I will send Him to you.
8 And when He is come, He will Reprove the World of sin and of Righteousness and of Judgment:
9 Of sin, because they believe not, on Me;
10 Of Righteousness, because I go to <u>My Father</u> and you see <u>Me</u>, no more;
11 Of Judgment, because the prince of this World is Judged.
12 I have yet, many things to say to you, but you cannot bear them now.

13 <u>HOWBEIT, WHEN HE, THE SPIRIT OF TRUTH IS COME, HE WILL GUIDE YOU INTO ALL TRUTH. FOR HE SHALL NOT SPEAK OF HIMSELF, BUT WHATSOEVER, HE SHALL HEAR, THAT SHALL HE SPEAK AND HE WILL SHOW YOU THINGS TO COME.</u>
14 HE SHALL GLORIFY ME, FOR HE SHALL RECEIVE OF MINE AND SHALL SHOW IT TO YOU.
15 All things that The Father has, are Mine. Therefore said I that He shall take of Mine and shall Show it to you.
16 A little while and you shall not see Me and again, a little while and you shall see Me, because I go to The Father."

17 Then asked some of His disciples among themselves, "what is this that, He said to us, "'a little while and you shall not see Me and again, a little while and you shall see Me and because I go to the Father?'"
18 They asked therefore, "what is this that, He said, "'a little while?'" We cannot tell what He said."
19 Now, Jesus Knew that they were desirous to ask Him and said to them, "do you enquire among yourselves of that I said, "'a little while and you shall not see Me and again, a little while and you shall see Me?'"
20 Verily, verily, I say to you that, "'YOU SHALL WEEP AND LAMENT, BUT THE WORLD SHALL REJOICE. AND YOU SHALL BE SORROWFUL, BUT YOUR SORROW SHALL BE TURNED INTO JOY.'"
21 A woman, when she is in travail, has sorrow, because her hour is come. But, as soon as she is delivered of the child, she remembers no more, the anguish, for joy that a man is born into the World.
22 And you now therefore, have sorrow, but I will see you again and your heart shall Rejoice and your Joy, no man takes from you.
23 And in that day, you shall ask Me anything. Verily, verily, I say to you, "'whatsoever, you shall Ask The Father in My Name, He will Give it you.
24 Hereto, have you asked nothing. In My Name, Ask and you shall Receive that your Joy may be Full.'"
25 These things have I spoken to you in proverbs, but the time comes, when I shall no more speak to you in proverbs, but I shall show you plainly of The Father.
26 At that day, you shall Ask in My Name and I say not, to you that I will Pray The Father for you.
27 For the Father Himself, Loves you, because you have Loved Me and have Believed that I came out from God.
28 I came forth from The Father and am come into the World. Again, I leave the World and go to The Father."

29 His disciples said to Him, "lo now, speak Yourself plainly and speak no proverb.
30 Now, are we sure that You Know All things and need not that any man should ask You. By this, we Believe that You came forth from God."
31 Jesus answered them, "do you now, Believe?
32 Behold, the hour comes; yes, is now come that YOU SHALL BE SCATTERED; EVERY MAN, TO HIS OWN AND SHALL LEAVE ME, ALONE and yet, I am not alone, because The Father is with Me.
33 These things, I have spoken to you that in Me, you might have Peace. <u>In the World, you shall have tribulation, but be of good cheer, I have overcome the World."</u>

Chapter 17

1 These Words, spoke Jesus and lifted up His eyes to Heaven and said, "Father, the hour is come. Glorify Your Son that Your Son also, may Glorify You.
2 As You have Given Him Power over all flesh that He should Give Eternal Life to as many as You have Given Him.
3 And this is Life Eternal that: <u>they might Know You; The Only True God and Jesus Christ, Whom You have sent.</u>
4 I have Glorified You on the Earth. I have

Finished the Work, which You Gave Me to Do.

5 And now, O Father, Glorify You, Me with Your Own Self, with The Glory, which I had with You, before the World was.

6 I have manifested Your Name to the men, which You gave Me out of the World. Yours, they were and You gave them Me and they have Kept Your Word.

7 Now, they have known that all things whatsoever, You have Given Me are of You.

8 For I have Given to them The Words, which You Gave Me and they have Received them and have Known surely that, I came out from You and they have Believed that You did send Me.

9 I Pray for them. I Pray not, for the World, but for them, which You have given Me, for they are Yours.

10 And all Mine, are Yours and Yours, are Mine and I am Glorified in them.

11 And now, I am no more, in the World, but these are in the World and I come to You. Holy Father, Keep through Your Own Name, those whom, You have given Me that they may be one as We are.

12 While I was with them in the World, I Kept them in Your Name. Those that You gave Me, I have Kept and none of them is lost, but the son of perdition that The Scripture might be Fulfilled.

13 And now, I come to You and these things, I speak in the World that they might have My Joy fulfilled in them.

14 I have Given them Your Word and the World has hated them, because they are not of the World; even as I am not of the World.

15 I Pray not that You should take them out of the World, but that You should Keep them from the evil.

16 They are not of the World; even as I am not of the World.

17 Sanctify them through Your Truth. Your Word is Truth.

18 As You have sent Me into the World, even so, have I also, sent them into the World.

19 And for their sakes, I Sanctify Myself that they also, might be Sanctified through The Truth.

20 Neither Pray I for these alone, but for them also, which shall Believe on Me through their word

21 That they all may be one, as You, Father, are in Me and I in You that they also, may be one in Us that the World may Believe that You have sent Me.

22 And The Glory, which You gave Me, I have given them that they may be one; even as We are one;

23 I, in them and You in Me that they may be made perfect in one and that the World may know that You have sent Me and have Loved them, as You have Loved Me.

24 Father, I will that they also, whom You have given Me, be with Me where I am that they may behold My Glory, which You have given Me, for You Loved Me before the foundation of the World.

25 O Righteous Father, the World has not known You, but I have Known You and these have Known that You have sent Me.

26 And I have declared to them Your Name and will declare it that, the Love wherewith, You have Loved Me may be in them and I, in them."

Chapter 18

1 When Jesus had spoken these Words, He went forth with His disciples over the brook, Cedron; where was a garden, into the which, He entered and His disciples.

2 And Judas also, which betrayed Him, knew the place, for Jesus oftentimes resorted there, with His disciples.

3 Judas then, having received a band of men and officers from the chief priests and Pharisees, came there, with lanterns and torches and weapons.

4 Jesus therefore, Knowing all things that should come on Him, went forth and said to them, "Whom seek you?"

5 They answered Him, "Jesus of Nazareth." Jesus said to them, "I am He." And Judas also, which betrayed Him, stood with them.

6 As soon then, as He had said to them, "I am He," they went backward and fell to the ground.

7 Then asked He them again, "Whom seek you?" And they said, "Jesus of Nazareth."

8 Jesus answered, "I have told you that I am He. If therefore, you seek Me, let these, go their way"

9 That the saying might be Fulfilled, which He spoke, "of them, which You gave Me, have I lost none."

10 Then, Simeon Peter having a sword, drew it and struck the High Priest's servant and cut off his right ear. The servant's name was Malchus.

11 Then said Jesus to Peter, "put up your sword into the sheath. The Cup which My Father has Given Me, shall I not Drink it?"

12 Then, the band and the captain and officers of the Jews, took Jesus and bound Him
13 And led Him away to Annas, first. For he was father in law to Caiaphas (which was the high priest that same year.)
14 Now Caiaphas was he, which gave counsel to the Jews that it was expedient that one man should die for the people.
15 And Simeon Peter followed Jesus and so did another disciple. That disciple was known to the high priest and went in with Jesus into the palace of the high priest.
16 But, Peter stood at the door without. Then went out that other disciple, which was known to the high priest and spoke to her that kept the door and brought in Peter.
17 Then, asked the damsel that kept the door to Peter, "are not you also, one of this Man's disciples?" He said, "I AM NOT."
18 And the servants and officers stood there, who had made a fire of coals, for it was cold and they warmed themselves. And Peter stood with them and warmed himself.

19 The high priest then asked Jesus of His disciples and of His Doctrine.
20 Jesus answered him, "I spoke openly to the World. I ever Taught in the synagogue and in the temple, where the Jews always resort and in secret, have I said nothing.
21 Why ask you Me? Ask them, which Heard Me what I have said to them. Behold, they know what I said."
22 And when He had thus spoken, one of the officers, which stood by, STRUCK JESUS WITH THE PALM OF HIS HAND saying, "answer You, the High Priest, so?"
23 Jesus answered him, "if I have spoken evil, bear witness of the evil. But if well, why beat you, Me?"

24 Now, Annas had sent Him bound to Caiaphas (the high priest.)
25 And Simeon Peter, stood and warmed himself. They said therefore, to him, "are not you also, one of His disciples?" He denied it and said, "I AM NOT."
26 One of the servants of the high priest, being his kinsman whose ear Peter cut off, asked, "did not I see you in the garden with Him?"
27 PETER THEN DENIED, again and immediately, THE COCK CREW.

28 Then led they Jesus, from Caiaphas to the hall of judgement and it was early and they themselves, went not into the judgement hall, lest they should be defiled. But that they might eat the Passover.
29 Pilate then went out to them and said, "what accusation bring you, against this Man?"
30 They answered and said to Him, "if He were not a malefactor, we would not have delivered Him up to you."
31 Then said Pilate to them, "take you, Him and judge Him according to your law." The Jews therefore, said to him, "it is not lawful for us to put any man to death"
32 That the saying of Jesus, might be Fulfilled, which He spoke, signifying what death He should die.

33 Then, Pilate entered into the judgement hall again and called Jesus and said to Him, "are You The King of the Jews?"
34 Jesus answered him, "say you, this thing of yourself, or did others tell it you of Me?"
35 Pilate answered, "am I a Jew? Your Own nation and the chief priests have delivered You to me. What have you done?"
36 Jesus answered, "My Kingdom is not of this World. If My Kingdom were of this World, then would My servants fight that I should not be delivered to the Jews. But now, is My Kingdom not from, hence."
37 Pilate therefore, said to Him, "are you A King, then?" Jesus answered, "you say that I am A King. To this end, was I born. And for this cause, came I into the World that I should Bear Witness to The Truth. Every one that is of The Truth, Hears My Voice."
38 Pilate asked him, "what is Truth?" And when he had said this, he went out again, to the Jews and said to them, "I find in Him, no fault at all.
39 But, you have a custom that I should release to you one at The Passover. Will you therefore that I release to you, The King of the Jews?"
40 Then they cried all again saying, "not this man, but Barabbas!" Now, Barabbas was a robber.

Chapter 19

1 Then Pilate therefore, TOOK JESUS AND SCOURGED HIM.
2 And the soldiers PLATTED A CROWN

OF THORNS AND PUT IT ON HIS HEAD AND THEY PUT ON HIM A PURPLE ROBE

3 And said, "HAIL, KING OF THE JEWS!" AND THEY SLAPPED HIM WITH THEIR HANDS.

4 Pilate therefore, went forth again and said to them, "behold, I bring Him forth to you that you may know that I find no fault in Him."

5 Then came Jesus forth, wearing the crown of thorns and the purple robe. And Pilate said to them, "behold, The Man!"

6 When the chief priests therefore and officers saw Him, they cried out saying, "crucify Him! Crucify Him!" Pilate said to them, "you take Him and crucify Him, for I find no fault in him."

7 The Jews answered him, "we have a law and by our law, He ought to die, because He made Himself, The Son of God."

8 When Pilate therefore, heard that saying, he was the more afraid

9 And went again, into the judgement hall and asked Jesus, "from whence are you?" BUT, JESUS GAVE HIM NO ANSWER.

10 Then asked Pilate to Him, "speak You, not to me? Know You not that I have power to crucify You and have power to release You?"

11 Jesus answered, "you could have no Power at all against Me, except it were given you from above. Therefore, he that delivered Me to you has the greater sin."

12 And from thereforth, Pilate sought to release Him, but the Jews cried out saying, "if you let this man go, you are not Caesar's friend. Whosoever makes himself a king, speaks against Caesar."

13 When Pilate therefore, heard that saying, he brought Jesus forth and sat down in the judgement seat in a place that is called the Pavement, but in the Hebrew, Gabbatha.

14 And it was the preparation of The Passover and about the sixth hour and he said to the Jews, "behold, your King!"

15 But they cried out, "away with Him, away with Him, crucify him!" Pilate asked them, "shall I crucify your King?" The chief priests answered, "we have no king, but Caesar."

16 Then he delivered Him therefore, to them to be crucified. And they took Jesus and led Him away.

17 And He bearing His cross, went forth into a place called, the Place of a Skull, which is called in the Hebrew, Golgotha,

18 Where THEY CRUCIFIED HIM AND TWO OTHERS WITH HIM on either side, one and Jesus in the midst.

19 And Pilate wrote a title and put it on the cross. And the writing was, "Jesus of Nazareth, The King of the Jews."

20 This title, then read many of the Jews, for the place where Jesus was crucified was near to the city and it was written in Hebrew and Greek and Latin.

21 Then said the chief priests of the Jews to Pilate, "write not, "'The King of the Jews,'" but that, "'He said, "'I am, King of the Jews.'"

22 Pilate answered, "what I have written, I have written."

23 Then the soldiers, when they had CRUCIFIED JESUS, TOOK HIS GARMENTS AND MADE FOUR PARTS; TO EVERY SOLDIER, A PART AND ALSO, HIS COAT. Now, the coat was without seam; woven from the top, throughout.

24 They said therefore, among themselves, "LET US NOT REND IT, BUT CAST LOTS FOR IT; WHOSE IT SHALL BE" that, The Scripture might be Fulfilled, which says, "THEY PARTED MY RAIMENT AMONG THEMSELVES AND FOR MY VESTRUE, THEY DID CAST LOTS." These things therefore, the soldiers did.

25 Now, there stood by the cross of Jesus, His mother and His mother's sister, Mary, the wife of Cleophas and Mary Magdalene.

26 When Jesus therefore, saw His mother and the disciple standing by, whom He loved, He said to His mother, "woman, behold your Son."

27 Then, He said to the disciple, "behold, your mother." And from that hour that disciple took her to his own home.

28 After this, Jesus knowing that all things were now, Accomplished that The Scripture might be Fulfilled said, "I thirst."

29 Now, there was set a vessel full of vinegar. And THEY FILLED A SPONGE WITH VINEGAR AND PUT IT ON HYSSOP AND PUT IT TO HIS MOUTH.

30 When Jesus therefore, had received the vinegar, He said, "it is Finished" and He bowed His head and gave up The Ghost.

31 <u>The Jews therefore</u>, because it was the preparation that the bodies should not remain on the cross on the Sabbath Day, (for that Sabbath Day was a high day) <u>besought Pilate that, "their legs might be broken and that they might be taken away."</u>

32 Then came the soldiers and broke the legs of the first and of the other, which was crucified with Him.

33 BUT, WHEN THEY CAME TO JESUS AND SAW THAT HE WAS DEAD ALREADY, THEY BROKE NOT, HIS LEGS.

34 BUT, ONE OF THE SOLDIERS WITH A SPEAR, PIERCED HIS SIDE AND FORTHWITH, CAME THERE OUT BLOOD AND WATER.

35 And He that saw it, bare record and his record is True and he Knows that he says True that you might Believe.

36 For these things were done that The Scripture should be Fulfilled, "A BONE OF HIM SHALL NOT BE BROKEN."

37 And again, another Scripture says, "THEY SHALL LOOK ON HIM, WHOM THEY PEIRCED."

38 And after this, Joseph, of Arimathaea being a disciple of Jesus, but secretly, for fear of the Jews, besought Pilate that he might take away the Body of Jesus and Pilate gave him leave. He came therefore and took the Body of Jesus.

39 And there came also, Nicodemus, which at the first, came to Jesus by night and brought a mixture of myrrh and aloes, about one hundred pounds, weight.

40 Then, took they the Body of Jesus and wound it in linen clothes with the spices as the manner of the Jews is to bury.

41 Now in the place where He was crucified, there was a garden. And in the garden, a new sepulchre, wherein was never man, yet laid.

42 There laid they Jesus therefore, because of the Jews' preparation day, for the sepulchre was near at hand.

Chapter 20

1 The first day of the week, came Mary Magdalene early when it was yet dark, to the sepulchre and saw the stone taken away from the sepulchre.

2 Then she ran and came to Simeon Peter and to the other disciple, whom Jesus loved and said to them, "they have taken away The Lord out of the sepulchre and we know not where they have laid Him."

3 Peter therefore, went forth and that other disciple and came to the sepulchre.

4 So they ran, both together and the other disciple did outrun Peter and came first, to the sepulchre.

5 And he stooping down and looking in, saw the linen clothes lying, yet he went not in.

6 Then came Simeon Peter following him and went into the sepulchre and saw the linen clothes lie

7 And the cloth that was about His head, not lying with the linen clothes, but wrapped together in a place by itself.

8 Then went in also that other disciple, which came first, to the sepulchre and he saw and Believed.

9 For as yet, they knew not <u>The Scripture that</u> HE MUST RISE AGAIN, FROM THE DEAD.

10 Then, the disciples went away again, to their own home.

11 But Mary stood without, at the sepulchre weeping and as she wept, she stooped down and looked into the sepulchre

12 And saw two angels in white sitting; the one, at the head and the other, at the feet, where the Body of Jesus had laid.

13 And they said to her, "woman, why weep you?" She said to them, "because they have taken away my Lord and I know not, where they have laid Him."

14 And when she had thus said, she turned herself back and saw Jesus standing and knew not that it was Jesus.

15 Jesus asked, "woman, why weep you, whom Seek you?" She, supposing Him to be the gardener, said to Him, "Sir, if You have borne Him hence, tell me where You have laid Him and I will take Him away."

16 Jesus said to her, "Mary." She turned herself and said to Him, "Rabboni," (which is to say, Master.)

17 Jesus said to her, "touch Me not, for I am not yet ascended to My Father. But, go to My brothers and say to them, "'I ascend to My Father and your Father and to My God and your God.'"

18 Mary Magdalene came and told the disciples that she had, "seen The Lord and sthat He had spoken these things to her."

19 Then the same day at evening; being the first day of the week, when the doors were shut, where the disciples were

assembled, for fear of the Jews, came Jesus and stood in the midst and said to them, "Peace be to you."
20 And when He had so said, He showed to them His hands and His side. Then were the disciples Glad, when they saw The Lord.
21 Then said Jesus to them again, "Peace be to you. As My Father has sent Me, even so, I send you."
22 And when He had said this, He breathed on them and said to them, "Receive you, The Holy Ghost.
23 Whose soever sins you remit, they are remitted to them and whose soever sins you retain, they are retained."
24 But Thomas, one of the twelve, (called Didymus) was not with them when Jesus came.
25 The other disciples therefore, said to him, "we have seen The Lord." But, he said to them, "except I shall see in His hands, the print of the nails and put my finger into the print of the nails and thrust my hand into His side, I will not believe."
26 And after eight days again, His disciples were within and Thomas with them. Then came Jesus; the doors being shut and stood in the midst and said, "Peace be to you."
27 Then said He to Thomas, "reach here, your finger and behold, My hands and reach here, your hand and thrust it into My side and be not faithless, but Believing."
28 And Thomas answered and said to Him, "my Lord and my God."
29 Jesus said to him, "Thomas, because you have seen Me, you have Believed. Blessed are they that have not seen and yet, have Believed."
30 And many other Signs truly, did Jesus in the presence of His disciples, which are not written in this scroll.
31 But, these are written that you might Believe that Jesus is The Christ; The Son of God and that Believing, you might have Life through His Name.

Chapter 21

1 After these things, Jesus showed Himself again, to the disciples at the Sea of Tiberias and on this wise, He showed Himself.
2 There were together, Simeon Peter and Thomas (called Didymus) and Nathanael, of Cana in Galilee and the sons of Zabdi and two others of His disciples.
3 Simeon Peter said to them, "I go a fishing." They said to him, "we also, go with you." They went forth and entered into a ship immediately and that night, they caught nothing.
4 But, when the morning was now come, Jesus stood on the shore. But, the disciples knew not that it was Jesus.
5 Then Jesus asked them, "children, have you any meat?" They answered Him, "no."
6 And He said to them, "cast the net on the right side of the ship and you shall find." They cast therefore and now, they were not able to draw it, for the multitude of fish.
7 Therefore that disciple, whom Jesus loved, said to Peter, "it is The Lord." Now, when Simeon Peter heard that it was The Lord, he girt his fisher's coat to himself (for he was naked) and did cast himself, into the Sea.
8 And the other disciples came in a little ship, (for they were not far from land. But as it were, two hundred cubits) dragging the net with fish.
9 As soon then, as they had come to land, they saw a fire of coals there and fish laid thereon and bread.
10 Jesus said to them, "bring of the fish, which you have now, caught."
11 Simeon Peter went up and drew the net to land, full of great fish; one hundred and fifty and three. And for all there were so many, yet was not the net broken.
12 Jesus said to them, "come and dine." And none of the disciples did ask Him, "Who are You?," knowing that it was The Lord.
13 Jesus then, came and took bread and gave them and fish, likewise.
14 This is now, the third time that Jesus showed Himself to His disciples after that He was Risen from the dead.
15 So, when they had dined, Jesus asked to Simeon Peter, "Simeon, son of Jonah, Love you Me, more than these?" He said to Him, "Yes Lord, You know that I Love You." He said to him, "feed My lambs."
16 He asked him again, the second time, "Simeon, son of Jonah, Love you Me?" He said to Him, "yes Lord, You know that I Love You." He said to him, "feed My sheep."
17 He asked him the third time, "Simeon, son of Jonah, Love you Me?" Peter was grieved, because He asked him the third time, "Love you Me?" And he said to Him, "Lord, you Know all things. You know that I Love You." Jesus said to him, "feed My

sheep.
18 Verily, verily, I say to you, "'when you were young, you girded yourself and walked where you would, but when you shall be old, you shall stretch forth your hands and another shall gird you and carry you where you would not.'"
19 This He spoke, signifying by <u>what death He should Glorify God</u>. And when He had spoken this, He said to him, "Follow Me."

20 Then Peter, turning about, saw the disciple, whom Jesus loved following, which also, leaned on His breast at supper and said, "Lord, which is he that betrays You?"
21 Peter seeing him asked Jesus, "Lord and what shall this man do?"
22 Jesus asked him, "if I will that he tarries until I come, what is that to you? Follow you, Me."
23 Then went this saying abroad, among the brothers that that disciple should not die yet. Jesus said not, to him, "he shall not die, but if I will that he tarries until I come, what is that to you?"
24 This is the disciple, which Testifies of these things and wrote these things and we Know that his Testimony is True.
25 And there are also, many other things, which Jesus did, the which, if they should be written, every one, I suppose that even the World itself, could not contain the scrolls that should be written. Amen.

Acts

Chapter 1
1 The former treatise have I made, O Theophilus, of all that Jesus began, both to Do and Teach,
2 Until the day in which, He was Taken Up, after that He, through The Holy Ghost, had Given Commandments to the apostles, whom He had Chosen;
3 To whom also, He showed Himself Alive, after His passion by many Infallible Proofs, being seen of them, forty days and speaking of the things pertaining to the Kingdom of God
4 And being assembled together with them, Commanded them that they should not depart from Jerusalem, but "Wait for The Promise of The Father," which He said, "you have Heard of Me,
5 For John truly Baptized with water, but you shall be Baptized with The Holy Ghost not many days, hence."
6 When they therefore, had come together, they asked of Him saying, "Lord, will You at this time, restore again, the Kingdom to Israel?"

7 And He said to them, "it is not for you to know the times, or the seasons, which The Father has put in His Own Power.
8 But, YOU SHALL RECEIVE POWER, AFTER THAT THE HOLY GHOST IS COME ON YOU AND YOU SHALL BE WITNESSES TO ME, BOTH IN JERUSALEM AND IN ALL JUDAEA AND IN SAMARIA AND TO THE UTTERMOST PARTS OF THE EARTH."
9 And when He had spoken these things, while they beheld, He was Taken Up and A Cloud Received Him out of their sight.

10 And while they looked steadfastly toward Heaven, as He went up, behold, two men stood by them in white apparel,
11 Which also said, "you men of Galilee, why stand you gazing up into Heaven? This same Jesus, which is Taken Up from you, into Heaven, shall so come in like manner as you have seen Him go into Heaven."

12 Then returned they, to Jerusalem from the mount called, Olivet; which is from Jerusalem, a Sabbath Day's journey.
13 And when they had come in, they went up into an upper room, where abode also: Peter and James and John and Andrew, Philip and Thomas, Bartholomew and Matthew, James (the son of Alphaeus) and Simeon Zelous and Judah (the brother of James.)
14 <u>These all Continued with One Accord, in Prayer and Supplication</u>; with the women and Mary, the mother of Jesus and with His brothers.

15 And in those days, Peter stood up in the midst of the disciples and said, (the number of names together, were about one hundred and twenty)
16 "Men and brothers, this Scripture must needs have been Fulfilled, which <u>The Holy Ghost, by the mouth of David spoke</u> before concerning Judas, which was guide to them that took Jesus.

17 For he was numbered with us and had obtained part of this ministry.
18 Now this man, purchased a field with the reward of iniquity and falling headlong, he burst asunder, in the midst and all his bowels gushed out.
19 And it was known to all the dwellers at Jerusalem, insomuch as that field is called in their proper tongue, Aceldama (that is to say, The Field of Blood.)
20 For it is written in the scroll of Psalms, "'LET HIS HABITATION BE DESOLATE AND LET NO MAN DWELL, THEREIN AND HIS BISHOPRIC, LET ANOTHER TAKE.'"

21 Wherefore, of these men, which have accompanied with us all the time that The Lord Jesus went in and out among us,
22 Beginning from the Baptism of John, to that same day that He was Taken Up from us, must one be Ordained to be a witness with us of His Resurrection.
23 And they appointed two: Joseph (called Barsabas, who was surnamed, Justus) and Matthias.
24 And they Prayed and said, "You Lord, which Knows the hearts of all men, show whether of these two, You have Chosen
25 That he may take part of this ministry and apostleship, from which, Judas by transgression fell that he might go to his own place."
26 And they gave forth their lots. And the lot fell on Matthias and he was numbered with the eleven apostles.

Chapter 2
1 And when the day of Pentecost was fully come, they were all with one accord, in one place.
2 And suddenly, there came a sound from Heaven as of a rushing Mighty wind and it filled all the house, where they were sitting.
3 And there appeared to them, Cloven Tongues, like as of Fire and it sat on each of them.
4 And they were all Filled with The Holy Ghost and began to Speak with other Tongues as The Spirit Gave them Utterance.
5 And there were dwelling at Jerusalem, Jews; devout men, out of every nation under Heaven.

6 Now, when this was noised abroad, the multitude came together and were confounded, because that every man, heard them speak in his own language.
7 And they were all amazed and marveled saying one to another, "behold, are not all these, which speak Galilaeans?
8 And how hear we, every man in our own tongue, wherein we were born?:
9 Parthians and Medes and Elamites and the dwellers in Mesopotamia and in Judaea and Cappadocia, in Pontus and Asia,
10 Phrygia and Pamphylia, in Egypt and in the parts of Libya, about Cyrene and strangers of Rome; Jews and proselytes,
11 Cretes and Arabians. We do hear them Speak in our tongues, the Wonderful Works of God."
12 And they were all amazed and were in doubt saying one to another, "what means this?"
13 Others mocking said, "these men are full of new wine."

14 But Peter, standing up with the eleven, lifted up his voice and said to them, "you men of Judaea and all you that dwell at Jerusalem, be this known to you and listen to my words,
15 For these are not drunken, as you suppose, seeing it is but, the third hour of the day.
16 But this is that, which was spoken by the Prophet Joel,
17 "'And it shall come to pass in the last days, says God, "'I WILL POUR OUT OF MY SPIRIT ON ALL FLESH AND YOUR SONS AND YOUR DAUGHTERS, SHALL PROPHESY AND YOUR YOUNG MEN SHALL SEE VISIONS AND YOUR OLD MEN SHALL DREAM DREAMS
18 AND ON MY SERVANTS AND ON MY HANDMAIDENS, I WILL POUR OUT IN THOSE DAYS, OF MY SPIRIT AND THEY SHALL PROPHESY
19 AND I WILL SHOW WONDERS IN HEAVEN ABOVE AND SIGNS IN THE EARTH BENEATH; blood and fire and vapor of smoke.
20 The Sun shall be turned into darkness and the MOON INTO BLOOD, before the great and notable day of The Lord comes.
21 AND IT SHALL COME TO PASS THAT, WHOSOEVER, SHALL CALL ON THE NAME OF THE LORD, SHALL BE SAVED.'"
22 You men of Israel, Hear these words. Jesus of Nazareth, a Man Approved of God among you, by Miracles and Wonders and Signs, which God did by Him, in the midst of you, as you yourselves also know.

23 Him, being delivered by the determinate counsel and Foreknowledge of God, you HAVE TAKEN AND BY WICKED HANDS, HAVE CRUCIFIED AND SLAIN,
24 WHOM GOD HAS RAISED UP, HAVING LOOSED THE PAINS OF DEATH, because it was not possible that He should be held of it.
25 For David speaks concerning Him, "'I FORESAW THE LORD ALWAYS, BEFORE MY FACE, FOR HE IS ON MY RIGHT HAND THAT I SHOULD NOT BE MOVED.
26 THEREFORE, DID MY HEART REJOICE AND MY TONGUE WAS GLAD. MOREOVER ALSO, MY FLESH SHALL REST IN HOPE,
27 BECAUSE YOU WILL NOT LEAVE MY SOUL IN HELL, NEITHER WILL YOU SUFFER YOUR HOLY ONE, TO SEE CORRUPTION.
28 YOU HAVE MADE KNOWN TO ME THE WAYS OF LIFE. YOU SHALL MAKE ME FULL OF JOY, WITH YOUR COUNTENANCE.'"

29 Men and brothers, let me freely speak to you of the patriarch, David that he is both dead and buried and his sepulchre is with us to this day.
30 Therefore, being a prophet and knowing that God had sworn with an Oath to him that of the fruit of his loins, according to the flesh, He would raise up Christ to sit on His throne.
31 He seeing this before, spoke of the Resurrection of Christ that His soul was not left in Hell, neither His flesh did see corruption.
32 This Jesus, has God Raised Up, whereof we all are witnesses.
33 Therefore, being by The Right Hand of God, Exalted and having Received of The Father, the Promise of The Holy Ghost, He has shed forth this, which you now, See and Hear.
34 For David is not ascended into the Heavens, but he said himself, "'THE LORD SAID TO MY LORD , ""SIT YOURSELF AT MY RIGHT HAND,
35 UNTIL I MAKE YOUR FOES, YOUR FOOTSTOOL."'"
36 Therefore, let all the house of Israel know assuredly that God has made the same Jesus, Whom YOU HAVE CRUCIFIED; both Lord and Christ."

37 Now, when they heard this, they were pricked in their heart and said to Peter and to the rest of the apostles, "men and brothers, what shall we do?"
38 Then Peter said to them, "Repent and be Baptized, every one of you, in The Name of Jesus Christ, for the Remission of sins and you shall Receive The Gift of The Holy Ghost,
39 FOR THE PROMISE IS TO YOU AND TO YOUR CHILDREN AND TO ALL THAT ARE AFAR OFF; EVEN AS MANY AS THE LORD, OUR GOD SHALL CALL."
40 And with many other words, did he Testify and exhort saying, "save yourselves from this untoward generation."
41 Then, they that gladly received his word, were Baptized. And the same day, there were added to them about three thousand souls.
42 And they continued steadfastly, in the apostles' doctrine and fellowship and in breaking of bread and in Prayers.
43 And Fear came on every soul and many Wonders and Signs were done by the apostles.
44 And all that Believed, were together and had all things common
45 And sold their possessions and goods and parted them to all men, as every man had need.
46 And they, continuing daily with one accord, in the temple and breaking bread from house to house, did eat their meat with gladness and singleness of heart;
47 Praising God and having favor with all the people. And The Lord added to the church daily, such as should be Saved.

Chapter 3

1 Now, Peter and John went up together into the temple at the hour of Prayer; being the ninth hour.
2 And a certain man, lame from his mother's womb was carried; whom they laid daily at the gate of the temple, which is called, Beautiful to ask alms of them that entered into the temple,
3 Who seeing Peter and John about to go into the temple, asked an alms.
4 And Peter, fastening his eyes on him with John said, "look on us."
5 And he gave heed to them, expecting to receive something of them.

6 Then Peter said, "silver and gold have I none, but such as I have, I give you. In The Name of Jesus Christ of Nazareth, Rise

Up and Walk."

7 And he took him by the right hand and lifted him up and immediately, his feet and ankle bones Received Strength.

8 And he Leaping Up, Stood and Walked and entered with them into the temple; Walking and Leaping and Praising God.

9 And all the people saw him Walking and Praising God

10 And they knew that it was he, which sat for alms at the beautiful gate of the temple. And they were filled with wonder and amazement at that, which had happened to him.

11 And as the lame man which was Healed, held Peter and John, all the people ran together to them in the porch that is called Solomon's, greatly wondering.

12 And when Peter saw it, he answered to the people, "you men of Israel, why marvel you at this, or why look you, so earnestly on us, as though by our own power, or holiness we had made this man to walk?

13 The God of Abraham and of Isaac and of Jacob; The God of our fathers, has Glorified His Son, Jesus, Whom you delivered up and denied Him in the presence of Pilate, when he was determined to let Him go.

14 But, you denied the Holy One and The Just and desired a murderer to be granted to you

15 And killed the Prince of Life, Whom God has Raised from the dead, whereof we are witnesses.

16 And His Name, through Faith in His Name, has made this man strong, whom you see and know. Yes, the Faith which is by Him has given him this perfect soundness in the presence of you all.

17 And now brothers, I know that through ignorance you did it, as did also, your rulers.

18 But those things, which God before, had shown by the mouth of all His prophets that Christ SHOULD SUFFER, He has so, Fulfilled.

19 Repent you therefore and be Converted that your sins may be blotted out, when the times of refreshing shall come from the Presence of The Lord.

20 And He shall send Jesus Christ, which before was Preached to you,

21 Whom the Heaven must receive until the times of restitution of all things, which God has spoken by the mouth of all His Holy prophets since the World began.

22 For Moses truly said to the fathers, "'A PROPHET SHALL THE LORD YOUR GOD RAISE UP TO YOU OF YOUR BRETHREN, LIKE TO ME. HIM, SHALL YOU HEAR IN ALL THINGS WHATSOEVER, HE SHALL SAY TO YOU.

23 AND IT SHALL COME TO PASS THAT EVERY SOUL, WHICH WILL NOT, HEAR THAT PROPHET, SHALL BE DESTROYED FROM AMONG THE PEOPLE.'"

24 Yes and all the prophets from Samuel and those that follow after; as many as have spoken, have likewise, foretold of these days.

25 You are the children of the prophets and of The Covenant, which God made with our fathers saying to Abraham "'AND IN YOUR SEED, SHALL ALL THE KINDREDS OF THE EARTH BE BLESSED.'"

26 To you first, God having Raised Up His Son, Jesus, sent Him to Bless you, in Turning Away every one of you, from his iniquities.

Chapter 4

1 And as they spoke to the people, the priests and the captain of the temple and the Sadducees came on them,

2 Being grieved that they Taught the people and Preached through Jesus the Resurrection from the dead.

3 And they laid hands on them and put them in hold until the next day, for it was now, evening.

4 Howbeit, many of them which Heard The Word, Believed and the number of the men was about five thousand.

5 And it came to pass, on the morrow that their rulers and elders and scribes

6 And Annas, the high priest and Caiaphas and John and Alexander and as many as were of the kindred of the high priest, were gathered together at Jerusalem.

7 And when they had set them in the midst, they asked, "by what Power, or by what Name have you done this?"

8 Then Peter, Filled with The Holy Ghost said to them, "you rulers of the people and elders of Israel,

9 If we this day, be examined of the good deed, done to the impotent man, by what means he is Made Whole,

10 Be it known to you all and to all the people of Israel that by The Name of Jesus Christ, of Nazareth, Whom YOU CRUCIFIED, WHOM GOD RAISED FROM THE DEAD; even by Him, does this man stand here, before you Whole.

11 THIS IS THE STONE, WHICH WAS SET AT NAUGHT OF YOU BUILDERS, WHICH IS BECOME, THE HEAD OF THE CORNER.

12 <u>Neither is there Salvation in any other, for there is none other Name, under Heaven given among men, whereby we must be Saved."</u>

13 Now, when they saw the boldness of Peter and John and perceived that they were unlearned and ignorant men, they marveled and they took knowledge of them that they had been with Jesus.

14 And beholding the man, which was Healed Standing with them, they could say nothing against it.

15 But when they had commanded them to go aside out of the council, they conferred among themselves,

16 Saying, <u>"what shall we do to these men, for that indeed, a notable Miracle has been done by them is manifest to all them that dwell in Jerusalem and we cannot deny it.

17 But that it spreads no further among the people, let us straightly, threaten them that they speak henceforth, to no man in this Name."</u>

18 And they called them and commanded them, "not to speak at all, nor Teach in The Name of Jesus."

19 But, Peter and John answered and said to them, "whether it be right in the sight of God to hearken to you more than to God, judge yourselves.

20 <u>For we cannot, but speak the things, which we have Seen and Heard."</u>

21 So, when they had further threatened them, they let them go, finding nothing how they might punish them, because of the people, for all men Glorified God, for that which was done.

22 For the man was above forty years old on whom, this Miracle of Healing was shown.

23 And being let go, they went to their own company and reported all that the chief priests and elders had said to them.

24 And when they heard that, they lifted up their voice to God with one accord and said, "Lord, You are God, (which have made Heaven and Earth and the Sea and all that in them is,

25 Who by the mouth of Your servant David, has said, "'WHY DID THE HEATHEN RAGE AND THE PEOPLE IMAGINE VAIN THINGS?

26 THE KINGS OF THE EARTH STOOD UP AND THE RULERS WERE GATHERED TOGETHER, AGAINST THE LORD AND AGAINST HIS CHRIST.'"

27 For of a Truth, against Your Holy Child, Jesus, Whom You have Anointed, both Herod and Pontius Pilate, with the gentiles and the people of Israel, were gathered together,

28 For to do whatsoever Your hand and Your counsel determined before to be done.

29 And now, Lord, behold their threatenings and grant to Your servants that with all boldness, they may speak Your Word,

30 By stretching forth your hand to Heal and that Signs and Wonders may be done by The Name of Your Holy Child, Jesus.)"

31 And when they had Prayed, the place was shaken where they were assembled, together and they were all Filled with The Holy Ghost and they Spoke The Word of God with Boldness.

32 And the multitude of them that Believed, were of one heart and of one soul, neither said any of them that, nothing of the things which he possessed was his own, but they had all things common.

33 And with Great Power, gave the apostles witness of the Resurrection of The Lord, Jesus and Great Grace was on them all.

34 Neither was there any, among them that lacked, for as many as were possessors of lands, or houses sold them and brought the prices of the things that were sold

35 And laid them down at the Apostles' feet and distribution was made to every man, according as he had need.

36 And Joseph, who by the Apostles was surnamed, Barnabas, (which is, being interpreted, the son of consolation) a Levite and of the country of Cyprus;

37 Having land, sold it and brought the money and laid it at the Apostles' feet.

Chapter 5

1 But, a certain man named Hananiah, with Sapphira, his wife sold a possession

2 And kept back part of the price. His wife also, being privy to it and brought a certain part and laid it at the Apostles' feet.

3 But Peter said, "Hananiah, why has Satan filled your heart to lie to The Holy Ghost and to keep back part of the price of the land?

4 While it remained, was it not your own and after it was sold, was it not in your own power? Why have you conceived this thing in your heart? You have not lied to men, but to God."

5 And Hananiah hearing these words, fell down and gave up the ghost and great Fear came on all them that heard these things.

6 And the young men arose, wound him up and carried him out and buried him.

7 And it was about the space of three hours after, when his wife, not knowing what was done, came in.

8 And Peter answered to her, "tell me whether you sold the land for so much." And she said, "yes, for so much."

9 Then Peter said to her, "how is it that you have agreed together, to tempt The Spirit of The Lord? Behold, the feet of them, which have buried your husband are at the door and shall carry you out."

10 Then she fell down straightway at his feet and yielded up the ghost and the young men came in and found her dead and carrying her forth, buried her by her husband.

11 And great Fear came on all the church and on as many as heard these things.

12 And by the hands of the apostles, were many Signs and Wonders Worked among the people and they were all with one accord in Solomon's porch.

13 And of the rest, did no man join himself to them, but the people magnified them.

14 And Believers were the more added to The Lord, multitudes; both of men and women

15 Insomuch that, they brought forth the sick into the streets and laid them on beds and couches that at the least, the shadow of Peter passing by, might overshadow some of them.

16 There came also, a multitude out of the cities, round about to Jerusalem, bringing sick people and them, which were vexed with unclean spirits and they were Healed, every one.

17 Then the high priest rose up and all they that were with him, (which is the sect of the Sadducees) and were filled with indignation

18 And laid their hands on the apostles and put them in the common prison.

19 But the angel of The Lord by night, Opened the prison doors and brought them forth and said,

20 "Go stand and speak in the temple to the people all the words of this life."

21 And when they heard that, they entered into the temple, early in the morning and Taught. But, the high priest came and they that were with him and called the council together and all the senate of the children of Israel and sent to the prison to have them brought.

22 But, when the officers came and found them not in the prison, they returned and told

23 Saying, "the prison truly, we found shut with all safety and the keepers standing without before the doors. But, when we had opened, we found no man within."

24 Now, when the high priest and the captain of the temple and the chief priests heard these things, they doubted of them whereunto, this would grow.

25 Then came one and told them saying, "behold, the men whom you put in prison are standing in the temple and Teaching the people."

26 Then went the captain with the officers and brought them without violence, for they feared the people, lest they should have been stoned.

27 And when they had brought them, they set them before the council and the high priest asked them

28 Saying, "did not we straightly, command you that you should not Teach in this Name? And behold, you have filled Jerusalem with your Doctrine and intend to bring this Man's blood on us."

29 Then Peter and the other apostles answered and said, "we ought to Obey God, rather than men."

30 The God of our fathers Raised Up Jesus, WHOM YOU SLEW AND HANGED ON A TREE.

31 Him, has God Exalted with His right hand to be a Prince and a Savior, for to Give Repentance to Israel and Forgiveness of sins.

32 And we are His Witnesses of these things and so is also, The Holy Ghost, whom God has Given to them that Obey

Him.

33 When they heard that, they were cut to the heart and took counsel to slay them.
34 Then stood there up one in the council, a Pharisee named, Gamaliel; a doctor of the Law, had in reputation among all the people and commanded to put the apostles forth a little space
35 And said to them, "you men of Israel, Take Heed to yourselves what you intend to do as touching these men.
36 For before these days, rose up Theudas, boasting himself to be somebody to whom a number of men, about four hundred joined themselves who was slain. And all, as many as obeyed him, were scattered and brought to naught.
37 After this man rose up, Judas, of Galilee (in the days of the taxing) and drew away much people after himself. He also, perished and all, even as many as obeyed him, were dispersed.
38 And now, I say to you, "refrain from these men and let them alone. For if this counsel, or this work is of men, it will come to naught.
39 <u>But, if it be of God, you cannot overthrow it, lest haply, you be found even to fight against God."</u>

40 And to him, they agreed and when they had called the apostles and beaten them, they commanded that, "they should not speak in The Name of Jesus" and let them go.
41 And they departed from the presence of the council, <u>Rejoicing that they were, "counted worthy to suffer shame, for His Name."</u>
42 And <u>daily in the temple and in every house, they ceased not to Teach and Preach Jesus Christ.</u>

Chapter 6

1 And in those days, when the number of the disciples were multiplied, there arose a murmuring of the Grecians against the Hebrews, because their widows were neglected in the daily ministration.
2 Then the twelve called the multitude of the disciples to themselves and said, "it is not reason that we should leave The Word of God and serve tables.
3 Wherefore brothers, look you out among yourselves, seven men of Honest report; Full of The Holy Ghost and Wisdom, whom we may appoint over this business.
4 But, we will give ourselves Continually, to Prayer and to the ministry of The Word."
5 And the saying pleased the whole multitude and they chose: Stephen (a man Full of Faith and of The Holy Ghost) and Philip and Prochorus and Nicanor and Timon and Parmenas and Nicolas (a proselyte of Antioch,
6 Whom they set before the apostles.) And when they had Prayed, they laid their hands on them.

7 And The Word of God increased and the number of the disciples multiplied in Jerusalem greatly and a great company of the priests were Obedient to The Faith.
8 And Stephen, Full of Faith and Power, did great Wonders and Miracles among the people.
9 Then there arose certain of the synagogue, (which is called the synagogue of the Libertines and Cyrenians and Alexandrians and of them of Cilicia and of Asia) disputing with Stephen.
10 And they were not able to resist the Wisdom and The Spirit by which he spoke.
11 Then they suborned men, which said, "we have heard him speak blasphemous words against Moses and against God."
12 And they stirred up the people and the elders and the scribes and came on him and caught him and brought him to the council
13 And set up false witnesses which said, "this man ceases not to speak blasphemous words against this Holy place and the law.
14 For we have heard him say that this Jesus, of Nazareth, shall destroy this place and shall change the customs, which Moses delivered us."
15 And all that sat in the council, looking steadfastly on him, saw his face as it had been the face of an angel.

Chapter 7

1 Then said the high priest, "are these things so?"
2 And he said, "men, brothers and fathers, hearken. The God of Glory appeared to our father, Abraham when he was in Mesopotamia, before he dwelled in Charran
3 And said to him, "'get yourself out of your country and from your kindred and come into THE LAND, WHICH I SHALL SHOW YOU.'"

4 Then, came he out of the land of the Chaldaeans and dwelled in Charran and from there, when his father was dead, he removed himself into this land wherein you now, dwell.
5 And He gave him no inheritance in it; no, not so much as to set his foot on, yet HE PROMISED THAT HE WOULD GIVE IT TO HIM FOR A POSSESSION AND TO HIS SEED AFTER HIM, when as yet, he had no child.

6 And God spoke on this wise that, "'HIS SEED SHOULD SOJOURN IN A STRANGE LAND AND THAT THEY SHOULD BRING THEM INTO BONDAGE AND ENTREAT THEM EVIL, FOUR HUNDRED YEARS
7 "'AND THE NATION TO WHOM, THEY SHALL BE IN BONDAGE, WILL I JUDGE,'" said God "'AND AFTER THAT, SHALL THEY COME FORTH AND SERVE ME IN THIS PLACE.'"
8 And He gave him the covenant of circumcision and so Abraham begat Isaac and circumcised him the eighth day. And Isaac begat Jacob and Jacob begat the twelve patriarchs.
9 And the patriarchs, moved with envy, sold Joseph into Egypt. But, God was with him
10 And delivered him out of all his afflictions and gave him Favor and Wisdom in the sight of Pharaoh, king of Egypt. And he made him governor over Egypt and all his house.

11 Now, there came a dearth over all the land of Egypt and Canaan and great affliction and our fathers found no sustenance.
12 But when Jacob heard that there was corn in Egypt, he sent out our fathers, first.
13 And at the second time, Joseph was made known to his brothers and Joseph's kindred was made known to Pharaoh.
14 Then sent Joseph and called his father, Jacob to himself and all his kindred, sixty and fifteen souls.
15 So, Jacob went down into Egypt and died; he and our fathers
16 And were carried over into Shechem and laid in the sepulchre that Abraham bought for a sum of money of the sons of Hamor, the father of Shechem.
17 But, when the time of The Promise drew near, which God had sworn to Abraham, the people grew and multiplied in Egypt,
18 Until another king arose, which knew not Joseph.
19 The same dealt subtly with our kindred and evilly entreated our fathers, so that they cast out their young children to the end, they might not live.
20 In which time, Moses was born and was exceedingly fair and nourished up in his father's house, three months.
21 And when he was cast out, Pharaoh's daughter took him up and nourished him for her own son.
22 And Moses was learned in all the wisdom of the Egyptians and was mighty in words and in deeds.
23 And when he was full, forty years old, it came into his heart to visit his brothers, the children of Israel.
24 And seeing one of them suffer wrong, he defended him and avenged him that was oppressed and slew the Egyptian,
25 For he supposed his brothers would have understood how that God by His hand, would Deliver them, but they understood not.

26 And the next day, he showed himself to them as they fought and would have set them at one, again saying, "'Sirs, you are brothers. Why do you wrong one to another?'"
27 But, he that did his neighbor wrong, thrust him away saying, "'who made you a ruler and a judge over us?
28 Will you kill me, as you did the Egyptian, yesterday?'"
29 Then fled Moses at this saying and was a stranger in the land of Midian, where he begat two sons.
30 And when forty years were expired, there appeared to him in the wilderness of Mount Sinai, an angel of The Lord in a Flame of Fire in a bush.
31 When Moses saw it, he wondered at the sight. And as he drew near to behold it, The Voice of The Lord came to him
32 Saying, "I am The God of your fathers; The God of Abraham and The God of Isaac and The God of Jacob. Then Moses trembled and did not behold.
33 Then said The Lord to him, "'put off your shoes from your feet, for the place where you stand is Holy ground.
34 I have seen, I have seen the affliction of My people, which is in Egypt and I have heard their groaning and am come down to Deliver them. And now, come, I will send you into Egypt.'"
35 This Moses, whom they refused saying,

"'who made you a ruler and a judge?,'" the same did God send to be a ruler and a deliverer by the hand of the angel, which appeared to him in the bush.

36 He brought them out, after that he had shown Wonders and Signs in the land of Egypt and in the Red Sea and in the wilderness, forty years.

37 This is that Moses, which said to the children of Israel, "'A PROPHET, SHALL THE LORD YOUR GOD RAISE UP TO YOU OF YOUR BRETHREN, LIKE TO ME. HIM, SHALL YOU HEAR.'"

38 This is he that was in the church in the wilderness with the angel, which spoke to him in the Mount Sinai and with our fathers who received the Lively Oracles to Give to us,

39 To whom our fathers would not obey, but thrust him from them and in their hearts, turned back again, into Egypt

40 Saying to Aaron, "'make us gods to go before us, for as for this Moses, which brought us out of the land of Egypt, we know not what is become of him.'"

41 And they made a calf in those days and offered sacrifices to the idol and rejoiced in the works of their own hands.

42 Then God turned and gave them up to worship the host of heaven as it is written in the scroll of the prophets, "'O you house of Israel, have you offered to Me slain beasts and sacrifices by the space of forty years in the wilderness?

43 Yes, you took up the tabernacle of Moloch and the star of your god, Remphan; figures, which you made to worship them and I will carry you away beyond Babylon.'"

44 Our fathers had the tabernacle of witness in the wilderness, as He had appointed, speaking to Moses that he should make it, according to the fashion that he had seen;

45 Which also, our fathers that came after, brought in with Jesus, into the possession of the gentiles, whom God drove out before the face of our fathers, to the days of David,

46 Who found Favor before God and desired to find a tabernacle for The God of Jacob.

47 But Solomon built Him a house.

48 Howbeit, The Most High dwells not in temples made with hands as asked the prophet,

49 "'Heaven is My throne and Earth is My footstool. What house will you build Me?,'" said The Lord, "'or what is the place of My rest?

50 Has not My hand made all these things?

51 You stiffnecked and uncircumcised in heart and ears, you do always, resist The Holy Ghost as your fathers did, so do you.

52 Which of the prophets have not your father's persecuted? And they have slain them, which showed before of the coming of The Just One of Whom, you have been now, the betrayers and murderers,

53 Who have received The Law by the disposition of angels and have not kept it.'"

54 When they heard these things, they were cut to the heart and they gnashed on him with their teeth.

55 But he, being Full of The Holy Ghost, looked up steadfastly into Heaven and saw The Glory of God and JESUS STANDING ON THE RIGHT HAND OF GOD

56 And said, "behold, I see the Heavens opened and The Son of Man, STANDING ON THE RIGHT HAND OF GOD."

57 Then, they cried out with a loud voice and stopped their ears and ran on him with one accord

58 And cast him out of the city and stoned him. And the witnesses laid down their clothes at a young man's feet, whose name was Saul.

59 And they stoned Stephen, (calling on God and saying) "Lord Jesus, receive my spirit."

60 And he kneeled down and cried with a loud voice, "Lord, lay not this sin to their charge!" And when he had said this, he fell asleep.

Chapter 8

1 And Saul was consenting to his death. And at that time, there was a great persecution against the church, which was at Jerusalem. And they were all scattered abroad throughout the regions of Judaea and Samaria, except the apostles.

2 And devout men, carried Stephen to his burial and made great lamentation over him.

3 As for Saul, he made havoc of the church, entering into every house and haling men and women; committed them to prison.

4 Therefore, they that were scattered abroad, went every where, Preaching The Word.

5 Then, Philip went down to the city of Samaria and Preached Christ to them.
6 And the people, with one accord, gave heed to those things, which Philip spoke, hearing and seeing the Miracles which he did.
7 For unclean spirits, crying with loud voices, came out of many that were possessed with them and many taken with palsies and that were lame, were Healed.
8 And there was great Joy in that city.

9 But, there was a certain man, called Simon, which beforetimes in the same city, used sorcery and bewitched the people of Samaria, giving out that himself was some great one,
10 To whom, they all gave heed; from the least to the greatest saying, "this man is the great power of god."
11 And to him, they had regard, because that of long time, he had bewitched them with sorceries.
12 But when they believed Philip, Preaching the things concerning the Kingdom of God and The Name of Jesus Christ, they were Baptized; both men and women.
13 Then Simon himself, Believed also and when he was Baptized, he continued with Philip and wondered; beholding the Miracles and Signs, which were done.
14 Now, when the apostles which were at Jerusalem, heard that Samaria had Received The Word of God, they sent to them, Peter and John,
15 Who when they had come down, Prayed for them that they might Receive The Holy Ghost
16 (For as yet, He was fallen on none of them. Only, they were Baptized in The Name of The Lord, Jesus.)
17 Then laid they their hands on them and they Received The Holy Ghost.

18 And when Simon saw that through Laying On of the apostles' Hands, The Holy Ghost was Given, he offered them money
19 Saying, "give me also, this Power that on whomsoever, I lay hands, he may receive The Holy Ghost."
20 But Peter said to him, "your money perish with you, because you have thought that The Gift of God may be purchased with money.
21 You have neither part, nor lot in this matter, for your heart is not right in the sight of God.

22 Repent therefore, of this, your wickedness and Pray God if perhaps, the thought of your heart may be Forgiven you.
23 For I perceive that you are in the gall of bitterness and in the bond of iniquity."
24 Then, answered Simon and said, "Pray you to The Lord for me that none of these things, which you have spoken come on me."

25 And they, when they had Testified and Preached The Word of The Lord, returned to Jerusalem and Preached The Gospel in many villages of the Samaritans.
26 And the angel of The Lord spoke to Philip saying, "arise and go toward the South, to the way that goes down from Jerusalem, to Gaza, which is desert."
27 And he rose and went. And behold, a man of Ethiopia, a eunuch of great authority, under Candace, queen of the Ethiopians who had the charge of all her treasure and had come to Jerusalem for to Worship,
28 Was returning and sitting in his chariot, read Isaiah, the prophet.
29 Then The Spirit said to Philip, "go near and join yourself to this chariot."
30 And Philip ran there to him and heard him read the Prophet Isaiah and said, "Understand you, what you read?"
31 And he said, "how can I, except some man should guide me?" And he desired Philip that he would come up and sit with him.
32 The place of The Scripture, which he read was this: HE WAS LED AS A SHEEP TO THE SLAUGHTER AND LIKE A LAMB, DUMB BEFORE HIS SHEARER, SO OPENED HE NOT HIS MOUTH.
33 IN HIS HUMILIATION, HIS JUDGMENT WAS TAKEN AWAY. AND WHO SHALL DECLARE HIS GENERATION? FOR HIS LIFE IS TAKEN FROM THE EARTH.
34 And the eunuch answered Philip and said, "I pray you, of Whom, speaks the prophet this, of himself, or of some other Man?"

35 Then, Philip opened his mouth and began at the same Scripture and Preached to him, Jesus.
36 And as they went on their way, they came to a certain water and the eunuch said, "see? Here is water. What does hinder me to be Baptized?"

37 And Philip said, "if you Believe with All your heart, you may." And he answered and said, "I Believe that Jesus Christ is The Son of God."
38 And he commanded the chariot to stand still and they went down, both into the water; both Philip and the eunuch and he Baptized him.
39 And when they had come up out of the water, The Spirit of The Lord caught away Philip that the eunuch saw him, no more and he went on his way, Rejoicing.
40 But Philip was found at Ashdod and passing through, he Preached in all the cities, until he came to Caesarea.

Chapter 9

1 And Saul, yet breathing out threatenings and slaughter against the disciples of The Lord, went to the high priest
2 And desired of him, letters to Damascus to the synagogues that if he found any of this Way, whether they were men, or women, he might bring them bound to Jerusalem.
3 And as he journeyed, he came near Damascus and suddenly, there Shined round about him, A Light from Heaven.
4 And he fell to the earth and Heard A Voice saying to him, "Saul, Saul, why persecute you Me?"
5 And he said, "who are You, Lord?" And The Lord said, "I am Jesus, Whom you persecute. It is hard for you to kick against the goads."
6 And he trembling and astonished said, "Lord, what will You have me to do?" And The Lord said to him, "arise and go into the city and it shall be told you, what you must do."
7 And the men, which journeyed with him, stood speechless; Hearing A Voice, but seeing no man.
8 And Saul arose from the earth and when his eyes were opened, he saw no man, but they led him by the hand and brought him into Damascus.
9 And he was three days, without sight and neither did eat, nor drink.

10 And there was a certain disciple at Damascus named, Hananiah and to him, said The Lord in a Vision, "Hananiah." And he said, "behold, I am here, Lord."
11 And The Lord said to him, "arise and go into the street, which is called, Straight and enquire in the house of Judas, for one called Saul, of Tarsus, for behold, he Prays
12 And has seen in a Vision, a man named, Hananiah coming in and putting his hand on him that he might Receive his Sight."
13 Then Hananiah answered, "Lord, I have heard by many of this man, how much evil he has done to Your saints at Jerusalem
14 And here, he has authority from the chief priests to bind all that Call on Your Name."
15 But The Lord said to him, "go your way, for he is a Chosen vessel to Me, to Bear My Name before the gentiles and kings and the children of Israel.
16 For I will show him how great things he must suffer for My Name's sake."

17 And Hananiah went his way and entered into the house and putting his hands on him said, "brother Saul, The Lord, even Jesus that appeared to you in the way as you came, has sent me that you might Receive your Sight and be Filled with The Holy Ghost."
18 And immediately, there fell from his eyes as it had been scales and he Received Sight, forthwith and arose and was Baptized.
19 And when he had received meat, he was strengthened. Then was Saul certain days with the disciples, which were at Damascus.
20 And straightway, he Preached Christ in the synagogues that, "He is The Son of God."
21 But all that heard him, were amazed and said, "is not this he that destroyed them, which called on this Name in Jerusalem and came here for that intent that he might bring them bound to the chief priests?"
22 But Saul increased the more in strength and confounded the Jews, which dwelled at Damascus; proving that, "this is very Christ."

23 And after that many days were fulfilled, the Jews took counsel to kill him,
24 But their laying wait was known of Saul and they watched the gates day and night to kill him.
25 Then the disciples took him by night and let him down by the wall in a basket.
26 And when Saul was come to Jerusalem, he assayed to join himself, to the disciples. But, they were all afraid of him and believed not that he was a disciple.
27 But Barnabas, took him and brought

him to the apostles and declared to them how he had seen The Lord in the way and that He had spoken to him and how he had Preached Boldly at Damascus, in The Name of Jesus.

28 And he was with them, coming in and going out at Jerusalem.

29 And he Spoke Boldly, in The Name of The Lord, Jesus and disputed against the Grecians, but they went about to slay him,

30 Which when the brothers knew, they brought him down to Caesarea and sent him forth to Tarsus.

31 Then had the churches rest, throughout all Judaea and Galilee and Samaria and were edified and Walking in the Fear of The Lord and in the comfort of The Holy Ghost, were multiplied.

32 And it came to pass, as Peter passed throughout all quarters, he came down also, to the saints, which dwelled at Lod.

33 And there, he found a certain man named, Aeneas, which had kept his bed eight years and was sick of the palsy.

34 And Peter said to him, "Aeneas, Jesus Christ Makes you Whole. Arise and make your bed." And he Arose, immediately.

35 And all that dwelled at Lod and Sharon, saw him and Turned To The Lord.

36 Now, there was at Joppa, a certain disciple named, Tabitha (which by interpretation is called, Dorcas.) This woman was full of good Works and Almsdeeds, which she did.

37 And it came to pass, in those days that she was sick and died, whom when they had washed, they laid her in an upper chamber.

38 And forasmuch as Lod was near to Joppa and the disciples had heard that Peter was there, they sent to him two men, desiring him that he would not delay to come to them.

39 Then, Peter arose and went with them. When he was come, they brought him into the upper chamber and all the widows stood by him weeping and showing the coats and garments, which Dorcas made while she was with them.

40 But Peter put them all forth and Kneeled Down and Prayed and turning himself to the body said, "Tabitha, Arise." And she Opened her eyes and when she saw Peter, she Sat Up.

41 And he gave her his hand and lifted her up. And when he had called the saints and widows, presented her alive.

42 And it was known throughout all Joppa and many Believed in The Lord.

43 And it came to pass that he tarried many days in Joppa with one, Simeon a tanner.

Chapter 10

1 There was a certain man in Caesarea called, Cornelius; a centurion of the band called, the Italian Band;

2 A devout man and one that Feared God with all his house, which gave much Alms to the people and Prayed to God, always.

3 He saw in a Vision evidently, about the ninth hour of the day, an angel of God coming in to him and saying to him, "Cornelius."

4 And when he looked on him, he was afraid and said, "what is it, lord?" And He said to him, "your Prayers and your Alms are come up for a memorial before God.

5 And now, send men to Joppa and call for one, Simeon, whose surname is Peter.

6 He lodges with one, Simeon, (a tanner) whose house is by the Sea side. He shall tell you what you ought to do."

7 And when the angel, which spoke to Cornelius was departed, he called two of his household servants and a devout soldier of them that waited on him, continually.

8 And when he had declared all these things to them, he sent them to Joppa.

9 On the morrow, as they went on their journey and drew near to the city, Peter went up on the housetop to Pray about the sixth hour.

10 And he became very hungry and would have eaten, but while they made ready, he fell into a trance

11 And saw Heaven opened and a certain vessel descending on himself; as it had been a great sheet, knit at the four corners and let down to the Earth,

12 Wherein, were all manner of four footed beasts of the Earth and wild beasts and creeping things and fowls of the air.

13 And there came A Voice to him, "rise Peter, kill and eat."

14 But Peter said, "not so Lord, for I have never eaten any thing that is common, or unclean."

15 And The Voice spoke to him again, the second time, "what God has cleansed, that call not you, common."

16 This was done thrice and the vessel was received up again, into Heaven.

17 Now, while Peter doubted in himself, what this Vision, which he had seen should mean, behold, the men which were sent from Cornelius had made inquiry for Simeon's house and stood before the gate
18 And called and asked whether Simeon (which was surnamed Peter) were lodged there.
19 While Peter thought on the Vision, The Spirit said to him, "behold, three men seek you.
20 Arise, therefore and get yourself down and go with them, doubting nothing, for I have sent them."
21 Then Peter went down to the men, which were sent to him from Cornelius and said, "behold, I am he, whom you seek. What is the cause wherefore, you are come?"
22 And they said, "Cornelius, the centurion, a Just man and one that Fears God and of good report among all the nation of the Jews, was warned from God by a Holy angel to send for you, into his house and to hear words of you."
23 Then, he called them in and lodged them. And on the morrow, Peter went away with them and certain brothers from Joppa accompanied him.

24 And the morrow after, they entered into Caesarea. And Cornelius waited for them and he had called together, his kinsmen and near friends.
25 And as Peter was coming in, Cornelius met him and fell down at his feet and worshipped him.
26 But Peter took him up saying, "stand up. I myself also, am a man."
27 And as he talked with him, he went in and found many that had come together.
28 And he said to them, "you know how that it is an unlawful thing for a man that is a Jew, to keep company, or come to one of another nation, but God has shown me that, I should not call any man, common or unclean.
29 Therefore, I came to you without gainsaying, as soon as I was sent. For I ask therefore, for what intent you have sent for me?"

30 And Cornelius said, "four days ago, I was Fasting until this hour and at the ninth hour, I Prayed in my house and behold, a man stood before me in bright clothing
31 And said, "'Cornelius, your Prayer is heard and your Alms are had in remembrance in the Sight of God.
32 Send therefore, to Joppa and call here, Simeon (whose surname is Peter.) He is lodged in the house of one, Simeon (a tanner) by the Sea side who when he comes, shall speak to you.'"
33 Immediately therefore, I sent to you and you have well done that you are come. Now therefore, are we all here present before God, to Hear all things that are Commanded you of God."

34 Then, Peter opened his mouth and said, "of a Truth, I perceive that God is no respecter of persons.
35 But in every nation, He that Fears Him and Works Righteousness, is accepted with Him.
36 The Word, which God sent to the children of Israel, Preaching Peace by Jesus Christ (He is Lord of all.)
37 That Word, I say, you know, which was published throughout all Judaea and began from Galilee, after the Baptism, which John Preached,
38 How God Anointed Jesus, of Nazareth with The Holy Ghost and with Power, Who went about Doing Good and Healing all that were oppressed of the Devil, for God was with Him.
39 And we are witnesses of all things, which He did, both in the land of the Jews and in Jerusalem, WHOM THEY SLEW AND HANGED ON A TREE.
40 Him, God RAISED UP THE THIRD DAY and showed Him openly;
41 Not to all the people, but to witnesses Chosen before God; even to us, who did eat and drink with Him after He Rose from the dead.
42 And He Commanded us to Preach to the people and to Testify that, "'it is He, which was Ordained of God to be the Judge of Quick and dead.'"
43 To Him, give all the prophets witness that, "'through His Name, whosoever, Believes in Him, shall Receive Remission of sins.'"

44 While Peter yet spoke these words, The Holy Ghost fell on all them, which Heard The Word.
45 And they of the circumcision which Believed, were astonished as many as came with Peter, because that on the gentiles also, was poured out The Gift of The Holy Ghost.
46 For they heard them Speak With Tongues and Magnify God. Then

answered Peter,

47 "Can any man forbid water that these should not be Baptized, which have Received The Holy Ghost, as well as we?"

48 And he commanded them to be Baptized in The Name of The Lord. Then, they prayed him to tarry certain days.

Chapter 11

1 And the apostles and brothers that were in Judaea, heard that the gentiles had also, Received The Word of God.

2 And when Peter was come up to Jerusalem, they that were of the circumcision, contended with him

3 Saying, "you went in to uncircumcised men and did eat with them."

4 But, Peter rehearsed the matter from the beginning and expounded it by order to them saying,

5 "I was in the city of Joppa Praying and in a trance, I saw a Vision. A certain vessel descend, as it had been a great sheet let down from Heaven by four corners and it came even to me,

6 On the which, when I had fastened my eyes, I considered and saw four footed beasts of the Earth and wild beasts and creeping things and fowls of the air.

7 And I heard A Voice saying to me, "'arise Peter, slay and eat.'"

8 But I said, "'not so, Lord, for nothing common, or unclean has at any time, entered into my mouth.'"

9 But, The Voice answered me again, from Heaven, "'what God has cleansed, that call you not, common.'"

10 And this was done three times and all were drawn up again, into Heaven.

11 And behold, immediately, there were three men, already come to the house where I was, sent from Caesarea to me.

12 And The Spirit Commanded me, "'go with them, nothing doubting.'" Moreover, these six brothers accompanied me and we entered into the man's house.

13 And he showed us how he had seen an angel in his house, which stood and said to him, "'send men to Joppa and call for Simeon, (whose surname is Peter)

14 Who shall tell you words, whereby you and all your house shall be Saved.'"

15 And as I began to speak, The Holy Ghost fell on them, as on us at the beginning.

16 Then I remembered, The Word of The Lord, how that He said, "John indeed, Baptized with water, BUT YOU SHALL BE BAPTIZED WITH THE HOLY GHOST."

17 Forasmuch then, as God gave them the like Gift as he did to us, who Believed on The Lord, Jesus Christ, what was I that I could withstand God?

18 When they heard these things, they held their peace and Glorified God saying, "then, HAS GOD ALSO, TO THE GENTILES GRANTED REPENTANCE TO LIFE."

19 Now, they which were scattered abroad on the persecution that arose about Stephen, traveled as far as Phenice and Cyprus and Antioch; Preaching The Word to none, but to the Jews only.

20 And some of them, were men of Cyprus and Cyrene, which, when they had come to Antioch, spoke to the Grecians; Preaching The Lord Jesus.

21 And the hand of The Lord was with them and a great number Believed and Turned To The Lord.

22 Then tidings of these things, came to the ears of the church, which was in Jerusalem and they sent forth Barnabas that he should go as far as Antioch.

23 Who, when he came and had seen the Grace of God, was glad and exhorted them all that with Purpose of heart, they would Cleave to The Lord.

24 For he was a good man and Full of The Holy Ghost and of Faith and much people were added to The Lord.

25 Then, departed Barnabas to Tarsus, for to seek Saul.

26 And when he had found him, he brought him to Antioch. And it came to pass that a whole year, they assembled themselves, with the church and Taught much people. And the disciples were called, Christians, first, in Antioch.

27 And in these days, came prophets from Jerusalem to Antioch.

28 And there stood up one of them named, Hagab and signified by The Spirit that, "there should be great dearth, throughout all the World, which came to pass in the days of Claudius Caesar."

29 Then the disciples, every man, according to his ability, determined to send relief to the brothers, which dwelled in Judaea,

30 Which also, they did and sent it to the elders by the hands of Barnabas and Saul.

Chapter 12

1 Now, about that time, Herod, the king stretched forth his hands to vex certain of the church.

2 And he killed James, the brother of John with the sword.

3 And because he saw it pleased the Jews, he proceeded further, to take Peter, also (then, were the days of Unleavened Bread.)

4 And when he had apprehended him, he put him in prison and delivered him to four quaternions of soldiers to keep him; intending after Easter to bring him forth, to the people.

5 Peter therefore, was kept in prison, but Prayer was made Without Ceasing of the church to God for him.

6 And when Herod would have brought him forth, the same night, Peter was sleeping between two soldiers; bound with two chains. And the keepers before the door kept the prison.

7 And behold, the angel of The Lord came on him and a Light showed in the prison. And he knocked Peter on the side and raised him up saying, "arise up, quickly." And his chains fell off from his hands.

8 And the angel said to him, "gird yourself and bind on your sandals." And so he did. And he said to him, "cast your garment about yourself and follow me."

9 And he went out and followed him and knew not that it was true, which was done by the angel, but thought he saw a Vision.

10 When they were past the first and the second ward, they came to the iron gate that leads to the city, which opened to them of his own accord. And they went out and passed on through one street and forthwith, the angel departed from him.

11 And when Peter was come to himself, he said, "now I know of a surety that The Lord has sent His angel and has Delivered me out of the hand of Herod and from all the expectation of the people of the Jews."

12 And when he had considered the thing, he came to the house of Mary, the mother of John, whose surname was Mark, where many were gathered together, Praying.

13 And as Peter knocked at the door of the gate, a damsel came to hearken named, Rhoda.

14 And when she knew Peter's voice, she opened not the gate for gladness, but ran in and told how Peter stood before the gate.

15 And they said to her, "you are mad." But, she constantly affirmed that it was even so. Then said they, "it is his angel."

16 But Peter continued knocking and when they had opened the door and saw him, they were astonished.

17 But he beckoning to them, with the hand to hold their peace, declared to them how, 'The Lord had brought him out of the prison.' And he said, "go show these things to James and to the brothers." And he departed and went into another place.

18 Now, as soon as it was day, there was no small stir among the soldiers, what was become of Peter.

19 And when Herod had sought for him and found him not, he examined the keepers and commanded that they should be put to death. And he went down from Judaea to Caesarea and there, abode.

20 And Herod was highly displeased with them of Tyre and Sidon, but they came with one accord to him and having made Blastus, the king's chamberlain, their friend, desired peace, because their country was nourished by the king's country.

21 And on a set day, Herod arrayed in royal apparel, sat on his throne and made an oration to them.

22 And the people gave a shout saying, "it is the voice of a god and not of a man!"

23 And immediately, the angel of The Lord struck him, because he gave not, God the Glory and he was eaten of worms and gave up the ghost.

24 But The Word of God grew and multiplied.

25 And Barnabas and Saul returned from Jerusalem, when they had fulfilled their ministry and took with them John (whose surname was Mark.)

Chapter 13

1 Now, there were in the church that was at Antioch, certain prophets and teachers, as Barnabas and Simeon that were called, Niger and Lucius, of Cyrene and Manaen, which had been brought up with Herod, the tetrarch and Saul.

2 As they ministered to The Lord and Fasted, <u>The Holy Ghost said</u>, "separate Me, Barnabas and Saul, for the work whereunto, I have called them."

3 And when they had Fasted and Prayed and Laid their Hands On them, they sent them away.

4 So they being <u>sent forth by The Holy Ghost</u>, departed to Seleucia and from there, they sailed to Cyprus.

5 And when they were at Salamis, they Preached The Word of God in the synagogues of the Jews and they had also, John to their minister.

6 And when they had gone through the isle to Paphos, they found a certain sorcerer; a false prophet; a Jew, whose name was, Barjesus,

7 Which was with the deputy of the country, Sergius Paulus; a prudent man, who called for Barnabas and Saul and desired to hear The Word of God.

8 But Elymas, <u>the sorcerer</u>, (for so is his name, by interpretation) withstood them, <u>seeking to turn away the deputy from the Faith</u>.

9 Then Saul, (who also, is called Paul) Filled with The Holy Ghost, set his eyes on him

10 And said, "O full of all subtlety and all mischief; <u>you child of the Devil</u>, you enemy of all Righteousness. Will you not cease to pervert The Right Ways of The Lord?"

11 And now, behold, the hand of The Lord is on you and you shall be blind; not seeing the Sun for a season. And immediately, there fell on him, a mist and a darkness and he went about seeking some to lead him by the hand.

12 Then the deputy, when he saw what was done, Believed, being astonished at <u>The Doctrine of The Lord</u>.

13 Now, when Paul and his company loosed from Paphos, they came to Perga, in Pamphylia. And John, departing from them, returned to Jerusalem.

14 But when they departed from Perga, they came to Antioch, in Pisidia and went into the synagogue on the Sabbath Day and sat down.

15 And after the reading of The Law and the Prophets, the rulers of the synagogue sent to them saying, "you men and brothers, if you have any word of exhortation for the people, say on."

16 Then, Paul stood up and beckoning with his hand said, "men of Israel and you that Fear God, give audience.

17 The God of this people of Israel, Chose our fathers and exalted the people when they dwelled as strangers in the land of Egypt and with a high arm, He brought them out of it

18 And about the time of forty years, suffered He, their manners in the wilderness.

19 And when He had destroyed seven nations in the land of Canaan, He divided their land to them by lot.

20 And after that, He gave to them, judges about the space of four hundred and fifty years, until Samuel, the prophet.

21 And afterward, they desired a king. And God gave to them, Saul, the son of Kish; a man of the tribe of Benjamin, by the space of forty years.

22 And when He had removed him, He raised up to them, David, to be their king, to whom also, He gave their Testimony and said, "'I HAVE FOUND DAVID, THE SON OF JESSE, A MAN AFTER MY OWN HEART, WHICH SHALL FULFILL ALL MY WILL'"

23 Of this man's seed, has God, according to His Promise, Raised to Israel, a Savior, Jesus.

24 When John had first Preached before His coming, the Baptism of Repentance to all the people of Israel

25 And as John fulfilled his course, he said, "'whom think you that I am? I am not He, but behold, there comes One after me, Whose shoes of his feet, I am not worthy to loose.'"

26 Men and brothers, children of the stock of Abraham and whosoever, among you Fears God, to you, is The Word of this Salvation sent.

27 For they that dwell at Jerusalem and their rulers, because they knew Him not, nor yet the voices of the prophets, which are read every Sabbath Day, they have Fulfilled them in CONDEMNING HIM.

28 And though they found no cause of death in Him, yet desired they, Pilate that He should be slain.

29 And when they had Fulfilled all that was written of Him, they took Him down from the tree and laid him in a sepulchre.

30 But God Raised Him from the dead.

31 And He was seen many days of them, which came up with Him from Galilee to Jerusalem; who are His witnesses to the people.

32 And we declare to you Glad Tidings, how that The Promise, which was made to the fathers,

33 God has Fulfilled the same to us, their children, in that, He has Raised Up Jesus

Again, as it is also, written in the Second Psalm, "'YOU ARE MY SON. THIS DAY, HAVE I BEGOTTEN YOU.'"

34 And as concerning that He Raised Him Up from the dead, now, no more to return to corruption, He said on this wise, "'I WILL GIVE YOU THE SURE MERCIES OF DAVID.'"

35 Wherefore, He says also, in another Psalm, "'YOU SHALL NOT SUFFER YOUR HOLY ONE TO SEE CORRUPTION.'"

36 For David, after he had served his own generation by The Will of God, fell on sleep and was laid to his fathers and saw corruption.

37 But He, Whom God Raised again, saw no corruption.

38 Be it known to you therefore, men and brothers that, through this Man is Preached to you, the Forgiveness of sins.

39 And by Him, all that Believe, are Justified from all things, from which, you could not be Justified by the law of Moses.

40 Beware therefore, lest that comes on you, which is spoken of in the Prophets,

41 "'BEHOLD, YOU DESPISERS AND WONDER AND PERISH. FOR I WORK A WORK IN YOUR DAYS; A WORK, WHICH YOU SHALL IN NO WISE BELIEVE, THOUGH A MAN DECLARE IT TO YOU.'"

42 And when the Jews were gone out of the synagogue, the gentiles besought that these Words might be Preached to them the next Sabbath.

43 Now, when the congregation was broken up, many of the Jews and religious proselytes, followed Paul and Barnabas who, speaking to them, persuaded them to continue in the Grace of God.

44 And the next Sabbath Day, came almost the whole city together, to Hear The Word of God.

45 But, when the Jews saw the multitudes, they were filled with envy and spoke against those things, which were spoken by Paul; contradicting and blaspheming.

46 Then Paul and Barnabas, waxed Bold and said, "it was necessary that The Word of God should first, have been spoken to you. But, seeing you put it from you and Judge yourselves unworthy of everlasting Life, lo, we turn to the gentiles.

47 For so, has The Lord Commanded us saying, "'I HAVE SET YOU TO BE A LIGHT OF THE GENTILES THAT YOU SHOULD BE FOR SALVATION TO THE ENDS OF THE EARTH.'"

48 And when the gentiles heard this, they were glad and Glorified The Word of The Lord. And as many as were Ordained to Eternal Life, Believed.

49 And The Word of The Lord was published throughout all the region.

50 But the Jews stirred up the devout and honorable women and the chief men of the city and raised persecution against Paul and Barnabas and expelled them out of their coasts.

51 But they shook off the dust of their feet against them and came to Iconium.

52 And the disciples were filled with Joy and with The Holy Ghost.

Chapter 14

1 And it came to pass, in Iconium that they went both together into the synagogue of the Jews and so spoke that a great multitude, both of the Jews and also, of the Greeks Believed.

2 But the unbelieving Jews, stirred up the gentiles and made their minds evilly affected against the brothers.

3 Long time therefore, they abode speaking Boldly in The Lord, which Gave Testimony to The Word of His Grace and granted Signs and Wonders to be done by their hands.

4 But the multitude of the city were divided and part held with the Jews and part with the apostles.

5 AND WHEN THERE WAS AN ASSAULT MADE, BOTH OF THE GENTILES AND ALSO, OF THE JEWS WITH THEIR RULERS TO USE THEM DESPITEFULLY AND TO STONE THEM,

6 THEY WERE AWARE OF IT AND FLED to Lystra and Derbe; cities of Lycaonia and to the region that lies, round about

7 And there, they Preached The Gospel.

8 And there sat a certain man at Lystra, impotent in his feet; being a cripple from his mother's womb, who never had walked.

9 The same heard Paul speak who steadfastly, beholding him and perceiving that he had Faith to be Healed,

10 Said with a loud voice, "Stand Upright on your feet!" And he Leaped and Walked.

11 And when the people saw what Paul had done, they lifted up their voices saying in the speech of Lycaonia, "the gods are come down to us in the likeness of men."

12 And they called Barnabas, Jupiter and Paul, Mercurius, because he was the chief speaker.

13 Then the priest of Jupiter, which was before their city, brought oxen and garlands to the gates and would have done sacrifice with the people,

14 Which when the apostles, Barnabas and Paul, heard of, they rent their clothes and ran in among the people crying out

15 And saying, "Sirs, why do you these things?! We also, are men of like passions with you and Preach to you that you should Turn From these vanities to The Living God, which made Heaven and Earth and the Sea and all things that are, therein,

16 Who in times past, suffered all nations to walk in their own ways.

17 Nevertheless, He left not Himself without witness, in that He did Good and gave us rain from heaven and fruitful seasons; filling our hearts with food and gladness.

18 And with these sayings, they scarcely, restrained the people that they had not done sacrifice to them.

19 And there came there, certain Jews from Antioch and Iconium, who persuaded the people and having stoned Paul, drew him out of the city, supposing he had been dead.

20 Howbeit, as the disciples stood, round about him, he rose up and came into the city and the next day, he departed with Barnabas to Derbe.

21 And when they had Preached The Gospel to that city and had Taught many, they returned again, to Lystra and to Iconium and Antioch,

22 Confirming the souls of the disciples and exhorting them to Continue in the Faith and that, "'we must through much tribulation, enter into the Kingdom of God.'"

23 And when they had Ordained themselves elders in every church and had Prayed with Fasting, they commended them to The Lord, on Whom they Believed.

24 And after they had passed throughout Pisidia, they came to Pamphylia.

25 And when they had Preached The Word in Perga, they went down into Attalia

26 And there sailed to Antioch, from whence they had been recommended to the Grace of God, for the Work which they fulfilled.

27 And when they had come and had gathered the church together, they rehearsed all that God had done with them and how He had opened The Door of Faith to the gentiles.

28 And there, they abode long time, with the disciples.

Chapter 15

1 And certain men, which came down from Judaea, taught the brothers and said, "except you be circumcised, after the manner of Moses, you cannot be Saved."

2 When therefore, Paul and Barnabas had no small dissension and disputation with them, they determined that Paul and Barnabas and certain other of them, should go up to Jerusalem to the apostles and elders, about this question.

3 And being brought on their way by the church, they passed through Phenice and Samaria, declaring the Conversion of the gentiles and they caused great Joy to all the brothers.

4 And when they had come to Jerusalem, they were received of the church. And of the apostles and elders and they declared all things that God had Done with them.

5 But there rose up certain of the sect of the Pharisees, which Believed saying that, "it was needful to circumcise them and to command them to keep the law of Moses."

6 And the apostles and elders came together, for to consider of this matter.

7 And when there had been much disputing, Peter rose up and said to them, "men and brothers, you know how that a good while ago, God made choice among us that the gentiles by my mouth, should Hear The Word of The Gospel and Believe.

8 And God, which Knows the hearts, bare them witness, Giving them The Holy Ghost; even as He did to us

9 And put no difference between us and them, Purifying their hearts by Faith.

10 Now therefore, why tempt you God, to put a yoke on the neck of the disciples, which neither our fathers, nor we, were able to bear?

11 But, we Believe that through the Grace of The Lord, Jesus Christ, we shall be Saved, even as they."

12 Then, all the multitude kept silence and gave audience to Barnabas and Paul, declaring what Miracles and Wonders God

had Worked among the gentiles by them.
13 And after they had held their peace, James answered saying, "men and brothers, hearken to me.
14 Simeon has declared how God, at the first, did visit the gentiles to take out of them, a people for His Name.
15 And to this, agree the words of the Prophets as it is written,
16 "'AFTER THIS, I WILL RETURN AND WILL BUILD AGAIN, THE TABERNACLE OF DAVID, WHICH IS FALLEN DOWN. AND I WILL BUILD AGAIN, THE RUINS THEREOF AND I WILL SET IT UP
17 THAT THE RESIDUE OF MEN, MIGHT SEEK AFTER THE LORD AND ALL THE GENTILES, ON WHOM, MY NAME IS CALLED,'" says The Lord, "'WHO DOES ALL THESE THINGS.'"

18 Known to God, are all His Works from the beginning of the World.
19 Wherefore, my sentence is that we trouble not them, which from among the gentiles are Turned To God,
20 But that we write to them that, "'they abstain from pollutions of idols and from fornication and from things strangled and from blood.'"
21 For Moses of old time, has in every city, them that Preach Him, being read in the synagogues every Sabbath Day."
22 Then, it pleased the Apostles and elders with the whole church, to send chosen men of their own company to Antioch with Paul and Barnabas, namely, Judah, surnamed Barsabas and Silas; chief men among the brothers.

23 And they wrote letters by themselves after this manner: "The apostles and elders and brothers send greeting to the brothers, which are of the gentiles in Antioch and Syria and Cilicia.
24 Forasmuch as we have heard that certain, which went out from us, have troubled you with words, subverting your souls saying, "'you must be circumcised and keep the law,'" to whom, we gave no such commandment.
25 It seemed good to us, being assembled with one accord, to send Chosen men to you with our beloved Barnabas and Paul;
26 Men that have hazarded their lives for The Name of our Lord Jesus Christ.
27 We have sent therefore, Judah and Silas, who shall also, tell you the same things by mouth.
28 For it seemed good to The Holy Ghost and to us, to lay on you no greater burden than these necessary things
29 That: you abstain from meats offered to idols and from blood and from things strangled and from fornication, from which if you keep yourselves, you shall do well. Fare you well."

30 So, when they were dismissed, they came to Antioch. And when they had gathered the multitude together, they delivered the epistle,
31 Which when they had read, they rejoiced for the consolation.
32 And Judah and Silas, being prophets also, themselves, exhorted the brothers with many words and Confirmed them.
33 And after they had tarried there a space, they were let go in peace from the brothers to the apostles.

34 Notwithstanding, it pleased Silas to abide there still.
35 Paul also and Barnabas, continued in Antioch, Teaching and Preaching The Word of The Lord; with many others, also.
36 And some days after, Paul said to Barnabas, "let us go, again and visit our brothers in every city, where we have Preached The Word of The Lord and see how they do."
37 And Barnabas determined to take with them, John (whose surname was Mark.)
38 But Paul thought not good to take him with them, who departed from them from Pamphylia and went not with them to the work.
39 And the contention was so sharp between them that they departed asunder; one from the other. And so, Barnabas took Mark and sailed to Cyprus.
40 And Paul chose Silas and departed, being recommended by the brothers to the Grace of God.
41 And he went through Syria and Cilicia, Confirming the churches.

Chapter 16

1 Then he came to Derbe and Lystra and behold, a certain disciple was there, named Timotheus, (the son of a certain woman, which was a Jewess and Believed, but his father was a Greek)
2 Which was well reported of by the brothers that were at Lystra and Iconium.
3 Him, would Paul have to go forth with himself and took and circumcised him, because of the Jews, which were in those

quarters, for they knew all that, his father was a Greek.

4 And as they went through the cities, they delivered them the Decrees for to Keep that were Ordained of the apostles and elders, which were at Jerusalem.

5 And so were the churches established in the Faith and increased in number daily.

6 Now, when they had gone throughout Phrygia and the region of Galatia and were forbidden of The Holy Ghost to Preach The Word in Asia,

7 After they had come to Mysia, they assayed to go into Bithynia, but The Spirit suffered them not.

8 And they passing by Mysia, came down to Troas.

9 And a Vision, appeared to Paul in the night: there stood a man of Macedonia and prayed him saying, "come over into Macedonia and help us."

10 And after he had seen the Vision, immediately, we endeavored to go into Macedonia, assuredly gathering that The Lord had called us for to Preach The Gospel to them.

11 Therefore, loosing from Troas, we came with a straight course to Samothracia and the next day, to Neapolis

12 And from there, to Philippi, which is the chief city of that part of Macedonia and a colony. And we were in that city abiding certain days.

13 And on the Sabbath, we went out of the city by a river side, where Prayer was wont to be made and we sat down and spoke to the women, which resorted there.

14 And a certain woman named Lydia, (a seller of purple, of the city of Thyatira) which Worshipped God, heard us, whose heart The Lord opened that she attended to the things, which were spoken of Paul.

15 And when she was Baptized and her household, she besought us saying, "if you have Judged me to be Faithful to The Lord, come into my house and abide there." And she constrained us.

16 And it came to pass, as we went to Prayer, a certain damsel, possessed with a spirit of divination met us, which brought her masters much gain by soothsaying.

17 The same followed Paul and us and cried saying, "these men are the servants of The Most High God, which show to us The Way of Salvation."

18 And this did she many days. But Paul, being grieved, turned and said to the spirit, "I Command you, in The Name of Jesus Christ to come out of her." And he came out, the same hour.

19 And when her masters saw that the hope of their gains was gone, they caught Paul and Silas and drew them into the marketplace to the rulers

20 And brought them to the magistrates saying, "these men, being Jews, do exceedingly, trouble our city

21 And Teach Customs, which are not lawful for us to receive, neither to observe, being Romans."

22 And the multitude rose up together, against them. And the magistrates rent off their clothes and commanded to beat them.

23 And when they had laid many stripes on them, they cast them into prison; charging the jailer to keep them safely,

24 Who having received such a charge, thrust them into the inner prison and made their feet fast in the stocks.

25 And at midnight, Paul and Silas Prayed and Sang Praises to God and the prisoners heard them.

26 And suddenly, there was a great earthquake, so that the foundations of the prison were shaken. And immediately, all the doors were Opened and every one's bands were Loosed.

27 And the keeper of the prison, waking out of his sleep and seeing the prison doors open, he drew out his sword and would have killed himself, supposing that the prisoners had been fled.

28 But Paul cried with a loud voice saying, "do yourself no harm, for we are all here."

29 Then he called for a light and sprang in and came trembling and fell down before Paul and Silas

30 And brought them out and said, "Sirs, what must I Do to be Saved?"

31 And they said, "Believe on The Lord, Jesus Christ and you shall be Saved and your house."

32 And they spoke to him The Word of The Lord and to all that were in his house.

33 And he took them the same hour of the night and washed their stripes and was Baptized; he and all his, straightway.

34 And when he had brought them into his house, he set meat before them and Rejoiced, Believing in God; with all his house.

35 And when it was day, the magistrates sent the sergeants saying, "let those men go."

36 And the keeper of the prison told this saying to Paul, "the magistrates have sent to let you go. Now therefore, depart and go in peace."

37 But Paul said to them, "they have beaten us openly, uncondemned; being Romans and have cast us into prison and now, do they thrust us out privily? No verily, but let them come themselves and fetch us out."

38 And the sergeants told these words to the magistrates and they feared, when they heard that they were Romans.

39 And they came and besought them and brought them out and desired them to depart out of the city.

40 And they went out of the prison and entered into the house of Lydia. And when they had seen the brothers, they comforted them and departed.

Chapter 17

1 Now, when they had passed through Amphipolis and Apollonia, they came to Thessalonica, where was a synagogue of the Jews.

2 And Paul, as his manner was, went in to them and three Sabbath Days, reasoned with them out of The Scriptures,

3 Opening and alleging that, "CHRIST MUST NEEDS HAVE SUFFERED AND RISEN AGAIN, FROM THE DEAD AND THAT THIS JESUS, Whom I Preach to you is, Christ."

4 And some of them Believed and consorted with Paul and Silas and of the devout Greeks; a great multitude of the chief women, not a few.

5 But the Jews, which believed not, moved with envy, took to themselves, certain lewd fellows of the baser sort and gathered a company and set all the city on an uproar and assaulted the house of Jason and sought to bring them out to the people.

6 And when they found them not, they drew Jason and certain brothers to the rulers of the city crying, "these that have turned the World upside down, are come here also,

7 Whom Jason has received and these all do contrary to the decrees of Caesar saying that, "'there is another King, one, Jesus.'"

8 And they troubled the people and the rulers of the city, when they heard these things.

9 And when they had taken security of Jason and of the others, they let them go.

10 And the brothers immediately, sent away Paul and Silas by night to Berea, who coming there, went into the synagogue of the Jews.

11 These were more noble than those in Thessalonica, in that they Received The Word with all readiness of mind and Searched The Scriptures daily; whether those things were so.

12 Therefore, many of them Believed also, of Honorable women, which were Greeks and of men, not a few.

13 But when the Jews of Thessalonica, had knowledge that The Word of God was Preached of Paul at Berea, they came there also, and stirred up the people.

14 And then immediately, the brothers sent away Paul, to go as it were to the Sea. But Silas and Timotheus, abode there still.

15 And they that conducted Paul, brought him to Athens and receiving a commandment to Silas and Timotheus, for to come to him with all speed, they departed.

16 Now, while Paul waited for them at Athens, his spirit was stirred in himself, when he saw the city, wholly given to idolatry.

17 Therefore, disputed he in the synagogue with the Jews and with the devout persons and in the market daily with them that met with him.

18 Then, certain philosophers of the Epicureans and of the Stoicks, encountered him. And some said, "what will this babbler say?" Others some, "he seems to be a setter forth of strange gods," because he Preached to them, Jesus and the Resurrection.

19 And they took him and brought him to Areopagus saying, "may we know what this New Doctrine, whereof you speak, is? 20 For you bring certain strange things to our ears. We would know therefore, what these things mean,"

21 (For all the Athenians and strangers, which were there, spent their time in nothing else, but either to tell, or to hear some new thing.)

22 Then Paul stood in the midst of Mars' Hill and said, "you men of Athens, I perceive that in all things, you are too superstitious.

23 For as I passed by and beheld your

devotions, I found an altar with this inscription, "'to The Unknown God,'" Whom therefore, you ignorantly Worship. Him, I declare to you,

24 God that made the World and all things therein, seeing that He is Lord of Heaven and Earth, dwells not, in temples made with hands.

25 Neither is worshipped with men's hands, as though He needed any thing; seeing He Gives to all, life and breath and all things

26 And has made of one blood, all nations of men, for to dwell on all the face of the Earth and has determined the times before appointed and the bounds of their habitation

27 That they should Seek The Lord, if haply, they might feel after Him and Find Him, though He is not far from every one of us.

28 For in Him, we live and move and have our being as certain also, of your own poets have said, for we are also, His offspring.

29 Forasmuch then, as we are the offspring of God, we ought not, to think that The Godhead is like to: gold, or silver, or stone; graven, by art and man's device.

30 <u>And the times of this ignorance, God winked at, but now, Commands all men every where, to Repent.</u>

31 Because He has appointed a day, in the which, He will Judge the World in Righteousness, by that Man, Whom He has Ordained whereof, He has Given assurance to all men, in that He has Raised Him from the dead."

32 And when they heard of <u>the Resurrection of the dead</u>, some mocked and others said, "we will hear you again, of this matter."

33 So, Paul departed from among them.

34 Howbeit, certain men clove to him and Believed, among the which, was Dionysius, the Areopagite and a woman named, Damaris and others with them.

Chapter 18

1 After these things, Paul departed from Athens and came to Corinth

2 And found a certain Jew named, Aquila, born in Pontus, lately come from Italy, with his wife, Priscilla (because that Claudius had commanded all Jews to depart from Rome) and came to them.

3 And because he was of the same craft, he abode with them and worked, for by their occupation they were tentmakers.

4 And he reasoned in the synagogue, every Sabbath and persuaded the Jews and the Greeks.

5 And when Silas and Timotheus had come from Macedonia, Paul was pressed in The Spirit and Testified to the Jews that, Jesus was Christ.

6 And when they opposed themselves and blasphemed, he shook his raiment and said to them, "your blood is on your own heads. I am clean from, henceforth. I will go to the gentiles."

7 And he departed there and entered into a certain man's house named, Justus; one that Worshipped God, whose house joined hard to the synagogue.

8 And Crispus, the chief ruler of the synagogue, Believed on The Lord with all his house and many of the Corinthians Hearing, Believed and were Baptized.

9 Then spoke The Lord to Paul in the night by a Vision, "be not afraid, but speak and hold not, your Peace.

10 For I am with you and no man, shall set on you to hurt you, for I have much people in this city."

11 And he continued there, a year and six months, Teaching The Word of God among them.

12 And when Gallio was the deputy of Achaia, the Jews made insurrection with one accord against Paul and brought him to the judgement seat

13 Saying, "this fellow, persuades men to Worship God, contrary to the law."

14 And when Paul was now, about to open his mouth, Gallio said to the Jews, "if it were a matter of wrong, or wicked lewdness, O you Jews, reason would that, I should bear with you.

15 But if it be a question of words and names and of your law, look yourselves to it, for I will be no judge of such matters."

16 And he drove them from the judgement seat.

17 Then all the Greeks took Sosthenes, the chief ruler of the synagogue and beat him before the judgement seat. And Gallio cared for none of those things.

18 And Paul, after this, tarried there yet a good while and then, took his leave of the brothers and sailed there, into Syria and with him, Priscilla and Aquila having shorn his head in Cenchrea, for he had a vow.

19 And he came to Ephesus and left them there. But he himself, entered into the

synagogue and reasoned with the Jews.

20 When they desired him to tarry longer times with them, he consented not,

21 But commanded them farewell saying, "I must by all means, keep this feast that comes in Jerusalem. But, I will return again, to you, if God wills." And he sailed from Ephesus.

22 And when he had landed at Caesarea and gone up and saluted the church, he went down to Antioch.

23 And after he had spent some time there, he departed and went over all the country of Galatia and Phrygia in order, strengthening all the disciples.

24 And a certain Jew named, Apollos, born at Alexandria; an eloquent man and mighty in The Scriptures, came to Ephesus.

25 This man was instructed in The Way of The Lord and being fervent in The Spirit, he spoke and Taught Diligently, the things of The Lord; knowing only, the Baptism of John.

26 And he began to Speak Boldly in the synagogue, whom when Aquila and Priscilla had heard, they took him to themselves and expounded to him, The Way of God, more perfectly.

27 And when he was disposed to pass into Achaia, the brothers wrote, exhorting the disciples to receive him, who when he was come, helped them much, which had Believed through Grace.

28 For he mightily convinced the Jews and that publicly, showing by The Scriptures that Jesus, was Christ.

Chapter 19

1 And it came to pass that, while Apollos was at Corinth, Paul having passed through the upper coasts, came to Ephesus and finding certain disciples,

2 He said to them, "have you Received The Holy Ghost since you Believed?" And they said to him, "we have not so much as heard whether there be any, Holy Ghost."

3 And he said to them, "to what then, were you Baptized?" And they said, "to John's Baptism."

4 Then Paul said, "John verily, Baptized with the Baptism of Repentance, saying to the people that, "'they should Believe on Him, which should come after him; that is, on Christ Jesus.'"

5 When they Heard this, they were Baptized, in The Name of The Lord, Jesus.

6 And when Paul had Laid his Hands On them, The Holy Ghost came on them and they Spoke With Tongues and Prophesied.

7 And all the men were about twelve.

8 And he went into the synagogue and spoke Boldly, for the space of three months; disputing and persuading the things concerning the Kingdom of God.

9 But, when diverse were hardened and believed not, but spoke evil of that Way before the multitude, he departed from them and separated the disciples; disputing daily, in the school of one, Tyrannus.

10 And this continued by the space of two years, so that all they, which dwelled in Asia, Heard The Word of The Lord, Jesus; both Jews and Greeks.

11 And God Worked special Miracles by the hands of Paul

12 So that, from his body, were brought to the sick, handkerchiefs, or aprons and the diseases departed from them and the evil spirits went out of them.

13 Then certain of the vagabond Jews, exorcists, took on themselves, to call over them, which had evil spirits, The Name of The Lord, Jesus saying, "we adjure you, by Jesus, whom Paul preaches..."

14 And there were seven sons of one, Sceva; a Jew and chief of the priests, which did so.

15 And the evil spirit answered and said, "Jesus, I know and Paul I know, but who are you?"

16 And the man in whom, the evil spirit was, leaped on them and overcame them and prevailed against them, so that they fled out of that house naked and wounded.

17 And this was known to all the Jews and Greeks also, dwelling at Ephesus and Fear fell on them all and The Name of The Lord, Jesus was Magnified.

18 And many that Believed, came and Confessed and showed their deeds.

19 Many of them also, which used curious arts, brought their scrolls together and burned them before all men. And they counted the price of them and found it, fifty thousand pieces of silver.

20 So mightily, grew The Word of God and Prevailed.

21 After these things were ended, Paul purposed in The Spirit, when he had passed through Macedonia and Achaia, to go to Jerusalem saying, "after I have been there, I must also, see Rome."

22 So, he sent into Macedonia, two of them that ministered to him: Timotheus and Erastus. But he himself, stayed in Asia for a season.
23 And the same time, there arose no small stir about that way.
24 <u>For a certain man named, Demetrius; a silversmith, which made silver shrines for Diana, brought no small gain to the craftsmen,</u>
25 <u>Whom he called together, with the workmen of like occupation and said, "Sirs, you know that by this craft we have our wealth.</u>
26 <u>Moreover, you see and hear that not alone at Ephesus, but almost throughout all Asia, this Paul has persuaded and turned away much people, saying that, "'they are no gods, which are made with hands'"</u>
27 So that, not only this, our craft is in danger to be set at naught. But, also that the temple of the great goddess, Diana, should be despised and her magnificence, should be destroyed, whom all Asia and the World worships."
28 And when they heard these sayings, they were full of wrath and cried out saying, "great is Diana, of the Ephesians!"
29 And the whole city was filled with confusion. And having caught Gaius and Aristarchus; men of Macedonia, Paul's companions in travel, they rushed with one accord, into the theatre.
30 And when Paul would have entered in to the people, the disciples suffered him not.
31 And certain of the chief of Asia, which were his friends, sent to him, desiring him that he would not adventure himself, into the theatre.
32 Some therefore, cried one thing and some another, for the assembly was confused and the more part knew not wherefore, they had come together.

33 And they drew Alexander out of the multitude; the Jews putting him forward. And Alexander, beckoned with the hand and would have made his defense to the people.
34 But, when they knew that he was a Jew, all with one voice, (about the space of two hours) cried out, "great is Diana, of the Ephesians!"
35 And when the town clerk had appeased the people, he said, "you men of Ephesus, what man is there that knows not how that the city of the Ephesians is a worshipper of the great goddess, Diana and of the image, which fell down from Jupiter?
36 Seeing then that these things cannot be spoken against, you ought to be quiet and to do nothing rashly.
37 For you have brought here these men, which are neither robbers of churches, nor yet blasphemers of your goddess.
38 Wherefore, if Demetrius and the craftsmen, which are with him, have a matter against any man, the law is open and there are deputies. Let them implead one another.
39 But, if you enquire any thing, concerning other matters, it shall be determined in a lawful assembly.
40 For we are in danger to be called in question for this day's uproar, there being no cause, whereby we may give an account of this concourse."
41 And when he had thus spoken, he dismissed the assembly.

Chapter 20

1 And after the uproar was ceased, Paul called to himself, the disciples and embraced them and departed for to go into Macedonia.
2 And when he had gone over those parts and had given them much exhortation, he came into Greece
3 And there abode three months. And when the Jews laid wait for him, as he was about to sail into Syria, he purposed to return through Macedonia.
4 And there accompanied him into Asia: Sopater, (of Berea and of the Thessalonians) Aristarchus and Secundus and Gaius (of Derbe) and Timotheus; and of Asia: Tychicus and Trophimus.
5 These going before, tarried for us, at Troas.
6 And we sailed away from Philippi after the days of Unleavened Bread and came to them, to Troas in five days, where we abode, seven days.

7 And on the first day of the week, when the disciples came together to break bread, Paul Preached to them, ready to depart on the morrow and continued his speech until midnight.
8 And there were many lights in the upper chamber, where they were gathered, together.
9 And there sat in a window, a certain young man, named Eutychus, being fallen into a deep sleep and as Paul was long Preaching, he sunk down with sleep and

fell down from the third loft and was taken up dead.

10 And Paul went down and fell on him and embracing him said, "trouble not yourselves, for his life is in him."

11 When he therefore, was come up again and had broken bread and eaten and talked a long while, even until break of day, so he departed.

12 And they brought the young man alive and were not a little comforted.

13 And we went before, to ship and sailed to Assos, there intending to take in Paul, for so had he appointed, minding himself to go afoot.

14 And when he met with us at Assos, we took him in and came to Mitylene.

15 And we sailed there and came the next day, over against Chios. And the next day, we arrived at Samos and tarried at Trogyllium. And the next day, we came to Miletus.

16 For Paul had determined to sail by Ephesus, because he would not spend the time in Asia, for he hasted, if it were possible for himself, to be at Jerusalem, the day of Pentecost.

17 And from Miletus, he sent to Ephesus and called the elders of the church.

18 And when they had come to him, he said to them, "you know from the first day that I came into Asia, after what manner I have been with you at all seasons,

19 Serving The Lord with all humility of mind and with many tears and temptations, which befell me by the lying in wait of the Jews

20 And how I kept back nothing that was profitable to you, but have shown you and have Taught you publicly and from house to house,

21 Testifying both to the Jews and also, to the Greeks, Repentance toward God and Faith toward our Lord, Jesus Christ.

22 And now, behold, I go bound in The Spirit to Jerusalem, not knowing the things that shall befall me there,

23 Save that, The Holy Ghost witnesses in every city, saying that bonds and afflictions abide me.

24 But none of these things move me, neither count I, my life dear to myself, so that I might finish my course with Joy and the ministry, which I have received of The Lord, Jesus, to Testify The Gospel of The Grace of God.

25 And now, behold, I know that you all, among whom, I have gone Preaching the Kingdom of God, shall see my face, no more.

26 Wherefore, I take you to record this day that I am pure from the blood of all men.

27 For I have not shunned to declare to you, all the Counsel of God.

28 Take Heed therefore, to yourselves and to all the flock, over the which, The Holy Ghost has made you overseers, to feed the church of God, which He has purchased with His Own Blood.

29 For I know this that, after my departing, shall grievous wolves enter in among you, not sparing the flock.

30 Also, of your own selves, shall men arise, speaking perverse things, to draw away disciples after themselves.

31 Therefore, watch and remember that, by the space of three years, I ceased not to warn every one, night and day with tears.

32 And now brothers, I commend you to God and to The Word of His Grace, which is able to build you up and to give you an inheritance among all them, which are Sanctified.

33 I have coveted no man's silver, or gold, or apparel.

34 Yes, you yourselves know that these hands have ministered to my necessities and to them that were with me.

35 I have shown you all things, how that so Laboring, you ought to support the weak and to remember The Words of The Lord, Jesus, how He said, "'it is more Blessed to Give, than to receive.'"

36 And when he had thus spoken, he Kneeled Down and Prayed with them all.

37 And they all wept sore and fell on Paul's neck and kissed him,

38 Sorrowing most of all, for the words, which he spoke that, "they should see his face no more." And they accompanied him to the ship.

Chapter 21

1 And it came to pass that after we were gotten from them and had launched, we came with a straight course to Coos and the day following, to Rhodes and from there, to Patara

2 And finding a ship sailing over to Phenicia, we went aboard and set forth.

3 Now, when we had discovered Cyprus, we left it on the left hand and sailed into

Syria and landed at Tyre, for there, the ship was to unlade her burden.

4 And finding disciples, we tarried there, seven days, who said to Paul through The Spirit that he, "SHOULD NOT GO UP TO JERUSALEM."

5 And when we had accomplished those days, we departed and went our way. And they all brought us on our way, with wives and children, until we were out of the city and we Kneeled Down on the shore and Prayed.

6 And when we had taken our leave, one of another, we took ship and they returned home again.

7 And when we had finished our course from Tyre, we came to Ptolemais and saluted the brothers and abode with them, one day.

8 And the next day, we that were of Paul's company, departed and came to Caesarea and we entered into the house of Philip, the evangelist, which was one of the seven and abode with him.

9 And the same man had four daughters; {virgins} which did Prophesy.

10 And as we tarried there many days, there came down from Judaea, a certain prophet named, Agabus.

11 And when he was come to us, he took Paul's girdle and bound his own hands and feet and said, "thus, says The Holy Ghost, "SO SHALL THE JEWS AT JERUSALEM, BIND THE MAN THAT OWNS THIS GIRDLE AND SHALL DELIVER HIM INTO THE HANDS OF THE GENTILES.'"

12 And when we heard these things, both we and they of that place, besought him not to go up to Jerusalem.

13 Then Paul answered, "what mean you to weep and to break my heart? For I am ready not to be bound only, but also, to die at Jerusalem for The Name of The Lord, Jesus."

14 And when he would not be persuaded, we ceased, saying, "The Will of The Lord be done."

15 And after those days, we took up our carriages and went up to Jerusalem.

16 There went with us also, certain of the disciples of Caesarea and brought with them one, Mnason, of Cyprus, an old disciple, with whom, we should lodge.

17 And when we had come to Jerusalem, the brothers received us gladly.

18 And the day following, Paul went in with us to James and all the elders were present.

19 And when he had saluted them, he declared particularly, what things God had Worked among the gentiles by his ministry.

20 And when they heard it, they Glorified The Lord and said to him, "you see brother, how many thousands of Jews there are, which Believe and they are all Zealous of The Law.

21 And they are informed of you that you Teach all the Jews, which are among the gentiles to forsake Moses saying that, "'they ought not to circumcise their children, neither to walk after the customs.'"

22 What is it therefore? The multitude must needs come together, for they will hear that you are come.

23 Do therefore, this that we say to you. We have four men, which have a vow on themselves.

24 Them, take and purify yourself, with them and be at charges with them that they may shave their heads. And all may know that those things, whereof they were informed concerning you, are nothing, but that you yourselves also, walk orderly and keep the Law.

25 As touching the gentiles, which Believe, we have written and concluded that, "they observe no such thing, save only that: they keep themselves, from things offered to idols and from blood and from strangled and from fornication."

26 Then, Paul took the men and the next day, purifying himself with them, entered into the temple, to signify the accomplishment of the days of purification, until that an offering should be offered for every one of them.

27 And when the seven days were almost ended, the Jews which were of Asia, when they saw him in the temple, stirred up all the people and laid hands on him,

28 Crying out, "men of Israel, help! This is the man that Teaches all men every where, against the people and the law and this place and further brought Greeks also, into the temple and has polluted this Holy place!"

29 (For they had seen before with him in the city, Trophimus, an Ephesian, whom they supposed that Paul had brought into the Temple.)

30 And all the city was moved and the

people ran, together and they took Paul and drew him out of the temple and forthwith, the doors were shut.

31 And as they went about to kill him, tidings came to the chief captain of the band that all Jerusalem was in an uproar,

32 Who immediately, took soldiers and centurions and ran down to them. And when they saw the chief captain and the soldiers, they left beating of Paul.

33 THEN THE CHIEF CAPTAIN, CAME NEAR AND TOOK HIM AND COMMANDED HIM TO BE BOUND WITH TWO CHAINS and demanded who he was and what he had done.

34 And some cried one thing, some another among the multitude. And when he could not know the certainty, for the tumult, he commanded him to be carried into the castle.

35 And when he came on the stairs, so it was that he was borne of the soldiers for the violence of the people,

36 For the multitude of the people followed after, crying, "away with him!"

37 And as Paul was to be led into the castle, he said to the chief captain, "may I speak to you?," who said, "can you speak Greek?

38 Are not you that Egyptian, which before these days, made an uproar and led out into the wilderness, four thousand men that were murderers?"

39 But Paul said, I am a man, which am a Jew, of Tarsus; a city in Cilicia, a citizen of no mean city and I beseech you, suffer me to speak to the people.

40 And when he had given him license, Paul stood on the stairs and beckoned with the hand to the people. And when there was made a great silence, he spoke to them in the Hebrew tongue saying,

Chapter 22

1 "Men, brothers and fathers, hear you my defense, which I make now, to you,

2 (And when they heard that he spoke in the Hebrew tongue to them, they kept the more silence) and he said,

3 "I am verily, a man which am a Jew, born in Tarsus; a city in Cilicia, yet brought up in this city at the feet of Gamaliel and Taught, according to the perfect manner of the Law of the fathers and was Zealous toward God, as you all are, this day.

4 And I persecuted this way, to the death; binding and delivering into prisons, both men and women.

5 As also, the high priest does bear me witness and all the estate of the elders from whom also, I received letters to the brothers and went to Damascus, to bring them, which were there, bound to Jerusalem, for to be punished.

6 And it came to pass that, as I made my journey and was come near to Damascus about noon, suddenly there Shone from Heaven a Great Light, round about me.

7 And I fell to the ground and heard A Voice saying to me, "'Saul, Saul, why persecute you Me?'"

8 And I answered, "'who are You, Lord?'" And He said to me, "'I am Jesus, of Nazareth, Whom you persecute.'"

9 And they that were with me saw indeed, The Light and were afraid. But, they heard not The Voice of Him that spoke to me.

10 And I said, "'what shall I do, Lord?'" And The Lord said to me, "'arise and go into Damascus and there, it shall be told you, of all things, which are appointed for you to do.'"

11 And when I could not see for The Glory of That Light, being led by the hand of them that were with me, I came into Damascus.

12 And one, Hananiah, a devout man, according to the Law; having a good report of all the Jews, which dwelled there,

13 Came to me and stood and said to me, "'brother Saul, Receive your Sight.'" And the same hour, I looked up on him.

14 And he said, "'The God of our fathers, has Chosen you that you should Know His Will and see that Just One and should Hear The Voice of His mouth.

15 For you shall be His witness to all men of what you have Seen and Heard.

16 And now, why tarry you? Arise and be Baptized and wash away your sins, Calling on The Name of The Lord.'"

17 And it came to pass that, when I was come again, to Jerusalem even while I Prayed in the temple, I was in a trance

18 And saw Him saying to me, "'make haste and get yourself, quickly out of Jerusalem. For they will not receive your Testimony concerning Me.'"

19 And I said, "'Lord, they know that I imprisoned and beat in every synagogue, them that Believed on You.

20 And when the blood of Your martyr, Stephen was shed, I also, was standing by and consenting to his death and kept the

raiment of them that slew him.'"
21 And He said to me, "'depart, for I will send you far hence, to the gentiles.'"
22 And they gave him audience to this word and then, lifted up their voices and said, "away with such a fellow from the Earth, for it is not fit that he should live!"
23 And as they cried out and cast off their clothes and threw dust into the air,
24 The chief captain commanded him to be brought into the castle and commanded that, "he should be examined by scourging that he might know wherefore, they cried so, against him."
25 And as they bound him with straps, Paul said to the centurion that stood by, "is it lawful for you to scourge a man that is a Roman and uncondemned?"
26 When the centurion heard that, he went and told the chief captain saying, "take heed what you do, for this man is a Roman."

27 Then the chief captain came and said to him, "tell me, are you a Roman?" He said, "yes."
28 And the chief captain answered, "with a great sum, I obtained this freedom." And Paul said, "but, I was free born."
29 Then straightway, they departed from him, which should have examined him. And the chief captain also, was afraid after he knew that he was a Roman and because he had bound him.
30 On the morrow, because he would have known the certainty wherefore, he was accused of the Jews, he loosed him from his bands and commanded the chief priests and all their council to appear and brought Paul down and set him before them.

Chapter 23

1 And Paul, earnestly beholding the council said, "men and brothers, I have lived in all good conscience before God until this day."
2 And the high priest, Hananiah commanded them that stood by him, to beat him on the mouth.
3 Then said Paul to him, "God shall strike you, you whited wall. For you sit to judge me after the law and command me to be beaten contrary to the law?"
4 And they that stood by said, "revile you, God's high priest?"
5 Then Paul said, "I knew not brothers that he was the high priest, for it is written, "'you shall not speak evil of the ruler of your people.'"

6 But when Paul perceived that the one part, were Sadducees and the other, Pharisees, he cried out in the council, "men and brothers, I am a Pharisee, the son of a Pharisee. Of the Hope and Resurrection of the dead, I am called in question."
7 And when he had so said, there arose a dissension between the Pharisees and the Sadducees and the multitude were divided.
8 For the Sadducees say that, "there is no resurrection, neither angel, nor spirit." But, the Pharisees confess both.
9 And there arose a great cry and the scribes that were of the Pharisees' part, rose and strove saying, "we find no evil in this man. But if a spirit, or an angel has spoken to him, let us not fight against God."
10 And when there arose a great dissension, the chief captain fearing, lest Paul should have been pulled in pieces of them, commanded the soldiers to, "go down and to take him by force, from among them and to bring him into the castle."

11 And the night following, The Lord stood by him and said, "be of good cheer, Paul. For as you have Testified of Me in Jerusalem, so must you Bear Witness also, at Rome."
12 And when it was day, certain of the Jews banded, together and bound themselves under a curse, saying that they would, "neither eat, nor drink until they had killed Paul."
13 And they were more than forty, which had made this conspiracy.
14 And they came to the chief priests and elders and said, "we have bound ourselves, under a great curse that, "'we will eat nothing, until we have slain Paul.'"
15 Now therefore, you with the council, signify to the chief captain that, "he brings him down to you tomorrow, as though you would enquire something more perfectly, concerning him and we, or ever he comes near, are ready to kill him."

16 And when Paul's sister's son, heard of their lying in wait, he went and entered into the castle and told Paul.
17 Then Paul called one of the centurions to himself and said, "bring this young man to the chief captain, for he has a certain

thing to tell him."

18 So, he took him and brought him to the chief captain and said, "Paul, the prisoner called me to himself and prayed me to bring this young man to you, who has something to say to you."

19 Then, the chief captain took him by the hand and went with him aside, privately and asked him, "what is that, you have to tell me?"

20 And he said, "the Jews have agreed to desire you that, "'you would bring down Paul tomorrow, into the council, as though they would enquire somewhat of him more perfectly.'"

21 But do not you, yield to them, for there lies in wait for him, of them, more than forty men, which have bound themselves, with an oath that they will, "'neither eat, nor drink until they have killed him'" and now, they are already, looking for a promise from you."

22 So, the chief captain then, let the young man depart and charged him, "see you tell no man that, "'you have shown these things to me.'"

23 And he called to himself, two centurions saying, "make ready, two hundred soldiers to go to Caesarea and horsemen, seventy and spearmen, two hundred at the third hour of the night

24 And provide them beasts that they may set Paul on and bring him safe to Felix, the governor."

25 And he wrote a letter after this manner:
26 "Claudius Lysias, to the most excellent, Governor, Felix sends greeting.
27 This man was taken of the Jews and should have been killed of them. Then I came with an army and rescued him, having understood that, he was a Roman.
28 And when I would have known the cause wherefore, they accused him, I brought him forth, into their council,
29 Whom I perceived to be accused of questions of their law, but to have nothing laid to his charge worthy of death, or of bonds.
30 And when it was told me how that the Jews laid wait for the man, I sent straightway, to you and gave commandment to his accusers also, to say before you, what they had against him. Farewell."

31 Then the soldiers, as it was commanded them, took Paul and brought him by night to Antipatris.
32 On the morrow, they left the horsemen, to go with him and returned to the castle,
33 Who when they came to Caesarea and delivered the epistle to the governor, presented Paul also, before him.
34 And when the governor had read the letter, he asked of what province he was. And when he understood that he was of Cilicia,
35 "I will hear you," he said, "when your accusers are also, come." And he commanded him to be kept in Herod's judgement hall.

Chapter 24

1 And after five days, Hananiah (the high priest) descended with the elders and with a certain orator named, Tertullus, who informed the governor against Paul.
2 And when he was called forth, Tertullus began to accuse him saying, "seeing that by you, we enjoy great quietness and that very worthy deeds are done to this nation by your providence,
3 We accept it always and in all places, most noble Felix, with all thankfulness.
4 Notwithstanding, that I be not further tedious to you, I pray you that you would hear us of your clemency, a few words.

5 For we have found this man, a pestilent fellow and a mover of sedition among all the Jews, throughout the World and a ringleader of the sect of the Nazarenes,
6 Who also, has gone about to profane the temple, whom we took and would have judged, according to our law.
7 But, the chief captain, Lysias came on us and with great violence, took him away out of our hands,
8 Commanding his accusers to come to you by examining of whom, yourself may take knowledge of all these things, whereof we accuse him."
9 And the Jews also, assented saying that, "'these things were so.'"

10 Then Paul, after that the governor had beckoned to him to speak, answered, "forasmuch as I know that you have been of many years, a judge to this nation, I do the more cheerfully, answer for myself,
11 Because that you may understand that there are yet, but twelve days, since I went up to Jerusalem for to Worship.
12 And they neither found me in the temple disputing with any man, neither raising up

the people; neither in the synagogues, nor in the city.
13 Neither can they prove the things whereof, they now, accuse me.

14 But this I confess to you that, after The Way, which they call heresy, so Worship I, The God of my fathers, Believing all things, which are written in the Law and in the Prophets
15 And have Hope toward God, which they themselves also, allow that there shall be a Resurrection of the dead; both of the Just and unjust.
16 And herein, do I exercise myself, to have always a conscience; void to offence, toward God and toward men.
17 Now after many years, I came to bring alms to my nation and offerings,
18 Whereupon, certain Jews from Asia found me purified in the temple, neither with multitude, nor with tumult,
19 Who ought to have been here before you and object, if they had anything against me.
20 Or else, let these same here, say if they have found any evil doing in me, while I stood before the council,
21 Except it be for this one voice that I cried, standing among them, touching the Resurrection of the dead, I am called in question by you this day."

22 And when Felix heard these things, having more perfect Knowledge of That Way, he deferred them and said, "when Lysias, (the chief captain) shall come down, I will know the uttermost of your matter."
23 And he commanded a centurion to keep Paul and to let him have liberty and that he should forbid none of his acquaintances to minister, or come to him.

24 And after certain days, when Felix came with his wife, Drusilla, which was a Jewess, he sent for Paul and heard him, concerning The Faith in Christ.
25 And as he reasoned of Righteousness, Temperance and Judgment to come, Felix trembled and answered, "go your way, for this time, when I have a convenient season, I will call for you."
26 He hoped also that money should have been given him of Paul that he might loose him. Wherefore, he sent for him the oftener and communed with him.
27 But after two years, Porcius Festus came into Felix' room and Felix, willing to show the Jews a pleasure, left Paul bound.

Chapter 25

1 Now, when Festus was come into the province, after three days, he ascended from Caesarea, to Jerusalem.
2 Then the high priest and the chief of the Jews informed him against Paul and besought him
3 And desired favor against him that he would send for him to Jerusalem; laying wait in the way to kill him.
4 But Festus answered that, "Paul should be kept at Caesarea and that he himself, would depart shortly there."
5 Let them therefore," he said, "which among you are able, go down with me and accuse this man, if there be any wickedness in him."
6 And when he had tarried among them more than ten days, he went down to Caesarea and the next day, sitting on the judgement seat, commanded Paul to be brought.

7 And when he was come, the Jews which came down from Jerusalem, stood round about and laid many and grievous complaints against Paul, which they could not prove.
8 While he answered for himself, "neither against the Law of the Jews, neither against the temple, nor yet against Caesar, have I offended any thing, at all."
9 But Festus, willing to do the Jews a pleasure, answered Paul and said, "will you go up to Jerusalem and there, be judged of these things before me?"
10 Then Paul said, "I stand at Caesar's judgement seat, where I ought to be judged. To the Jews, have I done no wrong, as you very well know.
11 For if I am an offender, or have committed any thing, worthy of death, I refuse not to die, but if there be none of these things whereof, these accuse me, no man may deliver me to them. I appeal to Caesar."
12 Then Festus, when he had conferred with the council answered, "have you appealed to Caesar? To Caesar, you shall go."

13 And after certain days, King Agrippa and Bernice came to Caesarea, to salute Festus.
14 And when they had been there many days, Festus declared Paul's cause to the king saying, "there is a certain man, left in

bonds by Felix,
15 About whom, when I was at Jerusalem, the chief priests and the elders of the Jews informed me, desiring to have judgement against him,
16 To whom I answered, "'it is not the manner of the Romans, to deliver any man to die, before that he which is accused, have the accusers face to face and have license to answer for himself, concerning the crime laid against him.'"

17 Therefore, when they had come here, without any delay, on the morrow, I sat on the judgement seat and commanded the man to be brought forth,
18 Against whom, when the accusers stood up, they brought no accusation of such things, as I supposed,
19 But had certain questions against him, of their own superstition and of one, Jesus, Which was dead, whom Paul affirmed to be Alive.
20 And because I doubted of such manner of questions, I asked him whether, "'he would go to Jerusalem and there, be judged of these matters.'"
21 But, when Paul had appealed to be reserved to the hearing of Augustus, I commanded him to be kept until I might send him to Caesar."

22 Then Agrippa said to Festus, "I would also, hear the man, myself. Tomorrow," he said, "you shall hear him."
23 And on the morrow, when Agrippa was come and Bernice, with great pomp and was entered into the place of hearing, with the chief captains and principal men of the city, at Festus' commandment, Paul was brought forth.
24 And Festus said, "King Agrippa and all men, which are here present with us, you see this man, about whom, all the multitude of the Jews have dealt with me; both at Jerusalem and also, here crying that he ought not to live any longer.
25 But, when I found that he had committed nothing worthy of death and that he himself, has appealed to Augustus, I have determined to send him,
26 Of whom, I have no certain thing to write to my lord. Wherefore, I have brought him forth, before you and especially before you, O, King Agrippa that, after examination, had I might have somewhat to write.
27 For it seems to me, unreasonable to send a prisoner and not withal, to signify the crimes laid against him."

Chapter 26

1 Then Agrippa said to Paul, "you are permitted to speak for yourself." Then Paul stretched forth the hand and answered for himself,
2 "I think myself happy, King Agrippa, because I shall answer for myself, this day before you, touching all the things, whereof I am accused of the Jews,
3 Especially, because I know you to be expert in all customs and questions, which are among the Jews. Wherefore, I beseech you to hear me, patiently.
4 My manner of life from my youth, which was at the first, among my own nation at Jerusalem, know all the Jews,
5 Which knew me from the beginning, if they would testify that after the most strait sect of our religion, I lived a Pharisee.
6 And now, I stand and am judged for the Hope of the Promise made of God, to our fathers,
7 To which, Promise our twelve tribes, instantly serving God, day and night, Hope to come, for which Hope's sake, King Agrippa, I am accused of the Jews.

8 Why should it be thought a thing incredible with you that God should Raise the dead?
9 I verily, thought with myself that I ought to do many things contrary to The Name of Jesus, of Nazareth,
10 Which thing I also, did in Jerusalem and many of the saints, I did shut up in prison, having received authority from the chief priests and when they were put to death, I gave my voice against them.
11 And I punished them often, in every synagogue and compelled them to blaspheme and being exceedingly mad against them, I persecuted them; even to strange cities.
12 Whereupon, as I went to Damascus with authority and commission from the chief priests,

13 At midday, O king, I saw in the way, A Light from Heaven; above the brightness of the Sun, Shining round about me and them which journeyed with me.
14 And when we were all fallen to the earth, I heard A Voice speaking to me and saying in the Hebrew tongue, "'Saul, Saul, why persecute you Me? It is hard for you to kick against the goads.'"

15 And I said, "'who are You, Lord?'" And He said, "'I am Jesus, whom you persecute.

16 But rise and stand on your feet, for I have appeared to you for this purpose; to make you a minister and a witness; both of these things, which you have seen and of those things in the which, I will appear to you,

17 Delivering you from the people and from the gentiles, to whom now, I send you;

18 To Open their eyes and to Turn them, from Darkness to Light and from the power of Satan, to God that they may Receive Forgiveness of sins and inheritance among them, which are Sanctified by Faith that is in Me.'"

19 Whereupon, O King Agrippa, I was not disobedient to the Heavenly Vision.

20 But showed first, to them of Damascus and at Jerusalem and throughout all the coasts of Judaea and then, to the gentiles that they should Repent and Turn To God and Do Works, Suitable for Repentance.

21 For these causes, the Jews caught me in the temple and went about to kill me.

22 Having therefore, obtained help of God, I continue to this day; Witnessing both, to small and great, saying none other things than those, which the prophets and Moses did say, "'should come

23 That Christ should suffer and that, He should be the first that should Rise from the dead and should show Light to the people and to the gentiles.'"

24 And as he thus spoke for himself, Festus said with a loud voice, "Paul, you are beside yourself! Much learning does make you mad!"

25 But he said, "I am not mad, most noble Festus, but speak forth, the Words of Truth and soberness.

26 For the king knows of these things, before whom also, I speak freely. For I am persuaded that none of these things are hidden from him, for this thing was not done in a corner.

27 King Agrippa, believe you the prophets? I know that you Believe."

28 Then Agrippa said to Paul, "you almost, persuade me to be a Christian."

29 And Paul said, "I would to God that not only you, but also, all that hear me this day, were both, almost and altogether, such as I am, except these bonds."

30 And when he had thus spoken, the king rose up and the governor and Bernice and they that sat with them

31 And when they were gone aside, they talked between themselves saying, "this man does nothing, worthy of death, or of bonds."

32 Then said Agrippa to Festus, "this man might have been set at liberty, if he had not appealed to Caesar."

Chapter 27

1 And when it was determined that we should sail into Italy, they delivered Paul and certain other prisoners to one named, Julius, a centurion of Augustus' band.

2 And entering into a ship of Adramyttium, we launched (meaning to sail by the coasts of Asia, one, Aristarchus, a Macedonian of Thessalonica, being with us.)

3 And the next day, we touched at Sidon. And Julius courteously, entreated Paul and gave him liberty to go to his friends to refresh himself.

4 And when we had launched from there, we sailed under Cyprus, because the winds were contrary.

5 And when we had sailed over the Sea of Cilicia and Pamphylia, we came to Myra, a city of Lycia.

6 And there, the centurion found a ship of Alexandria sailing into Italy and he put us, therein.

7 And when we had sailed slowly, many days and scarce had come over against Cnidus, the wind not suffering us, we sailed under Crete, over against Salmone

8 And hardly passing it, came to a place which is called, The Fair Havens near whereunto, was the city of Lasea.

9 Now, when much time was spent and when sailing was now dangerous, because the fast was now, already past, Paul admonished them

10 And said to them, "Sirs, I perceive that this voyage will be with hurt and much damage, not only of the lading and ship, but also, of our lives."

11 Nevertheless, the centurion believed the master and the owner of the ship, more than those things, which were spoken by Paul.

12 And because the haven was not commodious to winter in, the more part advised to depart there also, if by any means they might attain to Phenice and there, to winter, which is a haven of Crete

and lies toward the South, West and North West.

13 And when the South wind blew softly, supposing that they had obtained their purpose, loosing there, they sailed close by Crete.

14 But not long after, there arose against it, a tempestuous wind, called Euroclydon.
15 And when the ship was caught and could not bear up into the wind, we let her drive.
16 And running under a certain island, which is called Clauda, we had much work to come by the boat,
17 Which when they had taken up, they used helps, undergirding the ship and fearing, lest they should fall into the quicksand, struck sail and so, were driven.
18 And we being exceedingly tossed with a tempest the next day, they lightened the ship.

19 And the third day, we cast out with our own hands, the tackling of the ship.
20 And when neither Sun, nor stars in many days appeared and no small tempest laid on us, all hope that we should be saved was then taken away.
21 But, after long abstinence, Paul stood forth in the midst of them and said, "Sirs, you should have consented to me and not have loosed from Crete and to have gained this harm and loss.
22 And now, I exhort you to be of good cheer, FOR THERE SHALL BE NO LOSS OF ANY MAN'S LIFE AMONG YOU, BUT OF THE SHIP.
23 For there stood by me this night, the angel of God, Whose I am and Whom I serve
24 Saying, "'fear not, Paul, YOU MUST BE BROUGHT BEFORE CAESAR AND LO, GOD HAS GIVEN YOU, ALL THEM THAT SAIL WITH YOU.'"
25 Wherefore sirs, be of good cheer, for I Believe God that it shall be, even as it was told me.
26 Howbeit, we must be cast on a certain island."

27 But, when the fourteenth night was come, as we were driven up and down in Adria, about midnight, the shipmen deemed that they drew near to some country
28 And sounded and found it twenty fathoms. And when they had gone a little further, they sounded again and found it fifteen fathoms.
29 Then fearing, lest we should have fallen on rocks, they cast four anchors out of the stern and wished for the day.
30 And as the shipmen were about to flee out of the ship, when they had let down the boat into the Sea under color as though they would have cast anchors out of the foreship,
31 Paul said to the centurion and to the soldiers, "except these abide in the ship, you cannot be saved."
32 Then, the soldiers cut off the ropes of the boat and let her fall off.
33 And while the day was coming on, Paul besought them all to take meat saying, "this day, is the fourteenth day that you have tarried and continued fasting, having taken nothing.
34 Wherefore, I pray you to take some meat. For this is for your health, FOR THERE SHALL NOT A HAIR FALL FROM THE HEAD OF ANY OF YOU."
35 And when he had thus spoken, he took bread and Gave Thanks to God in presence of them all and when he had broken it, he began to eat.
36 Then were they all of good cheer and they also, took some meat.
37 And we were in all, in the ship, two hundred sixty and sixteen souls.
38 And when they had eaten enough, they lightened the ship and cast out the wheat into the Sea.

39 And when it was day, they knew not the land, but they discovered a certain creek with a shore, into the which, they were minded, if it were possible, to thrust in the ship.
40 And when they had taken up the anchors, they committed themselves to the Sea and loosed the rudder bands and hoisted up the mainsail to the wind and made toward shore.
41 And falling into a place where two seas met, they ran the ship aground and the forepart stuck fast and remained unmovable, but the hinder part was broken with the violence of the waves.
42 And the soldiers' counsel was to kill the prisoners, lest any of them should swim out and escape.
43 But the centurion, willing to save Paul, kept them from their purpose and commanded that, "they which could swim, should cast themselves first, into the Sea and get to land"
44 And the rest; some on boards and some

on broken pieces of the ship. And so it came to pass that, THEY ESCAPED ALL, SAFE TO LAND.

Chapter 28

1 And when they were escaped, then they knew that the island was called, Melita.
2 And the barbarous people showed us no little kindness, for they kindled a fire and received us every one, because of the present rain and because of the cold.
3 And when Paul had gathered a bundle of sticks and laid them on the fire, THERE CAME A VIPER OUT OF THE HEAT AND FASTENED ON HIS HAND.
4 And when the barbarians saw the venomous beast hang on his hand, they said among themselves, "no doubt, this man is a murderer, whom, though he has escaped the Sea, yet vengeance suffers not to live."
5 AND HE SHOOK OFF THE BEAST INTO THE FIRE AND FELT NO HARM.
6 Howbeit, they looked when he should have swollen, or fallen down dead suddenly, but AFTER THEY HAD LOOKED A GREAT WHILE AND SAW NO HARM COME TO HIM, they changed their minds and said that, "he was a god."

7 In the same quarters, were possessions of the chief man of the island, whose name was, Publius, who received us and lodged us, three days, courteously.
8 And it came to pass that the father of Publius, laid sick of a fever and of a bloody flux, to whom Paul entered in and Prayed and laid his hands on him and Healed him.
9 So, when this was done, others also, which had diseases in the island, came and were Healed,
10 Who also, honored us with many honors. And when we departed, they laded us with such things as were necessary.

11 And after three months, we departed in a ship of Alexandria, which had wintered in the isle, whose sign was Castor and Pollux.
12 And landing at Syracuse, we tarried there three days.
13 And from there, we fetched a compass and came to Rhegium. And after one day, the South wind blew and we came the next day to, Puteoli,
14 Where we found brothers and were desired to tarry with them, seven days. And so, we went toward Rome.

15 And from there, when the brothers heard of us, they came to meet us as far as Appii Forum and the three taverns, whom when Paul saw, he Thanked God and took courage.
16 And when we came to Rome, the centurion delivered the prisoners to the captain of the guard. But, Paul was suffered to dwell by himself, with a soldier that kept him.

17 And it came to pass that after three days, Paul called the chief of the Jews, together. And when they had come together, he said to them, "men and brothers, though I have committed nothing against the people, or customs of our fathers, YET WAS I DELIVERED PRISONER FROM JERUSALEM, INTO THE HANDS OF THE ROMANS,
18 Who when they had examined me, would have let me go, because there was no cause of death in me.
19 But, when the Jews spoke against it, I was constrained to appeal to Caesar, not that I had anything to accuse my nation of,
20 For this cause therefore, have I called for you, to see you and to speak with you, because that for the hope of Israel, I am bound with this chain."
21 And they said to him, "we neither received letters out of Judaea concerning you, neither any of the brothers that came, showed or spoke any harm of you.
22 But we desire to hear of you, what you think, for as concerning this sect, we know that every where, it is spoken against."

23 And when they had appointed him a day, there came many to him, into his lodging, to whom, he expounded and Testified the Kingdom of God, persuading them concerning, Jesus, both out of the Law of Moses and out of the Prophets, from morning until evening.
24 And some Believed the things, which were spoken and some believed not.
25 And when they agreed not among themselves, they departed. After that, Paul had spoken one word, "well spoke The Holy Ghost by Isaiah, the prophet to our fathers
26 Saying, "'GO TO THIS PEOPLE AND SAY, ""HEARING, YOU SHALL HEAR AND SHALL NOT UNDERSTAND AND SEEING, YOU SHALL SEE AND NOT PERCEIVE.
27 FOR THE HEART OF THIS PEOPLE IS WAXED GROSS AND THEIR EARS

ARE DULL OF HEARING AND THEIR EYES, HAVE THEY CLOSED, LEST THEY SHOULD SEE WITH THEIR EYES AND HEAR WITH THEIR EARS AND UNDERSTAND WITH THEIR HEART AND SHOULD BE CONVERTED AND I SHOULD HEAL THEM.'"

28 Be it known therefore, to you that, THE SALVATION OF GOD IS SENT TO THE GENTILES AND THAT, THEY WILL HEAR IT.'"

29 And when he had said these words, the Jews departed and had great reasoning among themselves.

30 And Paul dwelled two whole years in his own hired house and received all that came in to him,

31 Preaching the Kingdom of God and Teaching those things, which concern The Lord, Jesus Christ with all confidence, no man forbidding him.

Romans

Chapter 1

1 Paul, a servant of Jesus Christ, called to be an apostle; Separated to The Gospel of God,

2 Which He had Promised before by His prophets in The Holy Scriptures,

3 Concerning His Son, Jesus Christ, our Lord, which was made of the seed of David, according to the flesh

4 And declared to be The Son of God with Power, according to The Spirit of Holiness, by The Resurrection from the dead;

5 By Whom, we have received Grace and apostleship; for Obedience to The Faith among all nations, for His Name;

6 Among whom, are you also, the called of Jesus Christ.

7 To all that be in Rome, beloved of God, called to be saints: Grace to you and Peace from God our Father and The Lord, Jesus Christ,

8 First, I Thank my God, through Jesus Christ for you all that your Faith is spoken of throughout the whole World.

9 For God is my witness, Whom I serve with my spirit in The Gospel of His Son that without ceasing, I make mention of you always in my Prayers,

10 Making request, if by any means now, at length, I might have a prosperous journey by The Will of God to come to you.

11 For I long to see you that I may impart to you some spiritual gift, to the end you may be established.

12 That is that I may be comforted, together with you by the mutual Faith; both of you and me.

13 Now, I would not have you ignorant brothers that oftentimes, I purposed to come to you (but was let, hereto) that I might have some Fruit among you, also; even as among other gentiles.

14 I am debtor, both to the Greeks and to the barbarians; both to the wise and to the unwise.

15 So, as much as is in me, I am ready to Preach The Gospel to you that are at Rome, also.

16 For I am not ashamed of The Gospel of Christ, for it is The Power of God to Salvation, to every one that Believes; to the Jew, first and also, to the Greek.

17 For therein, is the Righteousness of God Revealed, from Faith to Faith. So it is written, "the Just shall Live by Faith."

18 For the wrath of God is revealed from Heaven against all ungodliness and unrighteousness of men; who hold The Truth in unrighteousness.

19 Because that, which may be Known of God, is Manifest in them, for God has Shown it to them.

20 For the invisible things of Him, from the Creation of the World are clearly seen; being understood by the things that are made; even His Eternal Power and Godhead, so that they are without excuse,

21 BECAUSE THAT, WHEN THEY KNEW GOD, THEY GLORIFIED HIM NOT, AS GOD, NEITHER WERE THANKFUL, BUT BECAME VAIN IN THEIR IMAGINATIONS AND THEIR FOOLISH HEART WAS DARKENED;

22 PROFESSING THEMSELVES TO BE WISE, THEY BECAME FOOLS

23 AND CHANGED THE GLORY OF THE INCORRUPTIBLE GOD, INTO AN IMAGE MADE LIKE TO: CORRUPTIBLE MAN AND TO BIRDS AND FOUR FOOTED BEASTS AND CREEPING THINGS.

24 WHEREFORE, GOD ALSO, GAVE THEM UP TO UNCLEANNESS, THROUGH THE LUSTS OF THEIR OWN HEARTS; TO DISHONOR THEIR OWN BODIES, BETWEEN THEMSELVES,
25 WHO CHANGED THE TRUTH OF GOD, INTO A LIE AND WORSHIPPED AND SERVED THE CREATURE, MORE THAN THE CREATOR; WHO IS BLESSED, FOR EVER. AMEN.
26 FOR THIS CAUSE, GOD GAVE THEM UP TO VILE AFFECTIONS. FOR EVEN THEIR WOMEN, DID CHANGE THE NATURAL USE INTO THAT, WHICH IS AGAINST NATURE.
27 AND LIKEWISE ALSO, THE MEN LEAVING THE NATURAL USE OF THE WOMAN, BURNED IN THEIR LUST, ONE TOWARD ANOTHER; MEN WITH MEN, WORKING THAT, WHICH IS UNSEEMLY AND RECEIVING IN THEMSELVES THAT RECOMPENSE OF THEIR ERROR, WHICH WAS NECESSARY.

28 AND EVEN AS THEY DID NOT LIKE TO RETAIN GOD IN THEIR KNOWLEDGE, GOD GAVE THEM OVER TO A REPROBATE MIND, TO DO THOSE THINGS, WHICH ARE NOT CONVENIENT;
29 BEING FILLED WITH ALL UNRIGHTEOUSNESS: FORNICATION, WICKEDNESS, COVETOUSNESS, MALICIOUSNESS, FULL OF ENVY, MURDER, DEBATE, DECEIT, MALIGNITY, WHISPERERS,
30 BACKBITERS, HATERS OF GOD, DESPITEFUL, PROUD, BOASTERS, INVENTORS OF EVIL THINGS, DISOBEDIENT TO PARENTS,
31 WITHOUT UNDERSTANDING, COVENANT BREAKERS, WITHOUT NATURAL AFFECTION, IMPLACABLE, UNMERCIFUL…;
32 Who knowing the Judgment of God that they, which commit such things, are worthy of death; not only do the same, but have pleasure in them that do them.

Chapter 2

1 Therefore, you are inexcusable, O man, whosoever you are that judges, for wherein you judge another, you condemn yourself, for you that judge, do the same things.
2 But we are sure that, The Judgment of God is according to Truth against them, which commit such things.
3 And think you this, O man that judges them, which do such things and do the same that you shall escape The Judgment of God?
4 Or, despise you the riches of His Goodness and forbearance and longsuffering, not knowing that The Goodness of God leads you to Repentance?
5 But after your hardness and impenitent heart, treasure up to yourself, wrath against the Day of Wrath and Revelation of The Righteous Judgment of God,
6 Who will render to every man, according to his deeds,
7 To them who by Patient Continuance in Well Doing, Seek for Glory and Honor and Immortality, Eternal Life.

8 But, to them that are contentious and do not obey The Truth, but obey unrighteousness: indignation and wrath,
9 Tribulation and anguish, on every soul of man that does evil; of the Jew, first and also, of the gentile,
10 But Glory, Honor and Peace to every man that Works good; to the Jew, first and also, to the gentile.
11 For there is no respect of persons with God.
12 For as many as have sinned without Law, shall also, perish without Law. And as many as have sinned in The Law, shall be Judged by The Law.
13 For not the hearers of The Law are just before God, but the Doers of The Law, shall be Justified.

14 For when the gentiles, which have not The Law, do by nature, the things contained in The Law, these having not The Law, are a Law to themselves,
15 Which show the Work of The Law, written in their hearts, their conscience also, bearing witness and their thoughts the mean while, accusing, or else, excusing one another
16 In the day when God shall Judge the secrets of men by Jesus Christ, according to my gospel.

17 Behold, you are called a Jew and rest in The Law and make your boast of God
18 And Know His Will and approve the things that are more excellent; being instructed out of The Law
19 And are confident that, you yourself, are a guide of the blind; a Light of them, which are in Darkness;
20 An instructor of the foolish, a teacher of

babes, which have the form of Knowledge and of The Truth in The Law.

21 You therefore, which Teaches another, you Teach not yourself? You that Preaches a man should not steal, do you steal?
22 You that say a man should not commit adultery, do you commit adultery? You that abhor idols, do you commit sacrilege?
23 You that make your boast of The Law, through breaking The Law, you dishonor God?
24 "For The Name of God is blasphemed among the gentiles through you," as it is written.

25 For circumcision verily profits, if you keep the law. But, if you be a breaker of the law, your circumcision is made uncircumcision.
26 Therefore, if the uncircumcision Keeps the Righteousness of the law, shall not his uncircumcision, be counted for circumcision?
27 And shall not uncircumcision, which is by nature, if it fulfills the law, Judge you, who by the letter and circumcision do transgress the law?
28 For he is not a Jew, which is one outwardly, neither is that circumcision, which is outward in the flesh,
29 But he is a Jew, which is one, inwardly and circumcision is that of the heart, in The Spirit and not in the letter, whose praise is not of men, but of God.

Chapter 3

1 What advantage then, has the Jew, or what profit is there, of circumcision?
2 Much every way chiefly, because that to them, were committed The Oracles of God.
3 For what if some did not believe? Shall their unbelief make The Faith of God without effect?
4 God forbid. Yes, LET GOD BE TRUE, BUT EVERY MAN A LIAR, as it is written that, "YOU MIGHT BE JUSTIFIED IN YOUR SAYINGS AND MIGHT OVERCOME, WHEN YOU ARE JUDGED."
5 But, if our unrighteousness, commends the Righteousness of God, what shall we say? Is God unrighteous who takes vengeance? (I speak as a man)
6 God forbid, for then, how shall God Judge the World?
7 For if The Truth of God has more abounded through my lie to His Glory, why yet, am I also, judged as a sinner?
8 And not rather, as we be slanderously reported and as some affirm that, we say, "let us do evil that good may come." Whose damnation is just?
9 What then, are we better than they? No, in no wise, for we have before, proved both Jews and gentiles that they are all under sin
10 As it is written, "there is none righteous, no, not one.
11 There is none that understands. There is none that seeks after God.
12 They are all gone out of The Way. They are together, become unprofitable. There is none that does good; no, not one.
13 Their throat is an open sepulchre. With their tongues, they have used deceit. The poison of asps is under their lips,
14 Whose mouth is full of cursing and bitterness.
15 Their feet are swift to shed blood.
16 Destruction and misery are in their ways
17 And the way of Peace, have they not known.
18 There is no fear of God, before their eyes."

19 Now, we know that what things soever, the law says, it says to them, who are under the law that, "every mouth may be stopped and all the World may become guilty before God."
20 Therefore, by the deeds of the law, there shall no flesh be justified in His sight, for by The Law is the Knowledge of sin.
21 But now, the Righteousness of God, without the law is manifested; being witnessed by The Law and the Prophets;
22 Even the Righteousness of God, which is by Faith of Jesus Christ to all and on all them that Believe, for there is no difference.

23 For all have sinned and come short of the glory of God;
24 Being Justified freely, by His Grace through the Redemption that is in Christ Jesus,
25 Whom God has set forth, to be a propitiation through Faith in His Blood, to declare His Righteousness for the Remission of sins that are past through the forbearance of God,

26 To declare, I say, at this time, His Righteousness that he might be Just and the Justifier of him, which Believes in Jesus.

27 Where is boasting then? It is excluded. By what law, of works? No, but by The Law of Faith.
28 Therefore, we conclude that, a man is Justified by Faith, without the deeds of the law.
29 Is He, The God of the Jews only? Is he not also, of the gentiles? Yes, of the gentiles also,
30 Seeing it is One God, which shall Justify the circumcision by Faith and uncircumcision through Faith,
31 Do we then, make void The Law through Faith? God forbid. Yes, we establish The Law.

Chapter 4
1 What shall we say then that Abraham, our father, as pertaining to the flesh has found?
2 For if Abraham were justified by works, he has whereof, to glory, but not before God.
3 For what says The Scripture? Abraham Believed God and it was counted to him for Righteousness.
4 Now, to him that works, is the reward not reckoned of Grace, but of debt.
5 But to him that works not, but Believes on Him that Justifies the un-Godly, his Faith is counted for Righteousness.
6 Even as David also, describes the blessedness of the man, to whom God imputes Righteousness without works
7 Saying, "Blessed are they, whose iniquities are Forgiven and whose sins are Covered.
8 Blessed is the man to whom, The Lord will not impute sin."

9 Comes this Blessedness then, on the circumcision only, or on the uncircumcision, also? For we say that Faith was reckoned to Abraham for Righteousness.
10 How was it then, reckoned? When he was in circumcision, or in uncircumcision? Not in circumcision, but in uncircumcision.
11 And he received the sign of circumcision; a seal of the Righteousness of The Faith, which he had, yet being uncircumcised that he might be the father of all them that Believe; though they be not circumcised that Righteousness might be imputed to them, also
12 And the father of circumcision, to them who are not of the circumcision only, but who also, Walk in the steps of that Faith of our father, Abraham, which he had, being yet, uncircumcised.

13 For The Promise that he should be the heir of the World, was not to Abraham, or to his seed, through the law, but through the Righteousness of Faith.
14 For if they, which are of the law be heirs, Faith is made void and The Promise, made of none effect,
15 Because The Law works wrath, for where no Law is, there is no transgression.
16 Therefore, it is of Faith that it might be by Grace to the end, The Promise might be Sure, to all the seed, not to that only, which is of the Law, but to that also, which is of The Faith of Abraham, who is the father of us all,
17 As it is written, "I have made you a father of many nations," before Him, Whom he Believed, even God, who Quickens the Dead and calls those things, which be not as though they were.
18 Who against Hope, Believed in Hope that he might become the father of many nations, according to that, which was spoken. So shall your seed be.
19 And being not weak in Faith, he considered not his own body now dead, when he was about one hundred years old, neither yet the deadness of Sarah's womb,
20 He staggered not at the Promise of God, through unbelief, but was strong in Faith; Giving Glory to God.
21 And being fully persuaded that, what He had Promised, He was able also, to Perform.
22 And therefore, it was imputed to him for Righteousness.

23 Now, it was not written for his sake alone that it was imputed to him,
24 But for us also, to whom it shall be imputed, if we Believe on Him that Raised Up Jesus, our Lord from the dead;
25 Who was Delivered for our offences and was Raised Again, for our Justification.

Chapter 5
1 Therefore, being Justified by Faith, we have Peace with God through our Lord,

Jesus Christ,

2 By Whom also, we have access by Faith, into this Grace, wherein we Stand and Rejoice in Hope of The Glory of God.

3 And not only so, but we Glory in tribulations, also; Knowing that Tribulation works Patience

4 And Patience, Experience and Experience, Hope.

5 And Hope makes not ashamed, because the Love of God is shed abroad in our hearts by The Holy Ghost, which is Given to us.

6 For when we were yet, without strength, in due time, Christ died for the un-Godly.

7 For scarcely, for a Righteous man, will one die, yet peradventure, for a good man, some would even dare to die.

8 But God commends His Love toward us, in that, while we were yet sinners, Christ died for us.

9 Much more then, being now Justified, by His Blood, we shall be Saved from wrath through Him.

10 For if when we were enemies, we were reconciled to God by the death of His Son, much more, being Reconciled, we shall be Saved by His Life.

11 And not only so, but we also, Joy in God, through our Lord, Jesus Christ; by Whom we have now, Received The Atonement.

12 Wherefore, as by one man, sin entered into the World. And Death, by sin and so, Death passed on all men; for that all have sinned

13 (For until The Law, sin was in the World, but sin is not imputed, when there is no Law.)

14 Nevertheless, Death reigned from Adam to Moses; even over them that had not sinned, after the similitude of Adam's transgression, who is the figure of Him that was to come,

15 But not as the offence, so also, is The Free Gift. For if through the offence of one, many be dead, much more The Grace of God and The Gift by Grace, which is by One Man, Jesus Christ has abounded to many.

16 And not as it was by one that sinned, so is The Gift, for the Judgment was by one to condemnation, but The Free Gift is of many offences to Justification.

17 For if by one man's offence, Death reigned by one, much more, they which Receive abundance of Grace and of the Gift of Righteousness, shall Reign in Life by one, Jesus Christ.

18 Therefore, as by the offence of one, Judgment came on all men to condemnation. Even so, by the Righteousness of One, The Free Gift came on all men, to Justification of Life.

19 For as by one man's disobedience, many were made sinners. So, by the Obedience of One, shall many be made Righteous.

20 Moreover, The Law entered that the offence might abound. But, where sin abounded, Grace did much more, abound

21 That as sin has reigned to Death, even so, might Grace Reign, through Righteousness, to Eternal Life, by Jesus Christ, our Lord.

Chapter 6

1 What shall we say then? Shall we continue in sin that Grace may abound?

2 God forbid. How shall we that are dead to sin, live any longer, therein?

3 Know you not that so many of us, as were Baptized into Jesus Christ, were Baptized into His death?

4 Therefore, we are buried with Him, by Baptism into death that like as Christ was Raised Up from the dead, by The Glory of The Father. Even so, we also, should Walk in Newness of Life.

5 For if we have been planted together, in the likeness of His death, we shall be also, in the likeness of His Resurrection.

6 Knowing this that, our old man is crucified with Him that the body of sin might be destroyed that henceforth, we should not serve sin.

7 For he that is dead is freed from sin.

8 Now, if we are dead with Christ, we Believe that, we shall also, Live with Him.

9 Knowing that Christ being Raised from the dead, dies no more, death has no more dominion over Him.

10 For in that He died, He died to sin, once. But in that, He Lives, He Lives to God.

11 Likewise, reckon you also, yourselves to be dead indeed to sin, but Alive to God through Jesus Christ, our Lord.

12 Let not sin therefore, reign in your mortal body that you should obey it, in the lusts, thereof.

13 Neither yield yourselves, your members as instruments of unrighteousness to sin, but yield yourselves, to God as those that are Alive from the Dead and your members as instruments of Righteousness to God.

14 For sin shall not have dominion over you, for you are not under the law, but under Grace.
15 What then? Shall we sin, because we are not under the law, but under Grace? God forbid.
16 Know you not that to whom, you yield yourselves servants to obey, his servants you are, to whom you obey; whether of sin to Death, or of Obedience to Righteousness?
17 But, God be Thanked that you were the servants of sin, but you have Obeyed from the heart that form of Doctrine, which was Delivered you.
18 Being then made Free from sin, you became the servants of Righteousness.

19 I speak after the manner of men, because of the infirmity of your flesh. For as you have yielded your members servants to uncleanness and to iniquity to iniquity, even so now, yield your members servants to Righteousness to Holiness.
20 For when you were the servants of sin, you were free from Righteousness.
21 What fruit had you then, in those things whereof, you are now, ashamed? For the end of those things, is Death.
22 But now, being made Free from sin and become servants to God, you have your Fruit to Holiness and the end, everlasting Life.
23 For the wages of sin is Death, but The Gift of God, is Eternal Life, through Jesus Christ, our Lord.

Chapter 7

1 Know you not brothers, (for I speak to them that Know The Law) how that The Law has dominion over a man, as long as he lives?
2 For the woman, which has a husband, is bound by The Law, to her husband, so long as he lives. But, if the husband be dead, she is Loosed from The Law of her husband.
3 So then, if while her husband lives, she is married to another man, she shall be called an adulteress. But, if her husband is dead, she is Free from that Law, so that, she is no adulteress; though she be married to another man.
4 Wherefore my brothers, you also, are become dead to the law, by the body of Christ that you should be married to another; even to Him, who is Raised from the dead that we should bring forth Fruit to God.

5 For when we were in the flesh, the motions of sins, which were by The Law, did work in our members to bring forth fruit to Death.
6 But now, we are Delivered from the law that being dead, wherein we were held that we should serve in Newness of Spirit and not in the oldness of the letter.

7 What shall we say then? Is The Law sin? God forbid. No, I had not known sin, but by The Law, for I had not known lust, except The Law had said, "you shall not covet."
8 But sin, taking occasion by The Commandments, worked in me all manner of concupiscence. For without The Law, sin was dead.
9 For I was Alive without The Law, once. But, when The Commandments came, sin revived and I Died.
10 And The Commandments, which were Ordained to Life, I found to be to Death.
11 For sin, taking occasion by The Commandments, deceived me and by it, slew me.
12 Wherefore, The Law is Holy and The Commandments, Holy and Just and Good.
13 Was then that, which is Good, made Death to me? God forbid. But sin that it might appear sin, working Death in me, by that, which is Good that sin by The Commandment, might become exceedingly sinful.
14 For we know that, The Law is Spiritual, but I am carnal, sold under sin.

15 For that, which I do, I allow not. For what I would, that do I not. But what I hate, that do I.
16 If then, I do that, which I would not, I consent to The Law that it is Good.
17 Now then, it is no more I that do it, but sin that dwells in me.
18 For I know that, in me (that is, in my flesh) dwells no good thing. For to will, is present with me, but how to perform that, which is good, I find not.
19 For the good that I would, I do not. But the Evil, which I would not, that I do.
20 Now, if I do that, I would not, it is no more I that do it, but sin that dwells in me.

21 I find then, a Law that, when I would do good, evil is present with me.
22 For I delight in The Law of God after the inward man.
23 But, I see another law in my members, warring against the law of my mind and

bringing me into captivity to the law of sin, which is in my members.
24 O wretched man that I am! Who shall Deliver me from the body of this Death?
25 I Thank God, through Jesus Christ, our Lord, so then, with the mind, I myself Serve The Law of God, but with the flesh, the law of sin.

Chapter 8

1 There is therefore now, no condemnation to them, which are in Christ Jesus; who walk not, after the flesh, but after The Spirit.
2 For The Law of The Spirit of Life in Christ Jesus, has made me Free from the law of sin and Death.
3 For what the law could not do, in that, it was weak through the flesh, God sending His Own Son, in the likeness of sinful flesh and for sin; condemned sin in the flesh
4 That the Righteousness of The Law, might be Fulfilled in us; who Walk not, after the flesh, but after The Spirit.
5 For they that are after the flesh, do mind the things of the flesh, but they that are after The Spirit, the things of The Spirit.
6 For to be carnally minded is Death, but to be Spiritually minded, is Life and Peace,
7 Because the carnal mind is enmity against God, for it is not subject to The Law of God, neither indeed can be.

8 So then, they that are in the flesh, cannot please God.
9 But, you are not in the flesh, but in The Spirit. If so, be that, The Spirit of God dwells in you. Now, if any man has not, The Spirit of Christ, he is none of His.
10 And if Christ be in you, the body is dead, because of sin, but The Spirit is Life, because of Righteousness.
11 But, if The Spirit of Him that Raised Up Jesus from the dead dwells in you, He that Raised Up Christ from the dead shall also, Quicken your mortal bodies by His Spirit that dwells in you.

12 Therefore brothers, we are debtors, not to the flesh, to live after the flesh.
13 For if you live after the flesh, you shall Die. But if you, through The Spirit, do Mortify the deeds of the body, you shall Live.
14 For as many as are led by The Spirit of God, they are the sons of God.
15 For you have not received the spirit of bondage again, to fear. But, you have received The Spirit of adoption, whereby we cry, "Abba, Father!"
16 The Spirit itself, Bears Witness with our spirit that, 'we are the children of God'
17 And if children, then heirs; heirs of God and joint-heirs, with Christ, if so be that, we suffer with Him that we may be also, Glorified together.

18 For I reckon that, the sufferings of this present time, are not worthy to be compared with the Glory, which shall be revealed in us.
19 For the earnest expectation of the creature waits for the manifestation of the sons of God.
20 For the creature was made subject to vanity, not willingly, but by reason of Him who has subjected the same in Hope,
21 Because the creature itself also, shall be Delivered from the bondage of corruption, into The Glorious Liberty of the children of God.
22 For we know that, the whole creation groans and travails in pain together, until now.
23 And not only they, but ourselves also, which have The Firstfruits of The Spirit. Even we ourselves, groan within ourselves, waiting for the adoption, to wit, the Redemption of our body.

24 For we are Saved by Hope, but Hope that is seen, is not Hope. For what a man sees, why does he yet, hope for?
25 But, if we Hope for that we See Not, then do we with patience, Wait for it.
26 Likewise, The Spirit also, Helps our infirmities. For we know not, what we should Pray for, as we ought. But The Spirit itself, makes Intercession for us with groanings, which cannot be uttered.
27 And He that Searches the hearts, Knows what is The Mind of The Spirit, because He makes Intercession for the saints, according to The Will of God.
28 And we know that, all things work together, for Good to them that Love God; to them, who are the Called, according to His purpose.

29 For whom He did Foreknow, He also, did Predestinate to be Conformed, to the Image of His Son that He might be the firstborn among many brothers.
30 Moreover, whom He did Predestinate, them He also, Called and whom He Called, them He also, Justified and whom,

He Justified, them, He also, Glorified.

31 What shall we then; say to these things? <u>If God is For us, who can be against us?</u>
32 He that spared not, His Own Son, but delivered Him up for us all, how shall He not with Him also, freely give us all things?
33 Who shall lay any thing to the charge of God's elect? It is God that Justifies.
34 Who is He that condemns? It is Christ that died; yes, rather that, is Risen Again, Who is even at The Right Hand of God, Who also, makes Intercession for us.
35 <u>Who shall separate us from The Love of Christ? Shall: tribulation, or distress, or persecution, or famine, or nakedness, or peril, or sword?</u>
36 As it is written, "FOR YOUR SAKE, WE ARE KILLED ALL THE DAY LONG. WE ARE ACCOUNTED AS SHEEP FOR THE SLAUGHTER."
37 No, in all these things, we are more than conquerors through Him that Loved us.
38 For I am persuaded that, neither: Death, nor Life, nor angels, nor principalities, nor powers, nor things present, nor things to come,
39 Nor height, nor depth, nor any other creature, shall be able to separate us from the Love of God, which is in Christ Jesus, our Lord.

Chapter 9

1 I say the Truth in Christ, I lie not; my conscience also, bearing me witness in The Holy Ghost
2 That I have great heaviness and continual sorrow in my heart.
3 For I could wish that myself, were accursed from Christ for my brothers; my kinsmen, according to the flesh,
4 Who are Israelites to whom pertains the Adoption and The Glory and The Covenants and the Giving of The Law and The Service of God and The Promises,
5 Whose are The Father's and of Whom, as concerning the flesh, Christ came, Who is Over All, God Blessed for ever. Amen.
6 Not as though, The Word of God has taken no effect, <u>for they are not all Israel, which are of Israel</u>
7 Neither, because they are the seed of Abraham, are they all children. But, "IN ISAAC, SHALL YOUR SEED BE CALLED"
8 That is they, which are <u>the children of the flesh</u>. These are not the children of God, but the children of The Promise are counted for the seed.

9 For this is The Word of Promise: AT THIS TIME, WILL I COME AND SARAH, SHALL HAVE A SON.
10 And not only this, but when Rebecca also, had conceived by one; even by our father, Isaac
11 (For the children being not yet born, neither having done any good, or evil that The Purpose of God, according to Election, might stand not of works, but of Him that calls.)
12 It was said to her, "THE ELDER SHALL SERVE THE YOUNGER."
13 As it is written, "Jacob, have I loved, but Esau, have I hated."
14 What shall we say then? Is there unrighteousness with God? God forbid.
15 For He said to Moses, "I will have Mercy on whom, I will have Mercy and I will have Compassion on whom, I Will have Compassion."
16 So then, it is not of him that wills, nor of him that runs, but of God that Shows Mercy.
17 For The Scripture says to Pharaoh, "even for this same purpose, have I raised you up that I might show My Power in you and that My Name might be declared throughout all the Earth."
18 Therefore, He has Mercy on whom He will have Mercy and whom He will, He hardens.
19 You will say then to me, "why does He yet, find fault? For who has resisted His Will?
20 No but, O man, who are you that replies against God? Shall the thing formed, say to Him that formed it, "why have you made me thus?"
21 Has not the potter, Power over the clay, of the same lump to make one vessel to honor and another, to dishonor?
22 What if God, willing to show His wrath and to make His Power Known, endured with much longsuffering, the vessels of wrath fitted to destruction
23 And that He might make Known the riches of His Glory on the vessels of Mercy, which He had before, prepared to Glory,
24 Even us, whom He has Called; not of the Jews only, but also, of the gentiles?

25 As He said also, in Osee, "I WILL CALL THEM MY PEOPLE, WHICH WERE NOT MY PEOPLE AND HER BELOVED, WHICH WAS NOT BELOVED."

26 And it shall come to pass that, in the place where it was said to them, "'YOU ARE NOT MY PEOPLE.'" THERE, SHALL THEY BE CALLED, "'THE CHILDREN OF THE LIVING GOD.'"

27 Isaiah also, cried concerning Israel, "THOUGH THE NUMBER OF THE CHILDREN OF ISRAEL, BE AS THE SAND OF THE SEA, A REMNANT SHALL BE SAVED,

28 FOR HE WILL FINISH THE WORK AND CUT IT SHORT IN RIGHTEOUSNESS, BECAUSE A SHORT WORK WILL THE LORD MAKE ON THE EARTH."

29 And as Isaiah said before, "EXCEPT THE LORD OF SABAOTH, HAD LEFT US A SEED, WE HAD BEEN AS SODOM AND BEEN MADE LIKE TO GOMORRHA."

30 What shall we say then that the gentiles, which followed not after Righteousness, have attained to Righteousness; even the Righteousness, which is of Faith?

31 But Israel, which followed after The Law of Righteousness, has not attained to The Law of Righteousness.

32 Wherefore? Because they sought it not by Faith, but as it were, by the works of the law. For they stumbled at that Stumbling Stone,

33 As it is written, "BEHOLD, I LAY IN SION, A STUMBLING STONE AND ROCK OF OFFENCE AND WHOSOEVER, BELIEVES ON HIM, SHALL NOT BE ASHAMEED."

Chapter 10

1 Brothers, my heart's desire and Prayer to God for Israel is that, they might be Saved.

2 For I bear them record that, they have a Zeal of God, but not according to Knowledge.

3 For they being ignorant of God's Righteousness and going about, to establish their own righteousness, have not submitted themselves to The Righteousness of God.

4 For Christ is the end of The Law, for Righteousness to every one that Believes.

5 For Moses describes the Righteousness, which is of The Law that, "the man which does those things, shall live by them."

6 But The Righteousness, which is of Faith, speaks on this wise, "say not, in your heart, "'who shall ascend into Heaven? (that is, to bring Christ down from above)'"

7 Or, "'who shall descend into the deep?'" (that is, to bring up Christ again, from the dead.)

8 But what says it? "The Word is near you, even in your mouth and in your heart that is, The Word of Faith, which we Preach

9 That if you shall Confess with your mouth, "'The Lord, Jesus and shall Believe in your heart that, God has Raised Him From the dead,'" you shall be Saved.

10 For with the heart, man Believes to Righteousness and with the mouth, Confession is made to Salvation.

11 For the Scripture says, "WHOSOEVER, BELIEVES ON HIM, SHALL NOT BE ASHAMED."

12 For there is no difference between the Jew and the Greek. For the same Lord over all, is rich to all that Call on Him.

13 "FOR WHOSOEVER, SHALL CALL ON THE NAME OF THE LORD, SHALL BE SAVED."

14 How then, shall they Call on Him, in Whom they have not believed and how shall they Believe in Him, of Whom, they have not heard and how shall they Hear, without a preacher?

15 And how shall they Preach, except they be sent? As it is written, "how beautiful are the feet of them that Preach The Gospel of Peace and bring Glad Tidings of Good things!"

16 But they have not all Obeyed The Gospel. For Isaiah says, "Lord, who has Believed our report?"

17 So then, Faith comes by Hearing and Hearing, by The Word of God.

18 But I say, "have they not heard? Yes verily, their sound went into all the Earth and their words to the ends of the World."

19 But I say, "did not Israel know? First, Moses said, "'I WILL PROVOKE YOU TO JEALOUSY BY THEM THAT ARE NO PEOPLE AND BY A FOOLISH NATION, I WILL ANGER YOU.'"

20 But, Isaiah is very bold and says, "I WAS FOUND OF THEM THAT SOUGHT ME NOT. I WAS MADE MANIFEST TO

THEM THAT ASKED NOT AFTER ME."
21 But to Israel He says, "all day long, I have stretched forth My hands to a disobedient and gainsaying people."

Chapter 11

1 I say then, "has God cast away His people? God forbid. For I also, am an Israelite, of the seed of Abraham; of the tribe of Benjamin.
2 God has not cast away His people, which He Foreknew. Know you not, what The Scripture says of Elijah, how he made Intercession to God against Israel saying,
3 "'Lord, they have killed Your prophets and dug down Your alters and I am left alone and they seek my life.'"
4 But what says the answer of God to him? "'I have reserved to Myself, seven thousand men, who have not bowed the knee to the image of Baal.'"
5 Even so then, at this present time also, there is a remnant, according to the election of Grace
6 And if by Grace, then is it no more of works. Otherwise, Grace is no more Grace. But, if it be of works, then it is no more Grace. Otherwise, work is no more work.

7 What then? Israel has not obtained that, which he seeks for, but the election has obtained it and the rest were blinded,
8 According as it is written, "GOD HAS GIVEN THEM THE SPIRIT OF SLUMBER, EYES THAT THEY SHOULD NOT SEE AND EARS THAT THEY SHOULD NOT HEAR,'" to this day.
9 And David said, "'LET THEIR TABLE BE MADE A SNARE AND A TRAP AND A STUMBLINGBLOCK AND A RECOMPENSE TO THEM.
10 LET THEIR EYES BE DARKENED THAT THEY MAY NOT SEE AND BOW DOWN THEIR BACK ALWAYS.'"
11 I say then, "'have they stumbled that they should fall? God forbid, but rather, through their fall, Salvation is come to the gentiles, for to provoke them to jealousy.
12 Now, if the fall of them be the riches of the World and the diminishing of them, the riches of the gentiles, how much more their fullness?'"

13 For I speak to you gentiles, in as much as I am the apostle of the gentiles, I magnify my office.
14 If by any means, I may provoke to emulation them, which are my flesh and might Save some of them.
15 For if the casting away of them be the reconciling of the World, what shall the receiving of them be, but Life from the Dead?
16 For if The Firstfruit is Holy, the lump is also, Holy and if the roots are Holy, so are the branches.
17 And if some of the branches be broken off and you, being a wild olive tree, were grafted in among them and with them, partakes of the root and fatness of the olive tree,
18 Boast not against the branches. But if you boast, you bear not the root, but the root, you.
19 You will say then, "'the branches were broken off that I might be grafted in.'"
20 Well, because of unbelief, they were broken off and you stand by Faith. Be not high minded, but Fear.
21 For if God spared not, the natural branches, take Heed, lest He also, spares not, you.
22 Behold therefore, The Goodness and Severity of God on them which fell, severity. But toward you, Goodness, if you continue in His Goodness. Otherwise, you also, shall be cut off.
23 And they also, if they abide not still, in unbelief, shall be grafted in, for God is able to graft them in, again.
24 For if you were cut out of the olive tree, which is wild by nature and were grafted contrary to nature, into a Good olive tree, how much more, shall these, which be the natural branches, be grafted into their own olive tree?
25 For I would not brothers that you should be ignorant of this Mystery, lest you should be wise in your own conceits that blindness in part is happened to Israel, until the Fullness of the gentiles is come in.
26 And so, all Israel shall be Saved as it is written, "'THERE SHALL COME OUT OF SION, THE DELIVERER AND SHALL TURN AWAY UNGODLINESS FROM JACOB.
27 FOR THIS IS MY COVENANT TO THEM, WHEN I SHALL TAKE AWAY THEIR SINS.'"

28 As concerning The Gospel, they are enemies, for your sakes. But as touching the Election, they are beloved for the fathers' sakes.
29 For the Gifts and Calling of God are

without repentance.
30 For as you in times past, have not believed God, yet have now, Obtained Mercy through their unbelief.
31 Even so, have these also, now not believed that through your Mercy they also, may obtain Mercy.
32 For God has concluded them all in unbelief that He might have Mercy on all."

33 O, the depth of the riches, both of the Wisdom and Knowledge of God! How unsearchable are His Judgments and His Ways, past finding out!
34 "For who has known the mind of The Lord, or who has been His counselor?
35 Or, who has first, given to Him and it shall be recompensed to him again?"
36 For of Him and through Him and to Him, are all things, to Whom is Glory, for ever. Amen.

Chapter 12

1 I beseech you therefore, bothers, by The Mercies of God that you present your bodies a Living Sacrifice; Holy, Acceptable to God, which is your reasonable Service.
2 And be not conformed to this World, but be you Transformed, by the Renewing of your mind that you may Prove what is that Good and Acceptable and Perfect, Will of God.
3 For I say, "through the Grace Given to me, to every man that is among you, not to think of himself more highly than he ought to think, but to think Soberly, according as God has dealt to every man the measure of Faith."
4 For as we have many members in one body and all members have not, the same office.
5 So, we being many, are one body in Christ and every one, members one of another.
6 Having then, Gifts differing, according to the Grace that is Given to us; whether Prophecy, let us Prophesy, according to the proportion of Faith;
7 Or Ministry, let us wait on our Ministering; or he that Teaches, on Teaching;
8 Or he that Exhorts, on Exhortation. He that Gives, let him do it with simplicity. He that rules, with diligence; he that shows mercy, with cheerfulness.

9 Let Love be without dissimulation: Abhor that, which is evil. Cleave to that, which is Good.
10 Be kindly affectioned, one to another with Brotherly Love, in Honor, preferring one another;
11 Not slothful in business; Fervent in Spirit, Serving The Lord,
12 Rejoicing in Hope; Patient in tribulation; Continuing, Instant in Prayer;
13 Distributing to the necessity of saints; Given to Hospitality.
14 Bless them which persecute you. Bless and curse not.
15 Rejoice with them that do rejoice and Weep with them that weep.
16 Be of the same mind, one toward another. Mind not high things, but condescend to men of low estate. Be not wise in your own conceits.

17 Recompense to no man evil for evil. Provide things Honest in the sight of all men.
18 If it be possible, as much as lies in you, live Peaceably, with all men.
19 Dearly beloved, avenge not yourselves, but rather give place to wrath, for it is written, "VENGEANCE IS MINE. I WILL REPAY," says The Lord.
20 Therefore, if your enemy hungers, feed him. If he thirsts, give him drink, for in so doing, you shall heap coals of fire on his head.
21 Be not overcome of evil, but overcome evil, with Good.

Chapter 13

1 Let every soul be subject to the higher powers. For there is no power, but of God. The powers that be, are Ordained of God.
2 Whosoever therefore, resists the power, resists the Ordinance of God and they that resist, shall receive to themselves, damnation.
3 For rulers are not a terror to good works, but to the evil. Will you then, not be afraid of the power? Do that, which is good and you shall have praise of the same.
4 For he is the minister of God to you for good. But, if you do that, which is evil, be afraid, for he bears not the sword in vain, for he is the minister of God; a revenger to execute wrath on him that does evil.
5 Wherefore, you must needs be subject, not only for wrath, but also, for conscience sake.

6 For, for this cause, pay yourselves tribute, also, for they are God's ministers; attending continually, on this very thing.
7 Render therefore, to all their dues; tribute to whom, tribute is due; custom to whom, custom; fear to whom, fear; honor to whom, honor.
8 Owe no man any thing, but to Love one another, <u>for he that Loves another, has fulfilled The Law:</u>
9 <u>For this, "you shall not commit adultery, you shall not kill, you shall not steal, you shall not bear false witness, you shall not covet and if there be any other Commandment, it is briefly comprehended in this saying: namely, you shall Love your neighbor as yourself."</u>
10 <u>Love works no ill to his neighbor. Therefore, Love is the fulfilling of The Law.</u>
11 And that, knowing the time that now, it is high time, to awake out of sleep, <u>for now, is our Salvation nearer than when we believed.</u>
12 The night is far spent, the day is at hand. Let us therefore, cast off the works of Darkness and let us put on the Armor of Light.
13 Let us walk Honestly, as in the day; not in rioting and drunkenness, not in chambering and wantonness, not in strife and envying.
14 But put yourselves, on The Lord, Jesus Christ and make no provision for the flesh, to fulfill the lusts, thereof.

Chapter 14

1 <u>Receive yourselves, him that is weak in The Faith, but not to doubtful disputations:</u>
2 For one believes that he may eat all things. Another, who is weak, eats herbs.
3 Let not him that eats, despise him that eats not and let not him, which eats not, judge him that eats, for God has received him.
4 Who are you that judges another man's servant? To his own master, he stands, or falls. Yes, he shall be held up, for God is able to make him stand.
5 One man esteems one day, above another. Another, esteems every day, alike. Let every man, be fully persuaded in his own mind.
6 He that regards the day, regards it to The Lord. And he that regards not the day, to The Lord, he does not regard it. He that eats, eats to The Lord, for he Gives God Thanks. And he that eats not, to The Lord, he eats not and Gives God Thanks.
7 For none of us lives to himself and no man dies to himself.
8 For whether we live, we live to The Lord and whether we die, we die to The Lord. Whether we live therefore, or die, we are The Lord's.
9 For to this end, Christ both died and Rose and Revived that He might be Lord, both of the dead and Living.
10 But, why do you judge your brother, or why do you set at naught, your brother? <u>For we shall all stand before the Judgment Seat of Christ.</u>
11 For it is written, "as I live, says The Lord, every knee shall bow to Me and every tongue, shall confess to God."
12 <u>So then, every one of us shall Give Account of himself, to God.</u>
13 Let us not therefore, judge one another any more, but Judge this rather that: no man put a stumblingblock, or an occasion to fall in his brother's way.
14 I know and am persuaded by The Lord, Jesus that, there is nothing unclean of itself. But to him that esteems any thing, to be unclean, to him it is unclean.
15 But, if your brother is grieved with your meat, now walk yourself, not charitably. Destroy not him with your meat, for whom Christ died.
16 Let not then, your good be evil spoken of.
17 <u>For the Kingdom of God is not meat and drink, but Righteousness and Peace and Joy in The Holy Ghost.</u>
18 For he that in these things, serves Christ, is acceptable to God and approved of men.
19 Let us therefore, follow after the things, which make for Peace and things wherewith, one may edify another.
20 <u>For meat destroys not The Work of God.</u> All things indeed, are pure, <u>but it is evil for that man, who eats with offence.</u>
21 It is good neither to eat flesh, nor to drink wine, nor any thing, whereby your brother stumbles, or is offended, or is made weak.
22 Have you Faith? Have it to yourself, before God. Happy is he that condemns not himself in that thing, which he allows.
23 But now, having no more place in these parts and having a great desire, these many years to come to you.
23 And he that doubts is damned if he eats, because he eats not, of Faith, <u>for</u>

whatsoever is not of Faith, is sin.

Chapter 15

1 We then that are strong, ought to bear the infirmities of the weak and not to please ourselves.
2 Let every one of us please his neighbor for his good to Edification.
3 For even Christ pleased not Himself, but as it is written, "the reproaches of them that reproached you, fell on Me."
4 For whatsoever things, were written beforetime, were written for our Learning that we through Patience and Comfort of The Scriptures might have Hope.
5 Now, The God of Patience and Consolation, grant you to be Likeminded, one toward another, according to Christ Jesus
6 That you may with one mind and one mouth, Glorify God; even The Father of our Lord, Jesus Christ.
7 Wherefore, receive yourselves one another, as Christ also, received us, to The Glory of God.

8 Now, I say that Jesus Christ was a minister of the circumcision, for The Truth of God, to Confirm the Promises made to the fathers
9 And that the gentiles might Glorify God, for His Mercy as it is written, "FOR THIS CAUSE, I WILL CONFESS TO YOU AMONG THE GENTILES AND SING TO YOUR NAME."
10 And again, He says, "REJOICE, YOU GENTILES, WITH HIS PEOPLE."
11 And again, "PRAISE THE LORD, ALL YOU GENTILES AND LAUD HIM, ALL YOU PEOPLE."
12 And again, Isaiah said, "THERE SHALL BE A ROOT OF JESSE AND HE THAT SHALL RISE, TO REIGN OVER THE GENTILES. IN HIM, SHALL THE GENTILES TRUST."

13 Now, The God of Hope, fill you with all Joy and Peace in Believing that you may abound in Hope, through The Power of The Holy Ghost.
14 And I myself also, am persuaded of you, my brothers that you also, are full of goodness, filled with all Knowledge, able also, to admonish one another.
15 Nevertheless brothers, I have written the more Boldly to you in some sort, as putting you in mind, because of the Grace that is Given to me of God

16 That I should be the minister of Jesus Christ to the gentiles; ministering The Gospel of God that the offering up of the gentiles might be acceptable, being Sanctified by The Holy Ghost.
17 I have therefore, whereof I may Glory through Jesus Christ in those things, which pertain to God.
18 For I will not dare to speak of any of those things, which Christ has not worked by me, to make the gentiles Obedient, by word and deed,
19 Through Mighty Signs and Wonders; by The Power of The Spirit of God, so that from Jerusalem and round about, to Illyricum, I have fully Preached The Gospel of Christ.
20 Yes, so I have striven to Preach The Gospel, not where Christ was named, lest I should build on another man's foundation,
21 But, as it is written, "TO WHOM, HE WAS NOT SPOKEN OF, THEY SHALL SEE AND THEY THAT HAVE NOT HEARD, SHALL UNDERSTAND."
22 For which cause also, I have been much hindered from coming to you
24 When soever, I take my journey into Spain, I will come to you, for I trust to see you in my journey and to be brought on my way there by you, if first, I am somewhat filled with your company.

25 But now, I go to Jerusalem to minister to the saints.
26 For it has pleased them of Macedonia and Achaia, to make a certain contribution for the poor saints, which are in Jerusalem.
27 It has pleased them, verily and their debtors they are, for if the gentiles have been made partakers of their spiritual things, their duty is also, to minister to them in carnal things.
28 When therefore, I have performed this and have Sealed to them this Fruit, I will come by you into Spain.
29 And I am sure that, when I come to you, I shall come in The Fullness of The Blessing of The Gospel of Christ.

30 Now I beseech you brothers, for The Lord, Jesus Christ's sake and for The Love of The Spirit that you Strive together with me in your Prayers to God for me
31 That I may be delivered from them that do not believe in Judaea and that my service, which I have for Jerusalem, may

be accepted of the saints
32 That I may come to you with Joy by The Will of God and may with you be refreshed.
33 Now, The God of Peace be with you all. Amen.

Chapter 16

1 I commend to you Phebe, our sister, which is a servant of the church, which is at Cenchrea
2 That you receive her in The Lord, as becomes saints and that you assist her in whatsoever, business she has need of you, for she has been a succorer of many and of myself, also.
3 Greet Priscilla and Aquila, my helpers in Christ Jesus,
4 Who have for my life, laid down their own necks to whom, not only I give thanks, but also, all the churches of the gentiles.
5 Likewise, greet the church that is in their house. Salute my well-beloved Epaenetus, who is the firstfruits of Achaia, to Christ.
6 Greet Mary, who bestowed much labor on us.

7 Salute Andronicus and Junia, my kinsmen and my fellow-prisoners, who are of note among the apostles, who also, were in Christ before me.
8 Greet Amplias, my beloved in The Lord.
9 Salute Urbane, our helper in Christ and Stachys, my beloved.
10 Salute Apelles, approved in Christ. Salute them, which are of Aristobulus' household.
11 Salute Herodion, my kinsman. Greet them that be of the household of Narcissus, which are in The Lord.
12 Salute Tryphena and Tryphosa, who Labor in The Lord. Salute the beloved Persis, which Labored much in The Lord.
13 Salute Rufus, Chosen in The Lord and his mother and mine.
14 Salute Asyncritus, Phlegon, Hermas, Patrobas, Hermes and the brothers which are with them.
15 Salute Philologus and Julia, Nereus and his sister and Olympas and all the saints which are with them.
16 Salute one another with a Holy kiss. The churches of Christ salute you.
17 Now, I beseech you brothers, mark them which cause divisions and offences contrary to the Doctrine, which you have Learned and Avoid them.
18 For they that are such, serve not, our Lord, Jesus Christ, but their own belly and by good words and fair speeches, deceive the hearts of the simple.
19 For your Obedience is come abroad to all men. I am glad therefore, on your behalf, but yet I would have you wise to that, which is good and simple concerning evil.
20 And The God of Peace, shall bruise Satan under your feet, shortly. The Grace of our Lord Jesus Christ, be with you. Amen.

21 Timotheus, my workfellow and Lucius and Jason and Sosipater, my kinsmen, salute you.
22 I Tertius, who wrote this epistle, salute you in The Lord.
23 Gaius, my host and of the whole church, salutes you. Erastus, the chamberlain of the city, salutes you and Quareus, a brother.
24 The Grace of our Lord, Jesus Christ be with you all. Amen.

25 Now, to Him that is of Power to Establish you, according to my gospel and the Preaching of Jesus Christ, according to the Revelation of the Mystery, which was kept secret since the World began,
26 But now, is made Manifest and by The Scriptures of the Prophets, according to The Commandment of the everlasting God, made Known to all nations for the Obedience of Faith,
27 To God only wise, be Glory through Jesus Christ, for ever. Amen.

1ˢᵗ Corinthians

Chapter 1

1 Paul, called to be an apostle of Jesus Christ, through The Will of God and Sosthenes, our brother,
2 To the church of God, which is at Corinth, to them that are Sanctified in Christ Jesus, Called to be saints, with all that in every place, Call on The Name of Jesus Christ, our Lord, both theirs and ours,
3 Grace be to you and Peace from God, our Father and from The Lord, Jesus Christ.

4 I Thank my God always on your behalf, for the Grace of God, which is Given you by Jesus Christ
5 That in every thing, you are Enriched by Him, in all utterance and in all Knowledge;
6 Even as The Testimony of Christ was Confirmed in you
7 So that, <u>you come behind in no Gift</u>; Waiting for the coming of our Lord, Jesus Christ,
8 Who shall also, Confirm you to the end that you may be blameless in the day of our Lord, Jesus Christ.
9 God is Faithful, by Whom you were Called to the Fellowship of His Son, Jesus Christ, our Lord.

10 Now I beseech you brothers, by The Name of our Lord, Jesus Christ that you all speak the same thing and that there be no divisions among you, but that you be perfectly joined together in the same mind and in the same Judgment.
11 For it has been declared to me of you, my brothers, by them which are of the house of Chloe that there are contentions among you.
12 Now this I say that, every one of you says, "I am of Paul" and "I, of Apollos" and "I, of Cephas" and "I, of Christ."
13 Is Christ divided? Was Paul crucified for you, or were you Baptized in the name of Paul?
14 I Thank God that, I Baptized none of you, but Crispus and Gaius,
15 Lest any should say that, "I had Baptized in my own name."
16 And I Baptized also, the household of Stephanas. Besides, I know not, whether I Baptized, any other.
17 For Christ sent me not to Baptize, but to Preach The Gospel; not with wisdom of words, lest the cross of Christ should be made of no effect.

18 <u>For the Preaching of the cross is to them that perish, foolishness. But to us, which are Saved, it is The Power of God.</u>
19 For it is written, "I WILL DESTROY THE WISDOM OF THE WISE AND WILL BRING TO NOTHING, THE UNDERSTANDING OF THE PRUDENT."
20 Where is the wise? Where is the scribe? Where is the disputer of this World? Has not God made foolish, the wisdom of this World?
21 For after that, in The Wisdom of God, the World by wisdom, knew not God, it Pleased God by the foolishness of Preaching to Save them that Believe.
22 For the Jews require a Sign and the Greeks seek after wisdom,
23 But <u>we Preach Christ crucified</u>; to the Jews, a stumblingblock and to the Greeks, foolishness.
24 But to them which are Called, both Jews and Greeks; Christ, The Power of God and The Wisdom of God,
25 Because the foolishness of God is Wiser than men and the weakness of God is Stronger than men.

26 For you see your calling brothers, how that not many wise men after the flesh, not many mighty, not many noble, are Called.
27 But God has Chosen the foolish things of the World to Confound the wise and God has Chosen the weak things of the World to Confound the things, which are mighty
28 <u>And base things of the World and things which are despised, has God Chosen;</u> yes and things which are not, to bring to nothing things that are
29 <u>That no flesh should glory in His presence.</u>
30 But of Him, are you in Christ Jesus, Who of God, is made to us, Wisdom and Righteousness and Sanctification and Redemption
31 That according as it is written, <u>"he that glories, let him Glory in The Lord."</u>

Chapter 2

1 And I brothers, when I came to you, came not with excellency of speech, or of wisdom, declaring to you The Testimony of God.
2 For I determined not to know any thing among you, save Jesus Christ and Him crucified.
3 And I was with you in weakness and in fear and in much trembling.
4 And my speech and my Preaching was not with enticing words of man's wisdom, but in demonstration of The Spirit and of Power
5 That your Faith should not stand in the wisdom of men, but in The Power of God.

6 Howbeit, we speak Wisdom among them that are perfect, yet not the wisdom of this world, nor of the princes of this World that comes to nothing,
7 But we speak The Wisdom of God in a Mystery, even the hidden Wisdom, which God Ordained before the World to our

Glory,

8 Which none of the princes of this World knew, for had they known it, they would not have crucified The Lord of Glory.

9 But as it is written, "Eye has not seen, nor ear heard, neither have entered into the heart of man, the things, which God has prepared for them that love Him."

10 But God has revealed them to us by His Spirit, for The Spirit searches all things; yes, the deep things of God.

11 <u>For what man knows the things of a man, save the spirit of man, which is in him? Even so, the things of God, knows no man, but The Spirit of God.</u>

12 Now, we have received not, the spirit of the World, but The Spirit, which is of God that we might Know the things that are Freely Given to us of God;

13 Which things also, we speak, not in the words, which man's wisdom teaches, but which The Holy Ghost Teaches; comparing Spiritual things with Spiritual.

14 <u>But, the natural man receives not the things of The Spirit of God, for they are foolishness to him. Neither can he know them, because they are Spiritually Discerned.</u>

15 But, he that is Spiritual, Judges all things, yet he himself, is judged of no man.

16 For who has known the mind of The Lord that he may instruct Him? But, we have the mind of Christ.

Chapter 3

1 And I brothers, could not speak to you as to Spiritual, but as to carnal; even as to babes in Christ.

2 I have fed you with milk and not with meat. For hitherto, you were not able to bear it, neither yet now, are you able.

3 For you are yet carnal, for whereas, there is among you, envying and strife and divisions. Are you not carnal and walk as men?

4 For while one says, "I am of Paul" and another, "I am of Apollos." Are you not carnal?

5 Who then, is Paul and who is Apollos, but ministers by whom, you Believed, even as The Lord gave to every man?

6 <u>I have planted. Apollos watered, but God Gave the Increase.</u>

7 <u>So then, neither is he that plants any thing, neither he that waters, but God that Gives the Increase.</u>

8 Now, he that plants and he that waters are one. And every man shall receive his own reward, according to his own Labor.

9 For we are Laborers, together with God. You are God's husbandry. You are God's building,

10 According to The Grace of God, which is Given to me, as a wise masterbuilder. I have laid the foundation and another builds, thereon. But let every man take Heed, how he builds, thereupon.

11 For other foundations can no man lay than that is laid, which is Jesus Christ.

12 Now, if any man builds on this foundation: gold, silver, precious stones, wood, hay, stubble…

13 Every man's work shall be made manifest, for the day shall declare it, because it shall be revealed by Fire and the Fire shall Try every man's work of what sort it is.

14 If any man's work abides, which he has built thereupon, he shall receive a Reward.

15 <u>If any man's work shall be burned, he shall suffer loss. But, he himself shall be Saved; yet so, as by Fire.</u>

16 <u>Know you not that you are the temple of God and that The Spirit of God dwells in you?</u>

17 <u>If any man, defiles the temple of God, him shall God destroy. For the temple of God is Holy, which temple you are.</u>

18 Let no man deceive himself. If any man among you, seems to be wise in this World, let him become a fool that he may be wise.

19 <u>For the wisdom of this World is foolishness with God. For it is written, "He takes the wise in their own craftiness."</u>

20 <u>And again, "The Lord knows the thoughts of the wise that they are vain."</u>

21 Therefore, let no man glory in men. For all things are yours;

22 Whether: Paul, or Apollos, or Cephas, or the World, or life, or death, or things present, or things to come. All are yours

23 And you are Christ's and Christ is God's.

Chapter 4

1 Let a man so account of us, as of the ministers of Christ and stewards of The Mysteries of God.

2 <u>Moreover, it is required in stewards that a man be found Faithful.</u>

3 But with me, it is a very small thing that I should be judged of you, or of man's

judgement. Yes, I judge not my own self.

4 For I know nothing by myself, yet I am not hereby, justified. But he that Judges me, is The Lord.

5 Therefore, judge nothing before the time, until The Lord comes, Who both will bring to Light the hidden things of Darkness and will make manifest, the counsels of the hearts. And then, shall every man have praise of God.

6 And these things brothers, I have in a figure, transferred to myself and to Apollos for your sakes that you might Learn in us, not to think of men above that, which is written, that no one of you be puffed up for one against another.

7 For who makes you to differ from another and what have you that you did not receive? Now, if you did receive it, why do you glory, as if you have not received it?

8 Now, you are full. Now, you are rich. You have reigned as kings without us and I would to God you did reign that we also, might reign with you.

9 For I think that God has set forth us, the apostles last, as it were appointed to death. For we are made a spectacle to the World and to angels and to men.

10 We are fools for Christ's sake, but you are Wise in Christ. We are weak, but you are strong. You are honorable, but we are despised.

11 Even to this present hour, we both hunger and thirst and are naked and are buffeted and have no certain dwelling place

12 And labor, working with our own hands being reviled. We Bless being persecuted. We suffer it.

13 Being defamed, we entreat. We are made as the filth of the World and are the offscouring of all things to this day.

14 I write not these things to shame you, but as my beloved sons, I warn you.

15 For though you have ten thousand instructors in Christ, yet you have not many fathers, for in Christ Jesus I have begotten you through The Gospel.

16 Wherefore I beseech you, be you followers of me.

17 For this cause, I have sent to you, Timotheus, who is my beloved son and Faithful in The Lord, who shall bring you into remembrance of my ways, which are in Christ, as I Teach every where, in every church.

18 Now, some are puffed up as though I would not come to you.

19 But I will come to you shortly, if The Lord wills and will know not the speech of them which are puffed up, but The Power.

20 For the Kingdom of God is not in word, but in Power.

21 What will you..? Shall I come to you with a rod, or in Love and in the spirit of Meekness?

Chapter 5

1 It is reported, commonly that there is fornication among you and such fornication, as is not so much as named among the gentiles that one should have his father's wife.

2 And you are puffed up and have not rather mourned that he that has done this deed, might be taken away from among you.

3 For I verily, as absent in body, but present in spirit, have Judged already, as though I were present, concerning him that has so done this deed.

4 In The Name of our Lord, Jesus Christ, when you are gathered together and my spirit, with The Power of our Lord, Jesus Christ,

5 To deliver such a one, to Satan for the destruction of the flesh that the spirit may be Saved in The Day of The Lord, Jesus.

6 Your glorying is not good. Know you not that a little leaven, leavens the whole lump?

7 Purge out therefore, the old leaven that you may be a new lump, as you are unleavened. For even Christ, our Passover is Sacrificed for us.

8 Therefore, let us Keep the feast, not with old leaven, neither with the leaven of malice and wickedness, but with the Unleavened Bread of Sincerity and Truth.

9 I wrote to you in an epistle, not to company with fornicators,

10 Yet not altogether, with the fornicators of this World, or with the covetous, or extortioners, or with idolaters, for then, must you needs go out of the World.

11 But now, I have written to you not to keep company, if any man that is called a brother be: a fornicator, or covetous, or an idolater, or a railer, or a drunkard, or an extortioner; with such a one; no, not to eat.

12 For what have I to do to judge them, also that are without? Do not you Judge

them that are within?

13 But them that are without, God Judges, "therefore, put away from among yourselves that wicked person."

Chapter 6

1 Dare any of you, having a matter against another, go to law before the unjust and not before the saints?

2 Do you not know that the saints shall Judge the World and if the World shall be Judged by you, are you unworthy to Judge the smallest matters?

3 Know you not that we shall judge angels? How much more things that pertain to this life?

4 If then, you have judgments of things pertaining to this life, set them to Judge who are least esteemed in the church.

5 I speak to your shame. Is it so that there is not a wise man among you; no, not one that shall be able to Judge between his brothers?

6 But brother goes to law with brother and that, before the unbelievers.

7 Now therefore, there is utterly a fault among you, because you go to law, one with another. Why do you not rather, take wrong? Why do you not rather, suffer yourselves to be defrauded?

8 No, you do wrong and defraud and that your brothers.

9 Know you not that the unrighteous shall not inherit the kingdom of God? Be not deceived, neither: fornicators, nor idolaters, nor adulterers, nor effeminate, nor abusers of themselves with mankind,

10 Nor thieves, nor covetous, nor drunkards, nor revilers, nor extortioners, shall inherit the Kingdom of God.

11 And such were some of you, but you are Washed, but you are Sanctified, but you are Justified in The Name of The Lord, Jesus and by The Spirit of our God.

12 All things are lawful to me, but all things are not expedient. All things are lawful for me, but I will not be brought under the power of any.

13 Meats for the belly and the belly for meats, but God shall destroy both it and them. Now, the body is not for fornication, but for The Lord and The Lord, for the body.

14 And God has both Raised Up The Lord and will also, Raise Up us by His Own Power.

15 Know you not that your bodies are the members of Christ? Shall I then, take the members of Christ and make them the members of a harlot? God forbid.

16 What? Know you not that he which is joined to a harlot is one body? "For two," says He, "shall be one flesh."

17 But, he that is joined to The Lord is one spirit.

18 Flee fornication. Every sin that a man does, is without the body, but he that commits fornication, sins against his own body.

19 What? Know you not that your body is the temple of The Holy Ghost, which is in you, which you have of God and you are not your own?

20 For you are bought with a price. Therefore, Glorify God in your body and in your spirit, which are God's.

Chapter 7

1 Now, concerning the things whereof, you wrote to me: it is good for a man, not to touch a woman.

2 Nevertheless, to avoid fornication, let every man have his own wife and let every woman have her own husband.

3 Let the husband render to the wife due Benevolence and likewise also, the wife to the husband.

4 The wife has not power of her own body, but the husband and likewise also, the husband has no power of his own body, but the wife.

5 Defraud yourselves not, one the other, except it be with consent for a time that you may give yourselves, to Fasting and Prayer and come together again that Satan tempts you not, for your incontinence.

6 But, I speak this by permission and not of commandment.

7 For I would that, all men were even as I, myself. But every man has his proper Gift of God; one after this manner and another, after that.

8 I say therefore, to the unmarried and widows, it is good for them, if they abide even as I.

9 But if they cannot contain, let them marry, for it is better to marry than to burn.

10 And to the married, I command, yet not I, but The Lord; let not the wife depart from her husband.

11 But and if she departs, let her remain

unmarried, or be reconciled to her husband and let not the husband put away his wife.

12 But to the rest I speak, not The Lord; <u>if any brother has a wife that believes not and she be pleased to dwell with him, let him not put her away.</u>

13 <u>And the woman, which has a husband that believes not and if he be pleased to dwell with her, let her not leave him.</u>

14 For the unbelieving husband is sanctified by the wife and the unbelieving wife is sanctified by the husband, else were your children unclean, but now, are they Holy.

15 <u>But, if the unbelieving departs, let him depart. A brother, or a sister is not under bondage in such cases. But God has called us to Peace.</u>

16 <u>For what know you, O wife, whether you shall Save your husband, or how know you, O man, whether you shall Save your wife?</u>

17 But as God has distributed to every man, as The Lord has called every one, so let him Walk. And so, Ordain I, in all churches.

18 Is any man called being circumcised? Let him not become uncircumcised. Is any called in uncircumcision? Let him not be circumcised.

19 <u>Circumcision is nothing and uncircumcision is nothing, but the Keeping of The Commandments of God.</u>

20 Let every man abide in the same calling, wherein he was called.

21 Are you called being a servant? Care not for it, but if you may be made free, use it rather.

22 For he that is called in The Lord, being a servant, is The Lord's Freeman. Likewise also, he that is Called, being Free, is Christ's servant.

23 You are bought with a price. Be not yourselves, the servants of men.

24 Brothers, let every man, wherein he is Called, therein abide with God.

25 Now concerning virgins, I have no commandment of The Lord, yet I give my judgement as one that has obtained Mercy of The Lord to be Faithful.

26 I suppose therefore that this is good for the present distress. I say that it is good for a man, so to be.

27 Are you bound to a wife? Seek not to be loosed. Are you loosed from a wife? Seek not a wife.

28 But and if you marry, you have not sinned and if a virgin marries, she has not sinned. Nevertheless, such shall have trouble in the flesh, but I spare you.

29 But this I say brothers, "the time is short. It remains that both they that have wives, be as though they had none

30 And they that weep, as though they wept not and they that rejoice, as though they rejoiced not and they that buy, as though they possessed not

31 And they that use this World, as not abusing it, for the fashion of this World passes away."

32 <u>But, I would have you without carefulness. He that is unmarried, cares for the things that belong to The Lord, how he may Please The Lord</u>

33 <u>But he that is married, cares for the things that are of the World, how he may please his wife.</u>

34 <u>There is difference also, between a wife and a virgin. The unmarried woman cares for the things of The Lord that she may be Holy; both in body and in spirit. But she that is married, cares for the things of the World, how she may please her husband.</u>

35 And this I speak for your own profit, not hat I may cast a snare on you, but for that, which is comely and that you may attend on The Lord without distraction.

36 But, if any man thinks that he behaves himself, uncomely toward his virgin, if she passes the flower of her age and needs so require, let him do what he will. He sins not. Let them marry.

37 Nevertheless, he that stands steadfast in his heart, having no necessity, but has power over his own will and has so decreed in his heart that he will keep his virgin, does well.

38 So then, he that gives her in marriage, does well. But, he that gives her not, in marriage does better.

39 <u>The wife is bound by The Law as long as her husband lives. But, if her husband is dead, she is at Liberty, to be married to whom she will; only in The Lord.</u>

40 But she is happier if she so abides, after my judgement and I think, also that I have The Spirit of God.

Chapter 8

1 Now, as touching things offered to idols, we know that we all have knowledge.

Knowledge puffs up, but Charity Edifies.
2 And if any man thinks that he knows any thing, he knows nothing, yet as he ought to know.
3 But, if any man Loves God, the same is Known of Him.
4 As concerning therefore, the eating of those things that are offered in sacrifice to idols, we know that an idol is nothing in the World and that there is no other God, but One.
5 <u>For though there is that are called gods;</u> whether in heaven, or on Earth, (as there be gods, many and lords, many)
6 <u>But to us, there is but, One God; The Father, of Whom are all things and we in Him and One Lord, Jesus Christ, by Whom are all things and we by Him.</u>
7 <u>Howbeit, there is not in every man that Knowledge. For some with conscience of the idol to this hour, eats it as a thing offered to an idol and their conscience being weak, is defiled.</u>

8 But, meat commends us not to God. For neither if we eat, are we the better, neither, if we eat not, are we the worse.
9 But take Heed, lest by any means, this Liberty of yours becomes a stumblingblock to them that are weak.
10 <u>For if any man sees you, which has knowledge, sit at meat in the idol's temple, shall not the conscience of him, which is weak, be emboldened to eat those things, which are offered to idols</u>
11 <u>And through your Knowledge, shall the weak brother perish, for whom Christ died?</u>
12 <u>But, when you sin so, against the brothers and wound their weak conscience, you sin against Christ.</u>
13 <u>Wherefore, if meat makes my brother to offend, I will eat no flesh, while the World stands, lest I make my brother to offend.</u>

Chapter 9

1 Am I not an apostle? Am I not Free? Have I not seen Jesus Christ, our Lord? Are not you my Work in The Lord?
2 If I be not an apostle to others, yet doubtless, I am to you. For the seal of my apostleship, are you in The Lord.
3 My answer to them that do examine me is this,
4 Have we not power to eat and to drink?
5 Have we not power to lead about a sister, a wife, as well as other apostles and as the brothers of The Lord and Cephas?
6 Or, I only and Barnabas, have we not power to forbear working?

7 Who goes at warfare any time at his own charges? Who plants a vineyard and eats not of the fruit, thereof, or who feeds a flock and eats not of the milk of the flock?
8 Say I these things as a man, or says not The Law the same, also?
9 For it is written in The Law of Moses, "you shall not muzzle the mouth of the ox that treads out the corn." Does God take care for oxen?
10 Or, says He it altogether, for our sakes? For our sakes no doubt, this is written that he that plows, should plow in Hope and that he that threshes in Hope, should be partaker of his Hope.
11 If we have sown to you Spiritual things, is it a great thing, if we shall reap your carnal things?
12 If others be partakers of this power over you, are not we rather? Nevertheless, we have not used this power. But suffer all things, lest we should hinder The Gospel of Christ.

13 <u>Do you not know that they which minister about Holy things, live of the things of the temple and they which wait at the altar are partakers with the altar?</u>
14 <u>Even so, has The Lord Ordained that they which Preach The Gospel should Live of The Gospel.</u>
15 But I have used none of these things, neither have I written these things that it should be so done to me, for it were better for me to die, than that any man should make my glorying void.

16 For though I Preach The Gospel, I have nothing to glory of, for necessity is laid on me. Yes, woe is to me, if I Preach not The Gospel!
17 For if I do this thing willingly, I have a Reward. But if against my will, a dispensation of The Gospel is committed to me.
18 What is my Reward then? Verily that when I Preach The Gospel, I may make The Gospel of Christ without charge that I abuse not my power in The Gospel.
19 For though I be free from all men, yet have I made myself servant to all that I might gain the more.

20 <u>And to the Jews, I became as a Jew that I might gain the Jews; to them that are</u>

under the law, as under the law that I might gain them that are under the law;
21 To them that are without law, as without law (being not without Law to God, but under The Law to Christ) that I might gain them that are without law.
22 To the weak, became I as weak that I might gain the weak. I am made all things to all men that I might by all means Save some.
23 And this I do for The Gospel's sake that I might be partaker thereof, with you.

24 Know you not that they which run in a race run all, but one receives the prize? So, Run that you may Obtain.
25 And every man that strives for the mastery is temperate in all things. Now, they do it to obtain a corruptible crown, but we an incorruptible.
26 I therefore, so run, not as uncertainly. So fight I, not as one that beats the air,
27 But I keep under my body and bring it into subjection, lest that by any means, when I have Preached to others, I myself should be a castaway.

Chapter 10
1 Moreover brothers, I would not that you should be ignorant, how that all our fathers were under The Cloud and all passed through the Sea
2 And were all baptized to Moses in The Cloud and in the Sea
3 And did all eat the same Spiritual Meat
4 And did all drink the same Spiritual Drink, for they drank of that Spiritual Rock that followed them and that Rock was Christ.
5 But with many of them, God was not well pleased, for they were overthrown in the wilderness.

6 Now, these things were our examples, to the intent we should not lust after evil things, as they also, lusted.
7 Neither be you idolaters, as were some of them, as it is written, "the people sat down to eat and drink and rose up to play."
8 Neither let us commit fornication, as some of them committed and fell in one day, three and twenty thousand.
9 Neither let us tempt Christ, as some of them also, tempted and were destroyed of serpents.
10 Neither murmur yourselves, as some of them also, murmured and were destroyed of the Destroyer.
11 Now, all these things happened to them for examples and they are written for our admonition on whom, the ends of the World are come.

12 Wherefore, let him that thinks he stands, take Heed, lest he fall.
13 There has no temptation taken you, but such as is common to man. But God is Faithful, who will not suffer you to be tempted above that, you are able. But, will with the temptation, also make a way to escape that you may be able to bear it.
14 Wherefore, my dearly beloved, flee from idolatry.
15 I speak as to wise men. Judge yourselves, what I say.
16 The cup of Blessing, which we Bless, is it not the Communion of The Blood of Christ? The Bread which we break, is it not the Communion of the Body of Christ?
17 For we being many, are one bread and one body. For we are all partakers of that one Bread.
18 Behold Israel, after the flesh. Are not they, which eat of the sacrifices, partakers of the altar?
19 What say I then that the idol is any thing, or that which is offered in sacrifice to idols, is any thing?
20 But I say that the things, which the gentiles sacrifice, they sacrifice to devils and not to God and I would not that you should have fellowship with devils.
21 You cannot Drink the Cup of The Lord and the cup of devils. You cannot be partakers of The Lord's Table and of the table of devils.
22 Do we provoke The Lord to Jealousy? Are we stronger than He?
23 All things are lawful for me, but all things are not expedient. All things are lawful for me, but all things edify not.
24 Let no man seek his own, but every man another's wealth.

25 Whatsoever, is sold in the shambles that eat, asking no question for conscience sake,
26 For the Earth is The Lord's and the fullness, thereof.
27 If any of them that believe not, bid you to a feast and you are disposed to go, whatsoever, is set before you, eat, asking no question for conscience sake.
28 But, if any man says to you, "this is offered in sacrifice to idols," eat not, for his sake that showed it and for conscience sake. For the Earth is The Lord's and the

fullness, thereof;
29 Conscience I say, not your own, but of the others. For why is my Liberty judged of another man's conscience?
30 For if I, by Grace, be a partaker, why am I evil spoken of, for that, for which, I Give Thanks?
31 Whether therefore, you eat, or drink, or whatsoever you do, Do All, to the Glory of God.

32 <u>Give no offence; neither to the Jews, nor to the gentiles, nor to the church of God.</u>
33 <u>Even as I please all men in all things, not seeking my own profit, but the profit of many that they may be Saved.</u>

Chapter 11

1 Be you followers of me, even as I also, am of Christ.
2 Now I praise you brothers that you remember me in all things and Keep the Ordinances, as I delivered them to you.
3 <u>But, I would have you know that the Head of every man, is Christ and the head of the woman, is the man and the Head of Christ, is God.</u>
4 Every man Praying, or Prophesying, having his head covered, dishonors his Head.

5 But every woman that Prays, or Prophesies with her head uncovered, dishonors her head. For that is even all one, as if she were shaven.
6 For if the woman is not covered, let her also, be shorn. But if it be a shame for a woman to be shorn, or shaven, let her be covered.
7 For a man indeed, ought not to cover his head, forasmuch as he is the image and glory of God, but the woman is the glory of the man.
8 For <u>the man is not of the woman, but the woman of the man.</u>
9 Neither was the man created for the woman, but the woman for the man.
10 For this cause, the woman ought to have power on her head, because of the angels.
11 Nevertheless, neither is the man, without the woman, neither the woman, without the man, in The Lord.
12 For as the woman is of the man, even so, is the man also, by the woman, but all things of God.

13 Judge in yourselves. Is it comely that a woman Pray to God uncovered?
14 Does not even nature, itself teach you that if a man has long hair, it is a shame to him?
15 <u>But if a woman has long hair, it is a Glory to her,</u> for her hair is given her, for a covering.
16 <u>But, if any man seems to be contentious, we have no such custom; neither the churches of God.</u>

17 Now in this that I declare to you, I praise you not that you come together; not for the better, but for the worse.
18 For first of all, when you come together in the church, I hear that there be divisions among you and I partly believe it.
19 <u>For there must be also, heresies among you that they which are Approved may be made manifest among you.</u>
20 When you come together therefore, into one place, this is not to eat The Lord's supper.
21 For in eating, every one takes before others, his own supper and one is hungry and another is drunken.
22 What? Have you no houses to eat and to drink in, or despise you the church of God and shame them that have not? What shall I say to you? Shall I praise you in this? I praise you not.
23 For I have received of The Lord that, which also, I delivered to you that The Lord Jesus, the same night in which He was betrayed, took bread.
24 And when He had Given Thanks, He broke it and said, "take, eat. This is My Body, which is broken for you. This Do, in Remembrance of Me."
25 After the same manner also, He took the cup, when He had supped saying, "this cup is The New Testament in My Blood. This Do yourselves, as often as you drink it, in Remembrance of Me."
26 For as often as you eat this bread and drink this cup, you do show The Lord's death, until He comes.
27 Wherefore <u>whosoever, shall eat this bread and drink this cup of The Lord, unworthily, shall be guilty of The Body and Blood of The Lord.</u>
28 But let a man examine himself and so, let him eat of that bread and drink of that cup.
29 <u>For he that eats and drinks unworthily,</u>

eats and drinks damnation to himself; not discerning The Lord's Body.
30 For this cause, many are weak and sickly among you and many sleep.

31 For if we would Judge ourselves, we should not be Judged.
32 But, when we are Judged, we are Chastened of The Lord that we should not be condemned with the World.
33 Wherefore my brothers, when you come together to eat, tarry one for another.
34 And if any man hungers, let him eat at home that you come not together to condemnation. And the rest will I set in order when I come.

Chapter 12

1 Now, concerning Spiritual Gifts brothers, I would not have you ignorant.
2 You know that you were gentiles, carried away to these dumb idols; even as you were led.
3 Wherefore, I give you to Understand that no man speaking by The Spirit of God, calls Jesus accursed and that no man can say that, "Jesus is The Lord," but by The Holy Ghost.
4 Now, there are diversities of Gifts, but the same Spirit.
5 And there are differences of administrations, but the same Lord.
6 And there are diversities of operations, but it is the same God, which Works all in all.
7 But the Manifestation of The Spirit is Given to every man to Profit, withal.

8 For to one, is Given by The Spirit: The Word of Wisdom; to another, The Word of Knowledge, by the same Spirit;
9 To another, Faith by the same Spirit; to another, The Gifts of Healing, by the same Spirit;
10 To another, the Working of Miracles; to another, Prophecy; to another, Discerning of spirits; to another, Diverse Kinds of Tongues; to another, The Interpretation of Tongues.

11 But all these Works that one and the same Spirit; dividing to every man, severally as He Will.
12 For as the body is one and has many members and all the members of that one body, being many, are one body. So also, is Christ.

13 For by one Spirit, are we all Baptized into one body; whether we be Jews, or Gentiles, whether we be bond, or free and have been all made to Drink into one Spirit.
14 For the body is not one member, but many.

15 If the foot shall say, "because I am not the hand, I am not of the body," is it therefore, not of the body?
16 And if the ear shall say, "because I am not the eye, I am not of the body," is it therefore, not of the body?
17 If the whole body were an eye, where were the hearing? If the whole were hearing, where were the smelling?
18 But now, has God set the members, every one of them in the body, as it has Pleased Himself.
19 And if they were all one member, where were the body?
20 But now are they many members, yet but one body.

21 And the eye cannot say to the hand, "I have no need of you," nor again, the head to the feet, "I have no need of you."
22 No, much more those members of the body, which seem to be more feeble, are necessary.
23 And those members of the body, which we think to be less honorable, on these, we bestow more abundant Honor and our uncomely parts have more abundant comeliness.
24 For our comely parts have no need, but God has tempered the body together; having given more abundant Honor to that part which lacked
25 That there should be no schism in the body, but that the members should have the same care, one for another.
26 And whether one member suffers, all the members suffer with it; or one member be Honored, all the members Rejoice with it.
27 Now, you are the Body of Christ and members in particular.

28 And God has set some in the church: first, apostles; secondarily, prophets; thirdly, teachers; after that, Miracles; then, Gifts of Healings, Helps, Governments, Diversities of Tongues.
29 Are all apostles? Are all prophets? Are all teachers? Are all Workers of Miracles?
30 Have all the Gifts of Healing? Do all

Speak With Tongues? Do all Interpret?
31 But covet earnestly, the best Gifts and yet, I show to you, a more excellent way.

Chapter 13

1 Though I Speak With the Tongues of men and of angels and have not Charity, I am become as sounding brass, or a tinkling cymbal.
2 And though I have the Gift of Prophecy and Understand All Mysteries and all Knowledge and though I have all Faith, so that I could remove mountains and have not Charity, I am nothing.
3 And though I bestow all my goods to Feed the Poor and though I give my body to be burned and have not Charity, it profits me nothing.
4 Charity Suffers Long and is Kind. Charity envies not. Charity vaunts not itself; is not puffed up,
5 Does not behave itself unseemly; seeks not her own, is not easily provoked, thinks no evil,
6 Rejoices not in iniquity, but Rejoices in The Truth;
7 Bears all things, believes all things, Hopes all things, Endures all things.
8 Charity never fails. But, whether there are Prophecies, they shall fail. Whether there are Tongues, they shall cease. Whether there is Knowledge, it shall vanish away.
9 For we know in part and we Prophesy in part.
10 But when that, which is Perfect is come, then that, which is in part, shall be done away.

11 When I was a child, I spoke as a child, I understood as a child, I thought as a child. But, when I became a man, I put away childish things.
12 For now, we see through a glass, darkly, but then, face to face. Now, I know in part, but then, shall I Know, even as also, I am known.
13 And now, abides: Faith, Hope, Charity; these three, but the greatest of these, is Charity.

Chapter 14

1 Follow after Charity and desire Spiritual Gifts, but rather that, you may Prophesy.
2 For he that Speaks in an Unknown Tongue, Speaks not to men, but to God. For no man understands him. Howbeit, in The Spirit he Speaks Mysteries.

3 But, he that Prophesies, speaks to men to Edification and Exhortation and Comfort.
4 He that Speaks in an Unknown Tongue, Edifies himself, but he that Prophesies, Edifies the church.

5 I would that, you all Spoke With Tongues, but rather that, you Prophesied. For greater is he that Prophesies, than he that Speaks With Tongues; except he Interprets that the church may Receive Edifying.
6 Now brothers, if I come to you Speaking With Tongues, what shall I profit you, except I shall Speak to you, either by Revelation, or by Knowledge, or by Prophesying, or by Doctrine?
7 And even things without Life giving Sound; whether pipe, or harp, except they give a distinction in the sounds, how shall it be known what is piped, or harped?
8 For if the trumpet gives an uncertain sound, who shall prepare himself, to the battle?

9 So likewise yourselves, except you utter by the tongue, words easy to be understood, how shall it be known what is spoken? For you shall speak into the air.
10 There are, it may be so many kinds of voices in the World and none of them is without signification.
11 Therefore, if I know not, the meaning of the voice, I shall be to him that speaks, a barbarian and he that speaks, shall be a barbarian to me.
12 Even so yourselves, forasmuch as you are Zealous of Spiritual Gifts, Seek that you may Excel to the Edifying of the church.

13 Wherefore, let him that Speaks in an Unknown Tongue, Pray that he may Interpret.
14 For if I Pray in an Unknown Tongue, my spirit Prays, but my understanding is unfruitful.
15 What is it then? I will Pray with The Spirit and I will Pray with the Understanding, also. I will Sing with The Spirit and I will Sing with the Understanding, also.
16 Else, when you shall Bless with The Spirit, how shall he that occupies the room of the unlearned say, "Amen" at your Giving of Thanks, seeing he understands not, what you say?

17 For you verily, Give Thanks well, but the other is not edified.

18 I thank my God, I Speak With Tongues more than you all.
19 Yet, in the church, I had rather speak five words with my Understanding that by my voice, I might Teach others also, than ten thousand words in an unknown Tongue.
20 Brothers, be not children in understanding. Howbeit, in malice, be you children, but in Understanding, be men.
21 In The Law it is written, "WITH MEN OF OTHER TONGUES AND OTHER LIPS, WILL I SPEAK TO THIS PEOPLE AND YET, FOR ALL THAT, WILL THEY NOT HEAR ME," says The Lord.

22 Wherefore, Tongues are for a Sign, not to them that Believe, but to them that believe not. But Prophesying, serves not for them that believe not, but for them, which Believe.
23 If therefore, the whole church is come together into one place and all Speak With Tongues and there comes in those that are unlearned, or unbelievers, will they not say that you are mad?
24 But, if all Prophesy and there comes in one that believes not, or one unlearned, he is convinced of all, he is judged of all.
25 And thus, are the secrets of his heart made manifest and so Falling Down on his face, he will Worship God and report that, God is in you of a Truth.

26 How is it then brothers, when you come together, every one of you has a Psalm, has a Doctrine, has a Tongue, has a Revelation, has an Interpretation. Let all things be done to Edifying.
27 If any man Speaks in an Unknown Tongue, let it be by two, or at the most, by three and that by course and let one Interpret.
28 But, if there be no Interpreter, let him keep silent in the church and let him Speak to himself and to God.

29 Let the Prophets Speak two, or three and let the others Judge.
30 If any thing, be Revealed to another that sits by, let the first hold his peace.
31 For you may all Prophesy, one by one that all may Learn and all may be Comforted.
32 And the spirits of the Prophets are subject to the Prophets.

33 For God is not the author of confusion, but of Peace, as in all churches of the saints.

34 Let your women keep silence in the churches, for it is not permitted to them to speak, but they are commanded to be under Obedience as also, says The Law.
35 And if they will Learn any thing, let them ask their husbands at home, for it is a shame for women to speak in the church.
36 What? Came The Word of God out from you, or came it to you, only?
37 If any man thinks himself to be a Prophet, or Spiritual, let him acknowledge that the things that I write to you are The Commandments of The Lord.
38 But, if any man is ignorant, let him be ignorant.
39 Wherefore brothers, covet to Prophesy and forbid not to Speak With Tongues.
40 Let all things be done Decently and In Order.

Chapter 15

1 Moreover brothers, I declare to you The Gospel, which I Preached to you, which also, you have Received and wherein, you Stand
2 By which also, you are Saved, if you Keep in memory what I Preached to you, unless you have believed in vain.
3 For I Delivered to you first of all that which I also, Received, how that Christ died for our sins, according to The Scriptures.
4 And that He was buried and that He Rose again, the third day, according to The Scriptures
5 And that He was seen of Cephas, then of the twelve.
6 After that, He was seen of above five hundred brothers at once, of whom, the greater part remain to this present, but some are fallen asleep.
7 After that, He was seen of James, then, of all the apostles.
8 And last of all, He was seen of me also, as of one born out of due time.

9 For I am the least of the apostles that am not meet to be called an apostle, because I persecuted the church of God.
10 But by the Grace of God, I am what I am and His Grace, which was bestowed on me was not in vain. But I labored more abundantly than they all, yet not I, but The Grace of God, which was with me.

11 Therefore, whether it were I, or they, so we Preach and so, you Believed.

12 Now, if Christ be Preached that He Rose from the dead, how say some among you that, "there is no Resurrection of the dead?"
13 But, if there is no Resurrection of the dead, then is Christ not Risen.
14 And if Christ is not Risen, then is our Preaching vain and your Faith is also, vain.
15 Yes and we are found false witnesses of God, because we have Testified of God that He Raised Up Christ, Whom He Raised not up, if so, be that, the dead Rise not.
16 For if the dead Rise not, then is not Christ Raised
17 And if Christ is not Raised, your Faith is vain. You are yet, in your sins.
18 Then they also, which are fallen asleep in Christ, are perished.
19 If in this life only, we have Hope in Christ, we are of all men, most miserable.
20 But now, is Christ Risen From the dead and become the Firstfruits of them that slept.

21 For since by man came Death, by man came also, the Resurrection of the Dead.
22 For as in Adam, all Die, even so, in Christ, shall all be made Alive.
23 But every man in his own order, Christ, the Firstfruits afterward, they that are Christ's at His coming.
24 Then comes the end, when He shall have Delivered up the Kingdom to God; even The Father, when He shall have put down all Rule and all Authority and Power.
25 For He must Reign, until He has put all enemies under His feet.
26 The last enemy that shall be destroyed is Death.
27 For He has put all things under His feet. But, when He said, "all things are put under Himself," it is manifested that He is excepted, which did put all things under Himself.
28 And when all things shall be subdued to Him, then shall The Son also, Himself be subject to Him that put all things under Him that God may be all in all.

29 Else, what shall they do, which are Baptized for the dead, if the dead Rise not at all? Why are they then, Baptized for the dead?

30 And why stand we in jeopardy every hour?
31 I protest by your rejoicing, which I have in Christ Jesus, our Lord, I die daily.
32 If after the manner of men, I have fought with beasts at Ephesus, what advantages it me, if the dead Rise not? Let us eat and drink, for tomorrow, we die.

33 Be not deceived, evil communications corrupt good manners.
34 Awake to Righteousness and sin not, for some have not the Knowledge of God. I speak this, to your shame.
35 But, some man will say, "how are the dead Raised up and with what body, do they come?"
36 You fool, that which you sow is not Quickened, except it dies.
37 And that, which you sow, you sow not that body that shall be, but bares grain, it may chance of wheat, or of some other grain.
38 But God gives it a body as it has Pleased Him and to every seed, his own body.

39 All flesh is not the same flesh. But, there is one kind of flesh of men; another flesh of beasts; another of fish and another of birds.
40 There are also, celestial bodies and bodies, terrestrial. But the glory of the celestial is one and the glory of the terrestrial, is another.
41 There is one glory of the Sun and another glory of the Moon and another glory of the stars. For one star, differs from another star in glory.
42 So also, is the Resurrection of the dead. It is sown in corruption. It is raised in incorruption.
43 It is sown in dishonor. It is raised in glory. It is sown in weakness. It is raised in Power.
44 It is sown a natural body. It is raised a spiritual body. There is a natural body and there is a spiritual body.

45 And so it is written, "the first man, Adam was made a Living soul. The last Adam, was made a Quickening Spirit."
46 Howbeit that was not first, which is spiritual, but that, which is natural and afterwards that, which is spiritual.
47 The first man, is of the Earth, earthy. The second man, is The Lord, from Heaven.

48 As is the earthy, such are they, also that are earthy and as is, the Heavenly, such are they, also that are Heavenly.
49 And as we have borne the image of the earthy, we shall also, bear the image of the Heavenly.
50 Now, this I say brothers that, "flesh and blood cannot inherit the Kingdom of God, neither does corruption, inherit incorruption."

51 Behold, I show you a mystery: we shall not all sleep, but we shall all be Changed,
52 In a moment, in the twinkling of an eye, at the last trump; for the trumpet shall sound and the dead shall be Raised incorruptible and we shall be Changed.
53 For this corruptible, must put on incorruption and this mortal, must put on immortality.
54 So, when this corruptible, shall have put on incorruption and this mortal, shall have put on immortality, then shall be brought to pass the saying that is written, "DEATH IS SWALLOWED UP IN VICTORY.
55 O DEATH, WHERE IS YOUR STING? O GRAVE, WHERE IS YOUR VICTORY?"
56 The sting of Death is sin and the strength of sin is the Law.
57 But, Thanks be to God, which Gives us the Victory, through our Lord, Jesus Christ.
58 Therefore, my beloved brothers, be you steadfast, unmovable, always abounding in the Work of The Lord, forasmuch as you know that, your Labor is not in vain in The Lord.

Chapter 16

1 Now, concerning the collection for the saints, as I have given order to the churches of Galatia, even so, do yourselves.
2 On the first day of the week, let every one of you, lay by himself in store, as God has Prospered him that there be no gatherings when I come.
3 And when I come, whomsoever, you shall approve by your letters, them will I send to bring your Liberality, to Jerusalem.
4 And if it is meet that I go also, they shall go with me.

5 Now, I will come to you, when I shall pass through Macedonia, for I do pass through Macedonia.
6 And it may be that, I will abide; yes and winter with you that you may bring me on my journey wheresoever, I go.
7 For I will not see you now, by the way, but I trust to tarry a while with you, if The Lord permits.
8 But, I will tarry at Ephesus until Pentecost.
9 For a great door and effectual is opened to me and there are many adversaries.
10 Now, if Timotheus comes, see that he may be with you, without fear, for he Works The Work of The Lord, as I also, do.
11 Let no man therefore, despise him, but conduct himself forth in Peace that he may come to me. For I look for him with the brothers.
12 As touching our brother, Apollos, I greatly desired him to come to you with the brothers, but his will was not at all to come at this time, but he will come when he shall have convenient time.
13 Watch yourselves, Stand Fast in The Faith. Quit yourselves like men. Be strong.
14 Let all your things be done with Charity.

15 I beseech you brothers (you know the house of Stephanas that it is the firstfruits of Achaia and that they have addicted themselves, to the ministry of the saints)
16 That you submit yourselves to such and to every one that Helps with us and labors.
17 I am glad of the coming of Stephanas and Fortunatus and Achaicus for that, which was lacking on your part, they have supplied.
18 For they have refreshed my spirit and yours. Therefore, acknowledge yourselves, them that are such.

19 The churches of Asia salute you. Aquila and Priscilla salute you much in The Lord, with the church that is in their house.
20 All the brothers greet you. Greet yourselves, one another with a Holy kiss.
21 The salutation of me, Paul with my own hand.
22 If any man loves not The Lord, Jesus Christ, let him be anathema. Maranatha.
23 The Grace of our Lord, Jesus Christ be with you.
24 My Love be with you all in Christ Jesus. Amen.

2ⁿᵈ Corinthians

Chapter 1

1 Paul, an apostle of Jesus Christ, by The Will of God and Timothy, our brother, to the church of God, which is at Corinth with all the saints which are in all Achaia,

2 Grace be to you and Peace from God our Father and from The Lord, Jesus Christ.
3 Blessed be God, even The Father of our Lord, Jesus Christ, The Father of Mercies and The God of all Comfort,
4 Who Comforts us in all our tribulation that we may be able to Comfort them, which are in any trouble; by the Comfort wherewith, we ourselves are Comforted of God.
5 For as the sufferings of Christ abound in us, so our consolation also, abounds by Christ.
6 And whether we be afflicted, it is for your Consolation and Salvation, which is effectual in the enduring of the same sufferings, which we also, suffer, or whether we be Comforted, it is for your Consolation and Salvation.
7 And our Hope of you is Steadfast, knowing that as you are partakers of the sufferings, so you shall be also, of the Consolation.

8 For we would not brothers, have you ignorant of our trouble, which came to us in Asia that we were pressed out of measure, above strength, insomuch that we despaired, even of life.
9 But, we had the sentence of death in ourselves that we should not trust in ourselves, but in God, which Raises the dead,
10 Who Delivered us from so great a Death and does Deliver in Whom we Trust that He will yet, Deliver us.
11 You also, helping together by Prayer for us that for the Gift bestowed on us by the means of many persons, thanks may be given by many on our behalf.
12 For our rejoicing is this: The Testimony of our conscience that in simplicity and Godly Sincerity, not with fleshly wisdom, but by the Grace of God, we have had our conversation in the World and more abundantly, to you-ward.
13 For we write no other things to you that what you read, or acknowledge and I trust you shall acknowledge, even to the end
14 As also, you have acknowledged us in part that we are your rejoicing, even as you also, are ours in the Day of The Lord, Jesus.
15 And in this confidence, I was minded to come to you before that you might have a second benefit
16 And to pass by you, into Macedonia and to come again, out of Macedonia to you and of you, to be brought on my way, toward Judaea.
17 When I therefore, was thus minded, did I use lightness, or the things that I purpose? Do I purpose, according to the flesh that with me, there should be yes, yes and no, no?

18 But, as God is True, our word toward you was not, yes and no.
19 For The Son of God, Jesus Christ who was Preached among you by us; even by me and Silvanus and Timotheus, was not yes and no, but in Him, was yes.
20 For all the Promises of God, in Him are yes and in Him, Amen, to The Glory of God, by us.
21 Now, He which establishes us with you in Christ and has Anointed us, is God,
22 Who has also, Sealed us and Given the Earnest of The Spirit in our hearts.
23 Moreover, I call God for a record on my soul that to spare you, I came not as yet to Corinth,
24 Not for that we have dominion over your Faith, but are Helpers of your Joy, for by Faith, you Stand.

Chapter 2

1 But, I determined this with myself that I would not come again, to you in heaviness.
2 For if I make you sorry, who is he then that makes me glad, but the same, which is made sorry by me?
3 And I wrote this same to you, lest when I came, I should have sorrow from them of whom, I ought to rejoice, having confidence in you all that my joy is the joy of you all.
4 For out of much affliction and anguish of heart, I wrote to you with many tears, not that you should be grieved, but that you might know the love, which I have more abundantly to you.

5 But, if any has caused grief, he has not grieved me, but in part that I may not overcharge you all.
6 Sufficient to such a man is this punishment, which was inflicted of many.
7 So that contrariwise, you ought rather, to Forgive him and Comfort him, lest perhaps, such a one, should be swallowed up with overmuch sorrow.
8 Wherefore, I beseech you that you would confirm your love toward him.
9 For to this end also, did I write that I might know the proof of you, whether you be obedient in all things.
10 To whom, you forgive any thing, I forgive also, for if I forgave any thing, to whom, I forgave it, for your sakes, forgave I it, in the person of Christ,
11 Lest Satan should get an advantage of us, for we are not ignorant of his devices.

12 Furthermore, when I came to Troas to Preach Christ's Gospel and a Door was Opened to me of The Lord,
13 I had no rest in my spirit, because I found not, Titus my brother. But, taking my leave of them, I went from there, into Macedonia.
14 Now, Thanks be to God, which always causes us to Triumph in Christ and makes manifest, the Savour of His Knowledge by us in every place.
15 For we are to God, a sweet savor of Christ, in them that are Saved and in them that perish.
16 To the one, we are the savor of death to death and to the other, the savor of life to Life. And who is sufficient for these things?
17 <u>For we are not as many, which corrupt The Word of God</u>, but as of Sincerity, but as of God, in the sight of God, we speak in Christ.

Chapter 3

1 Do we begin again, to commend ourselves, or need we as some others, epistles of commendation to you, or letters of commendation from you?
2 You are our epistle written in our hearts; known and read of all men.
3 Forasmuch as you are manifestly declared to be the epistle of Christ ministered by us, written not with ink, but with The Spirit of The Living God, not in tablets of stone, but in fleshy tables of the heart.
4 And such trust have we, through Christ to God-ward.
5 Not that we are sufficient of ourselves to think any thing, as of ourselves, but our sufficiency is of God,
6 <u>Who also, have made us able ministers of The New Testament, not of the letter, but of The Spirit, for the letter kills, but The Spirit Gives Life.</u>
7 But if the ministration of death, written and engraved in stones, was glorious so that the children of Israel could not steadfastly behold the face of Moses for the glory of his countenance, which glory was to be done away,
8 How shall not the ministration of The Spirit be rather Glorious?
9 For if the ministration of condemnation is glory, much more, does the ministration of Righteousness exceed in Glory.
10 For even that which, was made Glorious had no glory in this respect, by reason of the Glory that excels.
11 For if that, which is done away, was glorious, much more that, which remains, is Glorious.
12 Seeing then that we have such Hope, we use great plainness of speech.

13 And not as Moses, which put a veil over his face that the children of Israel could not steadfastly look to the end of that, which is abolished,
14 But their minds were blinded, for until this day remains, the same vail untaken away in the reading of The Old Testament, which vail is done away in Christ.
15 But even to this day, when Moses is read, the vail is on their heart.
16 Nevertheless, when it shall Turn To The Lord, the vail shall be taken away.
17 <u>Now, The Lord is that Spirit and where The Spirit of The Lord is, there is Liberty.</u>
18 But we all, with open face, beholding as in a glass, The Glory of The Lord, are changed into the same image; from glory to Glory, even as by The Spirit of The Lord.

Chapter 4

1 Therefore, seeing we have this Ministry, as we have received Mercy, we faint not,
2 <u>But have renounced the hidden things of dishonesty, not walking in craftiness, nor handling The Word of God deceitfully, but by manifestation of The Truth; commending ourselves to every man's conscience in the sight of God.</u>
3 <u>But, if our Gospel is hid, it is hid to them</u>

that are lost,

4 In whom, the god of this World has blinded the minds of them, which believe not, lest The Light of The Glorious Gospel of Christ, Who is The Image of God, should Shine to them.

5 For we Preach not ourselves, but Christ Jesus, The Lord and ourselves, your servants for Jesus' sake.

6 For God, Who Commanded The Light to Shine out of Darkness, has Shined in our hearts, to Give The Light of The Knowledge of The Glory of God in the face of Jesus Christ.

7 But, we have this Treasure in earthen vessels that the Excellency of The Power may be of God and not of us.

8 We are troubled on every side, yet not distressed. We are perplexed, but not in despair;

9 Persecuted, but not forsaken; cast down, but not destroyed;

10 Always bearing about in the body, the dying of The Lord, Jesus that the Life also, of Jesus might be made Manifest in our body.

11 For we which live are always delivered to death for Jesus' sake that the Life also, of Jesus might be made Manifest in our mortal flesh.

12 So then, death works in us, but Life in you.

13 We having the same Spirit of Faith, according as it is written, "I Believed and therefore, I have spoken." We also, Believe and therefore, speak,

14 Knowing that He which Raised Up The Lord, Jesus shall Raise Up us also, by Jesus and shall present us with you.

15 For all things are for your sakes that the abundant Grace might through the Thanksgiving of many, redound to The Glory of God.

16 For which cause, we faint not, but though our outward man perishes, yet the inward man is Renewed day by day.

17 For our light affliction, which is but for a moment, works for us, a far more exceeding and Eternal weight of Glory,

18 While we look not, at the things which are seen, but at the things, which are not seen, for the things which are seen, are temporal. But the things, which are Not Seen are Eternal.

Chapter 5

1 For we know that if our earthly house of this tabernacle were dissolved, we have a building of God; a house not made with hands, Eternal in the Heavens.

2 For in this, we groan earnestly; desiring to be clothed on with our house, which is from Heaven.

3 If so be that, being clothed, we shall not be found naked.

4 For we that are in this tabernacle do groan, being burdened not, for that, we would be unclothed, but clothed on that mortality might be swallowed up of Life.

5 Now, He that has Worked us for the same thing is God, who also, has Given to us, the Earnest of The Spirit.

6 Therefore, we are always confident knowing that, while we are at home in the body, we are absent from The Lord;

7 For we Walk by Faith, not by sight.

8 We are confident, I say and willing rather, to be absent from the body and to be present with The Lord.

9 Wherefore, we Labor that whether present, or absent we may be accepted of Him.

10 For we must all appear before the Judgment Seat of Christ that every one may receive the things done in his body, according to that he has done; whether it is good, or bad.

11 Knowing therefore, the terror of The Lord, we persuade men. But, we are made manifest to God and I trust also, are made manifest in your consciences.

12 For we commend not ourselves again, to you, but give you occasion to glory on our behalf that you may have somewhat to answer them, which glory in appearance and not in heart.

13 For whether we are beside ourselves, it is to God, or whether we are sober, it is for your cause.

14 For The Love of Christ constrains us, because we thus Judge that: if One died for all, then were all Dead

15 And that He died for all that they, which Live should not henceforth, live to themselves, but to Him, which died for them and Rose, Again.

16 Wherefore henceforth, know we no man after the flesh. Yes, though we have Known Christ after the flesh, yet now henceforth, know we him, no more.

17 Therefore, if any man is in Christ, he is

a New Creature. Old things are passed away. Behold, all things are become New.
18 And all things are of God, who has Reconciled us to Himself, by Jesus Christ and has given to us the ministry of Reconciliation.
19 To wit that, God was in Christ, Reconciling the World to Himself; not imputing their trespasses to them and has committed to us The Word of Reconciliation.

20 Now then, we are ambassadors for Christ. As though, God did beseech you by us, we Pray you in Christ's stead. Be yourselves Reconciled to God.
21 For He has made Him to be sin for us; Who knew no sin that we might be made the Righteousness of God, in Him.

Chapter 6
1 We then, as Workers together with Him, beseech you also that you receive not The Grace of God in vain.
2 For He said, "I have heard you in a time accepted and in the day of Salvation, I have succored you. Behold, now is the accepted time. Behold, now is the day of Salvation,
3 Giving no offence in any thing that the ministry be not blamed."
4 But in all things, approving ourselves as the ministers of God in much Patience: in afflictions, in necessities, in distresses,
5 In stripes, in imprisonments, in tumults, in Labors, in Watchings, in Fastings;
6 By Pureness, by Knowledge, by Long Suffering, by Kindness, by The Holy Ghost, by Love Unfeigned,
7 By The Word of Truth, by The Power of God, by the Armor of Righteousness; on the right hand and on the left;
8 By Honor and dishonor; by evil report and good report as; deceivers and yet, True;
9 As unknown and yet, well known; as dying and behold, we Live as Chastened and not killed;
10 As sorrowful, yet always Rejoicing; as poor, yet making many rich; as having nothing and yet possessing all things.

11 O you Corinthians, our mouth is open to you. Our heart is enlarged.
12 You are not straitened in us, but you are straitened in your own bowels.
13 Now, for a recompense in the same, (I speak as to my children) be yourselves also, enlarged.

14 Be you, not unequally yoked together, with unbelievers. For what fellowship has Righteousness with unrighteousness? And what communion has Light with Darkness?
15 And what concord has Christ with Belial, or what part has he that Believes with an infidel?
16 And what agreement has the temple of God with idols? For you are the temple of The Living God as God has said, "I WILL DWELL IN THEM AND WALK IN THEM AND I WILL BE THEIR GOD AND THEY SHALL BE MY PEOPLE.
17 WHEREFORE, COME OUT FROM AMONG THEM AND BE YOU SEPARATE," says The Lord and "TOUCH NOT THE UNCLEAN THING AND I WILL RECEIVE YOU.
18 AND WILL BE A FATHER TO YOU AND YOU SHALL BE MY SONS AND DAUGHTERS," says The Lord, Almighty.

Chapter 7
1 Having therefore, these Promises, dearly beloved, let us Cleanse ourselves from all filthiness of the flesh and spirit; Perfecting Holiness in The Fear of God.
2 Receive us. We have wronged no man. We have corrupted no man. We have defrauded no man.
3 I speak not this, to condemn you, for I have said before that, "you are in our hearts to die and live with you."
4 Great is my boldness of speech toward you. Great is my glorying of you. I am filled with comfort. I am exceedingly joyful in all our tribulation.
5 For when we had come into Macedonia, our flesh had no rest, but we were troubled on every side. Without, were fightings; within, were fears.
6 Nevertheless, God that Comforts those that are cast down, Comforted us by the coming of Titus.
7 And not by his coming only, but by the consolation wherewith, he was comforted in you, when he told us: your earnest desire, your mourning, your fervent mind toward me, so that I rejoiced the more.

8 For though I made you sorry with a letter, I do not repent. Though I did repent, for I perceive that the same epistle has made you sorry, though it were but for a season.
9 Now, I rejoice not that you were made

sorry, but that you sorrowed to Repentance. For you were made sorry after a Godly manner that you might receive damage by us in nothing.

10 For Godly sorrow works Repentance to Salvation, not to be repented of, but the sorrow of the World works Death.

11 For behold, this same thing that you sorrowed after a Godly sort, what carefulness it worked in you; yes, what clearing of yourselves; yes, what indignation; yes, what fear; yes, what vehement desire; yes, what zeal; yes, what revenge! In all things, you have approved yourselves, to be clear in this matter.

12 Wherefore, though I wrote to you, I did it not for his cause that had done the wrong, nor for his cause that suffered wrong, but that our care for you in the sight of God might appear to you.

13 Therefore, we were comforted in your comfort; yes and exceedingly the more joyous; we, for the joy of Titus, because his spirit was refreshed by you all.

14 For if I have boasted any thing, to him of you, I am not ashamed. But as we spoke all things to you in truth, even so, our boasting, which I made before Titus, is found a Truth.

15 And his inward affection is more abundant toward you, while he remembers the obedience of you all, how with Fear and Trembling you received him.

16 I rejoice therefore that I have confidence in you in all things.

Chapter 8

1 Moreover brothers, we do you to wit, of the Grace of God bestowed on the churches of Macedonia,

2 How that in a great trial of affliction, the abundance of their joy and their deep poverty abounded to the Riches of their Liberality.

3 For to their power, I bear record, yes and beyond their power, they were willing of themselves,

4 Praying us with much entreaty that we would receive the gift and take on us, the fellowship of the ministering to the saints.

5 And this they did, not as we hoped, but first gave their own selves to The Lord and to us, by The Will of God.

6 Insomuch that we desired Titus that as he had begun, so he would also, finish in you the same grace, also.

7 Therefore, as you abound in every thing, in Faith and Utterance and Knowledge and in all Diligence and in your love to us, see that you abound in this Grace, also.

8 I speak not by commandment, but by occasion of the forwardness of others and to prove the sincerity of your love.

9 For you know the Grace of our Lord, Jesus Christ that though He was rich, yet for your sakes, He became poor that you through His poverty, might be Rich.

10 And herein, I give my advice. For this is expedient for you, who have begun before, not only to do, but also, to be forward a year ago.

11 Now therefore, perform the doing of it that as there was a readiness to will, so there may be a performance also, out of that which you have.

12 For if there be first a willing mind, it is accepted, according to that a man has and not, according to that he has not.

13 For I mean not that other men be eased and you burdened

14 But by an equality that now, at this time, your abundance may be a supply for their want that their abundance also, may be a supply for your want that there may be equality.

15 As it is written, "he that had gathered much, had nothing over and he that had gathered little, had no lack."

16 But Thanks be to God, which put the same earnest care into the heart of Titus for you.

17 For indeed, he accepted the exhortation, but being more forward, of his own accord, he went to you.

18 And we have sent with him the brother, whose praise is in The Gospel, throughout all the churches

19 And not that only, but who was also, chosen of the churches to travel with us with this Grace, which is administered by us to the Glory of the same Lord and declaration of your ready mind.

20 Avoiding this that, no man should blame us in this abundance which is administered by us,

21 Providing for honest things, not only in the sight of The Lord, but also, in the sight of men.

22 And we have sent with them our brother, whom we have oftentimes proved Diligent in many things, but now, much more Diligent, on the great confidence, which I have in you.

23 Whether any does enquire of Titus, he is my partner and fellow helper concerning you, or our brothers, be enquired of, they are the messengers of the churches and the Glory of Christ.
24 Wherefore, show yourselves to them and before the churches, the proof of your love and of our boasting on your behalf.

Chapter 9

1 For as touching the ministering to the saints, it is superfluous for me to write to you.
2 For I know the forwardness of your mind, for which I boast of you to them of Macedoni that Achaia was ready a year ago and your Zeal has provoked very many.
3 Yet have I sent the brothers, lest our boasting of you should be in vain in this behalf that, as I said, "you may be ready,"
4 Lest haply, if they of Macedonia come with me and find you unprepared, we (that we say not, you) should be ashamed in this same confident boasting.
5 Therefore, I thought it necessary to exhort the brothers that they would go before to you and make up beforehand your bounty, whereof you had notice before that the same might be ready as a matter of bounty and not as of covetousness.

6 But this I say, "he which sows sparingly, shall reap also, sparingly and he which Sows Bountifully, shall Reap also, Bountifully."
7 Every man, according as he purposes in his heart, so let him Give, not grudgingly, or of necessity. For God Loves a Cheerful Giver.
8 And God is able to make all Grace abound toward you that you, always having all sufficiency in all things, may abound to every good work.
9 As it is written, He has dispersed abroad. He has Given to the poor. His Righteousness remains, forever.
10 Now, he that Ministers seed to the sower, both ministers bread for your food and multiply your seed sown and increase the Fruits of your Righteousness,
11 Being enriched in every thing, to all bountifulness, which causes through us Thanksgiving to God.

12 For the administration of this service, not only supplies the want of the saints, but is abundant also, by many Thanksgivings to God.
13 While by the experiment of this ministration, they Glorify God for your professed subjection to The Gospel of Christ and for your Liberal distribution to them and to all men
14 And by their Prayer for you, which long after you, for the exceeding Grace of God in you.
15 Thanks be to God for His unspeakable Gift.

Chapter 10

1 Now, I Paul myself, beseech you by the Meekness and Gentleness of Christ, who in presence, am base among you, but being absent, am bold toward you.
2 But, I beseech you that I may not be bold when I am present with that confidence, wherewith I think to be bold against some, which think of us as if we walked, according to the flesh.
3 For though we walk in the flesh, we do not War after the flesh.
4 For the Weapons of our Warfare are not carnal, but Mighty through God, to the pulling down of strong holds;
5 Casting down imaginations and every high thing that exalts itself, against the Knowledge of God and bringing into captivity, every thought to the Obedience of Christ
6 And having in a readiness, to revenge all disobedience, when your Obedience is fulfilled.

7 Do you look on things after the outward appearance? If any man trusts to himself that he is Christ's, let him of himself, think this again that, as he is Christ's, even so are we Christ's.
8 For though I should boast somewhat more of our authority, which The Lord has given us for edification and not for your destruction, I should not be ashamed,
9 That I may not seem as if I would terrify you by letters.
10 "For his letters," they say, "are weighty and powerful. But, His bodily presence is weak and his speech contemptible."
11 Let such a one think this that: such as we are in word by letters when we are absent, such will we be also, in deed when we are present.

12 For we dare not make ourselves of the number, or compare ourselves, with some that commend themselves. But they measuring themselves, by themselves

and comparing themselves, among themselves, are not wise.

13 But, we will not boast of things without our measure, but according to the measure of the rule, which God has distributed to us; a measure to reach, even to you.

14 For we stretch not ourselves beyond our measure, as though we reached not to you, for we are come as far as to you also, in Preaching The Gospel of Christ;

15 Not boasting of things without our measure that is, of other men's labors, but having Hope, when your Faith is increased that we shall be enlarged by you, according to our rule abundantly,

16 To Preach The Gospel in the regions beyond you and not to boast in another man's line of things made ready to our hand,

17 "But, he that glories, let him Glory in The Lord."

18 For not he that commends himself, is approved, but whom The Lord commends.

Chapter 11

1 Would to God, you could bear with me a little in my folly and indeed, bear with me.

2 For I am jealous over you, with Godly jealousy. For I have espoused you to one husband that I may present you as a chaste virgin to Christ.

3 But I fear, lest by any means, as the serpent beguiled Eve, through his subtlety, so your minds should be corrupted from the simplicity that is in Christ,

4 For if he that comes, preaches another Jesus, whom we have not Preached, or if you receive another spirit, which you have not received, or another gospel, which you have not accepted; you might well bear with him.

5 For I suppose I was not a whit behind the very chiefest apostles,

6 But though I be rude in speech, yet not in Knowledge. But, we have been throughly made manifest among you in all things.

7 Have I committed an offence in abasing myself that you might be exalted, because I have Preached to you The Gospel of God, freely?

8 I robbed other churches; taking wages of them, to do you service.

9 And when I was present with you and wanted, I was chargeable to no man for that, which was lacking to me the brothers, which came from Macedonia supplied and in all things, I have kept myself from being burdensome to you and so, will I keep myself.

10 As the Truth of Christ is in me, no man shall stop me of this boasting in the regions of Achaia.

11 Wherefore, because I love you not? God knows.

12 But what I do that I will do that I may cut off occasion from them, which desire occasion that wherein, they glory, they may be found even as we.

13 For such are false apostles: deceitful workers, transforming themselves, into the apostles of christ.

14 And no marvel, for Satan himself, is transformed into an angel of light.

15 Therefore, it is no great thing, if his ministers also, be transformed as the ministers of righteousness, whose end shall be, according to their works.

16 I say again, let no man think me a fool, if otherwise, yet as a fool, receive me that I may boast myself a little.

17 That which I speak, I speak it not after The Lord, but as it were foolishly, in this confidence of boasting.

18 Seeing that, many glory after the flesh, I will glory, also.

19 For you suffer fools gladly, seeing you yourselves are wise.

20 For you suffer: if a man brings you into bondage, if a man devours you, if a man takes of you, if a man exalts himself, if a man beats you on the face.

21 I speak as concerning reproach, as though we had been weak. Howbeit, wherein soever, any are bold, (I speak foolishly) I am bold, also.

22 Are they Hebrews? So am I. Are they Israelites? So am I. Are they the seed of Abraham? So am I.

23 Are they ministers of Christ? (I speak as a fool.) I am: more in labors, more abundant in stripes, above measure in prisons, more frequent in deaths, often.

24 Of the Jews; five times, I received forty stripes, save one.

25 Thrice, was I beaten with rods. Once, I was stoned. Thrice, I suffered shipwreck. A night and a day, I have been in the deep;

26 In journeyings often, in perils of waters, in perils of robbers, in perils by my own countrymen, in perils by the heathen, in perils in the city, in perils in the wilderness, in perils in the Sea, in perils among false brothers,

27 <u>In weariness and painfulness, in watchings often, in hunger and thirst, in fastings often, in cold and nakedness;</u>
28 Besides those things that are without that, which comes on me daily, the care of all the churches.

29 <u>Who is weak and I am not weak? Who is offended and I burn not?</u>
30 If I must needs glory, I will glory of the things, which concern my infirmities.
31 The God and Father of our Lord, Jesus Christ, which is Blessed for evermore, knows that I lie not.
32 In Damascus, the governor under Aretas, the king kept the city of the Damascenes with a garrison, desirous to apprehend me
33 And through a window in a basket, I was let down by the wall and escaped his hands.

Chapter 12

1 It is not expedient for me doubtless to glory. I will come to Visions and Revelations of The Lord.
2 I knew a man in Christ, above fourteen years ago, (whether in the body, I cannot tell, or whether out of the body, I cannot tell. God knows) such a one, <u>caught up to the third Heaven</u>.
3 And I knew such a man, (whether in the body, or out of the body, I cannot tell. God knows)
4 How that, he was <u>caught up into Paradise</u> and heard unspeakable words, which it is not Lawful for a man to utter.
5 Of such a one, I will glory, yet of myself, I will not glory, but in my infirmities.
6 For though I would desire to glory, I shall not be a fool. For I will say the truth, but now, I forbear, lest any man should think of me above that, which he sees me to be, or that he hears of me.

7 And lest I should be exalted above measure through the abundance of the Revelations, there was given to me a thorn in the flesh, the messenger of Satan to buffet me, lest I should be exalted above measure.
8 For this thing, I besought The Lord thrice that it might depart from me.
9 And He said to me, "My Grace is sufficient for you, for My Strength is made Perfect in weakness." Most gladly therefore, will I rather glory in my infirmities that, the Power of Christ may rest on me.

10 <u>Therefore, I take pleasure:</u> in infirmities, in reproaches, in necessities, in persecutions, in distresses for Christ's sake. For when I am weak, then am I strong.
11 I am become a fool in glorying. You have compelled me, for I ought to have been commended of you. For in nothing, am I behind the very chiefest apostles, though I am nothing.
12 Truly, the Signs of an apostle were worked among you in all patience; in Signs and Wonders and mighty Deeds.
13 For what is it, wherein you were inferior to other churches, except it is that I myself, was not burdensome to you? Forgive me this wrong.
14 Behold, the third time, I am ready to come to you and I will not be burdensome to you. For I seek not yours, but you, <u>for the children ought not to lay up for the parents, but the parents, for the children.</u>
15 And I will very gladly spend and be spent for you, though the more abundantly, I love you, the less I am loved.
16 But be it so, I did not burden you. Nevertheless, being crafty, I caught you with guile.
17 Did I make a gain of you by any of them, whom I sent to you?

18 I desired Titus and with him, I sent a brother. Did Titus make a gain of you? Walked we not, in the same Spirit? Walked we not, in the same steps?
19 Again, think yourselves that we excuse ourselves to you? We speak before God in Christ. But, we do all things, dearly beloved, for your edifying.
20 For I fear lest, when I come, I shall not find you such as I would. And that I shall be found to you, such as you would not, lest there be: debates, envyings, wraths, strifes, backbitings, whisperings, swellings, tumults.
21 And lest, when I come again, my God will humble me among you and that <u>I shall bewail many, which have sinned already and have not Repented of the uncleanness and fornication and lasciviousness, which they have committed.</u>

Chapter 13

1 This is the third time I am coming to you. <u>In the mouth of two, or three witnesses, shall every word be established.</u>

2 I told you before and foretell you, as if I were present, the second time and being absent, now I write to them, which heretofore, have sinned and to all others that, "if I come again, I will not spare."
3 Since you seek a proof of Christ Speaking in me, which to you-ward are not weak, but is Mighty in you.
4 For though He was crucified through weakness, yet He Lives by The Power of God. For we also, are weak in Him, but we shall Live with Him by The Power of God, toward you.

5 <u>Examine yourselves, whether you are in The Faith. Prove your own selves. Know you not, your own selves, how that Jesus Christ is in you, except you be reprobates?</u>
6 But, I trust that you shall know that we are not reprobates.
7 <u>Now, I Pray to God that you do no evil; not that we should appear approved, but that you should do that, which is Honest, though we be as reprobates.</u>
8 For we can do nothing against the Truth, but for the Truth.
9 For we are glad, when we are weak and you are strong and this also, we wish, even your perfection.
10 Therefore, I write these things being absent, lest being present, I should use sharpness, according to the power, which The Lord has given me to edification and not to destruction.

11 <u>Finally brothers, farewell. Be perfect, be of Good Comfort, be of one mind, live in Peace and The God of Love and Peace, shall be with you.</u>
12 Greet one another with a Holy kiss.
13 All the saints salute you.
14 The Grace of The Lord, Jesus Christ and the Love of God and The Communion of The Holy Ghost, be with you all. Amen.

Galatians

Chapter 1

1 Paul, an apostle (not of men, neither by man, but by Jesus Christ and God, The Father, who Raised Him from the dead)
2 And all the brothers, which are with me to the churches of Galatia,
3 Grace be to you and Peace from God, The Father and from our Lord, Jesus Christ,
4 Who gave Himself for our sins that He might Deliver us from this present evil World, according to The Will of God and our Father,
5 To Whom be Glory, for ever and ever. Amen.

6 <u>I marvel that you are so soon removed from Him that called you into The Grace of Christ, to another gospel,</u>
7 <u>Which is not another, but there are some that trouble you and would pervert The Gospel of Christ.</u>
8 <u>But though we, or an angel from Heaven, preach any other gospel to you than that, which we have Preached to you, let him be accursed.</u>

9 <u>As we said before, so I say now again, "if any man preach any other gospel to you than that, you have Received, let him be accursed."</u>
10 For do I now, persuade men, or God, or do I seek to please men? <u>For if I yet pleased men, I should not be the servant of Christ.</u>
11 <u>But, I certify you brothers that, The Gospel, which was Preached of me is not after man.</u>

12 For I neither received it of man, neither was I Taught it, but by the Revelation of Jesus Christ.
13 For you have heard of my conversation in times past, in the Jews' religion, how that beyond measure, I persecuted the church of God and wasted it
14 And profited in the Jews' religion above many, my equals in my own nation, being more exceedingly zealous of the traditions of my fathers.
15 But, when it Pleased God, Who separated me from my mother's womb and called me by His Grace,
16 To Reveal His Son in me that I might Preach Him among the heathen. Immediately, I conferred not with flesh and blood,
17 Neither went I up to Jerusalem to them, which were apostles before me, but I went into Arabia and returned again, to Damascus.

18 Then, after three years, I went up to Jerusalem to see Peter and abode with

him fifteen days.
19 But others of the apostles, I saw none, save James, The Lord's brother.
20 Now, the things which I write to you, behold, before God, I lie not.
21 Afterwards, I came into the regions of Syria and Cilicia
22 And was unknown by face to the churches of Judaea, which were in Christ.
23 But they had heard only that he, which persecuted us in times past, now, Preaches The Faith, which he once destroyed.

Chapter 2

1 Then, fourteen years after I went up again, to Jerusalem with Barnabas and took Titus with me, also
2 And I went up by Revelation and communicated to them that Gospel, which I Preach among the gentiles, but privately to them, which were of reputation, lest by any means, I should run, or had run, in vain.
3 But, neither Titus, who was with me, being a Greek was compelled to be circumcised
4 And that because of false brothers unawares brought in, who came in privily to spy out our Liberty, which we have in Christ Jesus that they might bring us into bondage,
5 To whom, we gave place by subjection; no, not for an hour that The Truth of The Gospel might continue with you.
6 But of these, who seemed to be somewhat, (whatsoever they were, it makes no matter to me. God accepts no man's person) for they who seemed to be somewhat in conference added nothing to me.

7 But contrariwise, when they saw that The Gospel of the uncircumcision was committed to me, as The Gospel of the circumcision was to Peter
8 (For he that worked effectually in Peter, to the apostleship of the circumcision, the same was mighty in me toward the gentiles.)
9 And when James, Cephas and John, who seemed to be pillars, perceived The Grace that was given to me, they gave to me and Barnabas, the right hands of fellowship that we should go to the heathen and they to the circumcision.
10 Only, they would that, we should remember the poor, the same which I also, was forward to do.

11 But when Peter was come to Antioch, I withstood him to the face, because he was to be blamed.

12 For before that certain came from James, he did eat with the gentiles. But when they had come, he withdrew and separated himself; fearing them, which were of the circumcision.
13 And the other Jews dissembled likewise, with him insomuch that, Barnabas also, was carried away with their dissimulation.
14 But when I saw that they walked not uprightly, according to The Truth of The Gospel, I said to Peter before them all, "if you, being a Jew, live after the manner of Gentiles and not as do the Jews, why compel you the gentiles to live as do the Jews?
15 We who are Jews by nature and not sinners of the gentiles,
16 Knowing that a man is not justified by the works of the law, but by The Faith of Jesus Christ, even we have Believed in Jesus Christ that we might be Justified by The Faith of Christ and not by the works of the law, for by the works of the law, shall no flesh be justified.
17 But if while we Seek to be Justified by Christ, we ourselves also, are found sinners. Is therefore, Christ the minister of sin? God forbid.
18 For if I build again, the things which I destroyed, I make myself a transgressor.
19 For I, through The Law, am dead to the law that I might Live to God.
20 I am crucified with Christ. Nevertheless, I Live. Yet not I, but Christ Lives in me and the life, which I now, live in the flesh, I Live by The Faith of The Son of God, who Loved me and gave Himself for me.
21 I do not frustrate The Grace of God, for if Righteousness comes by the law, then Christ is dead in vain."

Chapter 3

1 O foolish Galatians, who has bewitched you that you should not obey The Truth, before whose eyes, Jesus Christ has been evidently set forth, crucified among you?
2 This only, would I learn of you. Received you, The Spirit by the works of the law, or by the Hearing of Faith?
3 Are you so foolish having begun in The Spirit, are you now, made perfect by the flesh?
4 Have you suffered so many things in

vain? If it be yet in vain.

5 He therefore that ministers to you The Spirit and Works Miracles among you, does he it, by the works of the law, or by the Hearing of Faith?

6 Even as Abraham Believed God and it was accounted to him for Righteousness,
7 Know you therefore that, they which are of Faith, the same are the children of Abraham.
8 And The Scripture, foreseeing that God would Justify the heathen through Faith, Preached before, The Gospel to Abraham saying, "IN YOU, SHALL ALL NATIONS BE BLESSED."
9 So then, they which are of Faith are Blessed with Faithful Abraham.
10 For as many as are of the works of the law, are under the curse, for it is written, "cursed is every one that continues not, in all things, which are written in the scroll off the law to do them."
11 But that no man is justified by the law, in the sight of God, it is evident for, "THE JUST SHALL LIVE BY FAITH."

12 And the law is not of Faith but, "the man that does them, shall live in them."
13 Christ has Redeemed us From the curse of the law; being made a curse for us. For it is written, "CURSED IS EVERY ONE THAT HANGS ON A TREE"
14 That the Blessing of Abraham, might come on the gentiles through Jesus Christ that we might Receive The Promise of The Spirit through Faith.
15 Brothers, I speak after the manner of men. Though it is but a man's covenant, yet if it is confirmed, no man disannuls, or adds, thereto.
16 Now, to Abraham and his seed, were The Promises made. He said not and to seeds, as of many, but as of one and to your seed, which is Christ.
17 And this I say that The Covenant that was Confirmed before of God in Christ, the law, which was four hundred and thirty years after, cannot disannul that it should make The Promise of no effect.
18 For if the inheritance is of the law, it is no more of Promise, but God Gave it to Abraham by Promise.

19 Wherefore, then serves the law? It was added, because of transgressions, until the seed should come to whom, The Promise was made and it was Ordained by angels in the hand of a Mediator.

20 Now, a mediator is not a mediator of one, but God is One.
21 Is the law then, against The Promises of God? God forbid, for if there had been a law given, which could have given Life, verily, Righteousness should have been by the law.
22 But The Scripture has concluded, all under sin that The Promise by Faith of Jesus Christ might be Given to them that Believe.
23 But before Faith came, we were kept under the law; shut up to The Faith, which should afterwards, be revealed.
24 Wherefore, the law was our schoolmaster to bring us to Christ that we might be Justified by Faith.
25 But after that, Faith is come, we are no longer under a schoolmaster.
26 For you are all the children of God by Faith in Christ Jesus.
27 For as many of you as have been Baptized into Christ, have put on Christ.
28 There is neither Jew, nor Greek. There is neither bond, nor free. There is neither male, nor female, for you are all one, in Christ Jesus.
29 And if you be Christ's, then are you Abraham's seed and Heirs, according to The Promise.

Chapter 4

1 Now I say that, "the heir, as long as he is a child, differs nothing from a servant, though he be lord of all,
2 But is under tutors and governors, until the time appointed of The Father."
3 Even so, we, when we were children, were in bondage under the elements of the World,
4 But when the fullness of the time was come, God sent forth His Son; made of a woman, made under the Law;
5 To redeem them that were under the law that we might receive the adoption of sons.
6 And because you are sons, God has sent forth The Spirit of His Son into your hearts crying, "Abba, Father!"
7 Wherefore, you are no more a servant, but a son and if a son, then a heir of God, through Christ.

8 Howbeit then, when you knew not God, you did service to them, which by nature are not gods.
9 But now, after that you have Known God, or rather are Known of God, how turn you again, to the weak and beggarly elements,

whereunto, you desire again, to be in bondage?
10 You observe days and months and times and years.
11 I am afraid of you, lest I have bestowed on you, Labor in vain.

12 Brothers, I beseech you, be as I am, for I am as you are. You have not injured me at all.
13 You know how through infirmity of the flesh, I Preached The Gospel to you at the first.
14 And my temptation, which was in my flesh, you despised not, nor rejected, but received me as an angel of God; even as Christ Jesus.
15 Where is then, the blessedness you spoke of? For I bear you record that if it had been possible, you would have plucked out your own eyes and have given them to me.
16 Am I therefore, become your enemy, because I tell you the Truth?
17 They Zealously affect you, but not well. Yes, they would exclude you that you might affect them.
18 But, it is good to be Zealously affected always in a Good thing and not only, when I am present with you.
19 My little children, of whom I travail in birth again, until Christ is formed in you,
20 I desire to be present with you now and to change my voice, for I stand in doubt of you.

21 Tell me, you that desire to be under the law, do you not hear the law?
22 For it is written that, "Abraham had two sons; the one, by a bondmaid, the other, by a Freewoman."
23 But, he who was of the bondwoman, was born after the flesh, but he of the Freewoman, was by Promise.
24 Which things are an allegory, for these are the two Covenants: the one, from the Mount Sinai, which genders to bondage, which is Hagar.
25 For this Hagar, is Mount Sinai in Arabia and answers to Jerusalem, which now is and is in bondage with her children.
26 But, Jerusalem, which is above, is Free, which is the mother of us all.
27 For it is written, "rejoice you barren that bear not. Break forth and cry, you that travail not, for the desolate has many more children than she, which has a husband."

28 Now we brothers, as Isaac was, are the children of Promise.
29 But as then, he that was born after the flesh, persecuted him that was born after The Spirit; even so, it is now.
30 Nevertheless, what says The Scripture? "CAST OUT THE BONDWOMAN AND HER SON, FOR THE SON OF THE BONDWOMAN SHALL NOT BE HEIR WITH THE SON OF THE FREEWOMAN."
31 So then brothers, we are not children of the bondwoman, but of the Free.

Chapter 5

1 Stand Fast therefore, in the Liberty wherewith, Christ has made us Free and be not entangled again, with the yoke of bondage.
2 Behold, I Paul, say to you that, "if you be circumcised, Christ shall profit you nothing."
3 For I testify again, to every man that is circumcised that he is a debtor to do the whole Law.
4 Christ is become of no effect to you, whosoever of you, are justified by the law. You are fallen from Grace.
5 For we through The Spirit, wait for the Hope of Righteousness by Faith.
6 For in Jesus Christ, neither circumcision avails any thing, nor uncircumcision, but Faith, which Works by Love.
7 You did run well. Who did hinder you that you should not obey The Truth?
8 This persuasion comes not of Him that Calls you.
9 A little leaven leavens the whole lump.
10 I have confidence in you, through The Lord that you will be none otherwise minded. But, he that troubles you, shall bear his Judgment, whosoever he is.
11 And I brothers, if I yet preach circumcision, why do I yet, suffer persecution? Then, is the offence of the cross ceased.
12 I would they were even cut off, which trouble you.

13 For brothers, you have been called to Liberty. Only use not, Liberty for an occasion to the flesh, but by Love, serve one another.
14 For all The Law is Fulfilled in one Commandment, even in this: you shall Love your neighbor as yourself.

15 But, if you bite and devour one another, take Heed that you are not consumed, one of another.
16 This I say then, "Walk in The Spirit and you shall not fulfill the lust of the flesh.
17 For the flesh lusts against The Spirit and the spirit against the flesh and these are contrary, the one to the other, so that you cannot do the things that you would.
18 But, if you be led of The Spirit, you are not under the law."

19 Now, the works of the flesh are manifest, which are these: adultery, fornication, uncleanness, lasciviousness,
20 Idolatry, witchcraft, hatred, variance, emulations, wrath, strife, seditions, heresies,
21 Envyings, murders, drunkenness, revelings… and such like, of the which, I tell you before, as I have also, told you in times past that, "they which do such things, shall not inherit the Kingdom of God."

22 But, the Fruit of The Spirit is: Love, Joy, Peace, Longsuffering, Gentleness, Goodness, Faith,
23 Meekness, Temperance. Against such, there is no Law.
24 And they that are Christ's, have crucified the flesh, with the affections and lusts.
25 If we Live in The Spirit, let us also, Walk in The Spirit.
26 Let us not be desirous of vain glory; provoking one another, envying one another.

Chapter 6

1 Brothers, if a man be overtaken in a fault, you which are Spiritual, Restore such a one in The Spirit of Meekness, considering yourself, lest you also, be tempted.
2 Bear yourselves, one another's burdens and so, Fulfill The Law of Christ.
3 For if a man thinks himself to be something, when he is nothing, he deceives himself.
4 But, let every man Prove his own Work and then, he shall have rejoicing in himself, alone and not in another..
5 For every man, shall bear his own burden.
6 Let him that is Taught in The Word, communicate to him that Teaches in all Good things.
7 Be not deceived, God is not mocked. For whatsoever, a man sows that, shall he also, reap.
8 For he that sows to his flesh, shall of the flesh, reap corruption. But, he that Sows to The Spirit, shall of The Spirit, reap Life everlasting.
9 And let us not be weary in well doing, for in due season, we shall Reap, if we faint not.
10 As we have therefore, opportunity, let us Do good to all men; especially to them, who are of the household of Faith.
11 You see how large a letter I have written to you with my own hand.
12 As many as desire to make a fair show in the flesh, they constrain you to be circumcised; only, lest they should suffer persecution for the cross of Christ.
13 For neither they themselves, who are circumcised keep the Law, but desire to have you circumcised that they may glory in your flesh.
14 But God forbid that, I should glory, save in the cross of our Lord, Jesus Christ, by Whom the World is crucified to me and I to the World.
15 For in Christ Jesus, neither circumcision avails any thing, nor uncircumcision; but a New Creature.
16 And as many as Walk according to this rule, Peace be on them and Mercy and on the Israel of God.
17 From henceforth, let no man trouble me, for I bear in my body, the marks of The Lord, Jesus.
18 Brothers, The Grace of our Lord, Jesus Christ be with your spirit. Amen.

Ephesians

Chapter 1

1 Paul, an apostle of Jesus Christ, by The Will of God, to the saints which are at Ephesus and to the Faithful in Christ Jesus,
2 Grace be to you and Peace from God, our Father and from The Lord, Jesus Christ.
3 Blessed be The God and Father of our Lord, Jesus Christ; Who has Blessed us

with all Spiritual Blessings in Heavenly places in Christ,
4 According as He has Chosen us in Himself, before the foundation of the World that we should be Holy and without blame before Him in Love,
5 Having Predestinated us to the adoption of children by Jesus Christ to Himself, according to The Good Pleasure of His Will,
6 To the Praise of The Glory of His Grace, wherein, He has made us accepted in the beloved;
7 In whom, we have Redemption through His Blood; the Forgiveness of sins, according to the riches of His Grace,
8 Wherein, He has abounded toward us, in all Wisdom and Prudence,
9 Having made known to us, The Mystery of His Will, according to His Good Pleasure, which He has Purposed in Himself
10 That in the Dispensation of The Fullness of Times, He might gather together in one, all things in Christ; both which are in Heaven and which are on Earth; even in Him,
11 In whom also, we have obtained an inheritance, being Predestinated, according to The Purpose of Him, who works all things, after The Counsel of His Own Will
12 That we should be to the praise of His Glory, who first Trusted in Christ;
13 In whom you also, Trusted after that you Heard The Word of Truth; The Gospel of your Salvation in Whom also, after that you Believed, you were Sealed with that Holy Spirit of Promise,
14 Which is the earnest of our inheritance until the Redemption of the purchased possession, to the Praise of His Glory.

15 Wherefore, I also, after I heard of your Faith in The Lord, Jesus and Love to all the saints,
17 That The God of our Lord, Jesus Christ; The Father of Glory, may Give to you, The Spirit of Wisdom and Revelation
16 Cease not to Give Thanks for you, making mention of you in my Prayers in the Knowledge of Him,
18 The Eyes of your Understanding being Enlightened that you may Know what is the Hope of His Calling and what the Riches of The Glory of His inheritance in the saints
19 And what is the exceeding Greatness of His Power to us-ward who Believe, according to The Working of His Mighty Power,
20 Which He Wrought in Christ, when He Raised Him from the dead and set Him at His Own right hand in the Heavenly places,
21 Far above all principalities and power and might and dominion and every name that is named; not only in this World, but also, in that, which is to come
22 And has put all things under His feet and gave Him to be The Head over all things, to the church,
23 Which is His body; the Fullness of Him that fills all, in all.

Chapter 2

1 And you, has He Quickened, who were Dead in trespasses and sins,
2 Wherein, in times past, you walked according to the course of this World, according to the prince of the power of the air, the spirit that now, works in the children of disobedience,
3 Among whom also, we all had our conversation in times past, in the lusts of our flesh; fulfilling the desires of the flesh and of the mind and were by nature, the children of wrath, even as others.
4 But God, Who is Rich in Mercy, for His Great Love wherewith, He Loved us,
5 Even when we were Dead in sins, has Quickened us together, with Christ (by Grace you are Saved)
6 And has Raised us Up together and made us sit together in Heavenly places in Christ Jesus
7 That in the ages to come, He might show the exceeding Riches of His Grace in His Kindness, toward us, through Christ Jesus.

8 For by Grace, are you Saved, through Faith and that not of yourselves. It is The Gift of God;
9 Not of works, lest any man should boast.
10 For we are His Workmanship; Created in Christ Jesus, to good Works, which God has before, Ordained that we should Walk in them.
11 Wherefore, remember that you being in times past, gentiles in the flesh, who are called uncircumcision by that, which is called the circumcision in the flesh made by hands
12 That at that time, you were without Christ, being aliens from the commonwealth of Israel and strangers

from The Covenants of Promise; having no hope and without God in the World.

13 But now, in Christ Jesus, you who sometimes were far off, are made near, by The Blood of Christ.
14 For He is our Peace, Who has made both, one and has broken down the middle wall of partition between us;
15 Having abolished in His flesh, the enmity, even the Law of commandments contained in ordinances, for to make in Himself of two, One New Man, so making Peace
16 And that He might Reconcile both to God, in one body by the cross; having slain the enmity, thereby
17 And came and Preached Peace to you, which were afar off and to them that were near.
18 For through Him, we both have access, by One Spirit to The Father.

19 Now therefore, you are no more strangers and foreigners, but fellow citizens with the saints and of the household of God
20 And are built on the foundation of the apostles and prophets; Jesus Christ, Himself, being, "THE CHIEF CORNER STONE."
21 In Whom, all the building, fitly framed together, grows to a Holy temple in The Lord,
22 In Whom, you also, are built together, for a habitation of God, through The Spirit.

Chapter 3

1 For this cause, I Paul, the prisoner of Jesus Christ for you gentiles,
2 If you have heard of the Dispensation of The Grace of God, which is Given me, to you-ward,
3 How that, by Revelation, He made Known to me, the Mystery, (as I wrote before in few words,
4 Whereby, when you read, you may Understand my Knowledge in the Mystery of Christ)
5 Which in other ages, was not made known to the sons of men, as it is now, Revealed to His Holy apostles and prophets, by The Spirit
6 That the gentiles should be fellow Heirs and of the same body and partakers of His Promise in Christ by The Gospel.

7 Whereof, I was made a minister, according to The Gift of The Grace of God, Given to me by the effectual Working of His Power.
8 To me, who am less than the least of all saints, is this Grace Given that I should Preach among the gentiles the unsearchable riches of Christ
9 And to make all men see, what is the Fellowship of the Mystery, which from the beginning of the World, has been hid in God, who Created All things by Jesus Christ,
10 To the intent that now, to the principalities and powers in Heavenly places, might be known by the church, the Manifold Wisdom of God,
11 According to the Eternal Purpose, which He Purposed in Christ Jesus, our Lord,
12 In Whom, we have boldness and access with confidence by The Faith of Him.

13 Wherefore, I desire that you faint not at my tribulations for you, which is your glory.
14 For this cause, I Bow my Knees to The Father of our Lord, Jesus Christ,
15 Of Whom, the whole family in Heaven and Earth is Named
16 That He would Grant you, according to the Riches of His Glory, to be Strengthened with Might by His Spirit in the inner man
17 That Christ may dwell in your hearts by Faith that you, being rooted and grounded in Love,
18 May be able to comprehend with all saints, what is the breadth and length and depth and height
19 And to Know The Love of Christ, which passes Knowledge that you might be Filled with all The Fullness of God.
20 Now, to Him that is able to do exceeding abundantly, above all that we ask, or think, according to The Power that Works in us,
21 To Him, be Glory in the church by Christ Jesus, throughout all ages, World without end. Amen.

Chapter 4

1 I therefore, the prisoner of The Lord, beseech you that you Walk worthy of the vocation, wherewith you are Called,
2 With all Lowliness and Meekness, with Longsuffering, Forbearing one another in Love;
3 Endeavoring to Keep the Unity of The

Spirit in the bond of Peace.
4 There is one body and one Spirit, even as you are Called in one Hope of your Calling:
5 One Lord, one Faith, one Baptism,
6 One God and Father of all; Who is Above all and through all and in you all.
7 But to every one of us, is Given Grace, according to the measure of The Gift of Christ.

8 Wherefore, He said, "when He ascended up on High, He led captivity, captive and Gave Gifts to men."
9 Now that He ascended, what is it, but that He also, descended first, into the lower parts of the Earth?
10 He that descended is the same, also that ascended up far above all heavens that He might Fill all things.

11 And He gave some: apostles and some, prophets and some, evangelists and some, pastors and teachers
12 For the Perfecting of the saints, for the Work of the Ministry, for the Edifying of the body of Christ,
13 Until we all come in the Unity of The Faith and of the Knowledge of The Son of God; to a Perfect Man, to the measure of the stature of the Fullness of Christ
14 That we henceforth, be no more children, tossed to and from and carried about with every wind of doctrine, by the sleight of men and cunning craftiness, whereby, they lie in wait to deceive,
15 But speaking The Truth in Love, may grow up into Him in all things, which is The Head; even Christ,
16 From Whom, the whole body, fitly joined together and compacted by that, which every joint supplies, according to the effectual working in the measure of every part, makes increase of the body to the edifying of itself in Love.

17 This I say, therefore and Testify in The Lord that you henceforth, walk not as other gentiles walk, in the vanity of their mind;
18 Having the understanding Darkened, being alienated from the Life of God, through the ignorance that is in them, because of the blindness of their heart,
19 Who being, past feeling, have given themselves over to lasciviousness; to work all uncleanness with greediness.
20 But, you have not so learned Christ,
21 If so, be that, you have Heard Him and have been Taught by Him, as The Truth is in Jesus
22 That you put off, concerning the former conversations, the old man, which is corrupt, according to the deceitful lusts
23 And be renewed in The Spirit of your mind
24 And that you put on the New Man, which after God is Created in Righteousness and True Holiness.
25 Wherefore, putting away lying, speak every man, Truth with his neighbor, for we are members one of another.

26 Be you, angry and sin not. Let not, the Sun go down on your wrath,
27 Neither give place to the Devil.
28 Let him that stole, steal no more. But rather, let him labor, working with his hands the thing, which is good that he may have to give to him that needs.
29 Let no corrupt communication proceed out of your mouth, but that, which is good to the use of Edifying that it may minister Grace to the Hearers.
30 And grieve not, The Holy Spirit of God; whereby, you are Sealed to the Day of Redemption.
31 Let all: bitterness and wrath and anger and clamor and evil speaking, be put away from you; with all malice.
32 And be you Kind one to another; Tenderhearted, Forgiving one another; even as God, for Christ's sake, has Forgiven you.

Chapter 5

1 Be you therefore, Followers of God, as dear children.
2 And Walk in Love, as Christ also, has Loved us and has Given Himself for us, an Offering and a Sacrifice to God, for a Sweet Smelling Savor.
3 But fornication and all uncleanness, or covetousness, let it not be once, named among you, as becomes saints;
4 Neither filthiness, nor foolish talking, nor jesting; which are not convenient, but rather, Giving of Thanks.
5 For this you know that: no whoremonger, nor unclean person, nor covetous man, who is an idolater, has any inheritance in the Kingdom of Christ and of God.

6 Let no man deceive you with vain words, for because of these things, comes the wrath of God on the children of disobedience.
7 Be not you therefore, partakers with

them.
8 For you were sometimes Darkness, but now, you are Light in The Lord. Walk as children of Light.
9 For the Fruit of The Spirit is in all: Goodness and Righteousness and Truth,
10 Proving what is acceptable to The Lord.
11 And have no fellowship with the unfruitful works of Darkness, but rather reprove them.
12 For it is a shame even to speak of those things, which are done of them in secret.
13 But, all things that are reproved are made manifest by the Light. For whatsoever, does make manifest is Light.

14 Wherefore, He says, "awake you that sleep and Arise from the Dead and Christ shall Give you Light."
15 See then that you Walk Circumspectly, not as fools, but as Wise,
16 Redeeming the time, because the days are evil.
17 Wherefore, be you not unwise, but Understanding what The Will of The Lord is.
18 And be not drunk with wine, wherein is excess, but be Filled with The Spirit;
19 Speaking to yourselves in Psalms and Hymns and Spiritual Songs; Singing and Making Melody in your heart to The Lord;
20 Giving Thanks always, for all things to God and The Father in The Name of our Lord, Jesus Christ;
21 Submitting yourselves, one to another, in The Fear of God.

22 Wives, submit yourselves to your own husbands, as to The Lord.
23 For the husband is the head of the wife, even as Christ is The Head of the church and He is The Savior of the body.
24 Therefore, as the church is subject to Christ, so let the wives be to their own husbands in every thing.
25 Husbands, Love your wives, even as Christ also, Loved the church and Gave Himself for it
26 That He might Sanctify and Cleanse it with the washing of water by The Word
27 That He might present it to Himself, a glorious church; not having spot, or wrinkle, or any such thing, but that it should be Holy and without blemish.
28 So ought men to Love their wives as their own bodies. He that Loves his wife, loves himself.
29 For no man ever, yet hated his own flesh, but nourishes and cherishes it; even as The Lord, the church.
30 For we are members of His body, of His flesh and of His bones.
31 For this cause, "shall a man leave his father and mother and shall be joined to his wife and they two, shall be one flesh."
32 This is a great mystery, but I speak concerning Christ and the church.
33 Nevertheless, let every one of you in particular, so Love his wife, even as himself and the wife see that she Reverences her husband.

Chapter 6

1 Children, obey your parents in The Lord for this is right.
2 Honor your father and mother, which is The First Commandment with Promise,
3 That it may be well with you and you may live long on the Earth.

4 And you fathers, provoke not your children to wrath, but bring them up in the Nurture and Admonition of The Lord.
5 Servants, be obedient to them that are your masters, according to the flesh, with fear and trembling, in singleness of your heart, as to Christ;
6 Not with eye service as men pleasers, but as the servants of Christ; Doing The Will of God, from the heart,
7 With good will, Doing service as to The Lord and not to men,
8 Knowing that whatsoever, good thing any man does, the same, shall he receive of The Lord; whether he be bond, or free.
9 And you masters, do the same things to them; forbearing, threatening, knowing that your Master also, is in Heaven, neither is there respect of persons with Him.

10 Finally, my brothers, be Strong in The Lord and in The Power of His Might.
11 Put on the Whole Armor of God that you may be able to Stand Against the wiles of the Devil.
12 For we wrestle not against flesh and blood, but: against: principalities, against powers, against the rulers of the Darkness of this World; against spiritual wickedness in high places.
13 Wherefore, take to yourselves, the Whole Armor of God that you may be able to Withstand in the evil day and having Done All, to Stand.
14 Stand therefore: having your loins girt

about with Truth and having on the Breastplate of Righteousness
15 And your feet Shod with the Preparation of The Gospel of Peace;
16 Above all, taking the Shield of Faith, wherewith you shall be able to Quench All, the fiery darts of the wicked.
17 And take the Helmet of Salvation and the Sword of The Spirit, which is The Word of God,
18 Praying always, with all Prayer and Supplication in The Spirit and watching thereunto, with all Perseverance and Supplication for all saints.

19 And for me that utterance may be given to me that I may open my mouth Boldly, to make Known the Mystery of The Gospel,
20 For which, I am an ambassador in bonds that therein, I may speak Boldly, as I ought to speak,
21 But that you also, may know my affairs and how I do. Tychicus, a beloved brother and faithful minister in The Lord, shall make known to you all things,
22 Whom I have sent to you for the same purpose that you might know our affairs and that he might comfort your hearts.
23 Peace be to the brothers and Love with Faith, from God, The Father and The Lord, Jesus Christ.
24 Grace be with all them that Love our Lord, Jesus Christ in Sincerity. Amen.

Philippians

Chapter 1

1 Paul and Timotheus, the servants of Jesus Christ, to all the saints in Christ Jesus, which are at Philippi; with the bishops and deacons.
2 Grace be to you and Peace from God, our Father and from The Lord, Jesus Christ.
3 I Thank my God on every remembrance of you
4 Always in every Prayer of mine for you all, making requests with Joy,
5 For your fellowship in The Gospel, from the first day, until now.

6 Being confident of this very thing that He, which has begun a Good Work in you, will Perform it until the day of Jesus Christ,
7 Even as it is meet for me to think this of you all, because I have you in my heart in as much as both in my bonds and in the defense and confirmation of The Gospel, you all are partakers of my grace.
8 For God is my record, how greatly, I long after you all in the bowels of Jesus Christ.

9 And this I Pray that, your Love may abound, yet more and more in Knowledge and in all Judgment
10 That you may approve things that are excellent that you may be sincere and without offence until the day of Christ;
11 Being filled with the Fruits of Righteousness, which are by Jesus Christ, to The Glory and Praise of God.
12 But, I would you should understand brothers that the things, which happened to me have fallen out rather to the furtherance of The Gospel
13 So that, my bonds in Christ are manifest in all the palace and in all other places
14 And many of the brothers in The Lord, waxing confident by my bonds, are much more Bold to speak The Word without fear.

15 Some indeed Preach Christ, even of envy and strife and some also, of good will.
16 The one, Preaches Christ of contention, not sincerely; supposing to add affliction to my bonds.
17 But the other of Love, knowing that I am set for the defense of The Gospel.
18 What then? Notwithstanding, every way, whether in pretence, or in Truth, Christ is Preached and I therein, do rejoice; yes and will rejoice.
19 For I know that this shall turn to my Salvation through your Prayer and the supply of The Spirit of Jesus Christ,
20 According to my earnest expectation and my hope that in nothing, I shall be ashamed, but that with all Boldness, as always, so now also, Christ shall be Magnified in my body, whether it be by life, or by death.

21 For to me, to live is Christ and to die is gain.
22 But, if I Live in the flesh, this is the fruit of my labor. Yet, what I shall choose, I know not.
23 For I am in a strait between two; having a desire to depart and to be with Christ,

which is far better.
24 Nevertheless, to abide in the flesh, is more needful for you.
25 And having this confidence, I know that I shall abide and continue with you all, for your furtherance and Joy of Faith
26 That your rejoicing may be more abundant in Jesus Christ for me by my coming to you again.

27 Only, let your conversation be as it becomes The Gospel of Christ that whether I come and see you, or else be absent, I may hear of your affairs that you Stand Fast in one spirit, with one mind, striving together, for The Faith of The Gospel
28 <u>And in nothing terrified by your adversaries, which is to them an evident Token of perdition, but to you of Salvation and that of God.</u>
29 For to you, it is given in the behalf of Christ, not only to Believe on Him, but also, to suffer for His sake,
30 Having the same conflict, which you saw in me and now, hear to be in me.

Chapter 2
1 If there be therefore, any Consolation in Christ, if any Comfort of Love, if any Fellowship of The Spirit, if any bowels and Mercies,
2 Fulfill you my joy that you be likeminded: having the same Love, being of one accord, of one mind.
3 Let nothing be done through strife, or vainglory, but in Lowliness of mind. <u>Let each esteem others, better than themselves.</u>
4 Look not every man on his own things, but every man also, on the things of others.

5 Let this mind be in you, which was also, in Christ Jesus,
6 Who, being in the Form of God, thought it not robbery to be Equal with God,
7 But made Himself of no reputation and took on Himself, the form of a servant and was made in the likeness of men
8 And being found in fashion as a man, He Humbled Himself and became Obedient unto death; even the death of the cross.
9 Wherefore, God also, has highly Exalted Him and given Him a Name, which is Above every name
10 <u>That at The Name of Jesus, every knee should Bow</u>; of things in Heaven and things on Earth and things under the earth
11 <u>And that every tongue should Confess that, Jesus Christ is Lord; to The Glory of God, The Father.</u>

12 Wherefore, my beloved, as you have always Obeyed, not as in my presence only, but now, much more in my absence, <u>Work out your own Salvation with Fear and Trembling.</u>
13 For it is God, which Works in you; both to Will and to do of His Good Pleasure.
14 <u>Do all things without murmurings and disputings</u>
15 <u>That you may be blameless and harmless, the sons of God, without rebuke,</u> in the midst of a crooked and perverse nation, among whom, you Shine as Lights in the World
16 Holding forth, The Word of Life that I may rejoice in the day of Christ that I have not Run in vain, neither Labored in vain.
17 Yes and if I am offered on the sacrifice and service of your Faith, I joy and rejoice with you all.
18 For the same cause also, do you joy and rejoice with me.
19 But I trust in The Lord, Jesus to send Timotheus shortly, to you that I also, may be of good comfort, when I know your state.
20 For I have no man likeminded, who will naturally care for your state.
21 For all seek their own, not the things which are Jesus Christ's.
22 But, you know the proof of him that as a son with the father, he has served with me in The Gospel.
23 Him therefore, I hope to send presently, so soon as I shall see how it will go with me.
24 But I trust in The Lord that I also, myself shall come shortly.
25 Yet I supposed it necessary to send to you Epaphroditus, my brother and companion in labor and fellowsoldier, but your messenger and he that ministered to my wants.
26 For he longed after you all and was full of heaviness, because that, you had heard that he had been sick.
27 For indeed, he was sick near to death, but God had Mercy on him and not on him only, but on me also, lest I should have sorrow on sorrow.
28 I sent him therefore, the more carefully that when you see him again, you may rejoice and that I may be the less

sorrowful.
29 Receive him therefore, in The Lord with all gladness and hold such in reputation
30 Because, for the Work of Christ, he was near to death, not regarding his life, to supply your lack of service toward me.

Chapter 3

1 Finally my brothers, Rejoice in The Lord. To write the same things to you, to me indeed, is not grievous, but for you it is safe.
2 Beware of dogs: Beware of evil workers; beware of the concision.
3 For we are the circumcision, which Worship God in The Spirit and Rejoice in Christ Jesus and have no confidence in the flesh;
4 Though I might also, have confidence in the flesh. If any other man, thinks that he has whereof, he might trust in the flesh, I more;
5 Circumcised the eighth day; of the stock of Israel, of the tribe of Benjamin, a Hebrew of the Hebrews as touching the Law, a Pharisee;
6 Concerning Zeal, persecuting the church, touching the Righteousness, which is in the Law, blameless.
7 But, what things were gain to me, those, I counted loss for Christ.

8 Yes, doubtless and I count all things, but loss, for the excellency of the Knowledge of Christ Jesus, my Lord for Whom, I have suffered the loss of all things and do count them, but dung that I may win Christ
9 And be found in Him, not having my own righteousness, which is of the Law, but that, which is through The Faith of Christ, The Righteousness, which is of God by Faith
10 That I may Know Him and The Power of His Resurrection and the Fellowship of His sufferings; being made conformable to His death,
11 If by any means, I might attain to the Resurrection of the dead.
12 Not as though I had already attained, either were already perfect, but I follow after, if that I may apprehend that, for which also, I am apprehended of Christ Jesus.

13 Brothers, I count not myself to have apprehended, but this one thing I do: forgetting those things, which are behind and reaching forth to those things, which are before.

14 <u>I press toward the mark for the Prize of the High Calling of God in Christ Jesus.</u>
15 Let us therefore, as many as be perfect, be thus minded and if in any thing, you are otherwise minded, God shall reveal even this to you.
16 Nevertheless, whereto we have already attained, let us Walk by the same rule. Let us mind the same thing.

17 Brothers, be Followers together, of me and mark them, which Walk so (as you have us for an example):
18 <u>For many walk, of whom, I have told you often and now, tell you even weeping that, "they are the enemies of the cross of Christ;</u>
19 <u>Whose end is destruction, whose God is their belly and whose glory is in their shame, who mind earthly things."</u>
20 <u>For our conversation is in Heaven from where also, we look for The Savior, The Lord, Jesus Christ;</u>
21 Who shall change our vile body that it may be fashioned like to His Glorious body, according to the working whereby, He is able even to subdue all things to Himself.

Chapter 4

1 Therefore my brothers, dearly beloved and longed for, my joy and crown, so **Stand Fast in The Lord**, my dearly beloved.
2 I beseech Euodias and beseech Syntyche that they be of the same mind in The Lord.
3 And I entreat you also, true yokefellows, help those women, which Labored with me in The Gospel, with Clement also and with others, my fellow Laborers, <u>whose names are in The Scroll of Life</u>.
4 <u>Rejoice in The Lord always and again, I say, "Rejoice."</u>
5 Let your moderation be known to all men. The Lord is at hand.

6 Be careful for nothing, but in every thing, <u>by Prayer and Supplication with Thanksgiving, let your Requests be made known to God.</u>
7 <u>And the Peace of God, which passes all understanding, shall Keep your hearts and minds through Christ Jesus.</u>
8 <u>Finally brothers, whatsoever things are: True,</u> whatsoever things are <u>Honest,</u> whatsoever things are <u>Just,</u> whatsoever things are <u>Pure,</u> whatsoever things are <u>Lovely,</u> whatsoever things are of <u>Good</u>

Report, if there is any Virtue and if there is any Praise, think on these things.

9 Those things, which you have both Learned and Received and Heard and Seen in me, Do and The God of Peace shall be with you.
10 But, I Rejoiced in The Lord greatly that now, at the last, your care of me has flourished again, wherein you were also, careful, but you lacked opportunity.
11 Not that I speak in respect of want, for I have learned, in whatsoever state I am, therewith, to be Content.
12 I know both how to be abased and I know how to abound every where. And in all things, I am instructed both to be full and to be hungry, both to abound and to suffer need.
13 I can do all things through Christ, which strengthens me.

14 Notwithstanding, you have well done that you did communicate with my affliction.
15 Now you Philippians, know also that in the beginning of The Gospel, when I departed from Macedonia, no church communicated with me as concerning Giving and receiving, but you only.
16 For even in Thessalonica, you sent once and again, to my necessity.
17 Not because I desire a gift, but I desire fruit that may abound to your account.
18 But I have all and abound. I am full, having received of Epaphroditus, the things which were sent from you, an odor of a sweet smell; a sacrifice acceptable, wellpleasing to God.
19 But my God shall supply all your needs, according to His Riches in Glory by Christ Jesus.
20 Now, to God and our Father, be Glory, for ever and ever. Amen.
21 Salute every saint in Christ Jesus. The brothers which are with me greet you.
22 All the saints salute you, chiefly they that are of Caesar's household.
23 The Grace of our Lord, Jesus Christ be with you all. Amen.

Colossians

Chapter 1

1 Paul, an apostle of Jesus Christ, by The Will of God and Timotheus, our brother,
2 To the saints and Faithful brothers in Christ, which are at Colosse, Grace be to you and Peace, from God, our Father and The Lord, Jesus Christ.
3 We Give Thanks to God and The Father of our Lord, Jesus Christ, Praying always for you,
4 Since we heard of your Faith in Christ Jesus and of the Love, which you have to all the saints,
5 For the Hope, which is laid up for you in Heaven, whereof you Heard before in The Word of The Truth of The Gospel,
6 Which is come to you, as it is in all the World and brings forth Fruit, as it does also, in you since the day you heard of it and Knew The Grace of God in Truth,
7 As you also, learned of Epaphras, our dear fellow servant, who is for you, a Faithful minister of Christ,
8 Who also, declared to us your Love in The Spirit.

9 For this cause, we also, since the day we heard it, do not cease to Pray for you and to desire that you might be Filled with the Knowledge of His Will in all Wisdom and Spiritual Understanding
10 That you might Walk worthy of The Lord to all pleasing, being Fruitful in every good Work and Increasing in The Knowledge of God;
11 Strengthened with all Might, according to His Glorious Power, to all Patience and Longsuffering with Joyfulness;
12 Giving Thanks to The Father, which has made us qualified to be partakers of the inheritance of the saints in Light;
13 Who has Delivered us from the power of Darkness and has Translated us into the Kingdom of His Dear Son;
14 In Whom, we have Redemption through His Blood, even the Forgiveness of sins;
15 Who is the Image of The invisible God; the firstborn of every creature.
16 For by Him, were all things Created that are in Heaven and that are in Earth; visible and invisible, whether they be thrones, or dominions, or principalities, or powers. All things were Created by Him and for Him.
17 And He is before all things and by Him, all things consist.
18 And He is The Head of the body, (the church) who is the beginning, the firstborn

from the dead that in all things He might have the Preeminence.
19 <u>For it Pleased The Father that in Him, should all Fullness dwell</u>
20 <u>And having made Peace through The Blood of His cross, by Him, to Reconcile all things to Himself, by Him, I say, whether they are things in Earth, or things in Heaven.</u>

21 <u>And you that were sometimes alienated and enemies in your mind, by wicked works, yet now, has He Reconciled</u>
22 <u>In the body of His flesh through death, to present you Holy and unblameable and unreproveable in His Sight,</u>
23 <u>If you Continue in The Faith; grounded and settled and be not moved away from the Hope of The Gospel,</u> which you have Heard and which was Preached to every creature, which is under Heaven; whereof I, Paul am made a minister,
24 Who now, rejoice in my sufferings, for you and fill up that, which is behind of the afflictions of Christ in my flesh, for His body's sake, which is the church;
25 Whereof, I am made a minister, according to the Dispensation of God, which is Given to me for you, to fulfill The Word of God;
26 Even the Mystery, which has been hidden from ages and from generations, but now, is made Manifest to His saints;
27 To whom, God would make Known, what is the Riches of The Glory of this Mystery among the gentiles, which is Christ in you, the Hope of Glory;
28 <u>Whom we Preach, Warning every man and Teaching every man in all Wisdom that we may present every man perfect in Christ Jesus;</u>
29 Whereunto, I also, Labor; Striving according to His Working, which Works in me mightily.

Chapter 2

1 For I would that you knew what great conflict I have for you and for them at Laodicea and for as many as have not seen my face in the flesh
2 That their hearts might be comforted, being knit together in Love and to all riches of the full assurance of Understanding, to the acknowledgement of The Mystery of God and of The Father and of Christ;
3 In Whom, are hid all the Treasures of Wisdom and Knowledge.

4 And this I say, <u>lest any man should beguile you with enticing words,</u>
5 For though I be absent in the flesh, yet am I with you in The Spirit, joying and beholding your order and <u>the Steadfastness of your Faith in Christ.</u>
6 As you have therefore, Received Christ Jesus, The Lord, so Walk you in Him;
7 Rooted and built up in Him and Established in The Faith, as you have been Taught; abounding therein, with Thanksgiving.

8 <u>Beware, lest any man spoil you through philosophy and vain deceit; after the tradition of men, after the rudiments of the World and not after Christ.</u>
9 <u>For in Him, dwells All The Fullness of The Godhead, bodily.</u>
10 And you are complete in Him, which is The Head of all Principality and Power,
11 <u>In Whom also, you are Circumcised with the Circumcision made without hands, in putting off the body of the sins of the flesh, by the Circumcision of Christ;</u>
12 <u>Buried with Him in Baptism, wherein also, you are Risen with Him, through The Faith of the operation of God, who has Raised Him from the dead.</u>
13 <u>And you, being dead in your sins and the uncircumcision of your flesh, He has Quickened together with Himself, having Forgiven you, all trespasses;</u>
14 <u>Blotting out the handwriting of ordinances that was against us, which was contrary to us and took it out of the way; nailing it to His cross</u>
15 <u>And having spoiled principalities and powers, He made a show of them openly, triumphing over them in it.</u>
16 Let no man therefore, judge you in meat, or in drink, or in respect of a Holyday, or of the new Moon, or of the Sabbath Days,
17 Which are a shadow of things to come, but the body is of Christ.

18 <u>Let no man beguile you of your Reward in a voluntary humility and worshiping of angels</u>; intruding into those things, which he has not seen, <u>vainly puffed up by his fleshly mind,</u>
19 And not holding the head, from which all the body by joints and bands having nourishment ministered and knit together, increases with the increase of God.
20 Wherefore, if you are dead with Christ, from the rudiments of the World, why, as though Living in the World, are you subject to ordinances,

21 (Touch not. Taste not. Handle not.
22 Which all are to perish with the using) after the commandments and doctrines of men?
23 Which things have indeed a show of Wisdom in will, worship and humility and neglecting of the body, not in any honor, to the satisfying of the flesh.

Chapter 3

1 If you then, are Risen with Christ, Seek those things which are Above, where Christ sits on the right hand of God.
2 Set your affection on things Above, not on things on the Earth.
3 For you are dead and your life is hid with Christ in God.
4 When Christ, who is our Life, shall appear, then shall you also, appear with Him in Glory.
5 Mortify therefore, your members which are on the Earth: fornication, uncleanness, inordinate affection, evil concupiscence and covetousness, which is idolatry,
6 For which things' sake the wrath of God comes on the children of disobedience;
7 In the which you also, walked some times, when you lived in them.
8 But now, you also, put off all these: anger, wrath, malice, blasphemy, filthy communication out of your mouth.
9 Lie not one to another, seeing that you have put off the old man with his deeds
10 And have put on the New Man, which is Renewed in Knowledge, after the Image of Him that Created him,
11 Where there is neither: Greek, nor Jew; circumcision, nor uncircumcision, barbarian, Scythian; bond, nor free. But, Christ is all and in all.
12 Put on therefore, as the elect of God, Holy and beloved, bowels of: Mercies, Kindness, Humbleness of Mind, Meekness, Longsuffering;
13 Forbearing one another and Forgiving one another. If any man has a quarrel against any, even as Christ Forgave you, so also, Do you.
14 And above all these things, put on Charity, which is the bond of Perfectness.
15 And let the Peace of God rule in your hearts, to the which also, you are called in one body and be yourselves, Thankful.
16 Let The Word of Christ dwell in you richly in all Wisdom; Teaching and Admonishing one another in Psalms and Hymns and Spiritual songs, Singing with Grace in your hearts to The Lord.
17 And whatsoever you Do in Word, or Deed, Do all in The Name of The Lord Jesus, Giving Thanks to God and The Father by Him.
18 Wives, submit yourselves to your own husbands, as it is fit in The Lord.
19 Husbands, Love your wives and be not bitter against them.
20 Children, obey your parents in all things, for this is well Pleasing to The Lord.
21 Fathers, provoke not your children to anger, lest they be discouraged.
22 Servants, obey in all things, your masters, according to the flesh, not with eyeservice, as men pleasers, but in singleness of heart, Fearing God.
23 And whatsoever you do, do it heartily, as to The Lord and not to men,
24 Knowing that of The Lord, you shall receive the reward of the inheritance, for you serve The Lord, Christ.
25 But, he that does wrong shall receive for the wrong, which he has done and there is no respect of persons.

Chapter 4

1 Masters, give to your servants that, which is Just and Equal, knowing that you also, have a Master in Heaven.
2 Continue in Prayer and watch in the same with Thanksgiving,
3 Withal Praying also, for us that God would open to us a door of utterance, to speak the Mystery of Christ, for which I am also, in bonds
4 That I may make it manifest, as I ought to speak.
5 Walk in Wisdom, toward them that are without, redeeming the time.
6 Let your speech be always with Grace; seasoned with salt that you may know how you ought to answer every man.
7 All my state shall Tychicus declare to you, who is a beloved brother and a faithful minister and fellow servant in The Lord,
8 Whom I have sent to you for the same purpose that he might know your estate and comfort your hearts
9 With Onesimus, a Faithful and beloved brother, who is one of you. They shall make known to you all things, which are done here.
10 Aristarchus, my fellowprisoner salutes you and Marcus', sister's son to Barnabas, touching whom, you received

commandments if he comes to you, receive him

11 And Jesus, which is called Justus, who are of the circumcision. These only, are my fellow workers to the Kingdom of God, which have been a Comfort to me.

12 Epaphras, who is one of you; a servant of Christ, salutes you, always Laboring Fervently for you in Prayers that you may stand perfect and complete in all The Will of God.

13 For I bear him record that he has a great zeal for you and them that are in Laodicea and them, in Hierapolis.

14 Luke, the beloved physician and Demas, greet you.

15 Salute the brothers, which are in Laodicea and Nymphas and the church, which is in his house.

16 And when this epistle is read among you, cause that it be read also, in the church of the Laodiceans and that you likewise, read the epistle from Laodicea.

17 And say to Archippus, "take heed to the ministry which you have received in The Lord that you fulfill it."

18 The salutation by the hand of me, Paul, remember my bonds. Grace be with you. Amen.

1ˢᵗ Thessalonians

Chapter 1

1 Paul and Silvanus and Timotheus, to the church of the Thessalonians, which is in God, The Father and in The Lord, Jesus Christ, Grace be to you and Peace, from God, our Father and The Lord, Jesus Christ.

2 We Give Thanks to God always for you all, making mention of you in our Prayers,

3 Remembering without ceasing your Work of Faith and Labor of Love and Patience of Hope in our Lord, Jesus Christ, in the sight of God and our Father,

4 Knowing beloved brothers, your election of God.

5 For our Gospel came not to you in word only, but also, in Power and in The Holy Ghost and in much assurance, as you know what manner of men we were among you for your sakes.

6 And you became followers of us and of The Lord, having Received The Word in much affliction, with Joy of The Holy Ghost,

7 So that you were examples to all that Believe in Macedonia and Achaia.

8 For from you, sounded out The Word of The Lord not only in Macedonia and Achaia, but also, in every place, your Faith to God-ward is spread abroad, so that we need not to speak any thing.

9 For they themselves, show of us what manner of entering in we had to you and how <u>you Turned To God from idols to Serve the Living and True God</u>

10 <u>And to wait for His Son from Heaven, whom He Raised from the dead; even Jesus, which Delivered us from the wrath to come.</u>

Chapter 2

1 For yourselves brothers, know our entrance in to you that it was not in vain,

2 But even after that, we had suffered before and were shamefully entreated, as you know at Philippi, we were bold in our God to speak to you, The Gospel of God with much contention.

3 For our Exhortation was not of deceit, nor of uncleanness, nor in guile,

4 But as we were allowed of God to be put in trust with The Gospel, even so, <u>we speak not as pleasing men, but God, which Tries our hearts.</u>

5 <u>For neither at any time, we used flattering words, as you know, nor a cloke of covetousness; God is witness,</u>

6 <u>Nor of men, sought we glory, neither of you, nor yet of others, when we might have been burdensome, as the apostles of Christ.</u>

7 But, we were gentle among you, even as a nurse cherishes her children.

8 So, being affectionately desirous of you, we were willing to have imparted to you, not The Gospel of God only, but also, our own souls, because you were dear to us.

9 For you remember brothers, our Labor and Travail, for Laboring night and day, because we would not be chargeable to any of you, we Preached to you The Gospel of God.

10 You are witnesses and God also, how Holily and Justly and Unblameably we behaved ourselves among you that Believe.

11 As you know how we exhorted and comforted and charged every one of you, as a father does his children
12 That you would Walk worthy of God, who has called you to His Kingdom and Glory.

13 For this cause also, we Thank God without ceasing because, when you Received The Word of God, which you Heard of us, you received it not, as the word of men, but as it is in Truth, The Word of God, which effectually works also, in you that Believe.
14 For you brothers, became followers of the churches of God, which in Judaea are in Christ Jesus, for you also, have suffered like things of your own countrymen; even as they have of the Jews,
15 Who both killed The Lord, Jesus and their own prophets and have persecuted us and they Please not God and are contrary to all men,
16 Forbidding us to speak to the gentiles that they might be Saved, to fill up their sins always, for the wrath is come on them to the uttermost.

17 But we brothers, being taken from you for a short time in presence, not in heart, endeavored the more abundantly to see your face with great desire.
18 Wherefore, we would have come to you, even I Paul, once and again, but Satan hindered us.
19 For what is our hope, or joy, or crown of rejoicing? Are not even you, in the Presence of our Lord, Jesus Christ at His coming?
20 For you are our glory and joy.

Chapter 3
1 Wherefore, when we could no longer forbear, we thought it good to be left at Athens alone
2 And sent Timotheus, our brother and minister of God and our fellow laborer in The Gospel of Christ, to Establish you and to Comfort you concerning your Faith
3 That no man should be moved by these afflictions, for yourselves know that we are appointed, thereunto.
4 For verily, when we were with you, we told you before that we should suffer tribulation, even as it came to pass and you know.
5 For this cause, when I could no longer forbear, I sent to know your Faith, lest by some means the Tempter has tempted you and our labor is in vain.
6 But now, when Timotheus came from you to us and brought us good tidings of your Faith and Charity and that you have good remembrance of us always, desiring greatly to see us, as we also, to see you.
7 Therefore brothers, we were comforted over you in all our affliction and distress by your Faith
8 For now, we Live, if you Stand Fast in The Lord.
9 For what Thanks can we render to God again, for you, for all the joy wherewith, we joy, for your sakes before our God
10 Night and day Praying exceedingly that, we might see your face and might perfect that, which is lacking in your Faith?
11 Now, God Himself and our Father and our Lord Jesus Christ, direct our way to you.
12 And The Lord make you to increase and abound in Love, one toward another and toward all men, even as we do toward you,
13 To the end, He may Establish your hearts Unblameable in Holiness before God; even our Father, at the Coming of our Lord Jesus Christ with all His saints.

Chapter 4
1 Furthermore then, we beseech you, brothers and exhort you, by The Lord, Jesus that as you have received of us, how you ought to Walk and to Please God, so you would abound more and more.
2 For you know what commandments we gave you by The Lord, Jesus.
3 For this is The Will of God, even your Sanctification that you should abstain from fornication
4 That every one of you, should know how to possess his vessel in Sanctification and Honor,
5 Not in the lust of concupiscence; even as the gentiles, which know not, God;
6 That no man, go beyond and defraud his brother in any matter, because that, The Lord is The Avenger of all such, as we also, have Forewarned you and Testified.
7 For God has not called us to uncleanness, but to Holiness.

8 He therefore that despises, despises not man, but God, who has also, Given to us His Holy Spirit.
9 But as touching brotherly Love, you need not that I write to you, for you yourselves, are Taught of God to Love one another.

10 And indeed, you do it toward all the brothers, which are in all Macedonia. But, we beseech you brothers that, you increase more and more
11 And that you study to be quiet and to do your own business and to work with your own hands, as we commanded you
12 That you may Walk Honestly toward them that are without and that you may have lack of nothing.

13 But, I would not have you to be ignorant brothers, concerning them which are asleep that you sorrow not, even as others, which have no hope.
14 For if we Believe that Jesus died and Rose Again, even so them also, which sleep in Jesus, will God bring with Himself.
15 For this we say to you by The Word of The Lord that we which are alive and remain to the Coming of The Lord, shall not precede them, which are asleep.
16 For The Lord, Himself, shall descend from Heaven with a shout, with the voice of the archangel and with the trump of God and the dead in Christ, shall Rise, first.
17 Then, we which are alive and remain, shall be caught up together, with them in The Clouds, to meet The Lord in the air and so, shall we ever be with The Lord.
18 Wherefore, Comfort one another with these words.

Chapter 5

1 But, of the times and the seasons brothers, you have no need that I write to you.
2 For yourselves Know perfectly that The Day of The Lord, so comes as a thief in the night.
3 For when they shall say, "peace and safety," then sudden destruction comes on them, as travail on a woman with child and they shall not escape.
4 But you brothers, are not in Darkness that, that day should overtake you as a thief.
5 You are all the children of Light and the children of the day. We are not of the night, nor of Darkness.

6 Therefore, let us not sleep, as do others, but let us watch and be sober.
7 For they that sleep, sleep in the night and they that are drunken, are drunken in the night.
8 But, let us who are of the day, be sober; putting on the Breastplate of Faith and Love and for a Helmet, the Hope of Salvation.
9 For God has not appointed us to wrath, but to obtain Salvation by our Lord, Jesus Christ;
10 Who died for us that whether we wake, or sleep, we should Live together with Him.
11 Wherefore, Comfort yourselves, together and Edify one another; even as also, you do.
12 And we beseech you brothers, to know them, which Labor among you and are over you in The Lord and admonish you
13 And to esteem them very highly in Love for their work's sake. And be at Peace among yourselves.

14 Now, we exhort you brothers, Warn them that are unruly, Comfort the feebleminded, Support the weak, be Patient toward all men.
15 See that none, renders evil for evil, to any man, but ever follow that, which is Good; both among yourselves and to all men.
16 Rejoice evermore.
17 Pray Without Ceasing.
18 In every thing Give Thanks, for this is The Will of God in Christ Jesus, concerning you.
19 Quench not, The Spirit.
20 Despise not, Prophesyings.
21 Prove all things. Hold Fast that, which is Good.
22 Abstain from all appearances of evil.
23 And the very God of Peace, Sanctify you Wholly and I Pray God, your whole spirit and soul and body are preserved blameless to the Coming of our Lord, Jesus Christ.
24 Faithful is He that Calls you, who also, will do it.
25 Brothers, Pray for us.
26 Greet all the brothers with a Holy kiss.
27 I charge you by The Lord that, this epistle is read to all the Holy brothers.
28 The Grace of our Lord, Jesus Christ be with you. Amen.

2ⁿᵈ Thessalonians

Chapter 1

1 Paul and Silvanus and Timotheus, to the church of the Thessalonians in God, our Father and The Lord, Jesus Christ,

2 Grace to you and Peace, from God our Father and The Lord, Jesus Christ.

3 We are bound to Thank God always for you brothers, as it is suitable, because that your Faith grows exceedingly and the Charity of every one of you all, toward each other abounds,

4 So that we ourselves, glory in you in the churches of God for <u>your Patience and Faith in all your persecutions and tribulations that you endure,</u>

5 <u>Which is a manifest Token of the Righteous Judgment of God that you may be counted worthy of the Kingdom of God, for which you also, suffer.</u>

6 <u>Seeing it is a Righteous thing with God to Recompense Tribulation to them that trouble you</u>

7 <u>And to you who are troubled, rest with us, when The Lord Jesus, shall be revealed from Heaven with His mighty angels,</u>

8 <u>In flaming fire, taking vengeance on them that know not, God and that obey not, The Gospel of our Lord, Jesus Christ;</u>

9 <u>Who shall be punished with everlasting destruction,</u> from the presence of The Lord and from The Glory of His Power,

10 When He shall come to be Glorified in His saints and to be Admired in all them that Believe (because our Testimony among you was believed) in that day.

11 Wherefore also, we Pray always for you that our God would count you worthy of this Calling and fulfill all the Good Pleasure of His Goodness and the Work of Faith with Power

12 That the Name of our Lord, Jesus Christ may be Glorified in you and you in Him, according to The Grace of our God and The Lord, Jesus Christ.

Chapter 2

1 Now, we beseech you brothers, by the Coming of our Lord, Jesus Christ and by our gathering together to Him

2 That you are not soon shaken in mind, or are troubled; neither by spirit, nor by word, nor by letter as from us, as that the Day of Christ is at hand.

3 <u>Let no man deceive you by any means, for that day shall not come, except there comes a falling away, first and that man of sin is revealed; the son of Perdition;</u>

4 <u>Who opposes and exalts himself, above all that is called god, or that is worshipped, so that he as God, sits in the temple of God, showing himself that he is god.</u>

5 Remember you not that when I was yet with you, I told you these things?

6 And now you know, what withholds that he might be revealed in his time.

7 <u>For the mystery of iniquity does already work. Only He who now lets, will let, until He be taken out of the way.</u>

8 And then, shall that wicked be revealed, whom The Lord shall consume with The Spirit of His mouth and shall destroy with the Brightness of His Coming;

9 <u>Even him, whose coming is after the working of Satan, with all power and signs and lying wonders</u>

10 <u>And with all deceivableness of unrighteousness in them that perish, because they received not, The Love of The Truth that they might be Saved.</u>

11 <u>And for this cause, God shall send them strong delusion that they should believe a lie</u>

12 <u>That they all, might be damned who believed not, The Truth, but had pleasure in unrighteousness.</u>

13 But we are bound to Give Thanks always to God for you brothers, beloved of The Lord, because God has from the beginning Chosen you to Salvation, through Sanctification of The Spirit and Belief of The Truth,

14 Whereunto, He Called you by our Gospel, to the obtaining of The Glory of our Lord, Jesus Christ.

15 Therefore brothers, Stand Fast and hold the Traditions, which you have been Taught; whether by word, or our epistle.

16 Now our Lord, Jesus Christ, Himself and God; even our Father, which has Loved us and has Given us everlasting Consolation and Good Hope through Grace,

17 Comfort your hearts and establish

yourselves in every good Word and Work.

Chapter 3

1 Finally brothers, Pray for us that The Word of The Lord may have Free Course and be Glorified, even as it is with you
2 And that we may be delivered from unreasonable and wicked men, for all men have not faith.
3 But The Lord is Faithful, who shall establish you and Keep you from evil.
4 And we have confidence in The Lord, touching you that you both do and will do the things, which we command you.
5 And The Lord directs your hearts into The Love of God and into the Patient Waiting for Christ.

6 Now we command you brothers, in The Name of our Lord, Jesus Christ that you withdraw yourselves, from every brother that walks disorderly and not after the tradition, which he received of us.
7 For yourselves know how you ought to follow us, for we behaved not ourselves disorderly among you.
8 Neither did we eat any man's bread for nothing, but wrought with labor and travail, night and day that we might not be chargeable to any of you,
9 Not because we have not power, but to make ourselves an example to you to follow us.
10 For even when we were with you, this we commanded you that, "if any would not work, neither should he eat."
11 For we hear that there are some, which walk among you disorderly; working not at all, but are busybodies.
12 Now, them that are such, we command and exhort by our Lord, Jesus Christ that with quietness, they work and eat their own bread.
13 But you brothers, be not weary in well doing.
14 And if any man obeys not our word by this epistle, note that man and have no company with him that he may be ashamed.
15 Yet count him not as an enemy, but admonish him as a brother.

16 Now, The Lord of Peace, Himself Give you Peace always by all means. The Lord be with you all.
17 The salutation of Paul, with my own hand, which is the token in every epistle, so I write.
18 The Grace of our Lord, Jesus Christ be with you all. Amen.

1ˢᵗ Timothy

Chapter 1

1 Paul, an apostle of Jesus Christ, by the Commandment of God, our Savior and Lord, Jesus Christ, which is our Hope.
2 To Timothy, my own son in The Faith, Grace, Mercy and Peace, from God, our Father and Jesus Christ, our Lord.
3 As I besought you to abide still at Ephesus, when I went into Macedonia that you might charge some that they Teach no other doctrine,

4 Neither give heed to fables and endless genealogies, which minister questions, rather than Godly Edifying, which is in Faith, so Do.
5 Now, the end of The Commandment is Charity, out of a Pure heart and of a good conscience and of Faith, unfeigned,
6 From which, some having swerved have turned aside to vain jangling;
7 Desiring to be teachers of the law; understanding neither what they say, nor whereof, they affirm.

8 But we know that, the Law is Good, if a man uses it, Lawfully:
9 Knowing this that, The Law is not made for a Righteous man, but: for:the lawless and disobedient; for the un-Godly and for sinners, for un-Holy and profane, for murderers of fathers and murderers of mothers, for manslayers,
10 For whoremongers, for them that defile themselves with mankind, for men stealers, for liars, for perjured persons and if there is any other thing that is contrary to Sound Doctrine,
11 According to The Glorious Gospel of The Blessed God, which was committed to my trust.

12 And I Thank Christ Jesus, our Lord, Who has enabled me, for that He counted me Faithful, putting me into the ministry;
13 Who was before, a blasphemer and a persecutor and injurious. But I obtained Mercy, because I did it ignorantly in unbelief.

14 And The Grace of our Lord was exceedingly abundant, with Faith and Love, which is in Christ Jesus.
15 This is a Faithful saying and worthy of all acceptation that, "Christ Jesus came into the World to Save sinners"; of whom, I am chief.
16 Howbeit, for this cause, I obtained Mercy that in me first, Jesus Christ might show forth all Longsuffering, for a pattern to them, which should hereafter, Believe on Him to Life everlasting.

17 Now, to The King: Eternal, Immortal, Invisible; the only Wise God, be Honor and Glory, for ever and ever. Amen.
18 This charge, I commit to you, son, Timothy according to the Prophecies, which went before on you that you by them, might War a good Warfare,
19 Holding Faith and a good conscience; which some, having put away, concerning Faith, have made shipwreck
20 Of whom, is Hymenaeus and Alexander, whom I have delivered to Satan that they may learn not, to blaspheme.

Chapter 2

1 I exhort therefore that first of all, Supplications, Prayers, Intercessions and Giving of Thanks are made for all men,
2 For kings and for all that are in authority that we may lead a quiet and Peaceable life in all Godliness and Honesty.
3 For this is good and acceptable in the Sight of God, our Savior,
4 Who will have all men, to be Saved and to come to the Knowledge of The Truth.
5 For there is one God and one Mediator, between God and men; The Man, Christ Jesus,
6 Who gave Himself a ransom for all, to be Testified in due time.
7 Whereunto, I am Ordained a preacher and an apostle, (I speak the truth in Christ and lie not) a teacher of the gentiles in Faith and verity.

8 I will therefore that men Pray every where, Lifting Up Holy Hands, without wrath and doubting.
9 In like manner also that women adorn themselves in modest apparel, with shamefacedness and sobriety; not with broided hair, or gold, or pearls, or costly array;
10 But (which becomes women professing Godliness) with good Works.
11 Let the woman learn in silence with all subjection.
12 But, I suffer not a woman to Teach, nor to usurp authority over the man, but to be in silence.
13 For Adam was first formed, then Eve.
14 And Adam was not deceived, but the woman being deceived was in the transgression.
15 Notwithstanding, she shall be saved in childbearing, if they continue in Faith and Charity and Holiness with Sobriety.

Chapter 3

1 This is a true saying: if a man desires the office of a Bishop, he desires a Good Work.
2 A Bishop then must be Blameless, the husband of one wife, Vigilant, Sober, of good Behavior, Given to Hospitality, apt to Teach;
3 Not given to wine, no striker, not greedy of filthy lucre, but patient, not a brawler, not covetous;
4 One that rules well his own house, having his children in subjection with all gravity;
5 (For if a man knows not how to rule his own house, how shall he take care of the church of God?)
6 Not a novice, lest being lifted up with pride, he falls into the condemnation of the Devil.
7 Moreover, he must have a good report of them, which are without, lest he falls into reproach and the snare of the Devil.
8 Likewise, must the deacons be Grave; not double tongued, not given to much wine, not greedy of filthy lucre;
9 Holding the Mystery of The Faith in a Pure conscience.
10 And let these also, first be Proved. Then, let them use the office of a deacon; being found Blameless.
11 Even so, must their wives be Grave; not slanderers; sober, Faithful in all things.
12 Let the deacons be the husbands of one wife, ruling their children and their own houses well.
13 For they that have used the office of a deacon, well purchase to themselves, a good degree and Great Boldness in The Faith, which is in Christ Jesus.

14 These things, I write to you, hoping to come to you, shortly,
15 But if I tarry long that you may know

how you ought to behave yourself in the house of God, which is the church of The Living God, The Pillar and Ground of The Truth.
16 And without controversy, Great is the Mystery of Godliness: God was Manifested in the flesh, Justified in The Spirit, seen of angels, Preached to the gentiles, Believed on in the World, Received up into Glory.

Chapter 4
1 Now, The Spirit speaks expressly that, "IN THE LATTER TIMES, SOME SHALL DEPART FROM THE FAITH; GIVING HEED TO SEDUCING SPIRITS AND DOCTRINES OF DEVILS,
2 SPEAKING LIES IN HYPOCRISY, HAVING THEIR CONSCIENCE SEARED WITH A HOT IRON,
3 FORBIDDING TO MARRY AND COMMANDING TO ABSTAIN FROM MEATS, WHICH GOD HAS CREATED TO BE RECEIVED WITH THANKSGIVING OF THEM, WHICH BELIEVE AND KNOW THE TRUTH.
4 For every creature of God is good and nothing to be refused, if it be received with Thanksgiving,
5 For it is Sanctified by The Word of God and Prayer."

6 If you put the brothers in remembrance of these things, you shall be a good minister of Jesus Christ; nourished up in The Words of Faith and of Good Doctrine, whereunto you have attained.
7 But, refuse profane and old wives' fables and exercise yourself rather, to Godliness.
8 For bodily exercise profits little, but Godliness is Profitable to all things; having Promise of The Life that now is and of that, which is to come.
9 This is a Faithful saying and worthy of all acceptation.
10 For therefore, we both Labor and suffer reproach, because we Trust in The Living God, who is The Savior of all men, especially of those that Believe.

11 These things, command and Teach.
12 Let no man despise your youth, but be you an example of the Believers: in Word, in Conversation, in Charity, in Spirit, in Faith, in Purity.
13 Until I come, give attendance to Readings; to Exhortation, to Doctrine.
14 Neglect not the Gift that is in you, which was Given you by Prophecy, with the Laying On of the Hands of the Presbytery.
15 Meditate on these things. Give yourself wholly to them that your Profiting may appear to all.
16 Take Heed to yourselves and to The Doctrine. Continue in them, for in Doing this, you shall both, Save yourself and them that hear you.

Chapter 5
1 Rebuke not an elder, but entreat him as a father and the younger men, as brothers;
2 The elder women as mothers; the younger, as sisters, with all Purity.
3 Honor widows that are widows, indeed.
4 But, if any widow has children, or nephews, let them Learn first, to show Piety at home and to Requite their parents, for that is good and acceptable before God.
5 Now, she that is a widow, indeed and desolate, Trusts in God and Continues in Supplications and Prayers, night and day.
6 But, she that lives in wantonness is Dead while she lives.
7 And these things, give in charge that they may be blameless.

8 But, if any provides not for his own and especially, for those of his own house, he has denied The Faith and is worse than an infidel.

9 Let not a widow be taken into the number, under sixty years old; having been the wife of one man;
10 Well reported of, for good Works; if she has brought up children, if she has lodged strangers, if she has washed the saints' feet, if she has Relieved the afflicted, if she has Diligently Followed every good Work.

11 But the younger widows refuse. For when they have begun to wax wanton against Christ, they will marry;
12 Having damnation, because they have cast off their first Faith.
13 And withal, they learn to be idle, wandering about from house to house and not only idle, but tattlers, also and busybodies, speaking things, which they ought not.
14 I will therefore that the younger women marry, bear children, guide the house, give none occasion to the adversary to speak reproachfully.
15 For some are already turned aside after Satan.

16 If any man, or woman that Believes, has widows, let them relieve them and let not, the church be charged that it may relieve them that are widows, indeed.

17 Let the elders that rule well, be counted worthy of double Honor, especially they who Labor in The Word and Doctrine.
18 For The Scripture says, "you shall not muzzle the ox that treads out the corn. And the laborer is worthy of his Reward."
19 Against an elder, receive not an accusation, but before two, or three witnesses.

20 Them that sin, Rebuke before all that others also, may Fear.
21 I charge you before God and The Lord, Jesus Christ and the elect angels that you observe these things, without preferring one before another, doing nothing by partiality.
22 Lay hands suddenly on no man, neither be partaker of other men's sins. Keep yourself Pure.
23 Drink no longer water, but use a little wine for your stomach's sake and your often infirmities.
24 Some men's sins are open beforehand, going before to Judgment and some men, they follow after.
25 Likewise also, the good Works of some are manifest beforehand and they that are otherwise cannot be hid.

Chapter 6

1 Let as many servants as are under the yoke count their own masters worthy of all honor that The Name of God and His Doctrine is not blasphemed.
2 And they that have Believing masters, let them not despise them, because they are brothers, but rather, do them service, because they are Faithful and beloved; partakers of The Benefit. These things Teach and Exhort.
3 If any man teaches otherwise and consents not, to Wholesome Words, even The Words of our Lord, Jesus Christ and to The Doctrine, which is according to Godliness,
4 He is proud; knowing nothing, but doting about questions and strifes of words, whereof comes: envy, strife, railings, evil surmisings,
5 Perverse disputings of men of corrupt minds and destitute of The Truth, supposing that gain is Godliness. From such, withdraw yourselves.

6 But, Godliness with contentment is Great Gain.

7 For we brought nothing into this World and it is certain, we can carry nothing out.
8 And having food and raiment, let us be therewith, Content.
9 But, they that will be rich, fall into temptation and a snare and into many foolish and hurtful lusts, which drown men in destruction and perdition.
10 For the love of money is the root of all evil, which while some coveted after, they have erred from The Faith and pierced themselves through with many sorrows.

11 But you, O man of God, flee these things and follow after: Righteousness, Godliness, Faith, Love, Patience, Meekness.
12 Fight the Good fight of Faith. Lay hold on Eternal Life, whereunto you are also, Called and have professed a good profession before many witnesses.
13 I give you charge in the sight of God, who Quickens all things and before Christ Jesus, who before Pontius Pilate witnessed a good Confession
14 That you keep this commandment without spot, unrebukable, until the appearing of our Lord, Jesus Christ,
15 Which in His time, He shall show, Who is the Blessed and only Potentate; The King of kings and Lord of lords;
16 Who only has Immortality dwelling in The Light, which no man can approach; to Whom, no man has seen, nor can see; to Whom, is Honor and Power everlasting. Amen.

17 Charge them that are rich in this World that they are not high minded, nor trust in uncertain riches, but in The Living God, who Gives us Richly, all things to Enjoy
18 That they Do good, that they are rich in good Works; ready to distribute, willing to communicate,
19 Laying up in store for themselves a good foundation against the time to come that they may, lay hold on Eternal Life.

20 O Timothy, keep that, which is committed to your trust; avoiding profane and vain babblings and oppositions of science, falsely, so called,
21 Which some professing, have erred concerning The Faith. Grace be with you. Amen.

2ⁿᵈ Timothy

Chapter 1

1 Paul, an apostle of Jesus Christ by The Will of God, according to The Promise of Life, which is in Christ Jesus. 2 To Timothy, my dearly beloved son, Grace, Mercy and Peace, from God, The Father and Christ Jesus, our Lord.

3 I Thank God, whom I serve from my forefathers with Pure conscience that without ceasing, I have remembrance of you in my Prayers night and day
4 Greatly desiring to see you, being mindful of your tears that I may be filled with joy
5 When I call to remembrance the Unfeigned Faith that is in you, which dwelled first, in your grandmother, Lois and your mother, Eunice and I am persuaded that in you, also.

6 Wherefore, I put you in remembrance that, you Stir Up The Gift of God, which is in you by the Putting On of my Hands.
7 For God has not given us the spirit of fear, but of Power and of Love and of a Sound Mind.
8 Be not you therefore, ashamed of The Testimony of our Lord, nor of me, His prisoner, but be you, partaker of the afflictions of The Gospel, according to The Power of God,
9 Who has Saved us and Called us with a Holy Calling, not according to our works, but according to His Own Purpose and Grace, which was Given us in Christ Jesus before the World began,
10 But is now, made Manifest by the appearing of our Savior, Jesus Christ; Who has abolished Death and has brought Life and immortality to Light through The Gospel
11 Whereunto, I am appointed a preacher and an apostle and a teacher of the gentiles.
12 For the which cause I also, suffer these things. Nevertheless, I am not ashamed, for I know Whom I have Believed and am persuaded that, He is able to Keep that, which I have committed to Him against that day.
13 Hold Fast, the form of Sound Words, which you have heard of me, in Faith and Love, which is in Christ Jesus
14 That good thing, which was committed to you; Keep by The Holy Ghost, which dwells in us.

15 This you know that, all they which are in Asia are turned away from me of whom are Phygellus and Hermogenes.
16 The Lord give Mercy to the house of Onesiphorus, for he often refreshed me and was not ashamed of my chains,
17 But when he was in Rome, he sought me out very diligently and found me.
18 The Lord grant to him that he may find Mercy of The Lord in that day and in how many things he ministered to me at Ephesus, you know very well.

Chapter 2

1 You therefore, my son, be Strong in The Grace that is in Christ Jesus.
2 And the things that you have heard of me among many witnesses, the same commit yourself to Faithful men, who shall be able to Teach others, also.
3 You therefore, Endure hardships, as a good soldier of Jesus Christ.
4 No man that wars, entangles himself with the affairs of this life that he may Please Him who has Chosen him to be a soldier.
5 And if a man also, strives for masteries, yet is he not crowned, except he strives Lawfully.
6 The Husbandman that Labors, must be first, partaker of the fruits.
7 Consider what I say and The Lord give you Understanding in all things.

8 Remember that Jesus Christ, of the seed of David was Raised from the dead, according to my gospel
9 Wherein, I suffer trouble, as an evil doer, even to bonds, but The Word of God is not bound.
10 Therefore, I Endure all things for the elect's sake that they may also, obtain the Salvation, which is in Christ Jesus with Eternal Glory.
11 It is a Faithful saying, "for if we are dead with Him, we shall also, Live with Him.
12 If we suffer, we shall also, reign with Him. If we deny Him, He also, will deny us.
13 If we Believe not, yet He abides Faithful. He cannot deny Himself."
14 Of these things, put them in remembrance, charging them before The

Lord that, they strive not about words to no profit, but to the subverting of the Hearers.

15 Study to show yourself approved to God; a workman that needs not to be ashamed; Rightly Dividing The Word of Truth.
16 But, shun profane and vain babblings, for they will increase to more ungodliness.
17 And their word will eat as does a canker of whom, is Hymenaeus and Philetus,
18 Who concerning The Truth have erred, saying that, "The Resurrection is past, already" and overthrow The Faith of some.
19 Nevertheless, the Foundation of God Stands Sure, having this Seal, The Lord knows them that are His. And let every one that names The Name of Christ, depart from iniquity.

20 But in a great house, there are not only vessels of gold and of silver, but also, of wood and of earth and some to honor and some to dishonor.
21 If a man therefore, Purges himself from these, he shall be a vessel to Honor, Sanctified and meet for the Master's use and prepared to every good Work.
22 Flee also, youthful lusts. But, follow: Righteousness, Faith, Charity, Peace, with them that call on The Lord out of a Pure heart.
23 But, foolish and unlearned questions avoid, knowing that they do gender strifes.
24 And the servant of The Lord must not strive. But, be gentle to all men, apt to Teach, Patient,
25 In Meekness, Instructing those that oppose themselves, if God peradventure, will give them Repentance to the acknowledging of The Truth
26 And that they may recover themselves out of the snare of the Devil, who are taken captive by him at his will.

Chapter 3
1 This know also that, in the last days, PERILOUS TIMES SHALL COME.
2 FOR MEN SHALL BE: LOVERS OF THEIR OWN SELVES, COVETOUS, BOASTERS, PROUD, BLASPHEMERS, DISOBEDIENT TO PARENTS, UNTHANKFUL, UNHOLY,
3 WITHOUT NATURAL AFFECTION, TRUCEBREAKERS, FALSE ACCUSERS, INCONTINENT, FIERCE, DESPISERS OF THOSE THAT ARE GOOD,
4 TRAITORS, HEADY, HIGH MINDED, LOVERS OF PLEASURES MORE THAN LOVERS OF GOD,
5 HAVING A FORM OF GODLINESS, BUT DENYING THE POWER, THEREOF. FROM SUCH, TURN AWAY.
6 FOR OF THIS SORT ARE THEY, WHICH CREEP INTO HOUSES AND LEAD CAPTIVE, SILLY WOMEN, LADEN WITH SINS; LED AWAY WITH DIVERSE LUSTS;
7 EVER LEARNING AND NEVER ABLE TO COME TO THE KNOWLEDGE OF THE TRUTH.
8 Now, as Jannes and Jambres withstood Moses, SO DO THESE ALSO, RESIST THE TRUTH; MEN OF CORRUPT MINDS, REPROBATE CONCERNING THE FAITH.
9 But, they shall proceed no further, for their folly shall be manifest to all men, as theirs also, was.
10 But, you have fully known my doctrine, manner of Life, Purpose, Faith, Longsuffering, Charity, Patience,
11 Persecutions, afflictions, which came to me at Antioch, at Iconium, at Lystra; what persecutions I endured, but out of them all, The Lord Deliverd me.
12 Yes and all that will Live Godly in Christ Jesus, shall suffer persecution.

13 But, EVIL MEN AND SEDUCERS SHALL WAX WORSE AND WORSE; DECEIVING AND BEING DECEIVED.
14 But, continue you in the things, which you have Learned and have been assured of, knowing of whom you have Learned them
15 And that from a child, you have Known The Holy Scriptures, which are able to make you Wise to Salvation through Faith, which is in Christ Jesus.
16 All Scripture is Given by Inspiration of God and is: Profitable for Doctrine, for Reproof, for Correction, for Instruction in Righteousness
17 That the man of God may be Perfect, thoroughly furnished to all good Works.

Chapter 4
1 I charge you therefore, before God and The Lord, Jesus Christ, Who shall Judge the Quick and the Dead at His appearing and His Kingdom.
2 Preach The Word. Be Instant in season, out of season: Reprove, Rebuke, Exhort with all Long Suffering and Doctrine.
3 FOR THE TIME WILL COME, WHEN THEY WILL NOT ENDURE SOUND

DOCTRINE, BUT AFTER THEIR OWN LUSTS, THEY SHALL HEAP TO THEMSELVES TEACHERS, HAVING ITCHING EARS.

4 AND THEY SHALL TURN AWAY THEIR EARS FROM THE TRUTH AND SHALL BE TURNED TO FABLES.

5 But, watch yourself in all things. Endure afflictions. Do the Work of an Evangelist. Make full proof of your ministry.

6 For I am now, ready to be offered and the time of my departure is at hand.

7 I have Fought a Good Fight. I have finished my course. I have Kept The Faith.

8 Henceforth, there is laid up for me a Crown of Righteousness, which The Lord, The Righteous Judge, shall Give me at that day and not to me only, but to all them, also that Love His appearing.

9 Do your diligence to come shortly, to me.

10 For Demas has forsaken me, having loved this present World and is departed to Thessalonica; Crescens to Galatia; Titus to Dalmatia.

11 Only Luke is with me. Take Mark and bring him with you, for he is profitable to me, for the ministry.

12 And Tychicus, have I sent to Ephesus.

13 The cloke that I left at Troas with Carpus, when you come, bring with you and the scrolls, but especially, the parchments.

14 Alexander the coppersmith did me much evil. The Lord reward him, according to his works.

15 Of whom, are you aware also, for he has greatly withstood our words.

16 At my first answer, no man stood with me, but all men forsook me. I Pray God that it may not be laid to their charge.

17 Notwithstanding, The Lord Stood with me and Strengthened me that by me, the Preaching might be fully Known and that all the gentiles might Hear and I was Delivered out of the mouth of the lion.

18 And The Lord shall Deliver me from every evil work and will Preserve me to His Heavenly Kingdom to Whom, be Glory, for ever and ever. Amen.

19 Salute Prisca and Aquila and the household of Onesiphorus.

20 Erastus abode at Corinth, but Trophimus have I left at Miletum, sick.

21 Do your diligence to come before Winter. Eubulus greets you and Pudens and Linus and Claudia and all the brothers.

22 The Lord, Jesus Christ be with your spirit. Grace be with you. Amen.

Titus

Chapter 1

1 Paul, a servant of God and an apostle of Jesus Christ, according to The Faith of God's elect and the acknowledging of The Truth, which is after Godliness,

2 In Hope of Eternal Life, which God that cannot lie, Promised before the World began,

3 But has in due times Manifested His Word through Preaching, which is committed to me, according to the Commandment of God, our Savior.

4 To Titus, my own son after the common Faith, Grace, Mercy and Peace, from God, The Father and The Lord, Jesus Christ, our Savior.

5 For this cause, I left you in Crete that you should set in order the things that are wanting and Ordain elders in every city, as I had appointed you;

6 If any is Blameless; the husband of one wife, having Faithful children, not accused of riot, or unruly.

7 For a bishop must be Blameless; as the steward of God: not self willed, not soon angry, not given to wine, no striker, not given to filthy lucre;

8 But, a lover of Hospitality, a lover of good men, Sober, Just, Holy, Temperate,

9 Holding Fast The Faithful Word as he has been Taught that he may be able by Sound Doctrine, both to Exhort and to Convince the gainsayers.

10 For there are many unruly and vain talkers and deceivers, especially they of the circumcision,

11 Whose mouths must be stopped, who subvert whole houses, teaching things, which they ought not, for filthy lucre's sake.

12 One of them, even a prophet of their own, said, "the Cretians are always liars, evil beasts, slow bellies."

13 This witness is true. Wherefore, rebuke them sharply that they may be Sound in The Faith;

14 Not giving heed to Jewish fables and

commandments of men that turn from The Truth.
15 <u>To the Pure, all things are Pure, but to them that are defiled and unbelieving is nothing pure, but even their mind and conscience is defiled.</u>
16 <u>They profess that they Know God, but in works, they deny Him; being abominable and disobedient and to every good Work, reprobate.</u>

Chapter 2
1 But speak yourselves the things which become Sound Doctrine:
2 That the aged men be Sober, Grave, Temperate; Sound in Faith, in Charity, in Patience.
3 The aged women likewise that, they are in behavior as becomes Holiness; not false accusers, not given to much wine, teachers of good things
4 That they may Teach the young women to be: Sober, to Love their husbands, to Love their children,
5 To be Discreet, Chaste, Keepers at home, good, obedient to their own husbands that The Word of God be not blasphemed.

6 Young men likewise, Exhort to be Sober Minded
7 In all things, showing yourselves a pattern of good Works in Doctrine, showing: Uncorruptness, Gravity, Sincerity,
8 Sound Speech that cannot be condemned that he that is of the contrary part, may be ashamed; having no evil thing to say of you.
9 Exhort servants to be obedient to their own masters and to please them well, in all things, not answering again,
10 Not purloining, but showing all good Fidelity that they may adorn The Doctrine of God, our Savior in all things.

11 For The Grace of God that brings Salvation has appeared to all men,
12 <u>Teaching us that, denying ungodliness and worldly lusts, we should live Soberly, Righteously and Godly, in this present World;</u>
13 Looking for that Blessed Hope and the Glorious appearing of The Great God and our Savior, Jesus Christ;
14 Who Gave Himself for us that He might Redeem us From all iniquity and Purify to Himself, a peculiar people; <u>Zealous of good Works.</u>

15 <u>These things speak and Exhort and Rebuke, with all authority.</u> Let no man despise you.

Chapter 3
1 Put them in mind: to be subject to principalities and powers, to obey magistrates; to be ready to every good Work,
2 To speak evil of no man, to be no brawlers; but Gentle, showing all Meekness to all men.
3 For we ourselves also, were sometimes: foolish, disobedient, deceived, serving diverse lusts and pleasures, living in malice and envy, hateful and hating one another.
4 <u>But, after that the Kindness and Love of God, our Savior toward man appeared,</u>
5 <u>Not by Works of Righteousness, which we have Done, but according to His Mercy, He Saved us, by the Washing of Regeneration and Renewing of The Holy Ghost,</u>
6 <u>Which He shed on us abundantly, through Jesus Christ, our Savior</u>
7 <u>That being Justified by His Grace, we should be made Heirs, according to the Hope of Eternal Life.</u>

8 <u>This is a Faithful saying and these things I will that, "you affirm constantly that, they which have Believed in God, might be careful to maintain good Works." These things are good and profitable to men.</u>
9 But, avoid: foolish questions and genealogies and contentions and strivings about the Law, for they are unprofitable and vain.
10 <u>A man that is a heretic, after the first and second Admonition, Reject,</u>
11 <u>Knowing that he that is such, is subverted and sins; being condemned of himself.</u>

12 When I shall send Artemas to you, or Tychicus, be diligent to come to me to Nicopolis, for I have determined there to winter.
13 Bring Zenas, the lawyer and Apollos on their journey diligently that nothing is wanting to them.
14 And let ours also, <u>Learn to maintain good Works, for necessary uses that they are not unfruitful.</u>
15 All that are with me, salute you. Greet them that love us in The Faith. Grace be with you all. Amen.

Philemon

1 Paul, a prisoner of Jesus Christ and Timothy, our brother. To Philemon, our dearly beloved and fellow laborer
2 And to our beloved Apphia and Archippus, our fellowsoldier and to the church in your house,
3 Grace to you and Peace from God, our Father and The Lord, Jesus Christ.
4 I Thank my God, making mention of you always in my Prayers,
5 Hearing of your Love and Faith, which you have toward The Lord, Jesus and toward all saints
6 That the Communication of your Faith may become Effectual by the acknowledging of every good thing, which is in you, in Christ Jesus.
7 For we have great joy and consolation in your love, because the bowels of the saints are refreshed by you, brother.
8 Wherefore, though I might be much Bold in Christ, to enjoin you that, which is convenient,
9 Yet for love's sake, I rather beseech you, being such a one as Paul, the aged and now also, a prisoner of Jesus Christ.
10 I beseech you for my son, Onesimus, whom I have begotten in my bonds,
11 Which in times past, was to you unprofitable, but now, profitable to you and to me,
12 Whom I have sent you again, therefore, receive him that is my own bowels,
13 Whom I would have retained with me that in your stead, he might have ministered to me in the bonds of The Gospel.
14 But without your mind, I would do nothing that your benefit should not be as it were of necessity, but willingly.
15 For perhaps he therefore, departed for a season that you should receive him, for ever,
16 Not now, as a servant, but above a servant; a beloved brother, especially to me, but how much more to you; both in the flesh and in The Lord?
17 If you count me therefore, a partner, receive him as myself.
18 If he has wronged you, or owes you anything, put that on my account.
19 I Paul, have written it with my own hand. I will repay it. Albeit, I do not say to you, how you owe to me, even your own self, besides.
20 Yes brother, let me have joy of you in The Lord. Refresh my bowels in The Lord.
21 Having confidence in your obedience, I wrote to you, knowing that you will also, do more than I say.
22 But withal, prepare me also, a lodging for I trust that through your Prayers, I shall be given to you.
23 There, salute you Epaphras, my fellowprisoner in Christ Jesus;
24 Marcus, Aristarchus, Demas, Lucas, my Fellow laborers.
25 The Grace of our Lord, Jesus Christ be with your spirit. Amen.

Hebrews

Chapter 1

1 God, Who at sundry times and in diverse manners, spoke in times past to the fathers by the prophets,
2 Has in these last days, spoken to us by His Son, Whom He has appointed Heir of all things, by Whom also, He made the Worlds,
3 Who being the Brightness of His Glory and the express Image of His Person and upholding all things by The Word of His Power, when he had by Himself, Purged our sins, sat down on the right hand of the Majesty on High,
4 Being made so much Better than the angels, as He has by inheritance, obtained a more excellent Name than they.
5 For to which, of the angels said He at any time, "YOU ARE MY SON, THIS DAY HAVE I BEGOTTEN YOU? AND AGAIN, I WILL BE TO HIM, A FATHER AND HE SHALL BE TO ME, A SON?"
6 And again, when He brought in the Firstbegotten into the World, He said, "AND LET ALL THE ANGELS OF GOD, WORSHIP HIM."
7 And of the angels He says, "Who makes

His angels, spirits and His ministers, a flame of fire."
8 But, to The Son He says, "YOUR THRONE, O GOD, IS FOR EVER AND EVER. A SCEPTRE OF RIGHTEOUSNESS IS THE SCEPTRE OF YOUR KINGDOM.
9 YOU HAVE LOVED RIGHTEOUSNESS AND HATED INIQUITY. THEREFROE GOD, EVEN YOUR GOD, HAS ANOINTED YOU WITH THE OIL OF GLADNESS, ABOVE YOUR FELLOWS."
10 And You Lord, in the beginning, have laid the foundation of the Earth and the heavens are the works of Your hands.
11 They shall perish, but You remain and they all shall wax old as does a garment.
12 And as a vesture, shall You fold them up and they shall be changed, but You are the same and Your years shall not fail."
13 But, to which of the angels said he at any time, "SIT ON MY RIGHT HAND UNTIL I MAKE YOUR ENEMIES YOUR FOOTSTOOL?"
14 Are they not all ministering spirits, sent forth to minister for them who shall be Heirs of Salvation?

Chapter 2

1 Therefore, we ought to give the more Earnest Heed to the things, which we have Heard, lest at any time we should let them slip.
2 For if the word spoken by angels was steadfast and every transgression and disobedience received a Just Recompense of reward,
3 How shall we escape, if we neglect so Great Salvation, which at the first, began to be spoken by The Lord and was Confirmed to us by them that Heard Him.
4 God also, bearing them witness, both with Signs and Wonders and with diverse Miracles and Gifts of The Holy Ghost, according to His Own Will?
5 For to the angels, He has not put in subjection, the World to come, whereof we speak.
6 But, one in a certain place Testified saying, "WHAT IS MAN THAT YOU ARE MINDFUL OF HIM, OR THE SON OF MAN THAT YOU VISIT HIM?
7 YOU MADE HIM A LITTLE LOWER THAN THE ANGELS. YOU CROWNED HIM WITH GLORY AND HONOR AND DID SET HIM OVER THE WORKS OF YOUR HANDS.
8 YOU HAVE PUT ALL THINGS IN SUBJECTION UNDER HIS FEET." For in that, He put all in subjection under Him, He left nothing that is not put under Him. But now, we see not yet, all things put under Him.
9 But, we see Jesus, who was made a little lower than the angels, for the suffering of death, Crowned with Glory and Honor that He, by The Grace of God should taste death for every man.
10 For it became Him, for whom are all things and by whom are all things, in bringing many sons to glory, to make the Captain of their Salvation, Perfect through sufferings.
11 For both He that Sanctifies and they who are Sanctified are all of one, for which cause, He is not ashamed to call them brothers
12 Saying, "I WILL DECLARE YOUR NAME TO MY BRETHREN. IN THE MIDST OF THE CHURCH, WILL I SING PRAISE TO YOU."
13 And again, "I WILL PUT MY TRUST IN HIM AND AGAIN, BEHOLD, I AND THE CHILDREN, WHICH GOD HAS GIVEN ME."
14 Forasmuch then, as the children are partakers of flesh and blood, He also, Himself likewise, took part of the same that through death, He might destroy him that had the power of Death; that is, the Devil
15 And Deliver them, who through fear of death, were all their lifetime, subject to bondage.
16 For verily, He took not on Himself, the nature of angels, but He took on Himself, the seed of Abraham.
17 Wherefore, in all things it behooved Him to be made like to His brothers that He might be a Merciful and Faithful High Priest in things pertaining to God, to make Reconciliation for the sins of the people.
18 For in that, He Himself, has suffered being tempted, He is able to Succor them, that are tempted.

Chapter 3

1 Wherefore, Holy brothers, partakers of the Heavenly Calling, consider The Apostle and High Priest of our Profession, Christ Jesus
2 Who was Faithful to Him that Appointed Him, as also, Moses was Faithful in all his house.
3 For this Man, was Counted Worthy of More Glory than Moses, in as much as He Who has built the house has More Honor

than the house.

4 For every house is built by some man, but He that created all matter is God.

5 And Moses verily, was Faithful in all his house as a servant for a Testimony of those things, which were to be spoken after,

6 But Christ as a Son over His own house, whose house we are, if we Hold Fast the Confidence and the Rejoicing of the Hope, firm to the end.

7 Wherefore, as The Holy Ghost said, "TODAY, IF YOU WILL HEAR HIS VOICE,
8 HARDEN NOT YOUR HEARTS, AS IN THE PROVOCATION, IN THE DAY OF TEMPTATION IN THE WILDERNESS
9 WHEN YOUR FATHERS TEMPTED ME, PROVED ME AND SAW MY WORKS, FORTY YEARS.
10 WHEREFORE, I WAS GRIEVED WITH THAT GENERATION" AND SAID, "THEY DO ALWAYS ERR IN THEIR HEART AND THEY HAVE NOT KNOWN MY WAYS.
11 SO I SWORE IN MY WRATH, THEY SHALL NOT ENER INTO MY REST."

12 Take Heed brothers, lest there be in any of you, an evil heart of unbelief; in departing from The Living God.

13 But, exhort one another daily, while it is called today, lest any of you be hardened, through the deceitfulness of sin.

14 For we are made partakers of Christ, if we Hold the beginning of our Confidence, Steadfast to the end.

15 While it is said, "TODAY, IF YOU WILL HEAR HIS VOICE, HARDEN NOT YOUR HEARTS, AS IN THE PROVOCATION."

16 For some, when they had heard, did provoke. Howbeit, not all that came out of Egypt by Moses.

17 But with whom, was He grieved, forty years? Was it not, with them that had sinned, whose carcasses fell in the wilderness?

18 And to whom swore He that they should not enter into His rest, but to them that believed not?

19 So, we see that they could not enter in because of unbelief.

Chapter 4

1 Let us therefore, Fear, lest a Promise being left us of entering into His rest, any of you should seem to come short of it.

2 For to us, was The Gospel Preached, as well as to them, but The Word Preached, did not profit them; not being mixed with Faith in them that Heard it.

3 For we which have Believed, do enter into rest, as He said, "AS I HAVE SWORN IN MY WRATH, IF THEY SHALL ENTER INTO MY REST," although, the works were finished from the foundation of the World.

4 For He spoke in a certain place of the seventh day on this wise and God did rest the seventh day, from all His Works.

5 And in this place again, "IF THEY SHALL ENTER INTO MY REST…"

6 Seeing therefore, it remains that some must enter, therein and they to whom it was first Preached, entered not in, because of unbelief.

7 Again, He limits a certain day, saying in David, "today, after so long a time as it is said, "'TODAY, IF YOU WILL HEAR HIS VOICE, HARDEN NOT YOUR HEARTS.'"

8 For if Jesus had given them rest, then He would not afterward, have spoken of another day.

9 There remains therefore, a rest to the people of God.

10 For he that is entered into His rest, he also, has ceased from his own works, as God did from His.

11 Let us Labor therefore, to enter into that rest, lest any man fall after the same example of unbelief.

12 For The Word of God is Quick and Powerful and Sharper than any two edged sword, piercing even to the dividing asunder of soul and spirit and of the joints and marrow and is a Discerner of the thoughts and intents of the heart.

13 Neither is there any creature that is not manifested in His sight, but all things are naked and opened to the eyes of Him with Whom, we have to do.

14 Seeing then that, we have a Great High Priest that is passed into the Heavens, Jesus, The Son of God, let us Hold Fast our Profession.

15 For we have not a High Priest, which cannot be touched with the feeling of our infirmities, but was in all points, tempted like as we are, yet without sin.

16 Let us therefore, come boldly to the Throne of Grace that we may obtain Mercy and find Grace to help in times of need.

Chapter 5

1 For every high priest taken from among men is ordained for men in things pertaining to God that he may offer both gifts and sacrifices for sins,

2 Who can have compassion on the ignorant and on them that are out of The Way, for that he himself also, is compassed with infirmity.

3 And by reason hereof, he ought as for the people, so also, for himself, to offer for sins.

4 And no man takes this Honor to himself, but he that is called of God, as was Aaron.

5 So also, Christ Glorified not, Himself to be made A High Priest, but He that said to Him, "YOU ARE MY SON. TODAY, HAVE I BEGOTTEN YOU."

6 As He says also, in another place, "YOU ARE A PRIEST FOR EVER, AFTER THE ORDER OF MELCHISEDEC."

7 Who in the days of his flesh, when He had offered up Prayers and Supplications with strong crying and tears to Him that was able to Save Him from death and was heard in that, He Feared.

8 Though He were a son, yet Learned He, Obedience by the things, which He suffered.

9 And being made Perfect, He became The Author of Eternal Salvation to all them that Obey Him;

10 Called of God, A High Priest, after the order of Melchisedec,

11 Of whom, we have many things to say and hard to be uttered, seeing you are dull of Hearing.

12 For when, for the time you ought to be Teachers, you have need that one Teach you again, which is the first Principles of The Oracles of God and are become such as have need of milk and not of strong meat.

13 For every one that uses milk is unskillful in The Word of Righteousness, for He is a babe.

14 But, strong meat belongs to them that are of full age, even those who by reason of use have their senses exercised to Discern both Good and evil.

Chapter 6

1 Therefore, leaving the principles of The Doctrine of Christ, let us go on to Perfection, not laying again, the foundation of Repentance from dead works and of Faith, toward God,

2 Of the Doctrine of Baptisms and of Laying On of Hands and of Resurrection of the dead and of Eternal Judgment.

3 And this will we do, if God permits.

4 For it is impossible for those who were once Enlightened and have tasted of the Heavenly Gift and were made partakers of The Holy Ghost

5 And have tasted The Good Word of God and The Powers of the World to come,

6 If they shall fall away, to Renew them again, to Repentance, seeing they crucify to themselves, The Son of God afresh and put Him to an open shame.

7 For the earth, which drinks in the rain that comes often on it and brings forth herbs, meet for them by whom it is dressed, receives Blessing from God,

8 But that which bears thorns and briers is rejected and is near to cursing, whose end is to be burned.

9 But beloved, we are persuaded better things of you and things that accompany Salvation, though we thus, speak.

10 For God is not unrighteous to forget your Work and Labor of Love, which you have shown toward His Name in that, you have ministered to the saints and do minister.

11 And we desire that every one of you do show the same Diligence to the full assurance of Hope to the end

12 That you be not slothful, but followers of them who through Faith and Patience inherit The Promises.

13 For when God made Promise to Abraham, because He could swear by no greater, He swore by Himself

14 Saying, "SURELY, BLESSING I WILL BLESS YOU AND MULTIPLYING, I WILL MULTIPLY YOU."

15 And so, after he had patiently endured, he obtained The Promise.

16 For men verily, swear by the greater and an oath for confirmation, is to them an end of all strife.

17 Wherein, God willing more abundantly, to show to the Heirs of Promise, the immutability of His counsel, Confirmed it by an Oath

18 That by two immutable things, in which it was impossible for God to lie, we might have a Strong Consolation, who have fled for refuge to Lay Hold on the Hope set before us,

19 Which Hope we have as an Anchor of the soul, both Sure and Steadfast and which enters into that, within the veil
20 Where the forerunner is for us entered, even Jesus, made a High Priest for ever, after the order of Melchisedec.

Chapter 7

1 For this Melchisedec, king of Salem, priest of The Most High God, who met Abraham returning from the slaughter of the kings and blessed him,
2 To whom also, Abraham gave a tenth part of all, first being by interpretation, king of Righteousness and after that also, king of Salem, which is, king of Peace;
3 Without father, without mother, without descent; having neither beginning of days, nor end of life, but made like to The Son of God, abides a priest, continually.
4 Now, consider how great this man was, to whom even the Patriarch, Abraham gave the tenth of the spoils.
5 And verily, they that are of the sons of Levi, who receive the office of the priesthood, have a Commandment to take tithes of the people, according to The Law that is, of their brothers, though they come out of the loins of Abraham.
6 But, he whose descent is not counted from them, received tithes of Abraham and blessed him that had The Promises.
7 And without all contradiction, the less is Blessed of The Better.
8 And here men that die, receive tithes, but there, he receives them, of Whom it is witnessed that He Lives.
9 And as I may so say, Levi also, who receives tithes, paid tithes in Abraham.
10 For he was yet in the loins of his father, when Melchisedec met him.

11 If therefore, Perfection were by the Levitical priesthood, (for under it, the people received the Law) what further need was there that another Priest should rise after the order of Melchisedec and not be called after the order of Aaron?
12 For the priesthood being changed, there is made of necessity a change also, of the Law.
13 For He of whom, these things are spoken, pertains to another tribe, of which no man gave attendance at the altar.
14 For it is evident that our Lord sprang out of Judah, of which tribe, Moses spoke nothing concerning priesthood.
15 And it is yet far more evident for that after the similitude of Melchisedec there arises another Priest,
16 Who is made, not after the law of a carnal commandment, but after The Power of an endless Life.
17 For He testifies, "YOU ARE A PRIEST FOR EVER, AFTER THE ORDER OF MELCHISEDEC."
18 For there is verily, a disannulling of the commandment going before, for the weakness and unprofitableness, thereof.
19 For the law made nothing perfect, but the bringing in of a Better Hope did, by the which, we Draw Near To God.
20 And in as much as not, without an oath He was made Priest
21 For those priests were made without an oath, but this, with an Oath by Him that said to Him, "THE LORD SWORE AND WILL NOT REPENT, YOU ARE A PRIEST FOR EVER, AFTER THE ORDER OF MELCHISEDEC."
22 By so much was Jesus made a surety, of a Better Testament.
23 And they truly, were many priests, because they were not suffered to continue by reason of death,

24 But this Man, because He continues ever, has an Unchangeable Priesthood.
25 Wherefore, He is able also, to Save them to the uttermost that come to God by Himself, seeing He ever Lives to make Intercession for them.
26 For such a High Priest became us; Who is Holy, Harmless, Undefiled, Separate from sinners and made Higher than the Heavens,
27 Who needs not daily, as those high priests, to offer up sacrifices, first for his own sins and then, for the people's; for this He did once, when He offered up Himself.
28 For the law makes men high priests, which have infirmity, but The Word of The Oath, which was since the Law, makes The Son, Who is Consecrated, for evermore.

Chapter 8

1 Now, of the things which we have spoken, this is the sum: we have such A High Priest, Who is set on The Right Hand of The Throne of The Majesty in the Heavens;
2 A Minister of the sanctuary and of the True Tabernacle, which The Lord pitched and not man.
3 For every high priest is ordained to offer gifts and sacrifices. Wherefore, it is of

necessity that this Man have somewhat also, to offer.

4 For if He were on Earth, He should not be a priest, seeing that there are priests that offer gifts, according to the law,

5 Who serve to the example and shadow of Heavenly things, as Moses was admonished of God, when he was about to make the tabernacle for, "see," He says that, "you make all things, according to the pattern shown to you in the mount."

6 But now, He has obtained a more excellent Ministry, by how much also, He is The Mediator of a Better Covenant, which was Established on Better Promises.

7 For if that first Covenant had been faultless, then should no place have been sought for the second.

8 For finding fault with them, He says, "BEHOLD, THE DAYS COME," says The Lord, "WHEN I WILL MAKE A NEW COVENANT WITH THE HOUSE OF ISRAEL AND WITH THE HOUSE OF JUDAH,

9 NOT ACCORDING TO THE COVENANT THAT I MADE WITH THEIR FATHERS IN THE DAY WHEN I TOOK THEM BY THE HAND TO LEAD THEM OUT OF THE LAND OF EGYPT, BECAUSE THEY CONTINUED NOT, IN MY COVENANT AND I REGARDED THEM NOT," says The Lord.

10 "FOR THIS IS THE COVENANT THAT I WILL MAKE WITH THE HOUSE OF ISRAEL AFTER THOSE DAYS," says The Lord, "I WILL PUT MY LAWS INTO THEIR MIND AND WRITE THEM IN THEIR HEARTS AND I WILL BE TO THEM, A GOD AND THEY SHALL BE TO ME A PEOPLE

11 AND THEY SHALL NOT TEACH EVERY MAN, HIS NEIGHBOR AND EVERY MAN, HIS BROTHER SAYING, "'KNOW, THE LORD,'" FOR ALL SHALL KNOW ME, FROM THE LEAST TO THE GREATEST.

12 FOR I WILL BE MERCIFUL TO THEIR UNRIGHTEOUSNESS AND THEIR SINS AND THEIR INIQUITIES, WILL I REMEMBER, NO MORE,"

13 In that He says, "A NEW COVENANT, HE HAS MADE THE FIRST, OLD," Now, that which decays and waxes old is ready to vanish away.

Chapter 9

1 Then verily, the first Covenant had also, ordinances of Divine Service and a worldly, sanctuary.

2 For there was a tabernacle made, the first wherein, was the candlestick and the table and the showbread, which is called the sanctuary.

3 And after the second veil, the tabernacle, which is called the Holiest of all,

4 Which had the golden censer and The Ark of The Covenant overlaid, round about with gold, wherein was the golden pot that had manna and Aaron's rod that budded and the tablets of The Covenant.

5 And over it, the cherubims of glory shadowing the mercyseat of which, we cannot now speak, particularly.

6 Now, when these things were thus ordained, the priests went always into the first tabernacle, accomplishing the service of God.

7 But into the second, went the high priest alone, once every year, not without blood, which he offered for himself and for the errors of the people.

8 The Holy Ghost, this signifying that the way into the Holiest of all, was not yet made manifest, while as the first tabernacle was yet standing,

9 Which was a figure for the time then present, in which were offered both gifts and sacrifices that could not make him that did the service, perfect, as pertaining to the conscience,

10 Which stood only in meats and drinks and diverse washings and carnal ordinances, imposed on them, until the time of Reformation.

11 But Christ being come A High Priest of Good things to come, by a Greater and More Perfect Tabernacle; not made with hands, that is to say, not of this building.

12 Neither by the blood of goats and calves, but by His Own Blood, He entered in once, into The Holy Place, having obtained Eternal Redemption for us.

13 For if the blood of bulls and of goats and the ashes of a heifer, sprinkling the unclean, sanctifies to the purifying of the flesh,

14 How much more, shall The Blood of Christ, who through The Eternal Spirit, Offered Himself without spot to God, Purge your Conscience from Dead works, to serve The Living God?

15 And for this cause, He is The Mediator of The New Testament that by means of death, for The Redemption of the transgressions that were under the First

Testament, they which are called, might receive The Promise of Eternal inheritance.

16 For where a testament is, there must also, of necessity, be the death of the testator.

17 For a testament is of force after men are dead. Otherwise, it is of no strength at all, while the testator lives.

18 Whereupon, neither the first Testament was dedicated without blood.

19 For when Moses had spoken every precept to all the people, according to the law, he took the blood of calves and of goats, with water and scarlet wool and hyssop and sprinkled both the scroll and all the people,

20 Saying, "THIS IS THE BLOOD OF THE TESTAMENT, WHICH GOD HAS ENJOINED TO YOU."

21 Moreover, he sprinkled with blood, both the tabernacle and all the vessels of the ministry.

22 And almost all things are by the Law, purged with blood and without shedding of blood, is no Remission.

23 It was therefore, necessary that the patterns of things in the Heavens should be purified with these, but the Heavenly things themselves, with Better Sacrifices than these.

24 For Christ is not entered into the Holy places made with hands, which are the figures of The True, but into Heaven itself, now to appear in The Presence of God for us.

25 Nor yet that, He should offer Himself often, as the high priest enters into the Holy place every year with blood of others,

26 For then, must He have often suffered, since the foundation of the World. But now, once in the end of the World, He has appeared to put away sin by The Sacrifice of Himself.

27 And as it is appointed to men once to die, but after this, The Judgment.

28 So, Christ was once offered to bear the sins of many and to them that look for Him, shall He appear the second time, without sin to Salvation.

Chapter 10

1 For the Law, having a shadow of Good things to come and not the very Image of the things, can never, with those sacrifices, which they offered year by year, continually make the comers thereunto, perfect.

2 For then, would they not have ceased to be offered, because that the worshippers once purged, should have had no more conscience of sins.

3 But in those sacrifices, there is a remembrance again, made of sins, every year.

4 For it is not possible that the blood of bulls and of goats should take away sins.

5 Wherefore, when He came into the World, He said, "SACRIFICE AND OFFERING YOU WOULD NOT, BUT A BODY, HAVE YOU PREPARED ME.

6 IN BURNT OFFERINGS AND SACRIFICES FOR SIN, YOU HAVE HAD NO PLEASURE."

7 THEN SAID I, "'LO, I COME (IN THE VOLUME OF THE SCROLL, IT IS WRITTEN OF ME) TO DO YOUR WILL, O GOD.'"

8 Above when He said, "'SACRIFICE AND OFFERING AND BURNT OFFERINGS AND OFFERING FOR SIN, YOU WOULD NOT, NEITHER HAVE PLEASURE, THEREIN'" which are offered by the law.

9 Then said He, "'lo, I come to do Your Will, O God.'" He takes away the first that He may Establish, The Second.

10 By the which, will, we are Sanctified through The Offering of The Body of Jesus Christ, once for all.

11 And every priest stands daily ministering and offering, oftentimes, the same sacrifices, which can never take away sins.

12 But this Man, after He had offered one sacrifice for sins, for ever, sat down on The Right Hand of God.

13 From henceforth, expecting until, "HIS ENEMIES ARE MADE HIS FOOTSTOOL."

14 For by one Offering, He has Perfected for ever, them that are Sanctified.

15 Whereof, The Holy Ghost also, is a Witness to us, for after that, He had said before,

16 "THIS IS THE COVENANT THAT I WILL MAKE WITH THEM, AFTER THOSE DAYS," says The Lord, "I WILL PUT MY LAWS INTO THEIR HEARTS AND IN THEIR MINDS, WILL I WRITE THEM

17 AND THEIR SINS AND INIQUITIES WILL I REMEMBER, NO MORE."

18 Now, where Remission of these is, there is no more, offering for sin,

19 Having therefore brothers, boldness to enter into the Holiest, by The Blood of Jesus,
20 By a New and Living Way, which He has Consecrated for us, through The Veil, that is to say, His Flesh
21 And having A High Priest over the house of God,
22 Let us draw near with a True Heart in Full Assurance of Faith, having our hearts sprinkled from an evil conscience and our bodies washed with pure water.
23 Let us Hold Fast the Profession of our Faith without wavering, for He is Faithful that Promised
24 And let us consider one another, to provoke to Love and to good Works;
25 Not forsaking the assembling of ourselves together, as the manner of some is, but Exhorting one another and so much the more, as you see the day approaching.

26 For if we sin willfully, after that, we have Received The Knowledge of The Truth, there remains no more Sacrifice for sins,
27 But a certain Fearful looking for of Judgment and Fiery Indignation, which shall devour the adversaries.
28 He that despised Moses' law, died without mercy under two, or three witnesses.
29 Of how much sorer Punishment, suppose you, shall he be thought worthy, who has trodden under foot, The Son of God and has counted The Blood of The Covenant, wherewith He was Sanctified, an un-Holy thing and has done despite, to The Spirit of Grace?
30 For we Know Him that has said, "VENGEANCE BELONGS TO ME, I WILL RECOMPENSE," says The Lord "AND AGAIN, THE LORD SHALL JUDGE HIS PEOPLE."
31 It is a Fearful thing to fall into the hands of The Living God.
32 But, call to remembrance the former days, in which, after you were Illuminated, you endured a great fight of afflictions.
33 Partly, while you were made a gazingstock, both by reproaches and afflictions and partly, while you became companions of them that were so used.

34 For you had compassion of me in my bonds and took joyfully the spoiling of your goods, knowing in yourselves that you have in Heaven a better and an enduring substance.

35 Cast not away therefore, your Confidence, which has great recompense of reward.
36 For you have need of Patience that, after you have Done The Will of God, you might Receive The Promise.
37 For yet, a little while and He that shall come, will come and will not tarry.
38 Now, the Just shall Live by Faith, but if any man draws back, My Soul shall have no pleasure in him.
39 But, we are not of them, who draw back to Perdition, but of them that Believe to the Saving of the soul.

Chapter 11

1 Now, Faith is the substance of things Hoped for, the evidence of things not seen.
2 For by it, the elders obtained a good report.
3 Through Faith, we understand that the Worlds were framed by The Word of God, so that things which are seen, were not made of things, which do appear.
4 By Faith, Abel offered to God a more excellent sacrifice than Cain, by which he obtained witness that he was Righteous, God Testifying of his gifts and by it, he being dead, yet speaks.
5 By Faith, Enoch was Translated that he should not see death and was not found, because God had Translated him, for before his Translation, he had this Testimony that he Pleased God.

6 But without Faith, it is impossible to Please Him, for he that comes to God, must Believe that He is and that He is a Rewarder of them that Diligently Seek Him.
7 By Faith, Noah being Warned of God of things not seen as yet, moved with Fear, prepared an ark to the saving of his house by the which, he condemned the World and became heir of the Righteousness, which is by Faith.

8 By Faith, Abraham, when he was called to go out into a place, which he should after receive for an inheritance, Obeyed and he went out, not knowing where he went.
9 By Faith, he sojourned in the land of Promise, as in a strange country; dwelling in tabernacles with Isaac and Jacob; the heirs with him of the same Promise.
10 For he looked for a city, which has

foundations, whose Builder and Maker is God.

11 Through Faith also, Sara herself, received Strength to conceive seed and was delivered of a child when she was past age, because she Judged Him Faithful who had Promised.

12 THEREFORE, SPRANG THERE EVEN OF ONE AND HIM AS GOOD AS DEAD, SO MANY AS THE STARS OF THE SKY IN MULTITUDE AND AS THE SAND, WHICH IS BY THE SEA SHORE, INNUMERABLE.

13 These all died in Faith, not having Received The Promises, but having seen them afar off and were persuaded of them and Embraced them and Confessed that they were strangers and pilgrims on the Earth.

14 For they that say such things, declare plainly that they seek a country.

15 And truly, if they had been mindful of that country, from whence they came out, they might have had opportunity to have returned.

16 But now, they desire a Better Country that is, a Heavenly, wherefore, God is not ashamed to be called their God, for He has prepared for them a city.

17 By Faith, Abraham, when he was Tried, offered up Isaac. And He that had received The Promises, offered up His only begotten Son,

18 Of whom, it was said that, "IN ISAAC, SHALL YOUR SEED BE CALLED,"

19 Accounting that God was able to Raise Him Up, even From the dead from where also, He received him in a figure.

20 By Faith, Isaac blessed Jacob and Esau concerning things to come.

21 By Faith, Jacob, when he was a dying, blessed both the sons of Joseph and Worshipped; leaning on the top of his staff.

22 By Faith, Joseph, when he died, made mention of the departing of the children of Israel and gave commandment concerning his bones.

23 By Faith, Moses, when he was born, was hid three months of his parents, because they saw he was a proper child and they were not afraid of the king's commandment.

24 By Faith, Moses, when he was come to years, refused to be called the son of Pharaoh's daughter,

25 Choosing rather to suffer affliction with the people of God, than to enjoy the pleasures of sin for a season,

26 Esteeming the reproach of Christ, greater riches than the treasures in Egypt. For he had respect to the recompense of the reward.

27 By Faith, he forsook Egypt, not fearing the wrath of the king, for he Endured as seeing Him who is invisible.

28 Through Faith, he Kept The Passover and the sprinkling of blood, lest he that destroyed the firstborn, should touch them.

29 By Faith, they passed through the Red Sea as by dry land, which the Egyptians assaying to do were drowned.

30 By Faith, the walls of Jericho fell down, after they were compassed about, seven days.

31 By Faith, the harlot, Rahab perished not, with them that believed not, when she had received the spies with Peace.

32 And what shall I say more? For the time would fail me to tell of Gideon and of Barak and of Samson and of Jephthah, of David, also and Samuel and of the prophets,

33 Who through Faith, subdued kingdoms, worked Righteousness, obtained Promises, stopped the mouths of lions,

34 Quenched the violence of fire, escaped the edge of the sword, out of weakness were made Strong, waxed valiant in fight, turned to flight the armies of the aliens.

35 Women received their dead Raised to life, again and others were tortured, not accepting deliverance that they might obtain a Better Resurrection

36 And others, had trial of cruel mockings and scourgings; yes moreover, of bonds and imprisonment.

37 They were stoned, they were sawn asunder, were tempted, were slain with the sword. They wandered about in sheepskins and goatskins being: destitute, afflicted, tormented

38 (Of whom, the World was not worthy.) They wandered in deserts and in mountains and in dens and caves of the earth.

39 And these all, having obtained a good report through Faith, received not The Promise.

40 God having provided some Better thing for us that they without us, should not be made Perfect.

Chapter 12

1 Wherefore, seeing we also, are

compassed about with so great a cloud of witnesses, let us lay aside every weight and the sin, which does so easily beset us and let us Run with Patience, the race that is set before us,

2 Looking to Jesus, The Author and Finisher of our Faith, Who for the Joy that was set before Him, Endured The Cross, despising the shame and is set down at The Right Hand of The Throne of God.

3 For consider Him that Endured such contradiction of sinners against Himself, lest you be wearied and faint in your minds.

4 You have not yet, resisted to blood, striving against sin.

5 And you have forgotten the Exhortation, which speaks to you as to children: My son, despise not yourself, the Chastening of The Lord, nor faint when you are Rebuked of Him.

6 For whom the Lord Loves, He Chastens and Scourges every son, whom He Receives.

7 If you Endure Chastening, God deals with you as with sons. For what son is he, whom The Father Chastens not?

8 But, if you be without Chastisement, whereof all are partakers, then are you bastards and not sons.

9 Furthermore, we have had fathers of our flesh, which corrected us and we gave them reverence. Shall we not much rather, be in Subjection to The Father of spirits and Live?

10 For they verily, for a few days, chastened us after their own pleasure, but He, for our Profit that we might be partakers of His Holiness.

11 Now, no Chastening for the present, seems to be a joyous, but grievous. Nevertheless afterward, it yields the Peaceable Fruit of Righteousness to them, which are exercised, thereby.

12 Wherefore, Lift Up the Hands, which hang down and the feeble knees

13 And make straight paths for your feet, lest that which is lame be turned out of the way. But, let it rather be healed.

14 Follow Peace with all men and Holiness, without which, no man shall see The Lord.

15 Looking Diligently, lest any man fail of The Grace of God, lest any root of bitterness springing up, trouble you and thereby, many be defiled.

16 Lest there be any fornicator, or profane person, as Esau, who for one morsel of meat, sold his birthright.

17 For you know how that afterward, when he would have inherited the Blessing, he was rejected, for he found no place of Repentance, though he sought it carefully with tears.

18 For you are not come to the mount that might be touched and that burned with Fire, nor to blackness and darkness and tempest

19 And the sound of a trumpet and The Voice of Words, Which Voice, they that Heard, entreated that The Word should not be spoken to them, any more.

20 (For they could not endure that, which was Commanded. And if so much as, a beast touches the mountain, it shall be stoned, or thrust through with a dart.

21 And so Fearful was the sight that Moses said, "I exceedingly Fear and quake")

22 But, you are come to Mount Sion and to the city of The Living God, the Heavenly Jerusalem and to an innumerable company of angels,

23 To the general assembly and church of the firstborn, which are written in Heaven and to God, The Judge of all and to the spirits of Just men made Perfect

24 And to Jesus, The Mediator of The New Covenant and to The Blood of sprinkling that speaks Better things than that of Abel.

25 See that you refuse not Him that speaks. For if they escaped not, who refused him that spoke on earth, much more, shall not we escape, if we turn away from Him that speaks from Heaven,

26 Whose Voice then, shook the Earth. But now, He has Promised saying, "yet once more, I shake not the Earth only, but also, Heaven."

27 And this Word, yet, once more, signifies the removing of those things that are shaken, as of things that are made that those things, which cannot be shaken, may remain.

28 Wherefore, we receiving a kingdom, which cannot be moved, let us have Grace, whereby we may serve God acceptably with Reverence and Godly Fear,

29 For our God is A Consuming Fire.

Chapter 13

1 Let Brotherly Love continue.

2 Be not forgetful to entertain strangers. For thereby, some have entertained angels unawares.
3 Remember them that are in bonds, as bound with them and them which suffer adversity, as being yourselves also, in the body.
4 Marriage is honorable in all and the bed undefiled, but whoremongers and adulterers, God will Judge.
5 Let your conversation be without covetousness and be content with such things as you have, for He has said, "I will never leave you, nor forsake you."
6 So that, we may Boldly say, "The Lord is my Helper and I will not fear what man shall do to me."
7 Remember them which have the rule over you, who have spoken to you The Word of God; whose Faith follow, considering the end of their conversation.

8 Jesus Christ: the same, yesterday and today and for ever.
9 Be not carried about with diverse and strange doctrines. For it is a good thing that the heart be established with Grace, not with meats, which have not profited them that have been occupied, therein.

10 We have an altar, whereof they have no right to eat, which serve the tabernacle.
11 For the bodies of those beasts, whose blood is brought into the sanctuary by the high priest for sin, are burned without the camp.
12 Wherefore Jesus, also that He might Sanctify the people with His Own Blood, suffered without the gate.
13 Let us go forth therefore, to Him without the camp, bearing His reproach.
14 For here have we no continuing city, but we seek one to come.
15 By Him therefore, let us offer the Sacrifice of Praise to God continually that is, the Fruit of our lips; Giving Thanks to His Name.
16 But, to Do good and to communicate, forget not, for with such Sacrifices, God is Well Pleased.
17 Obey them that have the rule over you and submit yourselves, for they watch for your souls, as they that must give account that they may do it with joy and not with grief, for that is unprofitable for you.

18 Pray for us, for we trust we have a good conscience, in all things; willing to live Honestly.
19 But, I beseech you the rather to do this that I may be restored to you the sooner.
20 Now, The God of Peace that brought again, from the dead, our Lord, Jesus that Great Shepherd of the sheep, through The Blood of the everlasting Covenant,
21 Make you perfect in every good Work to Do His Will; Working in you that, which is Wellpleasing in His Sight, through Jesus Christ, to Whom, be Glory, for ever and ever. Amen.
22 And I beseech you brothers, suffer the Word of Exhortation, for I have written a letter to you in few words.
23 Know you that our brother, Timothy is set at liberty with whom, if he comes shortly, I will see you.
24 Salute all them that have the rule over you and all the saints. They of Italy salute you.
25 Grace be with you all. Amen.

James

Chapter 1

1 James, a servant of God and of The Lord, Jesus Christ, to the twelve tribes which are scattered abroad, greetings.

2 My brothers, count it all Joy when you fall into diverse temptations,
3 Knowing this that, the Trying of your Faith Works Patience.
4 But, let Patience have her Perfect Work that you may be Perfect and entire, wanting nothing.

5 If any of you lacks Wisdom, let him Ask of God that Gives to all men, Liberally and upbraids not and it shall be Given him.
6 But let him Ask in Faith; nothing wavering. For he that wavers is like a wave of the Sea, driven with the wind and tossed.
7 For let not that man think that he shall receive any thing, of The Lord.
8 A double minded man is unstable in all his ways.

9 Let the brother of low degree Rejoice in that he is Exalted,
10 But the rich, in that he is made low,

because as the flower of the grass, he shall pass away.

11 For the Sun is no sooner risen with a burning heat, but it withers the grass and the flower thereof, falls and the grace of the fashion of it perishes. So also, shall the rich man fade away in his ways.

12 Blessed is the man that Endures temptation. For when he is Tried, he shall Receive the Crown of Life, which The Lord has Promised to them that Love Him.

13 Let no man say, when he is tempted, "I am tempted of God," for God cannot be tempted with evil, neither tempts He any man.

14 But, every man is tempted, when he is drawn away of his own lust and enticed.

15 Then, when lust has conceived, it brings forth sin and sin, when it is finished, brings forth Death.

16 Do not err, my beloved brothers.

17 Every Good Gift and every Perfect Gift is from above and comes down from The Father of Lights, with Whom is no variableness, neither shadow of turning.

18 Of His Own Will, He begat us with The Word of Truth that we should be a kind of Firstfruits of His creatures.

19 Wherefore, my beloved brothers, let every man be Swift to Hear, Slow to speak, Slow to wrath.

20 For the wrath of man works not, the Righteousness of God.

21 Wherefore, lay apart all filthiness and superfluity of naughtiness and receive with Meekness, The Engrafted Word, which is able to Save your souls.

22 But be yourselves, Doers of The Word and not hearers only; deceiving your own selves.

23 For if any be a hearer of The Word and not a Doer, he is like to a man beholding his natural face in a glass.

24 For he beholds, himself and goes his way and straightway, forgets what manner of man he was.

25 But, whosoever looks into the Perfect Law of Liberty and Continues therein, he being not, a forgetful Hearer, but a Doer of the Work, this man shall be Blessed in his Deed.

26 If any man among you, seems to be pious and bridles not his tongue, but deceives his own heart, this man's worship is vain.

27 Pure Worship and undefiled before God and The Father is this: to visit the fatherless and widows in their affliction and to Keep himself unspotted from the World.

Chapter 2

1 My brothers, have not The Faith of our Lord, Jesus Christ, The Lord of Glory, with respect of persons.

2 For if there comes to your assembly, a man with a gold ring, in goodly apparel and there comes in also, a poor man in vile raiment

3 And you have respect to him that wears the gay clothing and say to him, "sit you here," in a good place and say to the poor, "stand you there," or "sit here, under my footstool,"

4 Are you not then, partial in yourselves and are become judges of evil thoughts?

5 Hearken, my beloved brothers. Has not God Chosen the poor of this world, rich in Faith and Heirs of the Kingdom, which He has Promised to them that Love Him?

6 But, you have despised the poor. Do not rich men oppress you and draw you before the judgement seats?

7 Do not they blaspheme that Worthy Name by the which, you are Called?

8 If you Fulfill The Royal Law, according to The Scripture, You shall Love your neighbor as yourself, you do Well.

9 But, if you have respect to persons, you commit sin and are convicted of The Law as transgressors.

10 For whosoever, shall Keep The whole Law and yet offend in one point, he is guilty of all.

11 For he that said, "do not commit adultery," said also, "do not murder". Now, if you commit no adultery yet, if you murder, you are become a transgressor of The Law.

12 So, speak yourselves and so do, as they that shall be Judged by The Law of Liberty.

13 For he shall have Judgment without Mercy that has shown no mercy. And Mercy Rejoices against Judgment.

14 What does it profit, my brothers, though a man says, 'he has Faith and has not Works? Can Faith Save him?

15 If a brother, or sister is naked and destitute of daily food

16 And one of you says to them, "depart in peace, be you warmed and filled," notwithstanding, you give them not, those things, which are needful to the body, what does it profit?
17 Even so, faith, if it has not Works, is dead, being alone.
18 Yes, a man may say, "you have Faith and I have Works." Show me your faith without your works and I will show you my Faith By my Works.

19 You Believe that there is one God. You Do Well. The devils also, believe and tremble.
20 But, will you know, O vain man that faith without Works is dead?
21 Was not Abraham, our father, Justified by Works, when he had offered Isaac, his son on the altar?
22 See yourselves, how Faith Wrought with his Works and by Works was Faith made Perfect?
23 And The Scripture was Fulfilled which says, "ABRAHAM BELIEVED GOD AND IT WAS IMPUTED TO HIM FOR RIGHTEOUSNESS" and he was called the Friend of God.

24 You see then, how that by Works, a man is Justified and not by faith, only.
25 Likewise also, was not Rahab, the harlot Justified by Works, when she had received the messengers and had sent them out another way?
26 For as the body without the spirit is dead, so faith without Works, is dead, also.

Chapter 3

1 My brothers, be not many masters, knowing that we shall receive the greater condemnation.
2 For in many things, we offend all. If any man offends not in Word, the same is a perfect man and able also, to bridle the whole body.
3 Behold, we put bits in the horses' mouths that they may obey us and we turn about their whole body.
4 Behold also, the ships, which though they are so great and are driven of fierce winds, yet they are turned about with a very small helm, wheresoever, the governor lists.
5 Even so, the tongue is a little member and boasts great things. Behold, how great a matter a little fire kindles!
6 And the tongue is a fire; a World of iniquity. So is the tongue among our members that it defiles the whole body and sets on fire the course of nature and it is set on fire of Hell.
7 For every kind of beasts and of birds and of serpents and of things in the Sea, is tamed and has been tamed of mankind.
8 But the tongue, no man can tame. It is an unruly evil, full of deadly poison.
9 Therewith, we Bless God, even The Father and therewith, we curse men, which are made after the similitude of God.
10 Out of the same mouth, proceed blessings and cursings. My brothers, these things ought not, so to be.
11 Does a fountain send forth at the same place, sweet water and bitter?
12 Can the fig tree, my brothers, bear olive berries; either a vine, figs? So can no fountain, both yield salt water and fresh.
13 Who is a Wise man and Endued with Knowledge among you? Let him show out of a good conversation, his Works with Meekness of Wisdom.
14 But, if you have bitter envying and strife in your hearts, glory not and lie not, against The Truth.
15 This wisdom descends not, from above, but is: earthly, sensual, devilish.
16 For where envying and strife is, there is confusion and every evil work.
17 But, the Wisdom that is from Above is first, Pure, then Peaceable, Gentle and Easy to be Entreated, full of Mercy and Good Fruits, without partiality and without hypocrisy.
18 And the Fruit of Righteousness is sown in Peace of them that make Peace.

Chapter 4

1 From whence come wars and fightings among you? Come they not hence, even of your lusts that war in your members?
2 You lust and have not. You kill and desire to have and cannot obtain. You fight and war, yet you have not, because you ask not.
3 You ask and receive not, because you ask amiss that you may consume it on your lusts.

4 You adulterers and adulteresses, know you not that the friendship of the World is enmity with God? Whosoever therefore, will be a friend of the World is the enemy of God.

5 Do you think that The Scripture says in vain, "the spirit that dwells in us, lusts to envy?"
6 But, He Gives more Grace. Wherefore, He says, "God resists the proud, but Gives Grace to the Humble."

7 Submit yourselves therefore, to God. Opose the Devil and he will flee from you.
8 Draw Near to God and He will Draw Near to you. Cleanse your hands, you sinners and Purify your hearts, you double minded.
9 Be afflicted and mourn and weep. Let your laughter be turned to mourning and your joy to heaviness.
10 Humble yourselves in the sight of The Lord and He shall Lift you Up.
11 Speak not evil one of another, brothers. He that speaks evil of his brother and judges his brother, speaks evil of The Law and judges The Law. But, if you judge The Law, you are not a doer of The Law, but a judge.
12 There is one Lawgiver, who is able to Save and to destroy. Who are you that judges another?

13 Go to now, you that say, "today, or tomorrow, we will go into such a city and continue there a year and buy and sell and get gain."
14 Whereas, you know not, what shall be on the morrow. For what is your life? It is even a vapor that appears for a little time and then, vanishes away.
15 For that you ought to say, "if The Lord Wills, we shall live and do this, or that."
16 But now, you rejoice in your boastings. All such rejoicing is evil.
17 Therefore, to him that Knows to Do good and does it not, to him it is sin.

Chapter 5
1 Go to now, you rich men, weep and howl, for your miseries that shall come on you.
2 Your riches are corrupted and your garments are motheaten.
3 Your gold and silver is cankered and the rust of them, shall be a witness against you and shall eat your flesh as it were fire. You have heaped treasure together for the last days.
4 Behold, the hire of the laborers who have reaped down your fields, which is of you kept back by fraud, cries and the cries of them, which have reaped are entered into the ears of The Lord of Sabaoth.

5 You have lived in pleasure on the Earth and been wanton. You have nourished your hearts, as in a day of slaughter.
6 You have condemned and killed the Just and he does not resist you.

7 Be patient therefore, brothers to the Coming of The Lord. Behold, the husbandman waits for the precious fruit of the earth and has long patience for it, until he receives the early and latter rain.
8 Be you also, Patient. Establish your hearts, for the Coming of The Lord draws near.
9 Grudge not one against another, brothers, lest you be condemned. Behold, The Judge stands before the door.
10 Take my brothers, the prophets, who have spoken in The Name of The Lord, for an example of suffering, affliction and of patience.
11 Behold, we count them happy which Endure. You have heard of the patience of Job and have seen the end of The Lord that The Lord is very pitiful and of tender Mercy.
12 But above all things, my brothers, swear not, neither by Heaven, neither by the Earth, neither by any other oath, but let your yes be yes and your no, no, lest you fall into condemnation.

13 Is any among you afflicted? Let him Pray. Is any merry? Let him Sing psalms.
14 Is any sick among you? Let him call for the elders of the church and let them Pray over him, Anointing him with oil in The Name of The Lord.
15 And the Prayer of Faith, shall save the sick and The Lord shall Raise him Up. And if he has committed sins, they shall be Forgiven him.

16 Confess your faults one to another and Pray for one another that you may be Healed. The Effectual Fervent Prayer of a Righteous man avails much.
17 Elijah was a man subject to like passions as we are and he Prayed Earnestly that it might not rain and it rained not, on the earth by the space of three years and six months.
18 And he Prayed again and the heaven gave rain and the earth brought forth her fruit.
19 Brothers, if any of you do err from The Truth and one Converts him,
20 Let him know that he which Converts

the sinner from the error of his way, shall Save a soul from Death and shall hide a multitude of sins.

1st Peter

Chapter 1

1 Peter, an apostle of Jesus Christ. To the strangers scattered throughout: Pontus, Galatia, Cappadocia, Asia and Bithynia;
2 Elect according to the Foreknowledge of God, The Father, through Sanctification of The Spirit, to Obedience and sprinkling of The Blood of Jesus Christ. Grace to you and Peace be multiplied.

3 Blessed be The God and Father of our Lord, Jesus Christ, which according to His abundant Mercy has begotten us again, to a Lively Hope by the Resurrection of Jesus Christ From the dead,
4 To an inheritance, Incorruptible and Undefiled and that fades not away, reserved in Heaven for you,
5 Who are Kept by the Power of God through Faith to Salvation; ready to be revealed in the last time.
6 Wherein you greatly Rejoice, though now, for a season, if need be, you are in heaviness through manifold temptations
7 That the Trial of your Faith, being much more precious than of gold that perishes, though it be Tried with Fire, might be found to praise and honor and glory at the appearing of Jesus Christ;
8 Whom having not seen, you Love; in Whom, though now, you see Him not, yet Believing, you Rejoice with Joy unspeakable and Full of Glory;
9 Receiving the end of your Faith, even the Salvation of your souls;
10 Of which Salvation, the prophets have enquired and searched diligently; who Prophesied of the Grace that should come to you;
11 Searching what, or what manner of time, The Spirit of Christ, which was in them did signify, when it Testified beforehand, the sufferings of Christ and The Glory that should follow;
12 To Whom it was revealed that not to themselves, but to us they did minister the things, which are now, reported to you by them that have Preached The Gospel to you with The Holy Ghost sent down from Heaven; which things the angels desire to look into.

13 Wherefore, gird up the loins of your mind; be Sober and Hope to the end for The Grace that is to be brought to you at the Revelation of Jesus Christ
14 As Obedient children, not fashioning yourselves, according to the former lusts in your ignorance,
15 But as He, which has Called you is Holy, so be yourselves, Holy in all manner of conversation,
16 Because it is written, "be you Holy, for I am Holy."
17 And if you Call on The Father, Who without respect of persons, Judges, according to every man's Work, passes the time of your sojourning here in Fear,
18 Forasmuch as you know that you were not Redeemed with corruptible things, as silver and gold, from your vain conversation, received by tradition from your fathers,
19 But with The Precious Blood of Christ, as of a Lamb Without blemish and Without spot;
20 Who verily, was Foreordained before the foundation of the World, but was Manifested in these last times for you;
21 Who by Him, do Believe in God that Raised Him Up From the dead and gave Him Glory that your Faith and Hope might be in God.

22 Seeing you have Purified your souls in Obeying The Truth through The Spirit to unfeigned Love of the brothers, see that you Love one another with a Pure heart fervently;
23 Being Born Again, not of corruptible seed, but of incorruptible, by The Word of God, which Lives and Abides for ever.
24 "For all flesh is as grass and all the glory of man, as the flower of grass. The grass withers and the flower thereof, falls away.
25 But, The Word of The Lord endures for ever." And this is The Word, which by The Gospel is Preached to you.

Chapter 2

1 Wherefore, laying aside all malice and all guile and hypocrisies and envies and all evil speakings,

2 As newborn babes, desire the Sincere Milk of The Word that you may Grow, thereby.
3 If so, be you, have tasted that The Lord is Gracious.
4 To Whom coming, as to a Living Stone, disallowed indeed of men, but Chosen of God and Precious,
5 You also, as Lively stones, are built up a Spiritual house, a Holy priesthood, to offer up Spiritual Sacrifices, acceptable to God by Jesus Christ.

6 Wherefore also, it is contained in The Scripture, "BEHOLD, I LAY IN SION, A CHIEF CORNER STONE; ELECT, PRECIOUS AND HE THAT BLEIEVES ON HIM, SHALL NOT BE CONFOUNDED."
7 To you therefore, which Believe, He is Precious, but to them which are disobedient, "THE STONE, WHICH THE BUILDERS DISALLOWED, THE SAME IS MADE THE HEAD OF THE CORNER
8 AND A STONE OF STUMBLING AND A ROCK OF OFFENCE," even to them which stumble at The Word, being disobedient whereunto also, they were appointed.
9 But, you are a Chosen generation, a Royal priesthood, a Holy nation, a peculiar people that you should show forth the Praises of Him who has Called you out of Darkness into His Marvelous Light;
10 Which in times past were not a people, but are now, the people of God, which had not obtained Mercy, but now, have obtained Mercy.

11 Dearly beloved, I beseech you as strangers and pilgrims, abstain from fleshly lusts, which war against the soul,
12 Having your conversation Honest among the gentiles that, whereas they speak against you as evildoers, they may by your good Works, which they shall behold, Glorify God in the day of visitation.
13 Submit yourselves to every ordinance of man for The Lord's sake, whether it be to the king, as supreme,
14 Or to governors, as to them that are sent by Him for the punishment of evildoers and for the praise of them that do well.
15 For so is The Will of God that with well doing you may put to silence the ignorance of foolish men,
16 As Free and not using your Liberty for a cloke of maliciousness, but as the servants of God.
17 Honor all men. Love the brotherhood. Fear God. Honor The King.
18 Servants, be subject to your masters with all fear, not only to the good and gentle, but also, to the froward.
19 For this is thankworthy, if a man for conscience toward God Endures grief, suffering wrongfully.
20 For what glory is it, if when you are buffeted for your faults, you shall take it patiently? But, if when you do well and suffer for it, you take it patiently, this is acceptable with God.
21 For even hereunto, were you called because Christ also, suffered for us, leaving us an example that you should Follow His steps,
22 Who did no sin, neither was guile found in His mouth,
23 Who when He was reviled, reviled not again. When He suffered, He threatened not, but committed Himself, to Him that Judges Righteously;
24 Who His Own Self, bare our sins in His own body on the tree that we, being dead to sins, should Live to Righteousness by Whose stripes you were Healed.
25 "For you were as sheep going astray," but are now, Returned to The Shepherd and Bishop of your souls.

Chapter 3

1 Likewise, you wives, be in Subjection to your own husbands that, if any obey not The Word, they also, may without The Word, be won by the conversation of the wives
2 While they behold your Chaste conversation coupled with Fear,
3 Whose adorning, lets it not be that outward adorning of plaiting the hair and of wearing of gold, or of putting on of apparel,
4 But let it be the hidden man of the heart, in that which is not corruptible, even the Ornament of a Meek and Quiet spirit, which is in the Sight of God of Great Price.
5 For after this manner, in the old times, the Holy women also, who Trusted in God, adorned themselves, being in subjection to their own husbands,
6 Even as Sara obeyed Abraham, calling him lord, whose daughters you are, as long as you do well and are not afraid with any amazement.

7 Likewise, you husbands, dwell with them

according to Knowledge, giving Honor to the wife, as to the weaker vessel and as being Heirs together of The Grace of Life that your Prayers are not hindered.

8 Finally, be you all of one mind, having compassion one of another: Love as brothers, be Pitiful, be Courteous;
9 Not rendering evil for evil, or railing for railing, but contrariwise, Blessing, knowing that you are thereunto, Called that you should inherit a Blessing.
10 For he that will love life and see good days, let him refrain his tongue from evil and his lips that they speak no guile
11 Let him eschew evil and Do good. Let him seek Peace and ensue it.
12 For the eyes of The Lord are over the Righteous and His ears are Open to their Prayers, but the face of The Lord is against them that do evil.
13 And who is he that will harm you, if you are followers of that, which is good?
14 But and if you suffer for Righteousness' sake, happy are you. And be not afraid of their terror, neither be troubled.

15 But Sanctify The Lord, God in your hearts. And be ready always to give an answer to every man that asks you a reason of the Hope that is in you with Meekness and Fear,
16 Having a good conscience that, whereas they speak evil of you, as of evildoers, they may be ashamed that falsely accuse your good conversation in Christ.
17 For it is better, if The Will of God is so that you suffer for Well Doing, than for evil doing.
18 For Christ also, has once suffered for sins; The Just for the unjust that He might Bring us To God, being put to death in the flesh, but Quickened by The Spirit,
19 By which also, He went and Preached to the spirits in prison;
20 Which sometimes were disobedient, when once the Longsuffering of God waited in the days of Noah, while The Ark was a preparing, wherein few that is, eight souls were saved by water.
21 The like figure, whereunto even Baptism does also, now Save us (not the putting away of the filth of the flesh, but the answer of a good conscience toward God) by The Resurrection of Jesus Christ;
22 Who is gone into Heaven and is on the Right hand of God, angels and authorities and powers being made subject to Him.

Chapter 4

1 Forasmuch then, as Christ has suffered for us in the flesh, Arm yourselves likewise, with the same mind, for he that has suffered in the flesh has ceased from sin
2 That He no longer should live the rest of his time in the flesh to the lusts of men, but To The Will of God.
3 For the time past of our life, may suffice us to have worked the will of the gentiles, when we walked in: lasciviousness, lusts, excess of wine, revelings, banquetings and abominable idolatries.
4 Wherein, they think it strange that you run not with them to the same excess of riot, speaking evil of you,
5 Who shall give account to Him that is ready to Judge the Quick and the Dead.
6 For for this cause, The Gospel was Preached also, to them that are dead that they might be Judged, according to men in the flesh, but Live according to God in The Spirit.

7 But, the end of all things is at hand. Be you therefore, Sober and watch to Prayer.
8 And above all things, have Fervent Charity among yourselves, for Charity shall Cover the multitude of sins.
9 Use Hospitality one to another without grudging.
10 As every man has received The Gift, even so, minister the same one to another, as good stewards of the manifold Grace of God.
11 If any man speaks, let him speak as The Oracles of God. If any man ministers, let him do it as of the ability, which God Gives that God in all things, may be Glorified through Jesus Christ, to Whom is Praise and Dominion for ever and ever. Amen.

12 Beloved, think it not strange concerning the Fiery Trial, which is to Try you, as though some strange thing happened to you,
13 But Rejoice, in as much as you are partakers of Christ's sufferings that, when His Glory shall be revealed, you may be glad also, with exceeding Joy.
14 If you are reproached for The Name of Christ, happy are you, for The Spirit of Glory and of God rests on you. On their part, He is spoken evil of, but on your part, He is Glorified.
15 But, let none of you suffer as a murderer, or as a thief, or as an evildoer,

or as a busybody in other men's matters.
16 Yet if any man suffers as a Christian, let him not be ashamed, but let him Glorify God on this behalf.
17 For the time is come that Judgment must begin at the house of God. And if it first, begins at us, what shall the end be of them that obey not, The Gospel of God?
18 And if the Righteous, scarcely be Saved, where will the un-Godly and the sinner appear?
19 Wherefore, let them that suffer, according to The Will of God, commit the Keeping of their souls to Him in Well Doing, as to a Faithful Creator.

Chapter 5

1 The elders which are among you I exhort, who am also, an elder and a witness of the sufferings of Christ and also, a partaker of The Glory that shall be revealed
2 Feed the flock of God, which is among you, taking the oversight thereof; not by constraint, but willingly, not for filthy lucre, but of a ready mind;
3 Neither as being lords over God's heritage, but being examples to the flock.
4 And when The Chief Shepherd shall appear, you shall receive a Crown of Glory that fades not, away.
5 Likewise, you younger, submit yourselves to the elder. Yes, all of you be Subject one to another and be clothed with Humility, for God resists the proud and Gives Grace to the Humble.
6 Humble yourselves therefore, under The Mighty Hand of God that He may Exalt you in due time,
7 Casting all your cares on Him, for He Cares for you.

8 Be Sober, be Vigilant, because your adversary, the Devil, as a roaring lion, walks about, seeking whom he may devour;
9 Whom Resist, Steadfast in The Faith, Knowing that the same afflictions are accomplished in your brothers that are in the World.
10 But The God of all Grace, Who has Called us to His Eternal Glory by Christ Jesus, after that you have suffered a while, make you perfect; establish, strengthen, settle you.
11 To Him is Glory and Dominion, for ever and ever. Amen.

12 By Silvanus, a Faithful brother to you, as I suppose, I have written briefly, exhorting and testifying that this is The True Grace of God wherein, you stand.
13 The church that is at Babylon, elected together with you, salutes you and so does Marcus, my son.
14 Greet yourselves, one another with a kiss of Charity. Peace be with you all that are in Christ Jesus. Amen.

2nd Peter

Chapter 1

1 Simeon Peter, a servant and an apostle of Jesus Christ, to them that have obtained like Precious Faith with us through the Righteousness of God and our Savior, Jesus Christ,

2 Grace and Peace be multiplied to you, through The Knowledge of God and of Jesus, our Lord;
3 According as His Divine Power, has Given to us all things that pertain to Life and Godliness, through The Knowledge of Him that has called us to Glory and Virtue;
4 Whereby are Given to us exceedingly great and Precious Promises that by these, you might be partakers of the Divine Nature, having escaped the corruption that is in the World through lust.
5 And besides this, giving all Diligence, add to your Faith: Virtue and to Virtue, Knowledge
6 And to Knowledge, Temperance and to Temperance, Patience and to Patience, Godliness
7 And to Godliness, Brotherly Kindness and to Brotherly Kindness, Charity.
8 For if these things are in you and abound, they make you that you shall neither be barren nor unfruitful in The Knowledge of our Lord, Jesus Christ.
9 But, he that lacks these things is blind and cannot see afar off and has forgotten that he was Purged from his old sins.

10 Wherefore the rather brothers, give Diligence to make your Calling and Election sure, for if you Do these things, you shall never fall.
11 For so an entrance shall be ministered

to you abundantly into the everlasting Kingdom of our Lord and Savior, Jesus Christ.

12 Wherefore, I will not be negligent to put you always in remembrance of these things, though you know them and be Established in the present Truth.

13 Yes, I think it meet, as long as I am in this tabernacle, to stir you up by putting you in remembrance,

14 Knowing that shortly, I must put off this my tabernacle, even as our Lord, Jesus Christ has shown me.

15 Moreover, I will endeavor that you may be able, after my decease to have these things always in remembrance.

16 For we have not followed cunningly devised fables, when we made Known to you The Power and Coming of our Lord, Jesus Christ, but were eyewitnesses of His Majesty.

17 For He received from God, The Father, Honor and Glory when there came such A Voice to Him from the Excellent Glory, "THIS IS MY BELOVED SON, IN WHOM, I AM WELL PLEASED."

18 And this Voice, which came from Heaven, we Heard, when we were with Him in the Holy Mount.

19 We have also, a more Sure Word of Prophecy, whereunto you Do Well that you take Heed, as to a Light that Shines in a Dark place, until the day dawns and The Day Star arises in your hearts

20 Knowing this first that, no Prophecy of The Scripture is of any private interpretation.

21 For the Prophecy came not in old times by the will of man, but Holy men of God spoke as they were Moved by The Holy Ghost.

Chapter 2

1 But there were false prophets also, among the people, even as THERE SHALL BE FALSE TEACHERS AMONG YOU; WHO PRIVILY, SHALL BRING IN DAMNABLE HERESIES, EVEN DENYING THE LORD THAT BOUGHT THEM AND BRING ON THEMSELVES, SWIFT DESTRUCTION.

2 AND MANY SHALL FOLLOW THEIR PERNICIOUS WAYS BY REASON OF WHOM, THE WAY OF TRUTH SHALL BE EVIL SPOKEN OF

3 AND THROUGH COVETOUSNESS, SHALL THEY WITH FEIGNED WORDS, MAKE MERCHANDISE OF YOU, WHOSE JUDGMENT NOW, OF A LONG TIME LINGERS NOT AND THEIR DAMNATION SLUMBERS NOT.

4 For if God spared not the angels that sinned, but cast them down to Sheol and delivered them, into chains of Darkness, to be reserved to Judgment

5 And spared not the old world, but saved Noah, the eighth person, a preacher of Righteousness, bringing in the flood on the World of the un-Godly

6 And turning the cities of Sodom and Gomorrah into ashes; condemned them with an overthrow, making them an example to those that after, should live un-Godly

7 And Delivered just Lot, vexed with the filthy conversation of the wicked,

8 (For that righteous man dwelling among them, in seeing and hearing, vexed his righteous soul from day today with their unlawful deeds.)

9 The Lord knows how to Deliver the Godly out of temptations and to reserve the unjust to The Day of Judgement to be punished.

10 But chiefly, them that walk after the flesh in the lust of uncleanness and despise government; presumptuous are they, self willed. They are not afraid to speak evil of dignities.

11 Whereas angels, which are greater in power and might, bring not railing accusations against them before The Lord.

12 But these, as natural brute beasts, made to be taken and destroyed, speak evil of the things that they understand not and shall utterly perish in their own corruption

13 And shall receive the reward of unrighteousness, as they that count it pleasure to riot in the day time. Spots they are and blemishes; sporting themselves, with their own deceivings while they feast with you;

14 Having eyes full of adultery and that cannot cease from sin; beguiling, unstable souls; a heart they have exercised with covetous practices; cursed children,

15 Which have forsaken The Right Way and are gone astray; following the way of Balaam, the son of Bosor, who loved the wages of unrighteousness,

16 But was rebuked for his iniquity, the dumb ass speaking with man's voice, forbade the madness of the prophet.

17 These are wells without water; clouds that are carried with a tempest, to whom, the mist of Darkness is reserved, for ever.
18 For when they speak great swelling words of vanity, they allure through the lusts of the flesh, through much wantonness. Those that were clean, escaped from them, who live in error.
19 While they promise them liberty, they themselves are the servants of corruption. For of whom, a man is overcome, of the same, is he brought in bondage.

20 For if after they have escaped the pollutions of the World through The Knowledge of The Lord and Savior, Jesus Christ, they are again, entangled, therein and overcome. The latter end is worse with them, than the beginning.
21 For it had been better for them not to have Known The Way of Righteousness, than after they have Known it, to turn from The Holy Commandment Delivered to them.
22 But, it is happened to them, according to the True proverb, "the dog is turned to his own vomit, again and the sow that was washed to her wallowing, in the mire."

Chapter 3

1 This second epistle beloved, I now, write to you in both, which I stir up your Pure minds by way of remembrance
2 That you may be mindful of the words, which were spoken before, by the Holy prophets and of the commandment of us, the apostles of The Lord and Savior,
3 KNOWING THIS FIRST THAT, THERE SHALL COME IN THE LAST DAYS, SCOFFERS, WALKING AFTER THEIR OWN LUSTS
4 And saying, "where is The Promise of His coming? For since The Father's fell asleep, all things continue as they were, from the beginning of the Creation."
5 For this, they are willingly ignorant of that by The Word of God, the heavens were of old and the earth standing out of the water and in the water,
6 Whereby the World that then was, being overflowed with water, perished.
7 But, the heavens and the earth, which are now, by the same Word are kept in store, reserved to fire, against The Day of Judgement and perdition of un-Godly men.
8 But beloved, be not ignorant of this one thing that one day, is with The Lord, as a thousand years and a thousand years, as one day.
9 The Lord is not slack concerning His Promise, as some men count slackness, but is Longsuffering to us-ward; not willing that any should perish, but that all should come to Repentance.
10 But The Day of The Lord will come as a thief in the night in the which, the heavens shall pass away with a great noise and the elements shall melt with fervent heat; the Earth, also and the works that are therein, shall be burned up.
11 Seeing then that, all these things shall be dissolved, what manner of persons ought you to be in all Holy conversation and Godliness,
12 Looking for and hasting to the coming of The Day of God, wherein the heavens being on fire, shall be dissolved and the elements shall melt with fervent heat?
13 Nevertheless, we, according to His Promise, look for new heavens and a new Earth, wherein dwells Righteousness.
14 Wherefore beloved, seeing that you look for such things, be Diligent that you may be found of Him in Peace, without spot and Blameless.

15 And account that the Longsuffering of our Lord is Salvation, even as our beloved brother, Paul also, according to the Wisdom Given to him has written to you,
16 As also, in all his epistles, speaking in them of these things in which, are some things hard to be understood, which they that are unlearned and unstable wrest, as they do also, The Other Scriptures, to their own destruction.
17 You therefore beloved, seeing you know these things before, Beware, lest you also, being led away with the error of the wicked, fall from your own steadfastness.
18 But, grow in Grace and in The Knowledge of our Lord and Savior, Jesus Christ. To Him be Glory, both now and for ever. Amen.

1st John

Chapter 1

1 That which was from the beginning; which we have Heard, which we have Seen with our eyes, which we have looked on and our hands have handled, of The Word of Life

2 (For the Life was Manifested and we have Seen it and Bear Witness and show to you that Eternal Life, which was with The Father and was Manifested to us)

3 That which, we have Seen and Heard, we declare to you that you also, may have fellowship with us and truly, our fellowship is with The Father and with His Son, Jesus Christ.

4 And these things, we write to you that your Joy may be full.

5 This then, is The Message, which we have Heard of Him and declare to you that God is Light and in Him, is no Darkness at all.

6 If we say that we have Fellowship with Him and walk in Darkness, we lie and do not, The Truth

7 But, if we Walk in The Light, as He is in The Light, we have fellowship one with another and The Blood of Jesus Christ, His Son Cleanses us from all sin.

8 If we say that we have no sin, we deceive ourselves and The Truth is not in us.

9 If we Confess our sins, He is Faithful and Just to Forgive us our sins and to Cleanse us from All unrighteousness.

10 If we say that we have not sinned, we declare Him a liar and His Word is not, in us.

Chapter 2

1 My little children, these things write I to you that you sin not. And if any man sins, we have an Advocate with The Father, Jesus Christ, The Righteous.

2 And He is The Propitiation for our sins and not, for ours only, but also, for the sins of the whole World.

3 And hereby, we do know that, we Know Him if, we Keep His Commandments.

4 He that says, "I Know Him" and keeps not, His Commandments is a liar and The Truth is not, in him.

5 But whosoever, Keeps His Word, in him, verily, is The Love of God Perfected. Hereby, we know that we are in Him.

6 He that says "He Abides in him, ought himself also, so to Walk, even as He Walked."

7 Brothers, I write no New Commandment to you, but an Old Commandment, which you had from the beginning. The Old Commandment is, The Word, which you have Heard from the beginning.

8 Again, a New Commandment, I write to you, which thing is True in Him and in you, because the Darkness is past and The True Light now, Shines.

9 He that says "he is in The Light" and hates his brother, is in Darkness, even until now.

10 He that Loves his brother, Abides in The Light and there is no occasion of stumbling in him.

11 But, he that hates his brother is in Darkness and walks in Darkness and Knows not, where he goes, because that Darkness has blinded his eyes.

12 I write to you, little children, because your sins are Forgiven you, for His Name's sake.

13 I write to you fathers, because you have Known Him that is from the beginning. I write to you, young men, because you have Overcome the wicked one. I write to you, little children, because you have Known The Father.

14 I have written to you fathers, because you have Known Him that is from the beginning. I have written to you, young men, because you are strong and The Word of God Abides in you and you have Overcome the wicked one.

15 Love not, the World, neither the things that are in the World. If any man loves the World, the Love of The Father is not, in him.

16 For all that is in the World: the lust of the flesh and the lust of the eyes and the pride of life, is not of The Father, but is of the World.

17 And the World passes away and the lust thereof, but he that Does The Will of God Abides, for ever.

18 Little children, it is the last time and as you have heard that Antichrist shall come.

Even now, are there many antichrists, whereby we know that it is the last time.
19 They went out from us, but they were not of us. For if they had been of us, they would no doubt, have continued with us. But, they went out that they might be made manifested that they were not all of us.
20 But, you have an unction from the Holy One and you know all things.

21 I have not written to you because, you know not The Truth, but because you Know it and that no lie is of The Truth.
22 Who is a liar, but he that denies that, "Jesus is The Christ?" He is antichrist that denies The Father and The Son.
23 Whosoever denies The Son, the same has not, The Father. He that Acknowledges The Son, has The Father, also.
24 Let that therefore, abide in you, which you have Heard from the beginning. If that, which you have Heard from the beginning, shall Remain in you, you also, shall Continue in The Son and in The Father.
25 And this is The Promise that He has Promised us; even Eternal Life.

26 These things, have I written to you, concerning them that seduce you.
27 But the Anointing, which you have Received of Him, Abides in you and you need not that any man teach you. But, as the same Anointing Teaches you of all things and is Truth and is no lie. And even as it has Taught you, you shall Abide in Him.
28 And now, little children, Abide in Him that, when He shall appear, we may have confidence and not be ashamed before Him at His coming.
29 If you Know that He is Righteous, you Know that every one that Does Righteousness is Born of Him.

Chapter 3

1 Behold, what manner of Love The Father has Bestowed on us that we should be called the sons of God. Therefore, the World knows us not, because it knew Him, not.
2 Beloved, now are we the sons of God. And it does not yet, appear what we shall be, but we know that, when He shall appear, we shall be like Him, for we shall see Him as He is.
3 And every man that has this Hope in Him, Purifies himself, even as He is Pure.
4 Whosoever, commits sin, transgresses also, The Law, for sin is the transgression of The Law.
5 And you Know that He was Manifested to take away our sins and in Him, is no sin.
6 Whosoever, Abides in Him, sins not. Whosoever sins, has not seen Him, neither Known Him.
7 Little children, let no man deceive you, he that Does Righteousness is Righteous, even as He is Righteous.

8 He that continues sinning is of the Devil, for the Devil sins from the beginning. For this purpose, The Son of God was Manifested that He might destroy the works of the Devil.
9 Whosoever, is Born of God does not continue sinning, for His seed remains in him and he cannot sin, because he is Born of God.
10 In this, the children of God are manifested and the children of the Devil. Whosoever, does not, Righteousness is not, of God, neither he that loves not, his brother.

11 For this is The Message that you Heard from the beginning that we should Love one another.
12 Not as Cain, who was of that wicked one and slew his brother. And wherefore, slew he him? Because his own works were evil and his brother's Righteous.
13 Marvel not, my brothers, if the World hates you.
14 We know that we have passed from Death to Life, because we Love the brothers. He that loves not, his brother abides in Death.
15 Whosoever, hates his brother is a murderer and you Know that, no murderer has Eternal Life Abiding in him.
16 Hereby, perceive we The Love of God, because He laid down His life for us and we ought to lay down our lives for the brothers.
17 But whosoever, has this World's goods and sees his brother have need and shuts up his bowels of compassion from him, how dwells The Love of God in him?
18 My little children, let us not, love in word, neither in tongue, but in Deed and in Truth.
19 And hereby, we know that we are of The Truth and shall assure our hearts before Him.
20 For if our heart condemns us, God is Greater than our heart and Knows all

things.
21 Beloved, if our heart condemns us not, then have we confidence toward God.
22 And whatsoever we Ask, we Receive of Him, because we Keep His Commandments and Do those things that are Pleasing in His Sight.
22 And whatsoever we Ask, we Receive of Him, because we Keep His Commandments and Do those things that are Pleasing in His Sight.
23 And this is His Commandment that: we should Believe on The Name of His Son, Jesus Christ and Love one another, as He Gave us Commandment.
24 And he that Keeps His Commandments, Dwells in Him and He in him. And hereby, we know that, He Abides in us, by The Spirit, which He has Given us.

Chapter 4

1 Beloved, believe not, every spirit, but Try the spirits, whether they are of God, because many false prophets are gone out into the World.
2 Hereby, Know you, The Spirit of God: every spirit that Confesses that, "Jesus Christ is come in the flesh," is of God.
3 And every spirit that confesses not that, "Jesus Christ is come in the flesh" is not, of God and this is that spirit of Antichrist, whereof, you have Heard that it should come and even now, already is it in the World.
4 You are of God little children and have overcome them, because Greater is He that is in you, than he that is in the World.
5 They are of the World. Therefore, they speak of the World and the World hears them.
6 We are of God. He that Knows God, Hears us. He that is not, of God, Hears not, us. Hereby, we Know The Spirit of Truth and the spirit of error.

7 Beloved, let us Love one another, for Love is of God and every one that Loves is Born of God and Knows God.
8 He that Loves not, Knows not, God, for God is Love.
9 In this, was Manifested The Love of God toward us, because that, God sent His Only Begotten Son into the World that we might Live through Him.
10 Herein is Love: not that, we Loved God, but that He Loved us and sent His Son to be The Propitiation for our sins.

11 Beloved, if God so Loved us, we ought also, to Love one another.
12 No man has seen God at any time. If we Love one another, God dwells in us and His Love is Perfected in us.

13 Hereby, we know that, we Dwell in Him and He in us, because He has Given us of His Spirit.
14 And we have Seen and do Testify that The Father sent The Son to be The Savior of the World.
15 Whosoever, shall Confess that, "Jesus is The Son of God," God Dwells in Him and He in God.
16 And we have Known and Believed The Love that, God has to us. God is Love and he that Dwells in Love, Dwells in God and God in him.

17 Herein, is our Love made Perfect that we may have boldness in The Day of Judgement, because as He is, so are we in this World.
18 There is no fear in Love, but Perfect Love casts out fear, because fear has torment. He that fears is not made Perfect in Love.
19 We Love Him, because He first, Loved us.
20 If a man says, "I love God" and hates his brother, he is a liar, for he that Loves not, his brother, whom he has seen, how can he Love God, Whom he has not seen?
21 And this Commandment we have from Him that: he who Loves God, Love his brother, also.

Chapter 5

1 Whosoever, Believes that Jesus is The Christ is Born of God and every one that Loves Him that begat, Loves Him also that is Begotten of Him.
2 By this, we Know that, we Love the children of God, when we Love God and Keep His Commandments.
3 For this is The Love of God that we Keep His Commandments and His Commandments are not grievous.
4 For whatsoever, is Born of God, Overcomes the World and this is The Victory that Overcomes the World; even our Faith.
5 Who is he that Overcomes the World, but he that Believes that, Jesus is The Son of God?

6 This is He that, came by water and blood,

even Jesus Christ; not by water only, but by water and blood. And it is The Spirit that Bears Witness, because The Spirit is Truth.

7 For there are Three that bear record in Heaven: The Father, The Word and The Holy Ghost and these Three are One.
8 And there are Three that bear witness on Earth: The Spirit and The Water and The Blood and these Three Agree in One.
9 If we receive the witness of men, The Witness of God is Greater. For this is The Witness of God, which He has Testified of His Son.
10 He that Believes on The Son of God, has The Witness in himself. He that believes not, God has declared him a liar, because he believes not, The Record that God Gave of His Son
11 And this is the record that, God has Given to us, Eternal Life and this Life is in His Son.

12 He that has The Son, has Life and he that has not, The Son of God has not, Life.
13 These things have I written to you that Believe on The Name of The Son of God that you may Know that, you have Eternal Life and that you may Believe on The Name of The Son of God.

14 And this is The Confidence that we have in Him that if we ask any thing, according to His Will, He Hears us.
15 And if we Know that, He Hears us, whatsoever we Ask, we Know that, we have the petitions that, we desired of Him.
16 If any man, sees his brother sin a sin, which is not to Death, he shall ask and he shall give him Life for them that sin not to Death. There is a sin to Death. I do not say that, he shall Pray for it.
17 All unrighteousness is sin and there is a sin not to Death.
18 We know that, whosoever is Born of God sins not, but he that is Begotten of God, Keeps himself and that wicked one touches him not.
19 And we know that, we are of God and the whole World, lies in wickedness.
20 And we know that, The Son of God is come and has Given us an Understanding that we may Know Him that is True and we are in Him that is True; even in His Son, Jesus Christ. This is The True God and Eternal Life.
21 Little children, keep yourselves from idols. Amen.

2ⁿᵈ John

1 The elder, to the elect lady and her children, whom I Love in The Truth and not I only, but also, all they that have Known The Truth
2 For The Truth's sake, which Dwells in us and shall be with us, for ever.
3 Grace be with you; Mercy and Peace, from God, The Father and from The Lord, Jesus Christ, The Son of The Father, in Truth and Love.
4 I rejoiced greatly that I found of your children Walking in Truth, as we have received a Commandment from The Father.
5 And now, I beseech you, lady, not as though I wrote a new commandment to you, but that which we had from the beginning that we Love one another.
6 And this is Love that we Walk after His Commandments. This is The Commandment that: as you have Heard from the beginning, you should Walk in it.
7 For many deceivers are entered into the World, who Confess not that, "Jesus Christ is come in the flesh". This is a deceiver and an antichrist.
8 Look to yourselves that, we lose not, those things, which we have wrought, but that we receive a Full Reward.
9 Whosoever, transgresses and abides not, in The Doctrine of Christ, has not, God. He that Abides in The Doctrine of Christ, he has both, The Father and The Son.

10 If there comes any to you and brings not This Doctrine, receive him not, into your house, neither bid him God Speed
11 For he that bids him God Speed, is partaker of his evil deeds.

12 Having many things to write to you, I would not write with parchment and ink, but I trust to come to you and speak face to face that our joy may be full.
13 The children of your elect sister, greets you. Amen.

3rd John

1 The elder, to the well beloved Gaius, whom I Love in The Truth.

2 <u>Beloved, I wish above all things that you may Prosper and be in Health, even as your soul Prospers.</u>
3 For I Rejoiced greatly, when the brothers came and Testified of The Truth that is in you, even as you Walk in The Truth.
4 I have no greater Joy than to hear that my children Walk in Truth.
5 Beloved, you do Faithfully, whatsoever you do, to the brothers and to strangers,
6 Which have borne witness of your Charity before the church, whom if you bring forward on their journey after a Godly sort, you shall do well,
7 Because that for His Name's sake, they went forth, taking nothing of the gentiles.
8 We therefore, ought to receive such that we might be fellow Helpers to The Truth.
9 <u>I wrote to the church, but Diotrephes, who loves to have the preeminence among them, receives us not.</u>
10 <u>Wherefore, if I come, I will remember his deeds, which he does, prating against us with malicious words and not content therewith, neither does he himself receive the brothers and forbids them that would and casts them out of the church.</u>

11 Beloved, follow not that which is evil, but that, which is Good. He that Does good is of God, but he that does evil has not seen God.

12 Demetrius has good report of all men and of The Truth itself. Yes and we also, bear record and you know that, our record is true.
13 I had many things to write, but I will not with ink and stylus, write to you.
14 But I trust, I shall shortly see you and we shall speak face to face. Peace be to you. Our friends salute you. Greet the friends by name.

Jude

1 Jude, the servant of Jesus Christ and brother of James, to them that are Sanctified by God, The Father and preserved in Jesus Christ and Called.
2 Mercy to you and Peace and Love, be multiplied.
3 Beloved, when I gave all diligence to write to you of the common Salvation, it was needful for me to write to you and exhort you that <u>you should Earnestly Contend for The Faith</u>, which was once delivered to the saints.

4 <u>For there are certain men, crept in unawares, who were before of old, ordained to this condemnation;</u> un-Godly men, <u>turning the Grace of our God into lasciviousness</u> and denying The Only Lord, God and our Lord, Jesus Christ.
5 I will therefore, put you in remembrance, though you once Knew this, how that <u>The Lord, having Saved the people out of the land of Egypt, afterwards, destroyed them that believed not.</u>
6 And the angels, which kept not their first estate, but left their own habitation, He has reserved in everlasting chains under Darkness to The Judgment of The Great Day.
7 Even as Sodom and Gomorrah and the cities about them in like manner, <u>giving themselves over to fornication and going after strange flesh, are set forth for an example; suffering the vengeance of eternal fire.</u>

8 Likewise also, <u>these filthy dreamers defile the flesh</u>, despise dominion and speak evil of dignities.
9 Yet, Michael the archangel, when contending with the Devil, he disputed about the body of Moses, did not bring against him, a railing accusation, but said, "The Lord rebuke you."
10 <u>But, these speak evil of those things, which they know not, but what they know naturally, as brute beasts, in those things, they corrupt themselves.</u>
11 <u>Woe to them! For they have gone in the way of Cain and ran greedily after the error of Balaam for reward and perished in the gainsaying of Core.</u>
12 <u>These are spots in your feasts of Charity, when they feast with you; feeding</u>

themselves without Fear; clouds they are, without water, carried about of winds; trees, whose fruit withers, without fruit, twice Dead, plucked up by the roots;
13 Raging waves of the Sea, foaming out their own shame; wandering stars, to whom, is reserved the Blackness of Darkness, for ever.

14 And Enoch also, the seventh from Adam, Prophesied of these saying, "behold, The Lord comes with ten thousands of His saints,
15 To execute Judgment on all and to convict all that are un-Godly, among them, of all their un-Godly deeds, which they have un-Godly committed and of all their hard speeches, which un-Godly sinners have spoken against Him."

16 These are murmurers, complainers; walking after their own lusts and their mouth speaks great swelling words, having men's persons in admiration because of advantage.
17 But beloved, remember yourselves, The Words, which were spoken before of the apostles of our Lord, Jesus Christ,
18 How that they told you, "THERE SHOULD BE MOCKERS IN THE LAST TIME, WHO SHOULD WALK AFTER THEIR OWN UN-GODLY LUSTS."
19 These are they: who separate themselves, sensual, having not The Spirit.
20 But you, beloved, building up yourselves, on your most Holy Faith, Praying in The Holy Ghost,
21 Keep yourselves, in The Love of God; looking for The Mercy of our Lord, Jesus Christ, to Eternal Life.
22 And of some, have compassion, making a difference.
23 And others Save with Fear; pulling them out of the fire, hating even the garment spotted by the flesh.
24 Now, to Him that is able to Keep you from falling and to present you faultless before The Presence of His Glory with exceeding Joy,
25 To the only Wise God, our Savior, be Glory and Majesty, Dominion and Power, both now and ever. Amen.

Revelation

Chapter 1

1 The Revelation of Jesus Christ, which God Gave to Him, to show to His servants, things which must shortly come to pass and He sent and signified it by His angel to His servant, John,
2 Who Bare Record of The Word of God and of The Testimony of Jesus Christ and of all things that He saw.
3 Blessed is he that reads and they that Hear The Words of this Prophecy and Keeps those things, which are written therein, for the time is at hand.
4 John, to the seven churches which are in Asia, Grace be to you and Peace from Him, Which Is and Which Was and Which Is To Come and from the seven spirits, which are before His throne
5 And from Jesus Christ, Who is The Faithful Witness and The First Begotten of the dead and The Prince of the kings of the Earth, To Him that Loved us and Washed us from our sins in His Own Blood
6 And has made us kings and priests to God and His Father, to Him be Glory and Dominion, for ever and ever. Amen.
7 Behold, He comes with Clouds and every eye shall see Him. And they also, which pierced Him and all kindreds of the Earth, shall wail because of Him. Even so, Amen.

8 "I am Alpha and Omega; The Beginning and The Ending," says The Lord, "Which Is and Which Was and Which Is To Come, The Almighty."

9 I John, who also, am your brother and companion in tribulation and in The Kingdom and Patience of Jesus Christ, was in the isle that is called, Patmos, for The Word of God and for The Testimony of Jesus Christ.
10 I was in The Spirit on The Lord's Day and Heard behind me, A Great Voice, as of a trumpet,
11 Saying, "I am Alpha and Omega, The First and The Last. And what you see, write in a scroll and send it to the seven churches, which are in Asia: to Ephesus and to Smyrna and to Pergamos and to Thyatira and to Sardis and to Philadelphia

and to Laodicea."

12 And I turned to see The Voice that spoke with me. And being turned, I saw seven golden candlesticks

13 And in the midst of the seven candlesticks, one like to The Son of Man, clothed with a garment down to the foot and girt about the paps with a golden girdle.

14 His head and His hairs were white like wool; as white as snow and His eyes were as a Flame of Fire

15 And His feet like to fine brass, as if they burned in a furnace. And His Voice as the sound of many waters.

16 And He had in His right hand, seven stars. And out of His mouth went a sharp two edged Sword and His Countenance was as the Sun shines in his strength.

17 And when I saw Him, I fell at His feet as dead. And He laid His right hand on me, saying to me, "fear not. I am The First and The Last.

18 I am He that Lives and was dead and behold, I am Alive for Evermore, Amen and have the keys of Hell and of Death.

19 Write the things, which you have Seen and the things, which are and the things, which shall be, hereafter.

20 The Mystery of the seven stars, which you saw in My right hand and the seven golden candlesticks: the seven stars are the angels of the seven churches and the seven candlesticks, which you saw are the seven churches.

Chapter 2

1 To the angel of the church of Ephesus write, "'these things says He that holds the seven stars in His right hand, Who walks in the midst of the seven golden candlesticks,

2 ""I know your Works and your Labor and your Patience and how you can not bear them, which are evil and you have Tried them, which say they are apostles and are not and have found them liars

3 And have borne and have Patience and for My Name's sake, have Labored and have not fainted.

4 Nevertheless, I have somewhat against you, because you have left your First Love.

5 Remember therefore, from whence you are fallen and Repent and Do the first Works, or else, I will come to you quickly and will remove your candlestick out of his place, except you Repent.

6 But, this you have that you hate the deeds of the Nicolaitanes; which I also, hate.'""

7 He that has an ear, let him Hear what The Spirit says to the churches, "''to him that Overcomes, I will Give to eat of the Tree of Life, which is in the midst of The Paradise of God.'""

8 And to the angel of the church in Smyrna write, "'these things, says The First and The Last, which was dead and is Alive,

9 ""I know your Works and tribulation and poverty, but you are Rich and I know the blasphemy of them, which say they are Jews and are not, but are the synagogue of Satan.

10 Fear none of those things, which you shall suffer. Behold, the Devil shall cast some of you into prison that you may be Tried and you shall have tribulation ten days. Be you Faithful to death and I will Give you a Crown of Life.'""

11 He that has an ear, let him Hear what The Spirit says to the churches, "''he that Overcomes, shall not be hurt of the Second Death.'""

12 And to the angel of the church in Pergamos write, "'these things, says He Which has The sharp Sword with two edges,

13 I know your Works and where you dwell, even where Satan's seat is. And you Hold Fast My Name and have not, denied My Faith, even in those days wherein, Antipas was My Faithful Martyr; who was slain among you, where Satan dwells.

14 But, I have a few things against you: because you have there, them that hold the doctrine of Balaam, who taught Balac to cast a stumblingblock before the children of Israel; to eat things sacrificed to idols and to commit fornication.

15 So have you also, them that hold the doctrine of the Nicolaitanes, which thing I hate.

16 Repent, or else, I will come to you quickly and will fight against them with The Sword of My mouth.'""

17 He that has an ear, let him Hear what The Spirit says to the churches: "''to him that Overcomes, I will Give to eat of the hidden Manna and will give him a white

stone and in the stone, a new name written, which no man knows, saving he that receives it.'"

18 And to the angel of the church in Thyatira write, "'these things says The Son of God, who has His eyes like to a Flame of Fire and His feet are like fine brass,
19 ""I know your Works and Charity and Service and Faith and your Patience. And your Works and the last, to be more than the first.
20 Notwithstanding, I have a few things against you: because you suffer that woman, Jezebel, which calls herself a prophetess, to teach and to seduce my servants to commit fornication and to eat things sacrificed to idols.
21 And I gave her space to Repent of her fornication and she repented not.
22 Behold, I will cast her into a bed and them that commit adultery with her into great tribulation, except they Repent of their deeds.
23 And I will kill her children with death and all the churches shall know that I am He, which searches the reins and hearts and I will give to every one of you, according to your works.
24 But to you, I say and to the rest in Thyatira, as many as have not, this doctrine and which have not, known the depths of Satan, as they speak, I will put on you no other burden.
25 But that, which you have already, Hold Fast until I come.'"

26 "'And he that Overcomes and Keeps My Works to the end, to him will I give Power over the nations
27 And he shall rule them with a rod of iron, as the vessels of a potter, shall they be broken to shivers, even as I received of My Father.
28 And I will give Him The Morning Star.'"
29 He that has an ear, let him Hear what The Spirit says to the churches.

Chapter 3
1 And to the angel of the church in Sardis write, "'these things says He that has the seven spirits of God and the seven stars, ""I know your works that you have a name that you live and are Dead.
2 Be watchful and strengthen the things, which remain that are ready to die, for I have not found your works perfect before God.
3 Remember therefore, how you have Received and Heard and Hold Fast and Repent. If therefore, you shall not watch, I will come on you as a thief and you shall not, know what hour I will come on you.
4 You have a few names, even in Sardis, which have not defiled their garments and they shall Walk with Me in white, for they are worthy.'"

5 "'He that Overcomes, the same shall be clothed in white raiment. And I will not, blot out his name out of the Scroll of Life, but I will confess his name before My Father and before His angels.'"
6 He that has an ear, let him hear what The Spirit says to the churches.

7 And to the angel of the church in Philadelphia write, "'these things says He that is Holy; He that is True, He that has the key of David, He that opens and no man shuts and shuts and no man opens,
8 ""I know your works. Behold, I have set before you an open door and no man can shut it, for you have a little strength and have Kept My Word and have not denied My Name.
9 Behold, I will make them of the synagogue of Satan, which say they are Jews and are not, but do lie, behold, I will make them to come and worship before your feet and to know that I have Loved you.
10 Because you have Kept The Word of My Patience, I also, will Keep you from the hour of temptation, which shall come on all the World, to Try them that dwell on the Earth.
11 Behold, I come quickly. Hold Fast that, which you have that no man takes your crown.'"

12 "'Him that Overcomes, I will make a pillar in the temple of My God. And he shall go no more out and I will write on him, The Name of My God and the name of the city of My God, which is New Jerusalem, which comes down out of Heaven, from My God and I will write on Him My New Name.'"
13 He that has an ear, let him Hear what The Spirit says to the churches.

14 And to the angel of the church of the Laodiceans write, "'these things, says The Amen; The Faithful and True Witness; The Beginning of The Creation of God,
15 ""I know your works that you are neither cold, nor hot. I would you were cold, or hot.
16 So then, because you are lukewarm

and neither cold, nor hot, I will spew you out of My mouth,
17 Because you say, """I am rich and increased with goods and have need of nothing"'" and know not that you are wretched and miserable and poor and blind and naked.
18 I counsel you to buy of Me gold, Tried in the Fire that you may be rich and white raiment that you may be clothed and that the shame of your nakedness does not appear. And Anoint your eyes with eyesalve that you may See.
19 As many as I Love, I Rebuke and Chasten. Be Zealous, therefore and Repent.
20 Behold, I stand at The Door and knock. If any man Hears My Voice and Opens The Door, I will come in to him and will sup with him and he with Me."'"

21 "'To him that Overcomes, I will grant to sit with Me in My throne; even as I also, Overcame and am set down with My Father in His throne."'
22 He that has an ear, let him hear what The Spirit says to the churches."

Chapter 4

1 After this, I looked and behold, a door was opened in Heaven and the first Voice, which I Heard was as it were, of a trumpet talking with me which said, "come up here and I will show you things, which must be, hereafter."
2 And immediately, I was in The Spirit and behold, a throne was set in Heaven and One sat on the throne.
3 And He that sat, was to look on like a jasper and a sardine stone and there was a rainbow, round about the throne, in sight like to an emerald.
4 And round about, the throne were four and twenty seats. And on the seats, I saw four and twenty elders sitting clothed in white raiment and they had on their heads, crowns of gold.
5 And out of the throne proceeded Lightnings and Thunderings and voices. And there were seven lamps of fire burning before the throne, which are the seven spirits of God.
6 And before the throne, there was a Sea of glass like to crystal and in the midst of the throne and round about, the throne, were four beasts full of eyes before and behind.
7 And the first beast, was like a lion and the second beast, like a calf and the third beast, had a face as a man and the fourth beast, was like a flying eagle.
8 And the four beasts had each of them, six wings about him and they were full of eyes, within. And they rest not, day and night, saying, "Holy, Holy, Holy, Lord, God Almighty, which Was and Is and Is To Come."
9 And when those beasts give Glory and Honor and Thanks to Him that sat on the throne, who Lives, for ever and ever,
10 The four and twenty elders fall down before Him that sat on the throne and Worship Him that Lives, for ever and ever and cast their crowns before the throne saying,
11 "You are Worthy, O Lord, to receive Glory and Honor and Power for you have Created all things and for Your Pleasure, they are and were Created."

Chapter 5

1 And I saw in the right hand of Him that sat on the throne, a Scroll written within and on the backside, sealed with seven Seals.
2 And I saw a strong angel proclaiming with a loud voice, "Who is Worthy to open the Scroll and to loose the Seals, thereof?"
3 And no man in Heaven, nor on Earth, neither under the earth, was able to open the Scroll, neither to look, thereon.
4 And I wept much, because no man was found worthy to open and to read the Scroll, neither to look, thereon.
5 And one of the elders said to me, "weep not. Behold, The Lion of the Tribe of Judah; the Root of David, has Prevailed to open the Scroll and to loose the seven Seals, thereof."

6 And I beheld and lo, in the midst of the throne and of the four beasts and in the midst of the elders, stood a Lamb as it had been slain; having seven horns and seven eyes, which are the seven spirits of God sent forth into all the Earth.
7 And He came and took the Scroll out of the right hand of Him that sat on the throne.
8 And when He had taken the Scroll, the four beasts and four and twenty elders fell down before The Lamb; having every one of them, harps and golden vials full of odors, which are the Prayers of saints.

9 And they Sang a New Song saying, "You are Worthy to take the Scroll and to open the Seals thereof, for You were slain and have Redeemed us To God by Your Blood; out of every kindred and tongue and people and nation

10 And have made us to our God, kings and priests and we shall reign on the Earth."

11 And I beheld and I heard the voice of many angels, round about the throne. And the beasts and the elders and the number of them was ten thousand, times ten thousand and thousands of thousands

12 Saying with a loud voice, "Worthy is The Lamb that was slain to Receive Power and Riches and Wisdom and Strength and Honor and Glory and Blessing."

13 And every creature, which is in Heaven and on the Earth and under the earth and such as are in the Sea and all that are in them, I heard saying, "Blessing and Honor and Glory and Power, be to Him that sits on the throne and to The Lamb, for ever and ever."

14 And the four beasts said, "Amen." And the four and twenty elders fell down and Worshipped Him that Lives for ever and ever.

Chapter 6

1 And I saw when The Lamb opened one of the Seals and I heard, as it were, the noise of thunder, one of the four beasts saying, "come and see."

2 And I saw and behold, a white horse and he that sat on him, had a bow. And a crown was given to him and he went forth conquering and to conquer.

3 And when he had opened the second seal, I heard the second beast say, "come and see."

4 And there went out another horse that was red and power was given to him that sat thereon, to take Peace from the Earth and that they should kill one another. And there was given to him a great sword.

5 And when he had opened the third seal, I heard the third beast say, "come and see." And I beheld and lo, a black horse and he that sat on him had a pair of balances in his hand.

6 And I heard a voice in the midst of the four beasts say, "a measure of wheat for a penny and three measures of barley for a penny. And see you hurt not the oil and the wine."

7 And when he had opened the fourth seal, I heard the voice of the fourth beast say, "come and see."

8 And I looked and behold, a pale horse and his name that sat on him was Death. And Hell followed with him. And power was given to them over the fourth part of the Earth to kill with sword and with hunger and with Death and with the beasts of the Earth.

9 And when he had opened the fifth seal, I saw under the altar, the souls of them that were slain for The Word of God and for The Testimony, which they held.

10 And they cried with a loud voice saying, "how long, O Lord; Holy and True, do You not Judge and Avenge our blood on them that dwell on the Earth?"

11 And white robes were given to every one of them and it was said to them that, "they should rest yet, for a little season, until their fellow servants, also and their brothers that should be killed as they were, should be fulfilled."

12 And I beheld when He had opened the sixth seal and lo, there was a great earthquake. And the Sun became black as sackcloth of hair and the Moon became as blood

13 And the stars of heaven fell to the Earth; even as a fig tree casts her untimely figs, when she is shaken of a mighty wind.

14 And the heaven departed as a scroll when it is rolled together. And every mountain and island were moved out of their places.

15 And the kings of the Earth and the great men and the rich men and the chief captains and the mighty men and every bondman and every free man, hid themselves in the dens and in the rocks of the mountains

16 And said to the mountains and rocks, "fall on us and hide us from the face of Him that sits on the throne and from the wrath of The Lamb,

17 For the Great Day of His wrath is come. And who shall be able to stand?"

Chapter 7

1 And after these things, I saw four angels standing on the four corners of the Earth, holding the four winds of the Earth that the

wind should not blow on the Earth, nor on the Sea, nor on any tree.

2 And I saw <u>another angel</u> <u>ascending from the East</u>, having <u>the Seal of The Living God</u> and he cried with a loud voice to the four angels, to whom it was given to hurt the Earth and the Sea
3 Saying, <u>"hurt not the Earth, neither the Sea, nor the trees, until we have Sealed the servants of our God in their foreheads."</u>

4 And <u>I heard the number of them, which were Sealed and there were Sealed, one hundred and forty and four thousand of all the tribes of the children of Israel:</u>
5 Of the tribe of <u>Judah</u> were Sealed, <u>twelve thousand</u>; of the tribe of <u>Reuben</u> were Sealed, <u>twelve thousand</u>; of the tribe of <u>Gad</u> were Sealed, <u>twelve thousand</u>;
6 Of the tribe of <u>Asher</u> were Sealed, <u>twelve thousand</u>; of the tribe of <u>Naphtali</u> were Sealed, <u>twelve thousand</u>; of the tribe of <u>Manasseh</u> were Sealed, <u>twelve thousand</u>;
7 Of the tribe of <u>Simeon</u> were Sealed, <u>twelve thousand</u>; of the tribe of <u>Levi</u> were Sealed, <u>twelve thousand</u>; of the tribe of <u>Issachar</u> were Sealed, <u>twelve thousand</u>;
8 Of the tribe of <u>Zebulun</u> were Sealed, <u>twelve thousand</u>; of the tribe of <u>Joseph</u> were Sealed, <u>twelve thousand</u>; of the tribe of <u>Benjamin</u> were Sealed, <u>twelve thousand</u>.

9 After this, I beheld and lo, <u>a great multitude</u>, <u>which no man could number</u>, of <u>all nations</u> and <u>kindreds and people and tongues stood before the throne and before The Lamb</u>; clothed with white robes and palms in their hands
10 And cried with a loud voice saying, <u>"Salvation to our God, which sits on the throne and to The Lamb."</u>
11 And all the angels stood round about, the throne and about the elders and the four beasts and Fell before the throne on their faces and Worshipped God
12 Saying, "Amen, Blessing and Glory and Wisdom and Thanksgiving and Honor and Power and Might, be to our God, for ever and ever. Amen."

13 And one of the elders answered saying to me, <u>"what are these, which are arrayed in white robes and whence came they?"</u>
14 And I said to him, "Sir, you know." And he said to me, <u>"these are they, which came out of great tribulation and have washed their robes and made them white in The Blood of The Lamb.</u>
15 Therefore, they are before the throne of God and Serve Him day and night in His temple. And He that sits on the throne shall Dwell among them.
16 <u>They shall hunger no more, neither thirst any more, neither shall the Sun light on them, nor any heat.</u>
17 <u>For The Lamb, which is in the midst of the throne, shall feed them and shall lead them to Living Fountains of Waters. And God shall wipe away all tears from their eyes."</u>

Chapter 8

1 And when He had opened <u>the seventh seal, there was silence in Heaven about the space of half an hour.</u>

2 And I saw the <u>seven angels</u>, which stood before God and to them, were given <u>seven trumpets.</u>

3 And another angel came and stood at the altar, <u>having a golden censer and there was given to him much incense that he should offer it with the Prayers of all saints on the golden altar, which was before the throne.</u>
4 <u>And the smoke of the incense, which came with the Prayers of the saints, ascended up before God out of the angel's hand.</u>
5 And the angel took the censer and filled it with fire of the altar and cast it into the Earth. And there were voices and Thunderings and Lightnings and an earthquake.
6 And <u>the seven angels</u>, which had the <u>seven trumpets</u> prepared themselves to sound.

7 The <u>first angel sounded</u> and there, <u>followed hail and fire mingled with blood. And they were cast on the Earth and the third part of trees were burnt up and all green grass was burnt up.</u>

8 And the <u>second angel sounded</u> and <u>as it were, a great mountain burning with fire was cast into the Sea and the third part of the Sea became blood.</u>
9 <u>And the third part of the creatures, which were in the Sea and had life, died and the third part of the ships were destroyed.</u>

10 And the <u>third angel sounded</u> and <u>there fell a great star from heaven; burning as it</u>

were a lamp. And it fell on the third part of the rivers and on the fountains of waters.
11 And the name of the star is called, Wormwood. And the third part of the waters became wormwood and many men died of the waters, because they were made bitter.
12 And the fourth angel sounded and the third part of the Sun was stricken and the third part of the Moon and the third part of the stars, so as the third part of them, was darkened. And the day shone not, for a third part of it and the night, likewise.
13 And I beheld and heard an angel flying through the midst of Heaven saying with a loud voice, "woe, woe, woe, to the inhibitors of the Earth by reason of the other voices of the trumpet of the three angels, which are yet to sound!"

Chapter 9

1 And the fifth angel sounded and I saw a star fall from heaven to the Earth. And to him, was given the key of the Bottomless Pit.
2 And he opened the Bottomless Pit. And there arose a smoke out of the Pit; as the smoke of a great furnace. And the Sun and the air were darkened by reason of the smoke of the Pit.
3 And there came out of the smoke, locusts on the Earth. And to them, was given power as the scorpions of the Earth have power.
4 And it was Commanded them that they should not hurt the grass of the Earth; neither any green thing, neither any tree, but only those men, which have not, the Seal of God in their foreheads.
5 And to them, it was given that they should not kill them, but that they should be tormented five months. And their torment was as the torment of a scorpion, when he strikes a man.
6 And in those days, shall men seek death and shall not find it and shall desire to die and death shall flee from them.

7 And the shapes of the locusts were like unto horses prepared to battle. And on their heads were as it were, crowns like gold. And their faces were as the faces of men.
8 And they had hair as the hair of women. And their teeth were as the teeth of lions.
9 And they had breastplates, as it were breastplates of iron. And the sound of their wings was as the sound of chariots of many horses running to battle.
10 And they had tails like to scorpions. And there were stings in their tails and their power was to hurt men five months.
11 And they had a king over them, which is the angel of the Bottomless Pit; whose name in the Hebrew tongue is, Abaddon, but in the Greek tongue has his name, Apollyon.
12 One woe is past and behold, there comes two woes more, hereafter.

13 And the sixth angel sounded and I heard a voice from the four horns of the golden altar, which is before God,
14 Saying to the sixth angel, which had the trumpet, "loose the four angels, which are bound in the great river, Euphrates."
15 And the four angels were loosed, which were prepared for an hour and a day and a month and a year, for to slay the third part of men.

16 And the number of the army of the horsemen were two hundred thousand thousand and I heard the number of them.
17 And thus, I saw the horses in the Vision and them that sat on them, having breastplates of fire and of jacinth and brimstone. And the heads of the horses were as the heads of lions. And out of their mouths issued fire and smoke and brimstone.

18 By these three, were the third part of men killed, by the fire and by the smoke and by the brimstone, which issued out of their mouths.
19 For their power is in their mouth and in their tails, for their tails were like to serpents and had heads and with them, they do hurt.
20 And the rest of the men, which were not killed by these plagues yet, Repented not, of the works of their hands that they should not worship devils and idols of: gold and silver and brass and stone and of wood; which neither can see, nor hear, nor walk.
21 Neither Repented they: of their murders, nor of their sorceries, nor of their fornication, nor of their thefts.

Chapter 10

1 And I saw another mighty angel come down from Heaven, clothed with a cloud and a rainbow was on his head. And his face was as it were, the Sun and his feet, as pillars of fire.
2 And he had in his hand, a little scroll

open. And he set his right foot on the Sea and his left foot on the Earth

3 And cried with a loud voice, as when a lion roars. And when he had cried, seven thunders uttered their voices.

4 And when the seven thunders had uttered their voices, I was about to write and I heard a voice from Heaven saying to me, "seal up those things, which the seven thunders uttered and write them not."

5 And the angel, which I saw stand on the Sea and on the Earth lifted up his hand to Heaven

6 And swore by Him that Lives, for ever and ever, who Created Heaven and the things that therein, are and the Earth and the things that therein, are and the Sea and the things, which are therein that there should be time, no longer.

7 But in the days of the voice of the seventh angel, when he shall begin to sound, the mystery of God should be Finished, as He has declared to His servants, the prophets.

8 And the voice, which I heard from Heaven spoke to me again and said, "go and take the little scroll, which is open in the hand of the angel, which stands on the Sea and on the Earth."

9 And I went to the angel and said to him, "give me the little scroll." And he said to me, "take it and eat it up and it shall make your belly bitter, but it shall be in your mouth, sweet as honey."

10 And I took the little scroll out of the angel's hand and ate it up. And it was in my mouth, sweet as honey. And as soon as I had eaten it, my belly was bitter.

11 And he said to me, "you must Prophesy again, before many peoples and nations and tongues and kings."

Chapter 11

1 And there was given me a reed like to a rod. And the angel stood saying, "rise and measure the temple of God and the altar and them that Worship, therein.

2 But the court, which is without the temple, leave out and measure it not, for it is given to the gentiles. And the Holy city, shall they tread under foot forty and two months."

3 And I will give Power to My two witnesses. And they shall Prophesy one thousand two hundred and sixty days; clothed in sackcloth.

4 These are the two olive trees and the two candlesticks standing before The God of the Earth.

5 And if any man will hurt them, fire proceeds out of their mouth and devours their enemies. And if any man will hurt them, he must in this manner, be killed.

6 These have power to shut heaven that it rains not, in the days of their Prophecy and have power over waters to turn them to blood and to afflict the Earth with all plagues, as often as they will.

7 And when they shall have finished their Testimony, the beast that ascends out of the Bottomless Pit, shall make war against them and shall overcome them and kill them.

8 And their dead bodies, shall lie in the street of the great city, which spiritually is called, Sodom and Egypt, where also, our Lord was crucified.

9 And they of the people and kindreds and tongues and nations, shall see their dead bodies three days and a half and shall not suffer their dead bodies to be put in graves.

10 And they that dwell on the Earth, shall rejoice over them and make merry and shall send gifts, one to another, because these two prophets tormented them that dwelled on the Earth.

11 And after three days and a half, The Spirit of Life from God entered into them and they stood on their feet and Great Fear fell on them, which saw them.

12 And they heard A Great Voice from Heaven saying to them, "come up here." And they ascended up to Heaven in A Cloud and their enemies beheld them.

13 And the same hour, was there a great earthquake and the tenth part of the city fell. And in the earthquake, were slain of men, seven thousand and the remnant, were affrighted and Gave Glory to The God of Heaven.

14 The second woe is past and behold, the third woe, comes quickly.

15 And the seventh angel sounded and there were great voices in Heaven saying, "the kingdoms of this World are become the kingdoms of our Lord and of His Christ and He shall Reign, for ever and ever."

16 And the four and twenty Elders, which sat before God on their seats, fell on their faces and Worshipped God

17 Saying, "we Give You Thanks, O Lord, God Almighty, Which Are and Were and Are To Come, because You have taken to

Yourself, Your Great Power and have Reigned."
18 And the nations were angry. And Your wrath is come. And the time of the Dead that they should be Judged and that You should Give Reward to Your servants, the prophets and to the saints and them that Fear Your Name; small and great and should destroy them, which destroys the Earth.
19 And the temple of God was opened in Heaven and there was seen in His temple, The Ark of His Testament. And there were Lightnings and voices and Thunderings and an earthquake and great hail.

Chapter 12

1 And there appeared a great Wonder in heaven; a woman clothed with the Sun and the Moon under her feet and on her head, a crown of twelve stars.
2 And she being with child, cried travailing in birth and pained to be delivered.

3 And there appeared another Wonder in heaven and behold, <u>a great red dragon, having seven heads and ten horns and seven crowns on his heads.</u>
4 And his tail drew the third part of the stars of heaven and did cast them to the Earth. And the dragon stood before the woman, which was ready to be delivered, for to devour her child as soon as it was born.

5 <u>And she brought forth a Man Child, who was to Rule all nations with a rod of iron. And her child was caught up to God and to His throne.</u>
6 And the woman fled into the wilderness, where she has a place prepared of God that they should feed her there one thousand two hundred and sixty days.

7 <u>And there was war in Heaven. Michael and his angels fought against the dragon. And the dragon fought and his angels</u>
8 <u>And prevailed not, neither was their place found any more, in Heaven.</u>
9 <u>And the great dragon was cast out; that old serpent, called the Devil and Satan, which deceives the whole World; he was cast out into the Earth and his angels were cast out with him.</u>

10 <u>And I heard a loud voice saying in Heaven, "now, is come Salvation and Strength and the Kingdom of our God and The Power of His Christ, for the accuser of our brothers is cast down, which accused them before our God, day and night.</u>
11 <u>And they overcame him by The Blood of the Lamb and by The Word of their Testimony and they Loved not, their lives to the death.</u>
12 Therefore rejoice, you heavens and you that dwell in them. <u>Woe to the inhabiters of the Earth and of the Sea! For the Devil is come down to you, having great wrath, because he knows that he has but, a short time."</u>
13 And when the dragon saw that he was cast to the Earth, he persecuted the woman, which brought forth the Man Child.
14 And to the woman were given two wings of a great eagle that she might fly into the wilderness, into her place, where she is nourished for a time and times and half a time, from the face of the serpent.
15 And the serpent cast out of his mouth water as a flood after the woman that he might cause her to be carried away of the flood.
16 And the earth helped the woman. And the earth opened her mouth and swallowed up the flood, which the dragon cast out of his mouth.
17 <u>And the dragon was wroth with the woman and went to make war with the remnant of her seed, which Keep The Commandments of God and have The Testimony of Jesus Christ.</u>

Chapter 13

1 And I stood on the sand of the Sea and saw <u>a beast rise up out of the Sea, having seven heads and ten horns and on his horns, ten crowns and on his heads, the name of Blasphemy.</u>
2 And <u>the beast, which I saw was like to a leopard and his feet were as the feet of a bear and his mouth, as the mouth of a lion. And the dragon gave him his power and his seat and great authority.</u>
3 <u>And I saw one of his heads as it were wounded to death. And his deadly wound was healed. And all the World wondered after the beast.</u>

4 And <u>they worshipped the dragon</u>, which gave power to the beast. And <u>they worshipped the beast</u> saying, "who is like to the beast? Who is able to make war with him?"
5 And there was given to him, a mouth speaking great things and blasphemies.

And power was given to him to continue forty and two months.

6 And he opened his mouth in blasphemy against God, to blaspheme His Name and His tabernacle and them that dwell in Heaven.

7 <u>And it was given to him to make war with the saints and to overcome them. And power was given him, over all kindreds and tongues and nations.</u>

8 <u>And all that dwell on the Earth, shall worship him,</u> whose names are not written in the Scroll of Life of The Lamb Slain from the Foundation of the World.

9 If any man has an ear, let him Hear,

10 "He that leads into captivity, shall go into captivity. He that kills with the sword, must be killed with the sword. Here is the patience and the Faith of the saints."

11 And I beheld <u>another beast coming up out of the Earth.</u> And <u>he had two horns like a lamb and he spoke as a dragon.</u>

12 <u>And he exercises all the power of the first beast before him and causes the Earth and them, which dwell therein, to worship the first beast, whose deadly wound was healed.</u>

13 <u>And he does great wonders, so that he makes fire come down from heaven on the Earth in the sight of men</u>

14 <u>And deceives them that dwell on the Earth by the means of those miracles,</u> which he had power to do in the sight of the beast, saying to them that dwell on the Earth that, <u>"they should make an image to the beast, which had the wound by a sword and did live."</u>

15 <u>And he had power to give life to the image of the beast that the image of the beast should both speak and cause that as many as would not worship the image of the beast should be killed.</u>

16 <u>And he causes all; both small and great, rich and poor, free and bond, to receive a mark in their right hand, or in their foreheads</u>

17 <u>And that no man might buy, or sell save he that had the mark, or the name of the beast,</u> or the number of his name.

18 Here is Wisdom. Let him that has Understanding <u>count the number of the beast,</u> for <u>it is the number of a man. And his number is, six hundred sixty and six.</u>

Chapter 14

1 And I looked and lo, a Lamb stood on the Mount Sion and with Him, one hundred forty and four thousand having His Father's Name written in their foreheads.

2 And I Heard A Voice from Heaven, as the voice of many waters and as the voice of a great thunder. And I heard the voice of harpers, harping with their harps.

3 And they Sang as it were, a New Song before the throne and before the four beasts and the elders. And no man could learn that song, but the hundred and forty and four thousand, which were Redeemed from the Earth.

4 These are they, which were not defiled with women, for they are (virgins.) These are they, which follow The Lamb wheresoever, He goes. These were Redeemed from among men, being the Firstfruits to God and to The Lamb.

5 And in their mouths were found no guile, for they are without fault before the throne of God.

6 And I saw <u>another angel fly in the midst of Heaven,</u> having The Everlasting Gospel to Preach to them that dwell on the Earth and to every nation and kindred and tongue and people,

7 Saying with a loud voice, <u>"Fear God and Give Glory to Him, for the hour of His Judgment is come. And Worship Him that Made Heaven and Earth and the Sea and the fountains of waters!"</u>

8 And there followed <u>another angel</u> saying, <u>"Babylon is fallen, is fallen; that great city, because she made all nations drink of the wine of the wrath of her fornication."</u>

9 And <u>the third angel</u> followed them saying with a loud voice, <u>"if any man worships the beast and his image and receives his mark in his forehead, or in his hand,</u>

10 <u>The same shall drink of the wine of the wrath of God, which is poured out without mixture into the cup of His indignation and he shall be tormented with fire and brimstone in the presence of the Holy angels and in the Presence of The Lamb.</u>

11 <u>And the smoke of their torment ascends up for ever and ever! And they have no rest, day, nor night, who worship the beast and his image and whosoever, receives the mark of his name!"</u>

12 Here is the patience of the saints. Here are they that Keep The Commandments of God and The Faith of Jesus.

13 And I Heard A Voice from Heaven saying to me, "write, "Blessed are the dead, which die in The Lord from,

henceforth. Yes,'" says The Spirit that, "'they may rest from their Labors and their Works, do follow them.'"

14 And I looked and behold, A White Cloud. And on The Cloud, One sat like to The Son of Man; having on His head, a golden crown and in His hand, a sharp sickle.

15 And another angel came out of the temple crying with a loud voice to Him that sat on The Cloud, "thrust in Your sickle and reap, for the time is come for You to reap. For the harvest of the Earth is ripe!"

16 And He that sat on The Cloud, thrust in His sickle on the Earth and the Earth was reaped.

17 And another angel came out of the temple, which is in Heaven; he also, having a sharp sickle.

18 And another angel came out from the altar, which had power over fire and cried with a loud cry to him that had the sharp sickle saying, "thrust in your sharp sickle and gather the clusters of the vine of the Earth, for her grapes are fully ripe!"

19 And the angel thrust in his sickle into the Earth and gathered the vine of the Earth and cast it into the great winepress of the wrath of God.

20 And the winepress was trodden without the city. And blood came out of the winepress, even to the horse bridles, by the space of one thousand and six hundred furlongs.

Chapter 15

1 And I saw another Sign in Heaven; great and marvelous; seven angels having the seven last plagues. For in them, is filled up the wrath of God.

2 And I saw as it were, a Sea of glass, mingled with fire and them that had gotten the Victory over the beast and over his image and over his mark and over the number of his name, stand on the Sea of glass, having the harps of God.

3 And they Sing the song of Moses, the servant of God and the song of The Lamb saying, "Great and Marvelous are Your Works, Lord, God Almighty. Just and True are Your Ways, You King of saints.

4 Who shall not Fear You, O Lord and Glorify Your Name? For You only, are Holy. For all nations, shall come and Worship before You, for Your Judgments are made manifest."

5 And after that, I looked and behold, the temple of the tabernacle of The Testimony in Heaven was opened.

6 And the seven angels came out of the temple, having the seven plagues; clothed in pure and white linen and having their breasts girded with golden girdles.

7 And one of the four beasts gave to the seven angels, seven golden vials full of the wrath of God, who Lives for ever and ever.

8 And the temple was filled with smoke from The Glory of God and from His Power. And no man was able to enter into the temple, until the seven plagues of the seven angels were fulfilled.

Chapter 16

1 And I heard A Great Voice out of The Temple saying to the seven angels, "go your ways and pour out the vials of the wrath of God on the Earth."

2 And the first went and poured out his vial on the Earth. And there fell a noisome and grievous sore on the men, which had the mark of the beast and on them, which worshipped his image.

3 And the second angel poured out his vial on the Sea. And it became as the blood of a dead man. And every living soul died in the Sea.

4 And the third angel poured out his vial on the rivers and fountains of waters and they became blood.

5 And I heard the angel of the waters say, "You are Righteous, O Lord, Which Are and Were and Shall Be, because You have Judged, thus.

6 For they have shed the blood of saints and prophets and you have given them blood to drink, for they are worthy."

7 And I heard another out of the altar say, "even so, Lord, God Almighty, True and Righteous, are Your Judgments."

8 And the fourth angel poured out his vial on the Sun. And power was given to him to scorch men with fire.

9 And men were scorched with great heat and blasphemed The Name of God, which has Power over these plagues. And they Repented not, to give Him Glory.

10 And the fifth angel poured out his vial on the Seat of the beast. And his kingdom was full of Darkness and they gnawed

their tongues for pain,
11 And blasphemed The God of Heaven, because of their pains and their sores and Repented not, of their deeds.

12 And the sixth angel poured out his vial on the great river, Euphrates. And the water thereof, was dried up that the way of the kings of the East might be prepared.
13 And I saw three unclean spirits like frogs, come out of the mouth of the dragon and out of the mouth of the beast and out of the mouth of the false prophet.
14 For they are the spirits of devils, working miracles, which go forth to the kings of the Earth and of the whole World, to gather them to the battle of that Great Day of God Almighty.

15 "Behold, I come as a thief. Blessed is he that watches and Keeps his Garments, lest he walks naked and they see his shame."

16 And He gathered them together, into a place called in the Hebrew tongue, Armageddon.

17 And the seventh angel poured out his vial into the air. And there came A Great Voice out of the temple of Heaven, from the throne, saying, "it is done."
18 And there were voices and Thunders and Lightnings. And there was a great earthquake, such as was not, since men were on the Earth; so mighty an earthquake and so great.
19 And the great city was divided into three parts. And the cities of the nations fell. And great Babylon came in remembrance before God, to give to her, the cup of the wine of The fierceness of His wrath.
20 And every island fled away. And the mountains were not found.
21 And there fell on men, a great hail out of heaven; every stone, about the weight of a talent. And men blasphemed God, because of the plague of the hail, for the plague thereof, was exceedingly great.

Chapter 17

1 And there came one of the seven angels, which had the seven vials and talked with me, saying to me, "come here. I will show to you the Judgment of the great whore that sits on many waters,
2 With whom, the kings of the Earth have committed fornication and the inhabitants of the Earth have been made drunk with the wine of her fornication."

3 So, he carried me away in The Spirit into the wilderness. And I saw a woman sit on a scarlet colored beast; full of names of blasphemy, having seven heads and ten horns.
4 And the woman was arrayed in purple and scarlet color and decked with gold and precious stones and pearls; having a golden cup in her hand, full of abominations and filthiness of her fornication.
5 And on her forehead was a name written, "Mystery Babylon the great, the Mother of Harlots and Abominations of the Earth."
6 And I saw the woman drunken with the blood of the saints and with the blood of the martyrs of Jesus. And when I saw her, I wondered with great admiration.

7 And the angel said to me, "wherefore, did you marvel? I will tell you the mystery of the woman and of the beast that carries her, which has the seven heads and ten horns.
8 The beast that you saw, was and is not and shall ascend out of the Bottomless Pit and go into Perdition. And they that dwell on the Earth, shall wonder, whose names were not, written in the Scroll of Life, from the foundation of the World, when they behold the beast that was and is not and yet is.

9 And here is the mind, which has Wisdom: the seven heads are seven mountains, on which the woman sits.
10 And there are seven kings; five are fallen and one is. And the other, is not yet come. And when he comes, he must continue a short space.

11 And the beast that was and is not, even he is the eighth and is of the seven and goes into Perdition.

12 And the ten horns, which you saw are ten kings, which have received no kingdom as yet, but receive power as kings, one hour with the beast.
13 These have one mind and shall give their power and strength to the beast.
14 These shall make war with The Lamb and The Lamb shall overcome them, for He is Lord of lords and King of kings. And they that are with Him, are Called and

Chosen and Faithful."

15 And he said to me, "the waters which you saw, where the whore sits, are peoples and multitudes and nations and tongues.

16 And the ten horns, which you saw on the beast, these shall hate the whore and shall make her desolate and naked and shall eat her flesh and burn her with fire.
17 For God has put in their hearts to fulfill His Will and to agree and give their kingdom to the beast, until The Words of God, shall be Fulfilled.

18 And the woman, which you saw is that great city, which reigns over the kings of the Earth."

Chapter 18

1 And after these things, I saw another angel come down from Heaven, having great power. And the Earth was lightened with his glory.
2 And he cried mightily with a strong voice saying, "Babylon the great is fallen, is fallen and is become the habitation of devils and the hold of every foul spirit and a cage of every unclean and hateful bird.
3 For all nations have drunk of the wine of the wrath of her fornication and the kings of the Earth, have committed fornication with her. And the merchants of the Earth are waxed rich through the abundance of her delicacies!"

4 And I heard another Voice from Heaven saying, "come out of her My people that you are not partakers of her sins and that you receive not, of her plagues.
5 For her sins have reached to Heaven and God has remembered her iniquities.
6 Reward her, even as she rewarded you and double to her, double. According to her works in the cup, which she has filled, fill to her double.
7 How much she has glorified herself and lived deliciously. So much torment and sorrow, give her, for she says in her heart, "'I sit a queen and am no widow and shall see no sorrow.'"
8 Therefore, shall her plagues come in one day; death and mourning and famine and she shall be utterly burned with fire. For Strong is The Lord, God who Judges her.
9 And the kings of the Earth, who have committed fornication and lived deliciously with her, shall bewail her and lament for her, when they shall see the smoke of her burning,
10 Standing afar off, for the fear of her torment saying, "'alas, alas, that great city, Babylon, that mighty city! For in one hour, is her Judgment come!'"
11 And the merchants of the Earth, shall weep and mourn over her, for no man buys their merchandise, any more;
12 The merchandise: of gold and silver and precious stones and of pearls and fine linen and purple and silk and scarlet and all thyine wood and all manner, vessels of ivory and all manner, vessels of most precious wood and of brass and iron and marble
13 And cinnamon and odors and ointments and frankincense and wine and oil and fine flour and wheat and beasts and sheep and horses and chariots and slaves and souls of men.
14 And the fruits that your soul lusted after, are departed from you. And all things, which were dainty and goodly, are departed from you and you shall find them no more, at all.
15 The merchants of these things, which were made rich by her, shall stand afar off, for the fear of her torment; weeping and wailing
16 And saying, "'alas, alas, that great city that was clothed in: fine linen and purple and scarlet and decked with gold and precious stones and pearls!

17 For in one hour, so great riches are come to nothing.'" And every shipmaster and all the company in ships and sailors and as many as trade by Sea, stood afar off
18 And cried when they saw the smoke of her burning saying, "'what city is like to this great city?!'"
19 And they cast dust on their heads and cried; weeping and wailing saying, "'alas, alas, that great city, wherein were made rich; all that had ships in the Sea by reason of her costliness! For in one hour, is she made desolate!'"
20 Rejoice over her, you Heaven and you Holy apostles and prophets. For God has avenged you on her."
21 And a mighty angel took up a stone like a great millstone and cast it into the Sea saying, "thus, with violence shall that great city, Babylon be thrown down and shall be found no more at all.
22 And the voice of harpers and musicians and of pipers and trumpeters, shall be

heard no more at all in you. And no craftsman, of whatsoever craft he is, shall be found, any more in you. And the sound of a millstone, shall be heard no more, at all in you.

23 And the light of a candle, shall shine, no more at all in you. And the voice of the bridegroom and of the bride, shall be heard, no more at all in you, for your merchants were the great men of the Earth, for by your sorceries, were all nations deceived.

24 And in her, was found the blood of prophets and of saints and of all that were slain on the Earth."

Chapter 19

1 And after these things, I heard a great voice of much people in Heaven saying, "Alleluia! Salvation and Glory and Honor and Power to The Lord, our God!

2 For True and Righteous are His Judgments, for He has Judged the great whore, which did corrupt the Earth with her fornication and has avenged the blood of His servants at her hand!"

3 And again, they said, "Alleluia!" And her smoke rose up, for ever and ever.

4 And the four and twenty elders and the four beasts, fell down and Worshipped God that sat on the throne saying, "Amen! Alleluia!"

5 And A Voice came out of the throne saying, "Praise our God, all you, His servants and you that Fear Him, both small and great!"

6 And I Heard as it were, the voice of a great multitude and as the voice of many waters and as the voice of mighty Thunderings, saying, "Alleluia, for The Lord, God Omnipotent Reigns!

7 Let us be Glad and Rejoice and Give Honor to Him, for the Marriage of The Lamb is come and His wife has made herself ready!"

8 And to her, was granted that she should be arrayed in fine linen; clean and white, for the fine linen, is the Righteousness of saints.

9 And he said to me, "write, "'Blessed are they, which are Called to the Marriage Supper of The Lamb.'" And he said to me, "these are The True Sayings of God."

10 And I fell at his feet to worship him. And he said to me, "see you do it not. I am your fellow servant and of your brothers that have The Testimony of Jesus. Worship God. For The Testimony of Jesus, is The Spirit of Prophecy."

11 And I saw Heaven opened and behold, a white horse. And He that sat on him, was called, "Faithful and True." And in Righteousness, He does Judge and make war.

12 His eyes were as a Flame of Fire. And on His head, were many crowns. And He had a Name written that no man knew, but He, Himself.

13 And He was clothed with a vesture, dipped in Blood. And His Name is called, "The Word of God."

14 And the armies, which were in Heaven, followed Him on white horses; clothed in fine linen; white and clean.

15 And out of His mouth goes a sharp Sword that with it, He should afflict the nations. And He shall rule them, with a rod of iron. And He treads the winepress of the fierceness and wrath of Almighty God.

16 And He has on His vesture and on His thigh, a Name written, "King of kings and Lord of Lords."

17 And I saw an angel standing in the Sun. And he cried with a loud voice saying to all the fowls that fly in the midst of heaven, "come and gather yourselves, together to the supper of The Great God

18 That you may eat the flesh of kings and the flesh of captains and the flesh of mighty men and the flesh of horses and of them, that sit on them and the flesh of all men; both free and bond, both small and great."

19 And I saw the beast and the kings of the Earth and their armies, gathered together to make war against Him that sat on the horse and against His army.

20 And the beast was taken and with him, the false prophet that worked miracles before him, with which, he deceived them that had received the mark of the beast and them that worshipped his image. These both, were cast alive into a lake of fire, burning with brimstone.

21 And the remnant were slain, with The Sword of Him that sat on the horse, which Sword proceeded out of His mouth. And all the fowls were filled with their flesh.

Chapter 20

1 And I saw an angel come down from Heaven, having the key of the Bottomless Pit and a great chain in his hand.

2 And he laid hold on the dragon; that old

serpent, which is the Devil and Satan and bound him a thousand years

3 And cast him into the Bottomless Pit and shut him up and set a seal on him that he should deceive the nations no more, until the thousand years, should be Fulfilled. And after that, he must be loosed a little season.

4 And I saw thrones and they sat on them. And Judgment was Given to them. And I saw the souls of them that were beheaded for the witness of Jesus and for The Word of God and which had not worshipped the beast; neither his image, neither had received his mark on their foreheads, or in their hands. And they Lived and reigned with Christ a thousand years.

5 But, the rest of the dead Lived not again, until the thousand years were finished. This is the First Resurrection.

6 Blessed and Holy is he that has part in the First Resurrection. On such, the Second Death has no power, but they shall be priests of God and of Christ and shall reign with Him a thousand years.

7 And when the thousand years are expired, Satan shall be loosed out of his prison

8 And shall go out to deceive the nations, which are in the four quarters of the Earth; Gog and Magog, to gather them, together to battle, the number of whom, is as the sand of the Sea.

9 And they went up on the breadth of the earth and compassed the camp of the saints, about and the beloved city. And fire came down from God, out of Heaven and devoured them.

10 And the Devil that deceived them, was cast into the Lake of Fire and Brimstone, where the beast and the false prophet are and shall be tormented, day and night, for ever and ever.

11 And I saw a great white throne and Him that sat on it; from Whose face, the Earth and the Heaven fled away. And there was found no place for them.

12 And I saw the Dead, small and great, stand before God. And the scrolls were opened. And another scroll was opened, which is The Scroll of Life. And the Dead were Judged out of those things, which were written in the scrolls, according to their works.

13 And the Sea gave up the Dead, which were in it. And Death and Hell delivered up the Dead, which were in them. And they were Judged, every man, according to their works.

14 And Death and Hell were cast into the Lake of Fire. This is the Second Death.

15 And whosoever, was not found written in The Scroll of Life, was cast into the Lake of Fire.

Chapter 21

1 And I saw a new Heaven and a new Earth. For the first Heaven and the first Earth were passed away and there was no more Sea.

2 And I John, saw The Holy City, New Jerusalem, coming down from God out of Heaven, prepared as a bride, adorned for her Husband.

3 And I heard a great voice out of Heaven saying, "behold, the tabernacle of God is with men. And He will dwell with them and they shall be His people. And God Himself, shall be with them and be their God.

4 And God shall wipe away all tears from their eyes. And there shall be no more death; neither sorrow, nor crying, neither shall there be any more pain, for the former things are passed away."

5 And He that sat on the throne said, "behold, I make all things new." And He said to me, "write, "'for these Words are True and Faithful.'"

6 And He said to me, "it is done. I am Alpha and Omega; The Beginning and The End. I will Give to him that is athirst, of The Fountain of The Water of Life, Freely.

7 He that Overcomes, shall inherit all things. And I will be his God and he shall be My son.

8 But, the fearful and unbelieving and the abominable and murderers and whoremongers and sorcerers and idolaters and all liars, shall have their part, in the lake, which burns with fire and brimstone, which is the Second Death."

9 And there came to me, one of the seven angels, which had the seven vials, full of the seven last plagues and talked with me, saying, "come here, I will show you the bride, the Lamb's wife."

10 And he carried me away in The Spirit to a great and high mountain and showed me that great city, The Holy Jerusalem, descending out of Heaven from God.

11 Having The Glory of God. And her Light was like to a stone, most precious; even like a jasper stone, clear as crystal

12 And had a wall great and high and had twelve gates. And at the gates, twelve angels and names written thereon, which are the names of the twelve tribes of the children of Israel

13 On the East three gates, on the North three gates, on the South three gates and on the West three gates.

14 And the wall of the city had twelve foundations and in them, the names of the twelve apostles of The Lamb.

15 And he that talked with me, had a golden reed to measure the city and the gates, thereof and the wall, thereof.

16 And the city lies eighty and the length is as large as the breadth. And he measured the city with the reed, twelve thousand furlongs. The length and the breadth and the height of it are equal.

17 And he measured the wall thereof, one hundred and forty and four cubits, according to the measure of a man that is of the angel.

18 And the building of the wall of it, was of jasper. And the city was pure gold, like to clear glass.

19 And the foundations of the wall of the city, were garnished with all manner of precious stones. The first foundation was jasper; the second, sapphire; the third, a chalcedony; the fourth, an emerald;

20 The fifth, sardonyx; the sixth, sardius; the seventh, chrysolyte; the eighth, beryl; the ninth, a topaz; the tenth, a chrysoprasus; the eleventh, a jacinth; the twelfth, an amethyst.

21 And the twelve gates were twelve pearls; every several gate, was of one pearl. And the street of the city was pure gold, as it were transparent glass.

22 And I saw no temple therein, for The Lord, God Almighty and The Lamb are The Temple of it.

23 And the city had no need of the Sun, neither of the Moon, to shine in it, for The Glory of God did Lighten it and The Lamb is the Light, thereof.

24 And the nations of them, which are Saved, shall Walk in The Light of it and the kings of the Earth, do bring their glory and honor into it.

25 And the gates of it, shall not be shut at all by day, for there shall be no night there.

26 And they shall bring the glory and honor of the nations into it.

27 And there shall in no wise, enter into it, any thing that defiles, neither whatsoever, works abomination, or makes a lie, but they, which are written in The Lamb's Scroll of Life.

Chapter 22

1 And he showed me a Pure river of Water of Life; clear as crystal, proceeding out of The Throne of God and of The Lamb.

2 In the midst of the street of it and on either side of the river was there, the Tree of Life, which bares twelve manner of fruits and yielded her fruit every month. And the leaves of the tree, were for the Healing of the nations.

3 And there shall be no more curse. But The Throne of God and of The Lamb, shall be in it. And His servants, shall serve Him.

4 And they shall see His face. And His Name, shall be in their foreheads.

5 And there shall be no night there and they need no candle, neither light of the Sun, for The Lord, God gives them Light and they shall reign, for ever and ever.

6 And he said to me, "these sayings are Faithful and True." And The Lord, God of the Holy prophets sent His angel to show to His servants the things, which must shortly, be done.

7 "Behold, I come quickly. Blessed is he that Keeps The Sayings of The Prophecy of this scroll."

8 And I John, saw these things and Heard them. And when I had Heard and Seen, I fell down to worship before the feet of the angel, which showed me these things.

9 Then, he said to me, "see you do it not, for I am your fellow servant and of your brothers, the prophets and of them, which Keep the Sayings of this scroll. Worship God."

10 And he said to me, "seal not, the Sayings of The Prophecy of this scroll, for the time is at hand."

11 "He that is unjust, let him be unjust, still. And he which is filthy, let him be filthy, still. And he that is Righteous, let him be Righteous, still. And he that is Holy, let him be Holy, still.

12 And behold, I come quickly and My reward is with Me, to Give every man, accordingly, as his work, shall be.

13 I am Alpha and Omega; The Beginning and The End, The First and The Last.

14 Blessed are they that Do His Commandments that they may have right

to The Tree of Life and may enter in, through the gates into the city.

15 For without, are dogs and sorcerers and whoremongers and murderers and idolaters and whosoever, loves and makes a lie.

16 I Jesus, have sent My angel to Testify to you these things in the churches. I am the root and the offspring of David and The Bright and Morning Star."

17 And The Spirit and the bride says, "come and let him that Hears say, "'come.'" And let him that is athirst come and whosoever will, let him take the water of Life, Freely.

18 For I Testify to every man that Hears The Words of The Prophecy of this scroll, if any man shall add to these things, God shall add to him the plagues that are written in this scroll.

19 And if any man shall take away from The Words of the scroll of this Prophecy, God shall take away his part out of The Scroll of Life and out of the Holy city and from the things, which are written in this scroll."

20 He which Testifies these things says, "surely, I come quickly." Amen. Even so, come Lord, Jesus.

21 The Grace of our Lord, Jesus Christ be with you all. Amen.

www.ingramcontent.com/pod-product-compliance
Lightning Source LLC
Chambersburg PA
CBHW080241170426
43192CB00014BA/2525